BEING
PUNCTUAL

(About being punctual, as in the phrase "being punctual is important." *Def:*)

1. To be on time at a predetermined meeting spot or for a deadline.
2. To keep the power plug for your console game out of the wall socket, and/or, to not be let loose to freely roam the city nights.
3. An insincere bit of cant to be uttered at such times as something bad happens. Being punctual *is* important, but I guess I blew it in being three days late to meet someone, didn't I?

STORY AND ART BY
RIKDO KOSHI

EXCEL SAGA 04

STORY AND ART BY
RIKDO KOSHI

ENGLISH ADAPTATION BY
DAN KANEMITSU & CARL GUSTAV HORN

TRANSLATION
DAN KANEMITSU

LETTERING & TOUCH-UP BY
CATO

COVER DESIGN
BRUCE LEWIS

GRAPHIC DESIGNER
CAROLINA UGALDE

EDITOR
CARL GUSTAV HORN

MANAGING EDITOR
ANNETTE ROMAN

EDITOR IN CHIEF
WILLIAM FLANAGAN

PRODUCTION MANAGER
NOBORU WATANABE

SR. DIRECTOR OF LICENSING & ACQUISITIONS
RIKA INOUYE

VP OF SALES & MARKETING
LIZA COPPOLA

SR. VP OF EDITORIAL
HYOE NARITA

PUBLISHER
SEIJI HORIBUCHI

Published by VIZ, LLC
P.O. Box 77064
San Francisco, CA 94107

Action Edition
10 9 8 7 6 5 4 3 2 1
First printing, December 2003

For advertising rates or media kit, e-mail advertising@viz.com

www.viz.com

ANIMERICA
ANIME & MANGA MONTHLY
www.animerica-mag.com

store.viz.com

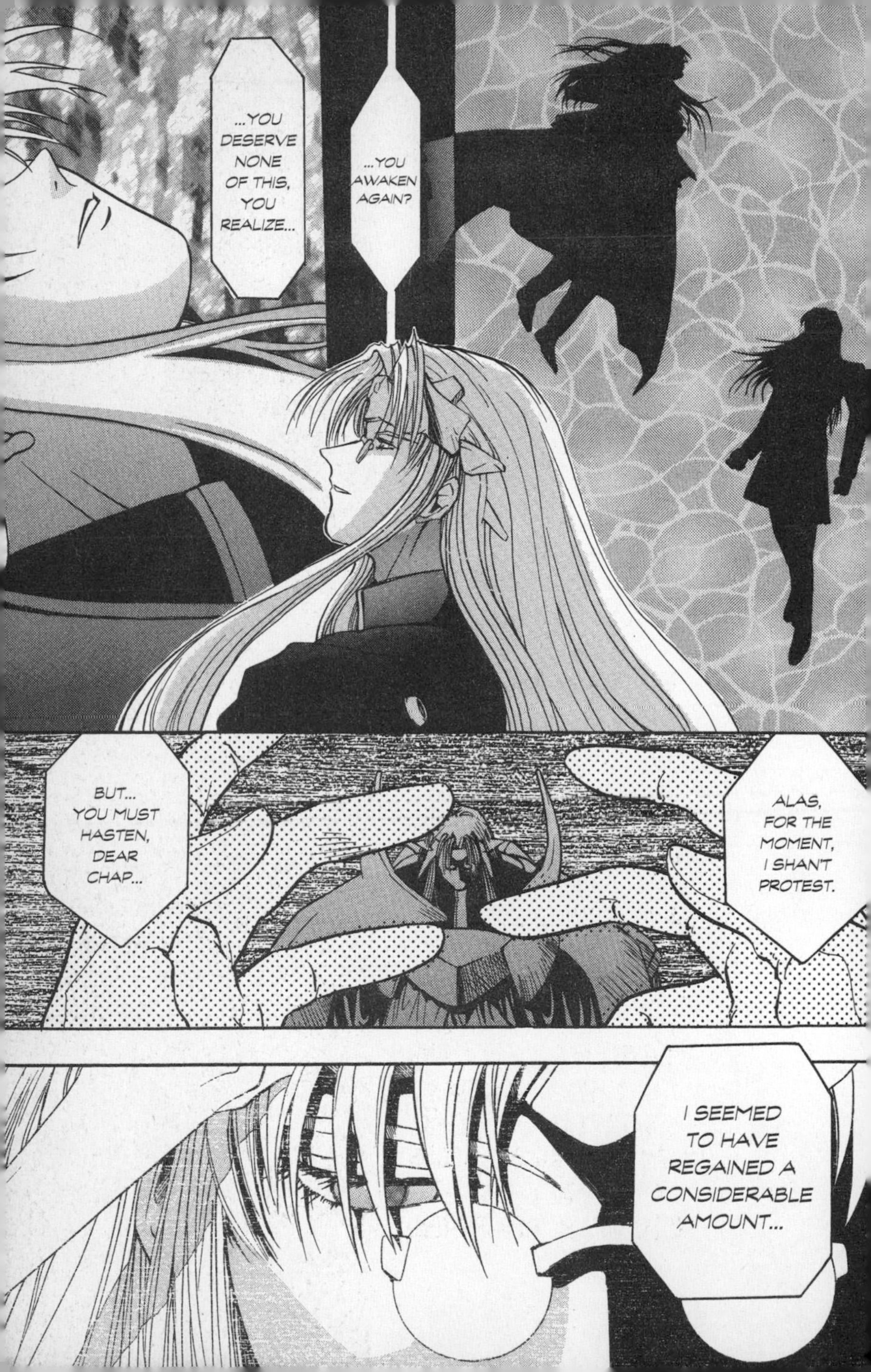
...YOU AWAKEN AGAIN?
...YOU DESERVE NONE OF THIS, YOU REALIZE...
ALAS, FOR THE MOMENT, I SHAN'T PROTEST.
BUT... YOU MUST HASTEN, DEAR CHAP...
I SEEMED TO HAVE REGAINED A CONSIDERABLE AMOUNT...

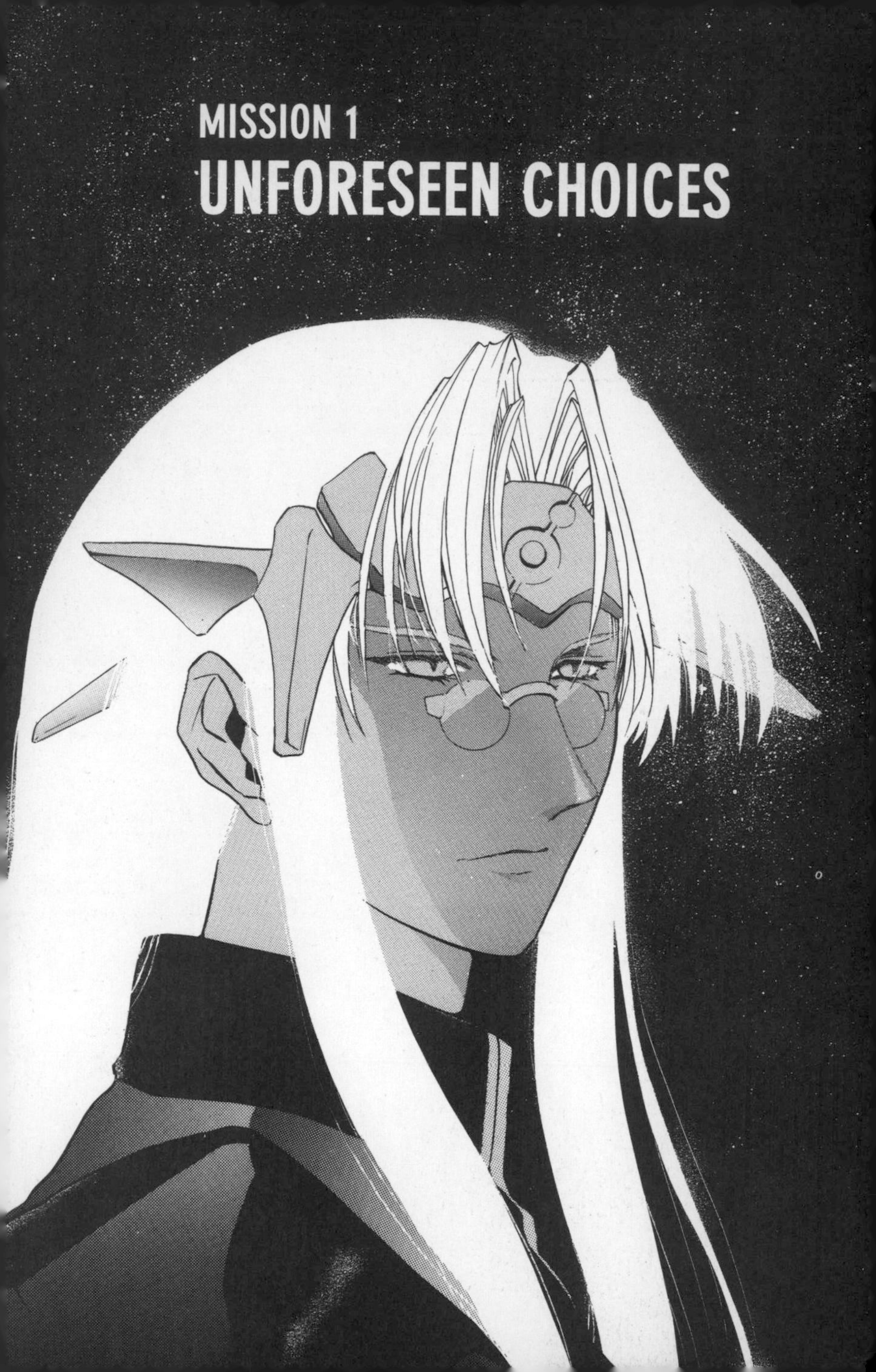
MISSION 1
UNFORESEEN CHOICES

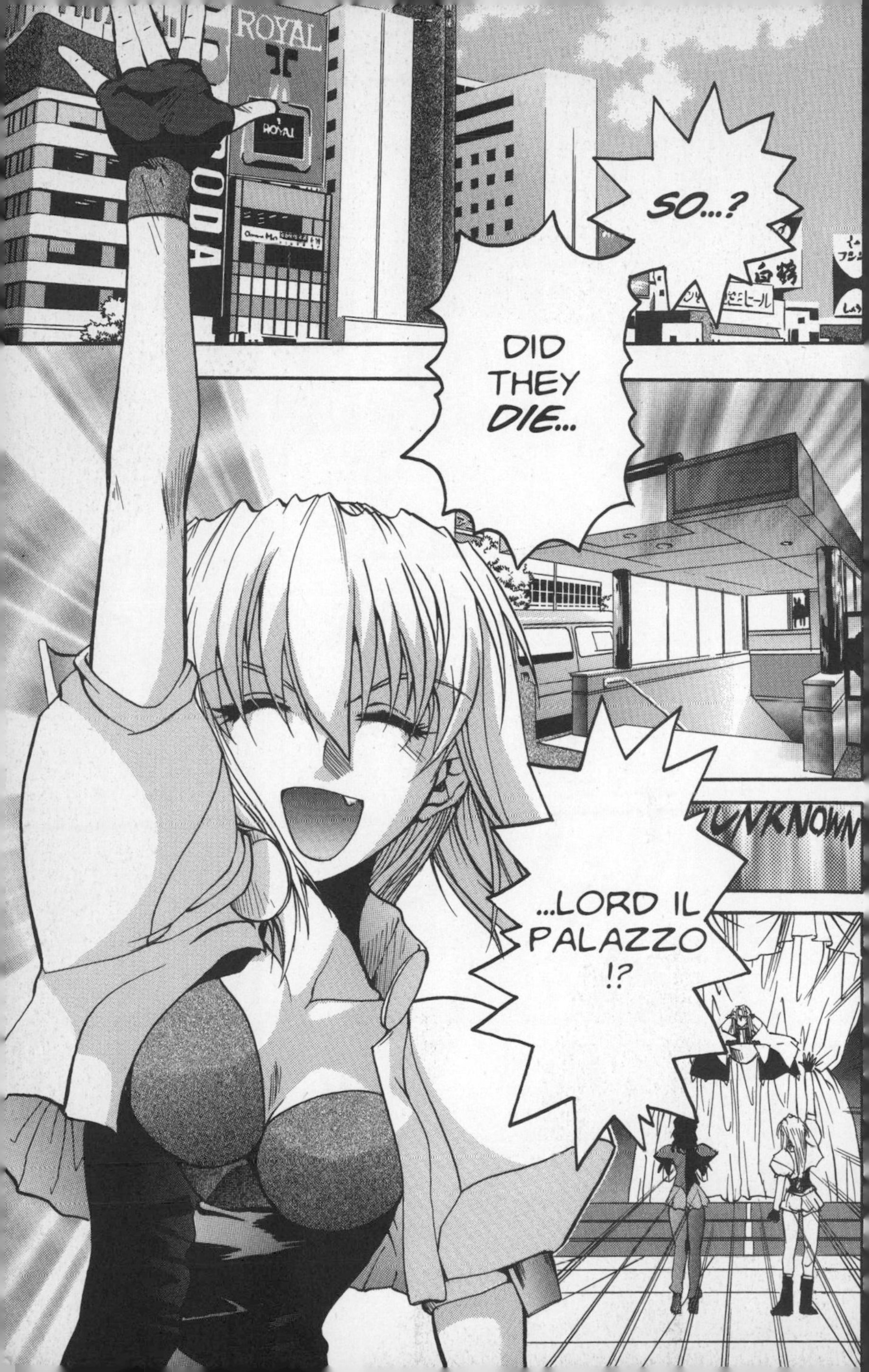
ROYAL
SO...?
DID THEY *DIE*...
UNKNOWN
...LORD IL PALAZZO !?

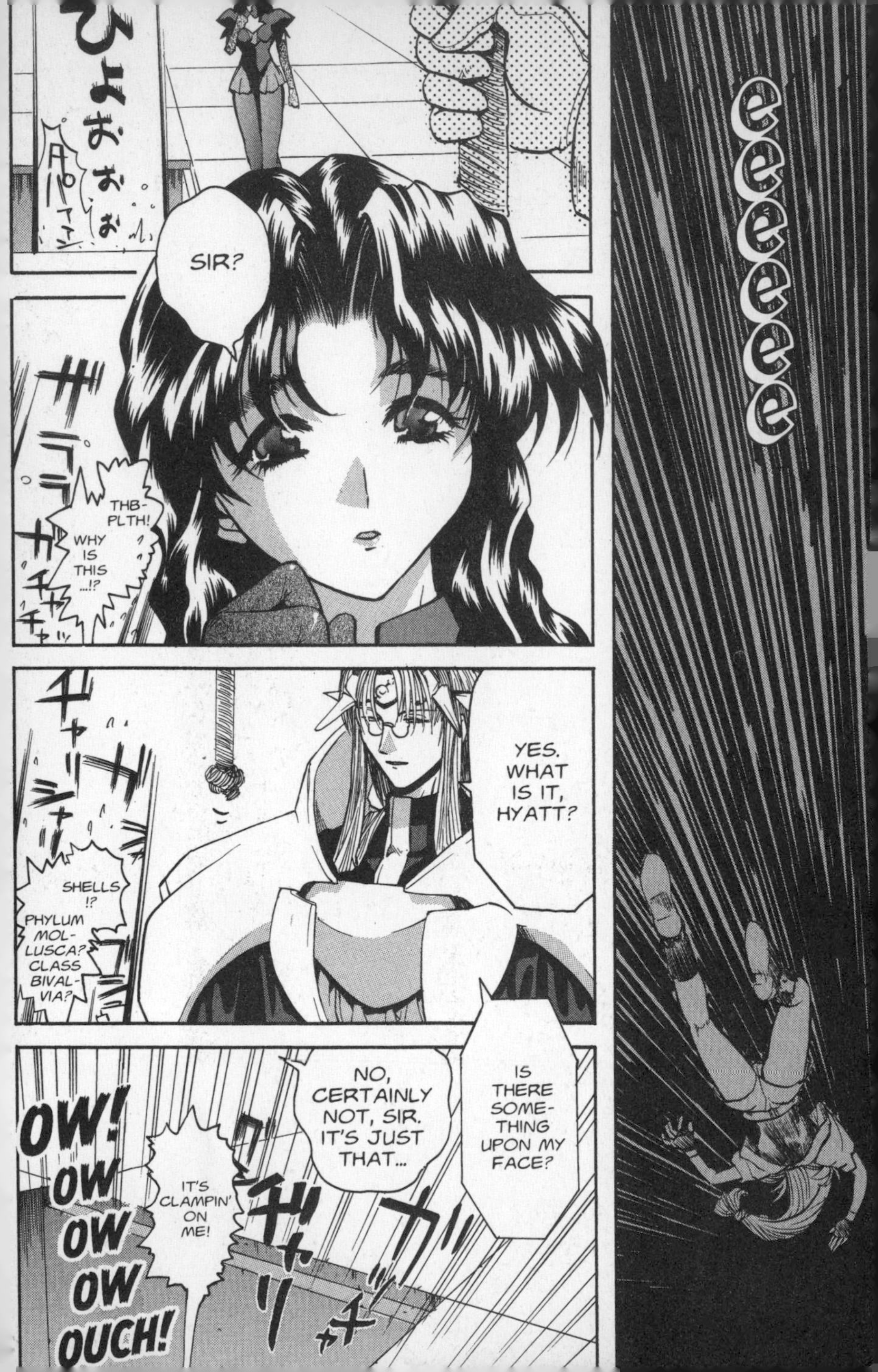
eeeeee
ひょおおお
SIR?
THB-PLTH! WHY IS THIS ...!?
YES. WHAT IS IT, HYATT?
SHELLS !? PHYLUM MOL-LUSCA? CLASS BIVAL-VIA?
IS THERE SOME-THING UPON MY FACE?
NO, CERTAINLY NOT, SIR. IT'S JUST THAT...
IT'S CLAMPIN' ON ME!
OW! OW OW OW OUCH!

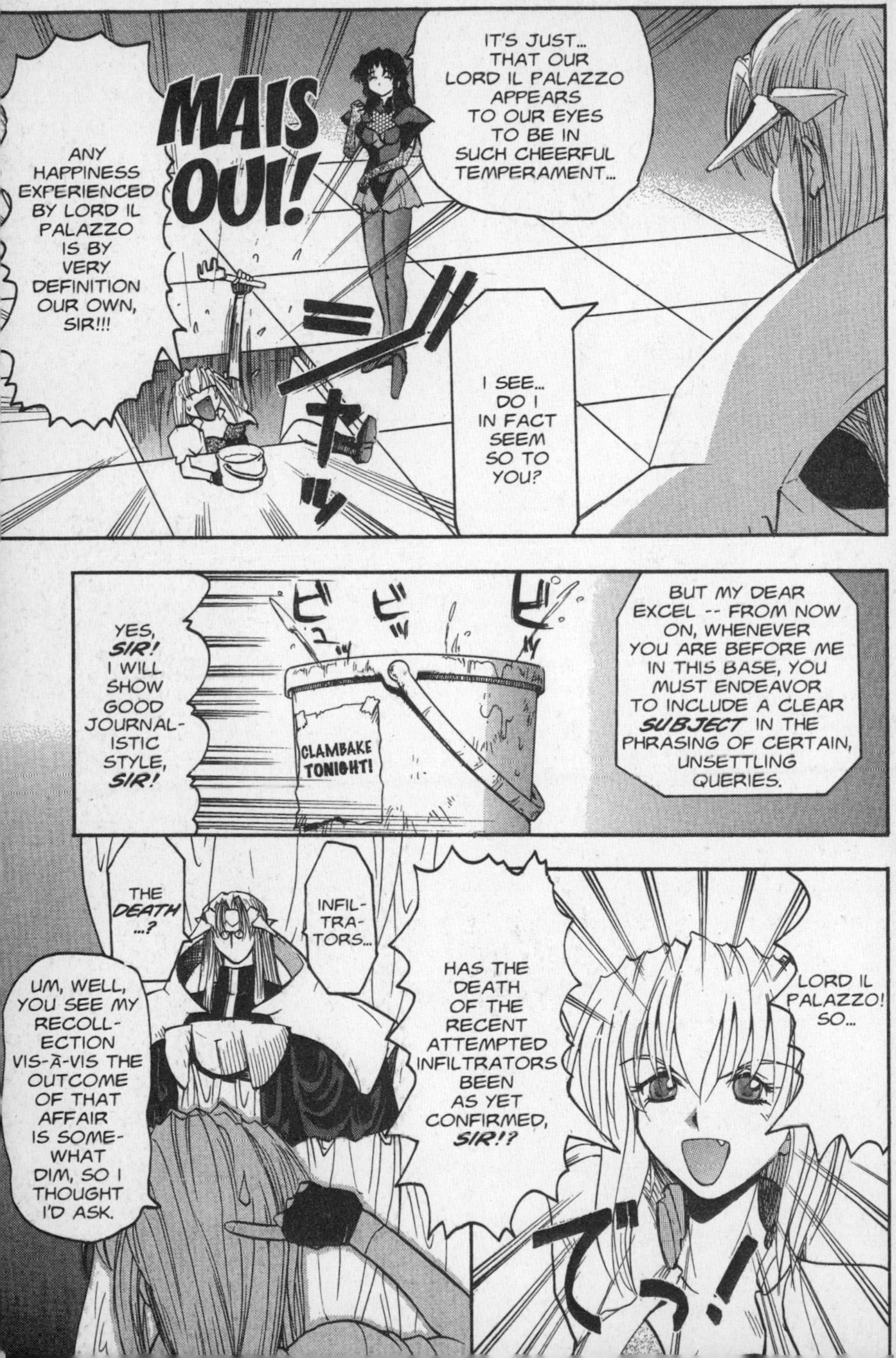
IT'S JUST... THAT OUR LORD IL PALAZZO APPEARS TO OUR EYES TO BE IN SUCH CHEERFUL TEMPERAMENT...
I SEE... DO I IN FACT SEEM SO TO YOU?
MAIS OUI!
ANY HAPPINESS EXPERIENCED BY LORD IL PALAZZO IS BY VERY DEFINITION OUR OWN, SIR!!!
BUT MY DEAR EXCEL -- FROM NOW ON, WHENEVER YOU ARE BEFORE ME IN THIS BASE, YOU MUST ENDEAVOR TO INCLUDE A CLEAR SUBJECT IN THE PHRASING OF CERTAIN, UNSETTLING QUERIES.
CLAMBAKE TONIGHT!
YES, SIR! I WILL SHOW GOOD JOURNAL-ISTIC STYLE, SIR!
LORD IL PALAZZO! SO...
HAS THE DEATH OF THE RECENT ATTEMPTED INFILTRATORS BEEN AS YET CONFIRMED, SIR!?
でっ!
INFIL-TRA-TORS...
THE DEATH ...?
UM, WELL, YOU SEE MY RECOLL-ECTION VIS-À-VIS THE OUTCOME OF THAT AFFAIR IS SOME-WHAT DIM, SO I THOUGHT I'D ASK.

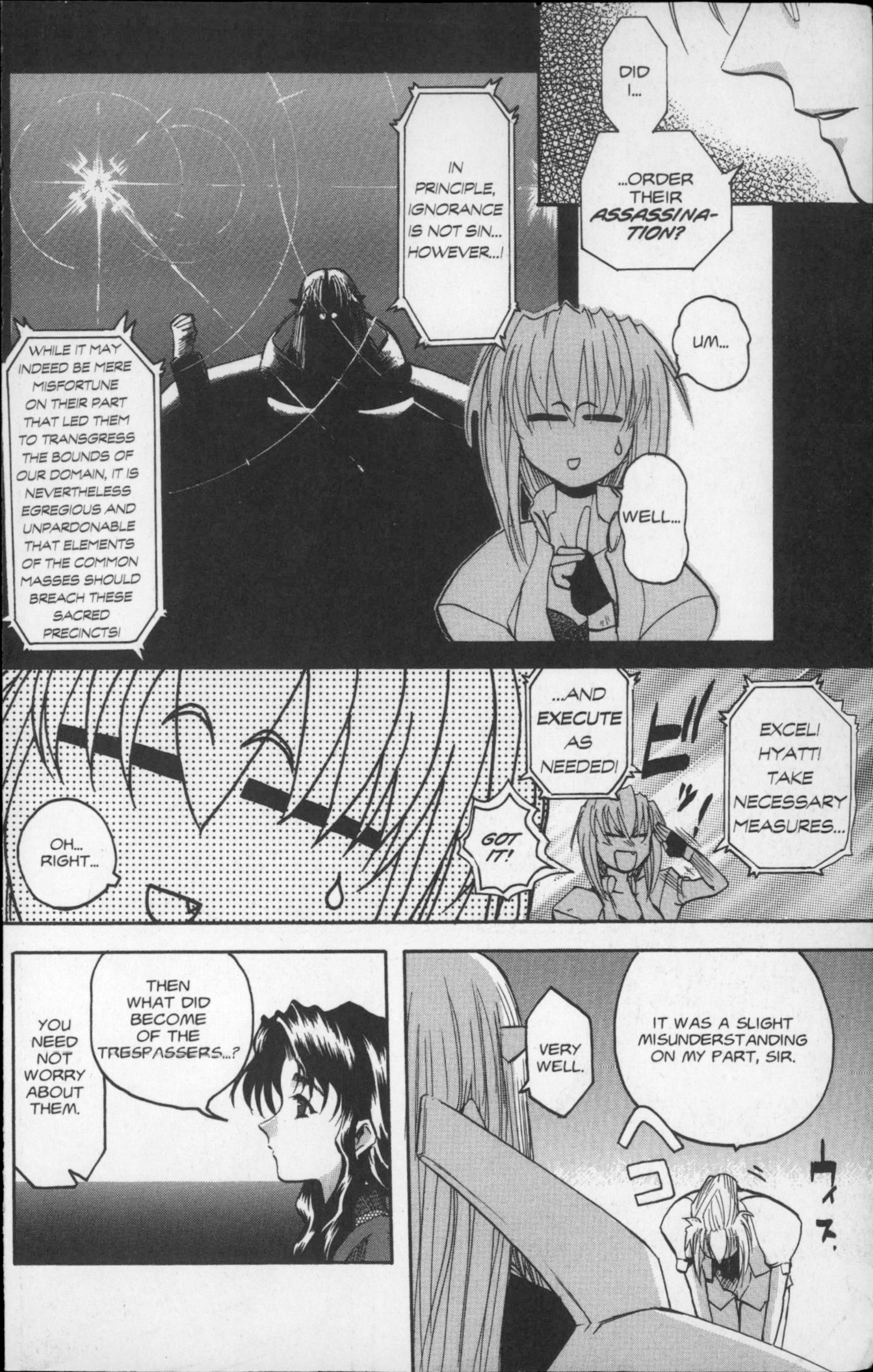
DID I...
...ORDER THEIR *ASSASSINATION?*
UM...
IN PRINCIPLE, IGNORANCE IS NOT SIN... HOWEVER...!
WELL...
WHILE IT MAY INDEED BE MERE MISFORTUNE ON THEIR PART THAT LED THEM TO TRANSGRESS THE BOUNDS OF OUR DOMAIN, IT IS NEVERTHELESS EGREGIOUS AND UNPARDONABLE THAT ELEMENTS OF THE COMMON MASSES SHOULD BREACH THESE SACRED PRECINCTS!
EXCEL! HYATT! TAKE NECESSARY MEASURES...
...AND EXECUTE AS NEEDED!
ビッ!
GOT IT!
OH... RIGHT...
IT WAS A SLIGHT MISUNDERSTANDING ON MY PART, SIR.
ヘコ
ウィス.
VERY WELL.
THEN WHAT DID BECOME OF THE TRESPASSERS...?
YOU NEED NOT WORRY ABOUT THEM.

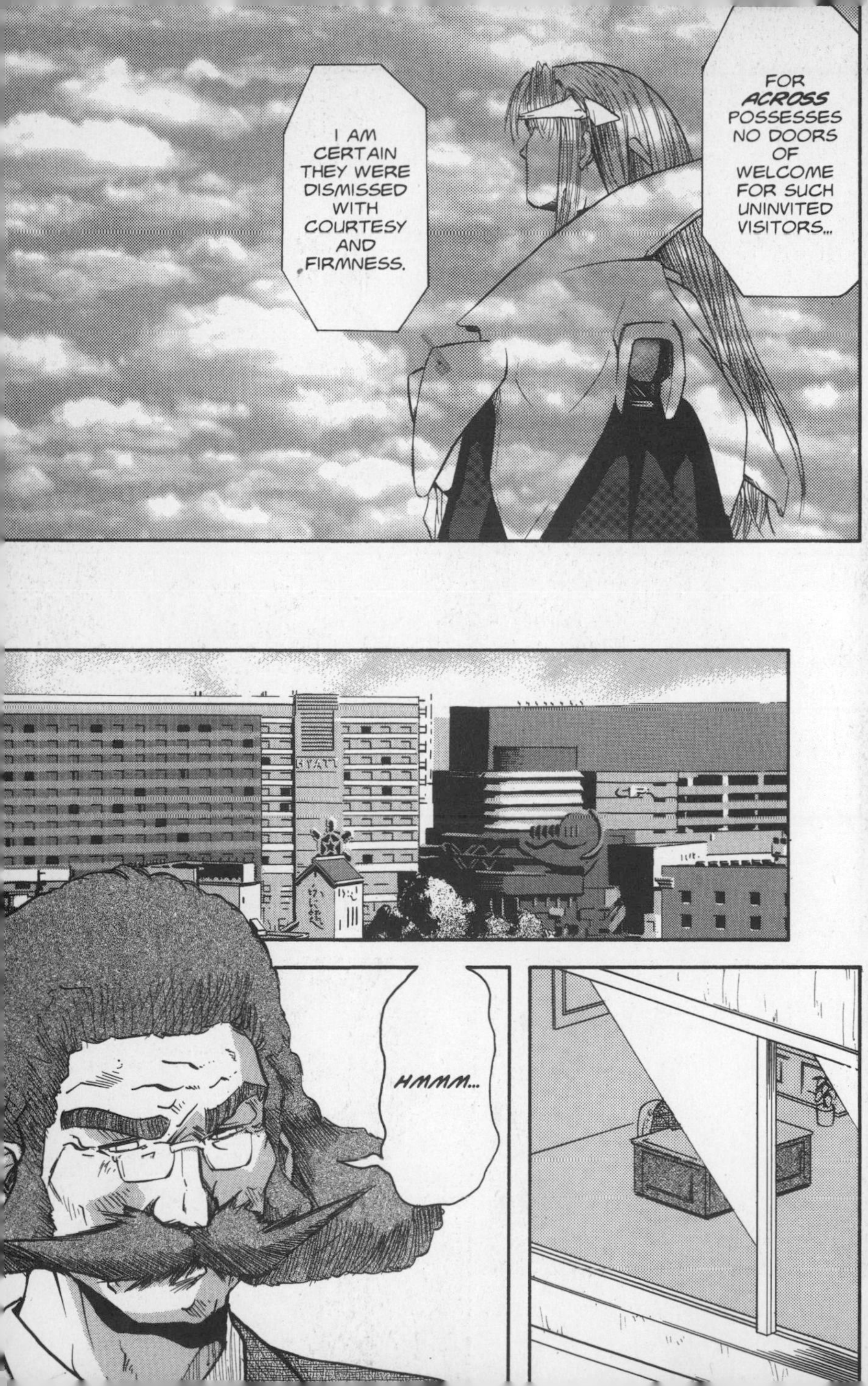
FOR ACROSS POSSESSES NO DOORS OF WELCOME FOR SUCH UNINVITED VISITORS...
I AM CERTAIN THEY WERE DISMISSED WITH COURTESY AND FIRMNESS.
HMMM...

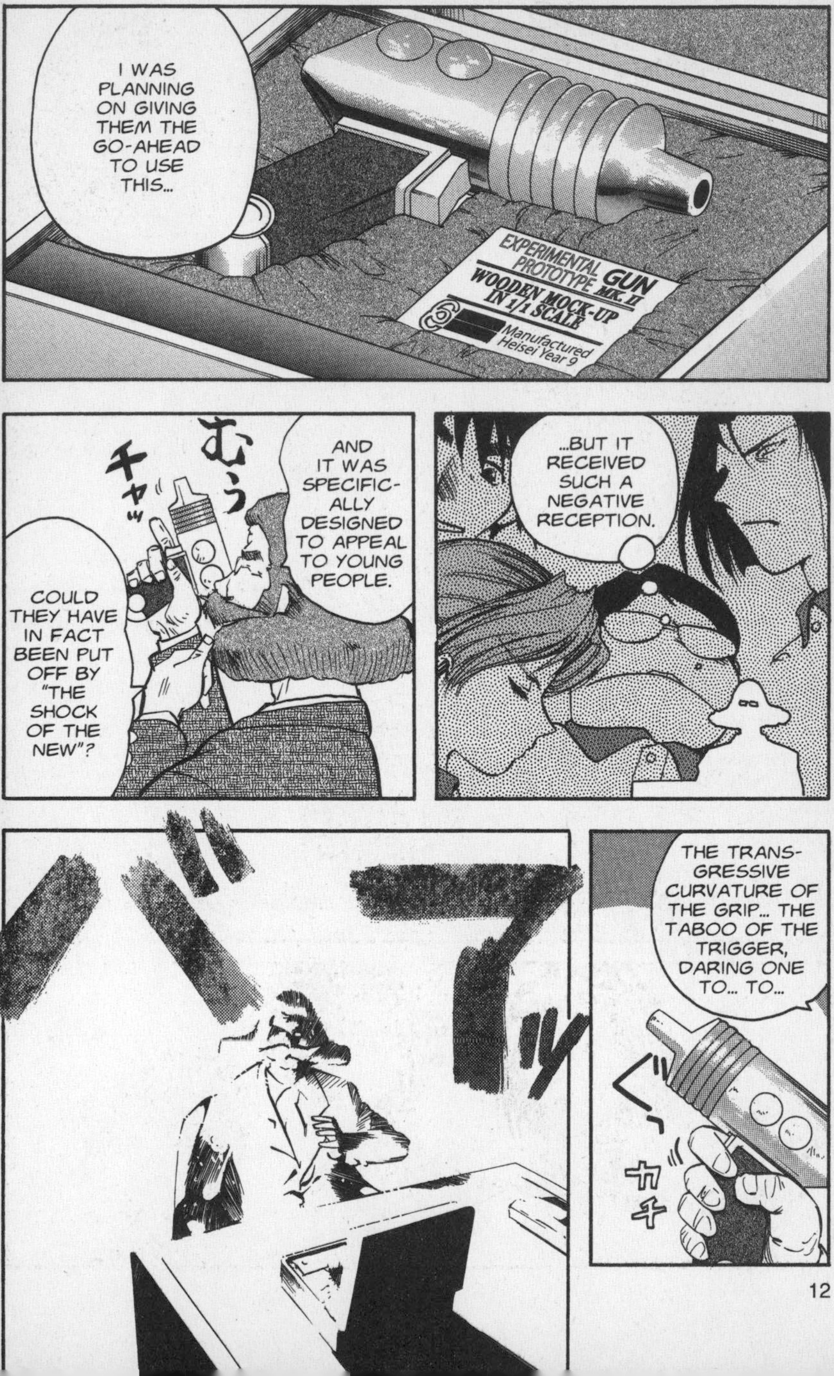
I WAS PLANNING ON GIVING THEM THE GO-AHEAD TO USE THIS...
EXPERIMENTAL PROTOTYPE GUN MK. II
WOODEN MOCK-UP IN 1/1 SCALE
Manufactured Heisei Year 9
...BUT IT RECEIVED SUCH A NEGATIVE RECEPTION.
むう
チャッ
AND IT WAS SPECIFIC-ALLY DESIGNED TO APPEAL TO YOUNG PEOPLE.
COULD THEY HAVE IN FACT BEEN PUT OFF BY "THE SHOCK OF THE NEW"?
THE TRANS-GRESSIVE CURVATURE OF THE GRIP... THE TABOO OF THE TRIGGER, DARING ONE TO... TO...
カチ

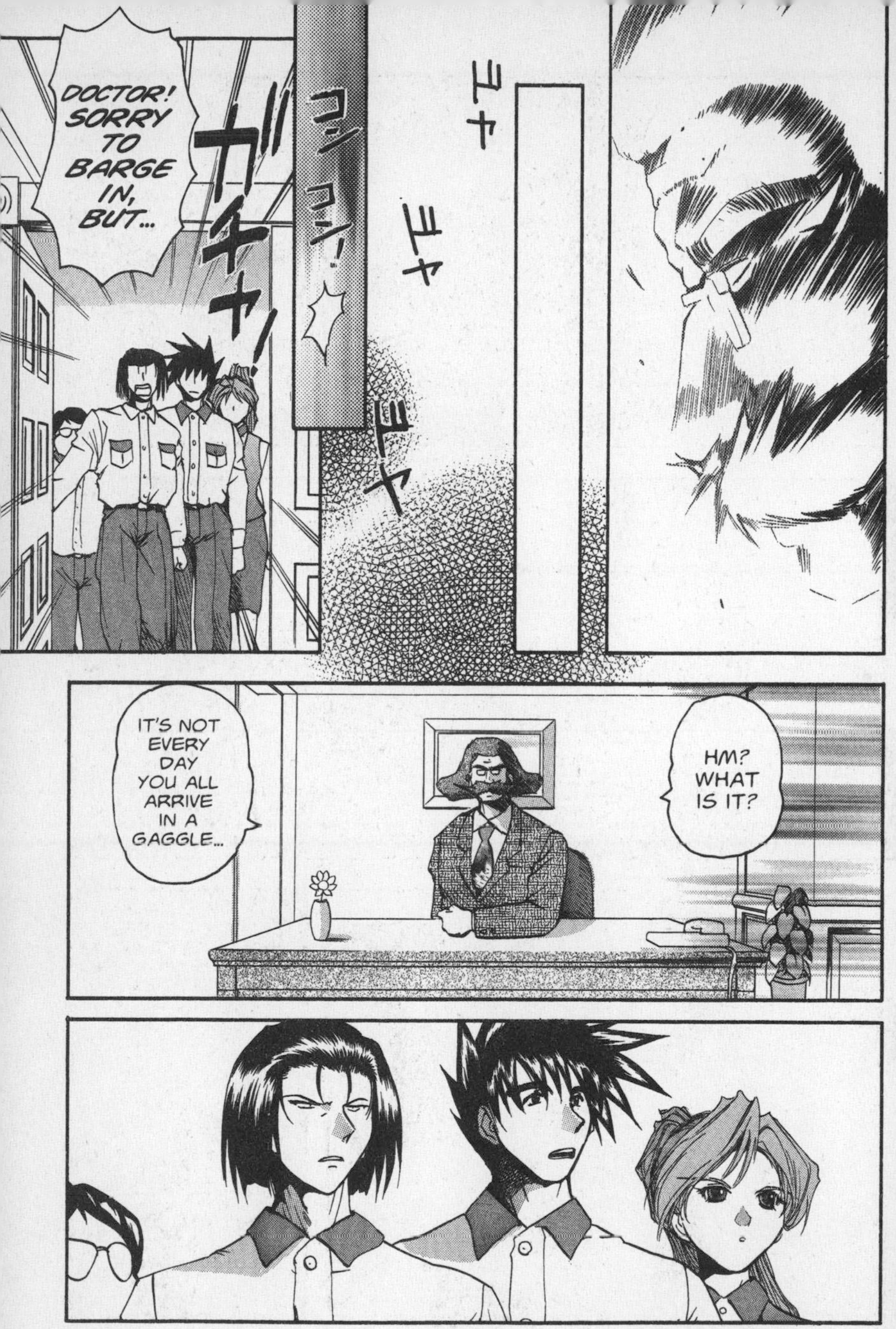
コンコン!
DOCTOR! SORRY TO BARGE IN, BUT...
ガチャ!
HM? WHAT IS IT?
IT'S NOT EVERY DAY YOU ALL ARRIVE IN A GAGGLE...

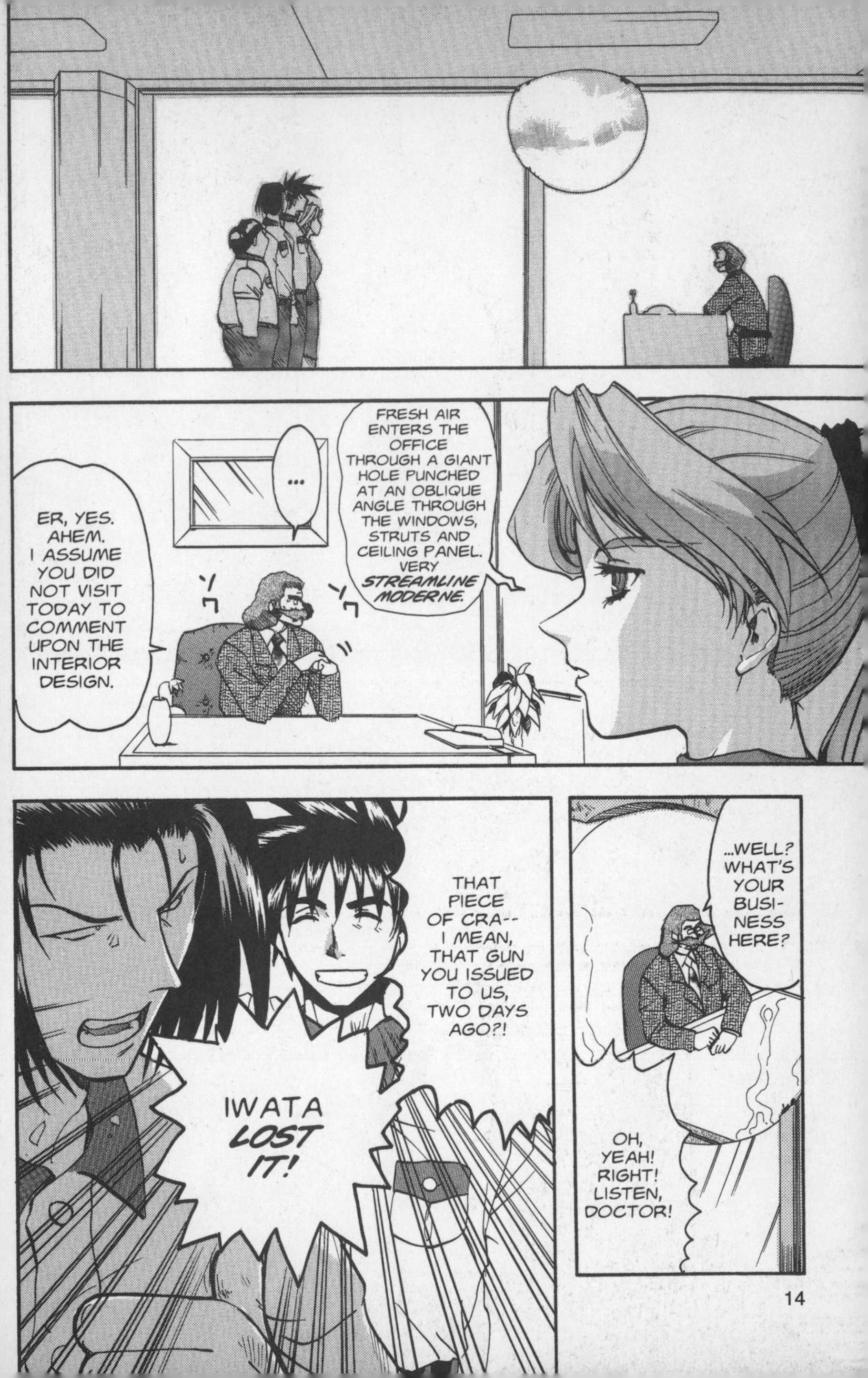
FRESH AIR ENTERS THE OFFICE THROUGH A GIANT HOLE PUNCHED AT AN OBLIQUE ANGLE THROUGH THE WINDOWS, STRUTS AND CEILING PANEL. VERY *STREAMLINE MODERNE.*
...
ER, YES. AHEM. I ASSUME YOU DID NOT VISIT TODAY TO COMMENT UPON THE INTERIOR DESIGN.
...WELL? WHAT'S YOUR BUSINESS HERE?
OH, YEAH! RIGHT! LISTEN, DOCTOR!
THAT PIECE OF CRA-- I MEAN, THAT GUN YOU ISSUED TO US, TWO DAYS AGO?!
IWATA *LOST IT!*

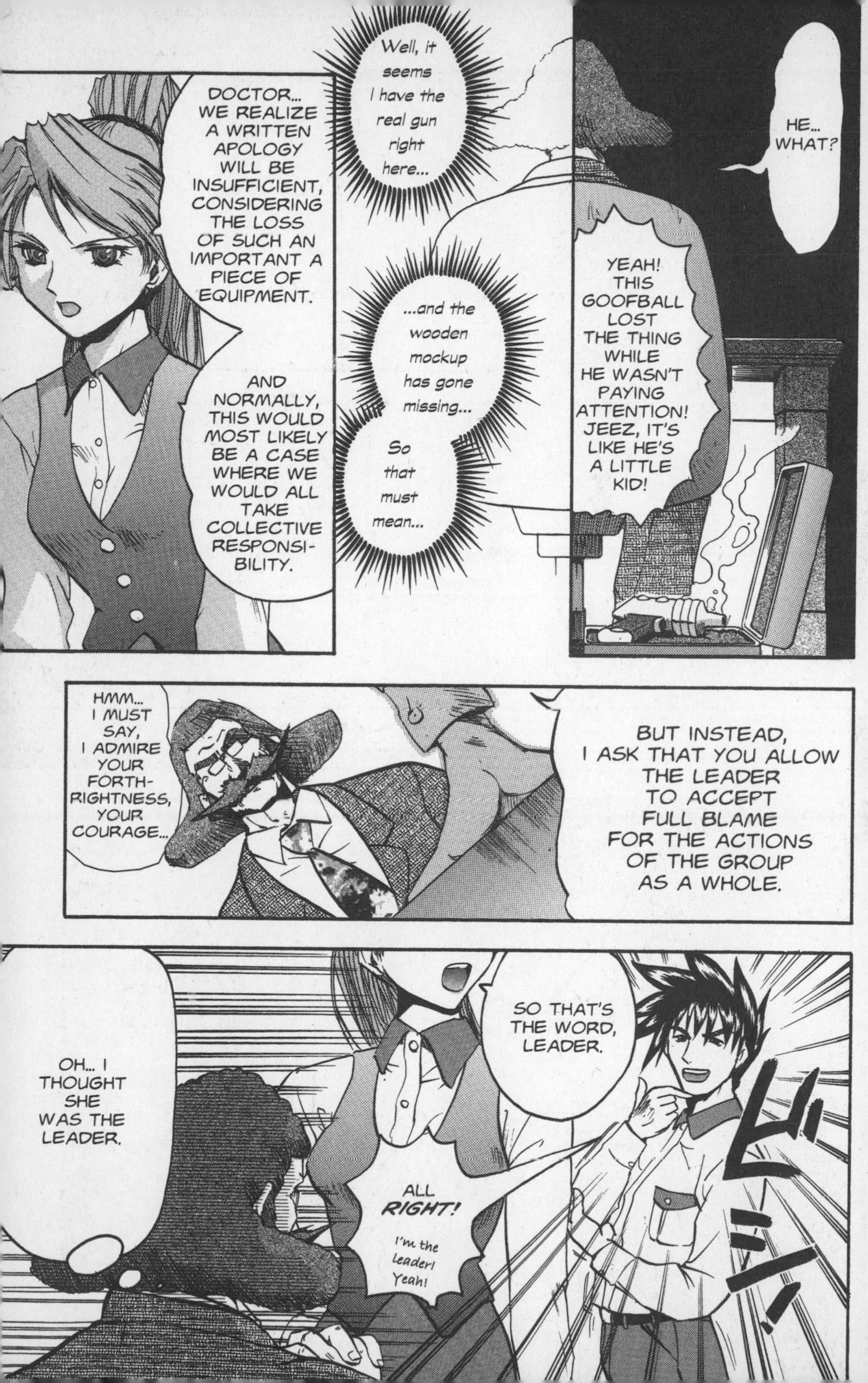
HE... WHAT?
YEAH! THIS GOOFBALL LOST THE THING WHILE HE WASN'T PAYING ATTENTION! JEEZ, IT'S LIKE HE'S A LITTLE KID!
Well, it seems I have the real gun right here...
...and the wooden mockup has gone missing...
So that must mean...
DOCTOR... WE REALIZE A WRITTEN APOLOGY WILL BE INSUFFICIENT, CONSIDERING THE LOSS OF SUCH AN IMPORTANT A PIECE OF EQUIPMENT.
AND NORMALLY, THIS WOULD MOST LIKELY BE A CASE WHERE WE WOULD ALL TAKE COLLECTIVE RESPONSI-BILITY.
BUT INSTEAD, I ASK THAT YOU ALLOW THE LEADER TO ACCEPT FULL BLAME FOR THE ACTIONS OF THE GROUP AS A WHOLE.
HMM... I MUST SAY, I ADMIRE YOUR FORTH-RIGHTNESS, YOUR COURAGE...
SO THAT'S THE WORD, LEADER.
ALL *RIGHT!*
I'm the leader! Yeah!
OH... I THOUGHT SHE WAS THE LEADER.

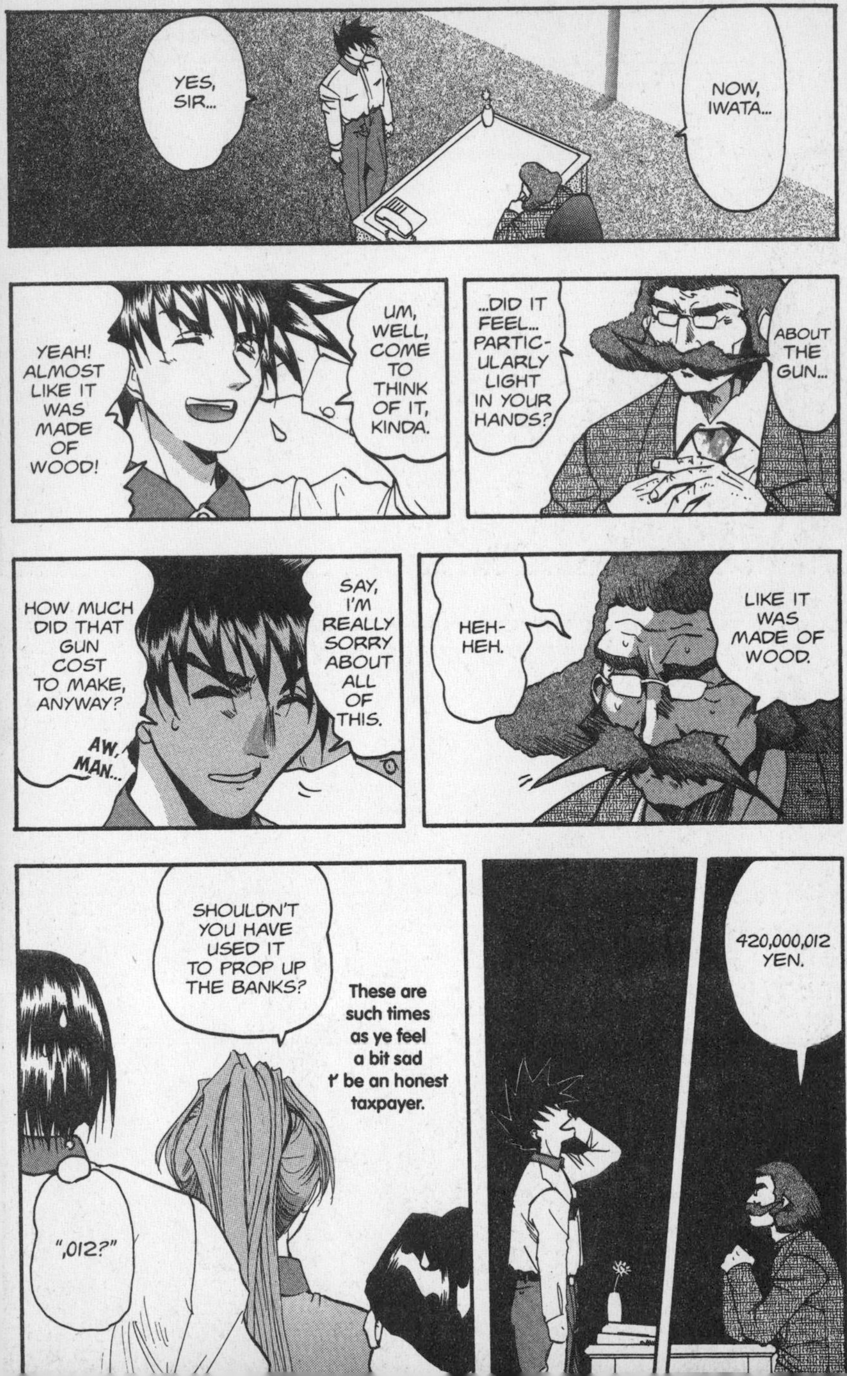
NOW, IWATA...
YES, SIR...
ABOUT THE GUN...
...DID IT FEEL... PARTICULARLY LIGHT IN YOUR HANDS?
UM, WELL, COME TO THINK OF IT, KINDA.
YEAH! ALMOST LIKE IT WAS MADE OF WOOD!
LIKE IT WAS MADE OF WOOD.
HEH-HEH.
SAY, I'M REALLY SORRY ABOUT ALL OF THIS.
HOW MUCH DID THAT GUN COST TO MAKE, ANYWAY?
AW, MAN...
420,000,012 YEN.
SHOULDN'T YOU HAVE USED IT TO PROP UP THE BANKS?
These are such times as ye feel a bit sad t' be an honest taxpayer.
",012?"

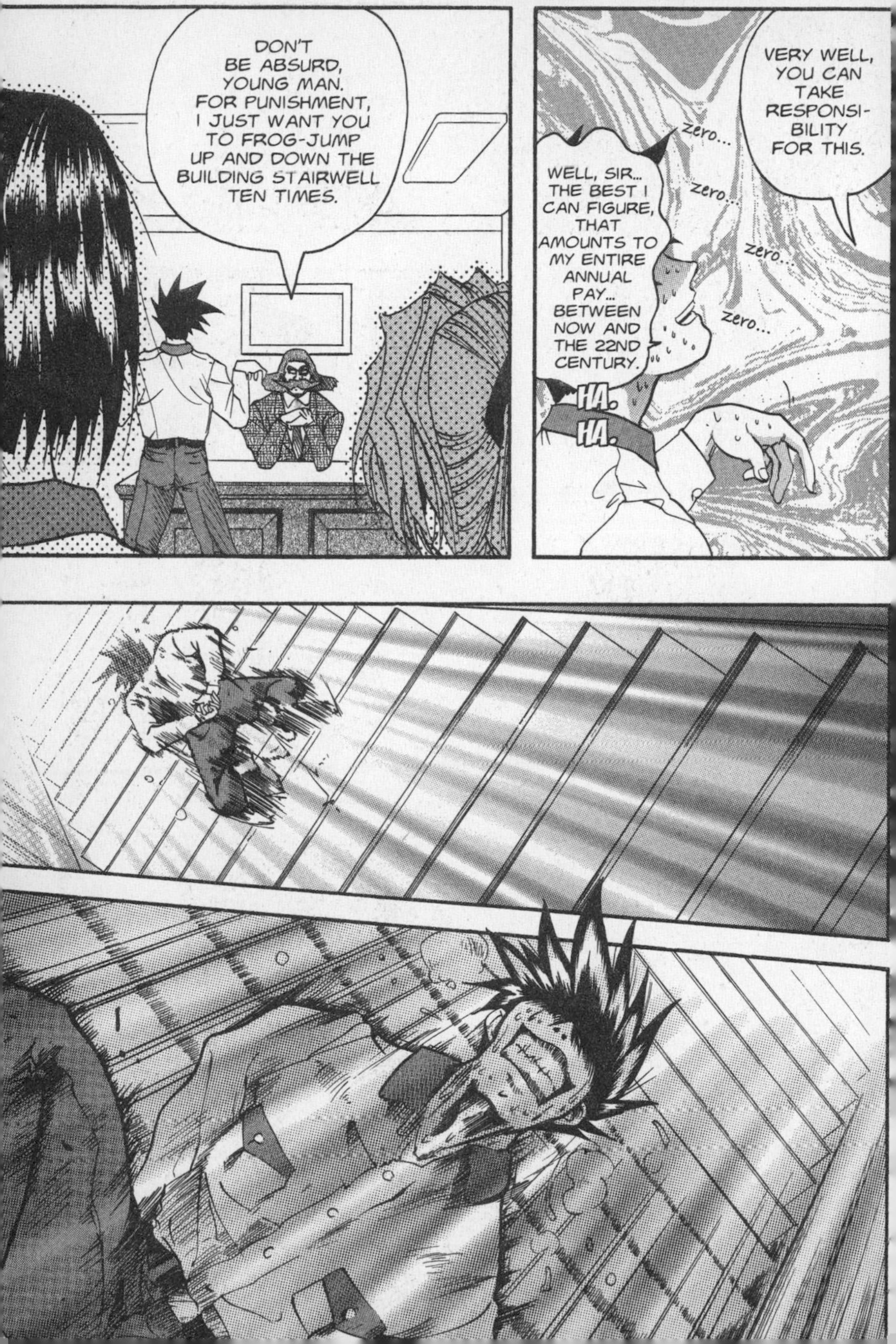
VERY WELL, YOU CAN TAKE RESPONSIBILITY FOR THIS.
zero... zero... zero... zero...
WELL, SIR... THE BEST I CAN FIGURE, THAT AMOUNTS TO MY ENTIRE ANNUAL PAY... BETWEEN NOW AND THE 22ND CENTURY.
HA. HA.
DON'T BE ABSURD, YOUNG MAN. FOR PUNISHMENT, I JUST WANT YOU TO FROG-JUMP UP AND DOWN THE BUILDING STAIRWELL TEN TIMES.

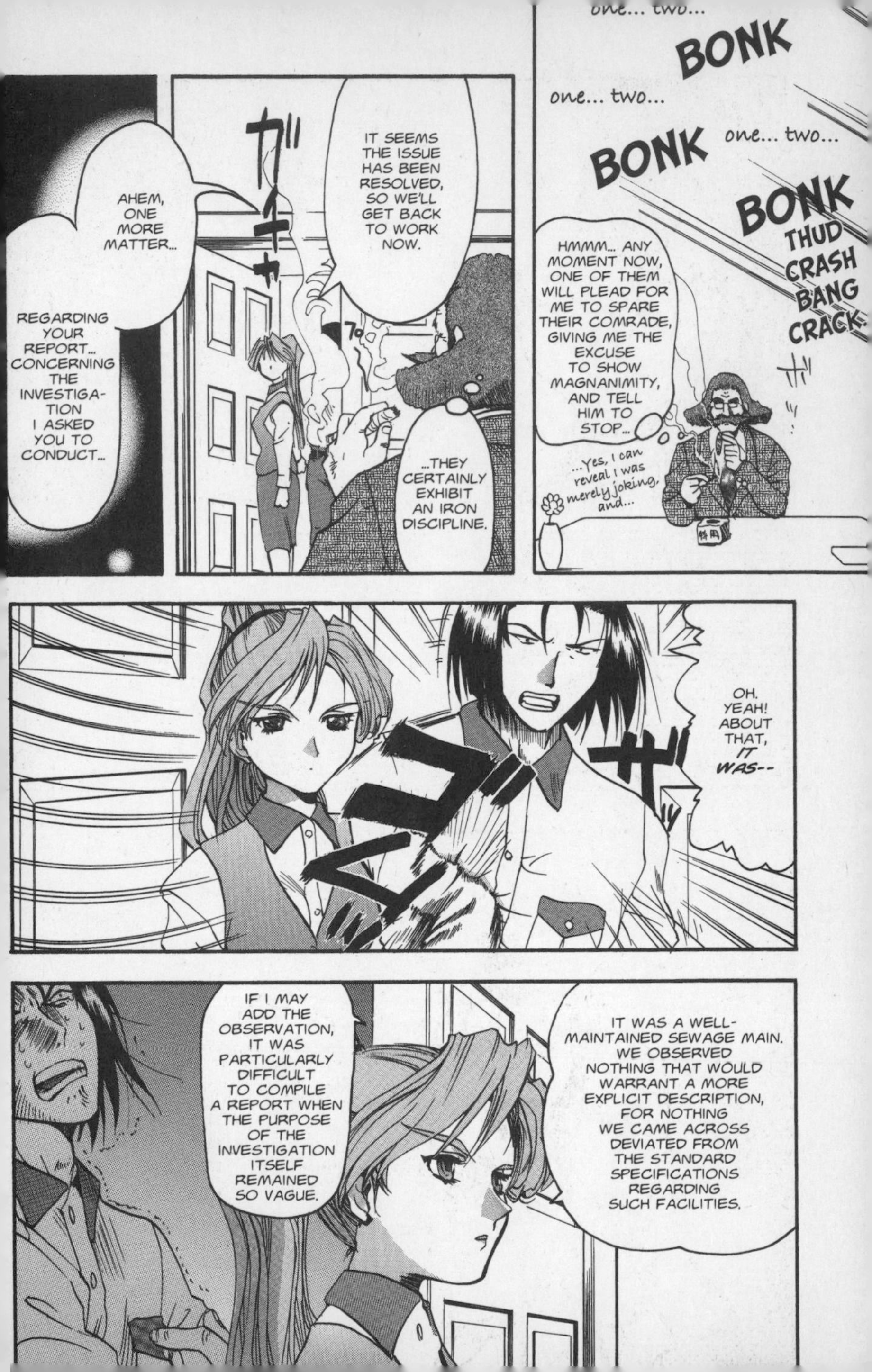
one... two...
BONK
one... two...
BONK
one... two...
BONK
THUD
CRASH
BANG
CRACK
HMMM... ANY MOMENT NOW, ONE OF THEM WILL PLEAD FOR ME TO SPARE THEIR COMRADE, GIVING ME THE EXCUSE TO SHOW MAGNANIMITY, AND TELL HIM TO STOP...
...Yes, I can reveal I was merely joking, and...
IT SEEMS THE ISSUE HAS BEEN RESOLVED, SO WE'LL GET BACK TO WORK NOW.
...THEY CERTAINLY EXHIBIT AN IRON DISCIPLINE.
AHEM, ONE MORE MATTER...
REGARDING YOUR REPORT... CONCERNING THE INVESTIGA-TION I ASKED YOU TO CONDUCT...
OH. YEAH! ABOUT THAT, IT WAS--
IT WAS A WELL-MAINTAINED SEWAGE MAIN. WE OBSERVED NOTHING THAT WOULD WARRANT A MORE EXPLICIT DESCRIPTION, FOR NOTHING WE CAME ACROSS DEVIATED FROM THE STANDARD SPECIFICATIONS REGARDING SUCH FACILITIES.
IF I MAY ADD THE OBSERVATION, IT WAS PARTICULARLY DIFFICULT TO COMPILE A REPORT WHEN THE PURPOSE OF THE INVESTIGATION ITSELF REMAINED SO VAGUE.

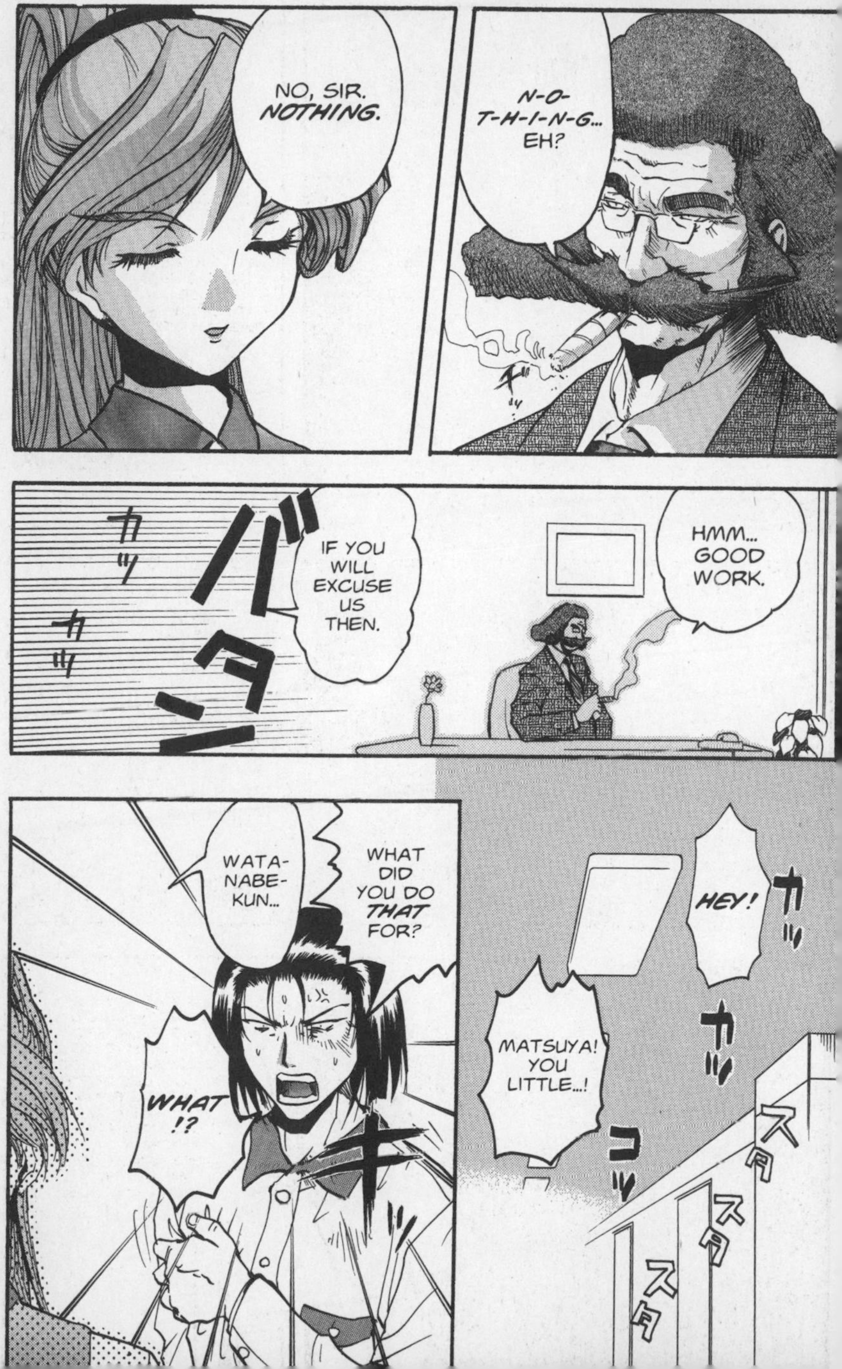
N-O-
T-H-I-N-G...
EH?
NO, SIR.
NOTHING.
HMM...
GOOD
WORK.
IF YOU
WILL
EXCUSE
US
THEN.
バタン
カッ
カッ
HEY!
MATSUYA!
YOU
LITTLE...!
WHAT
DID
YOU DO
THAT
FOR?
WATA-
NABE-
KUN...
*WHAT
!?*

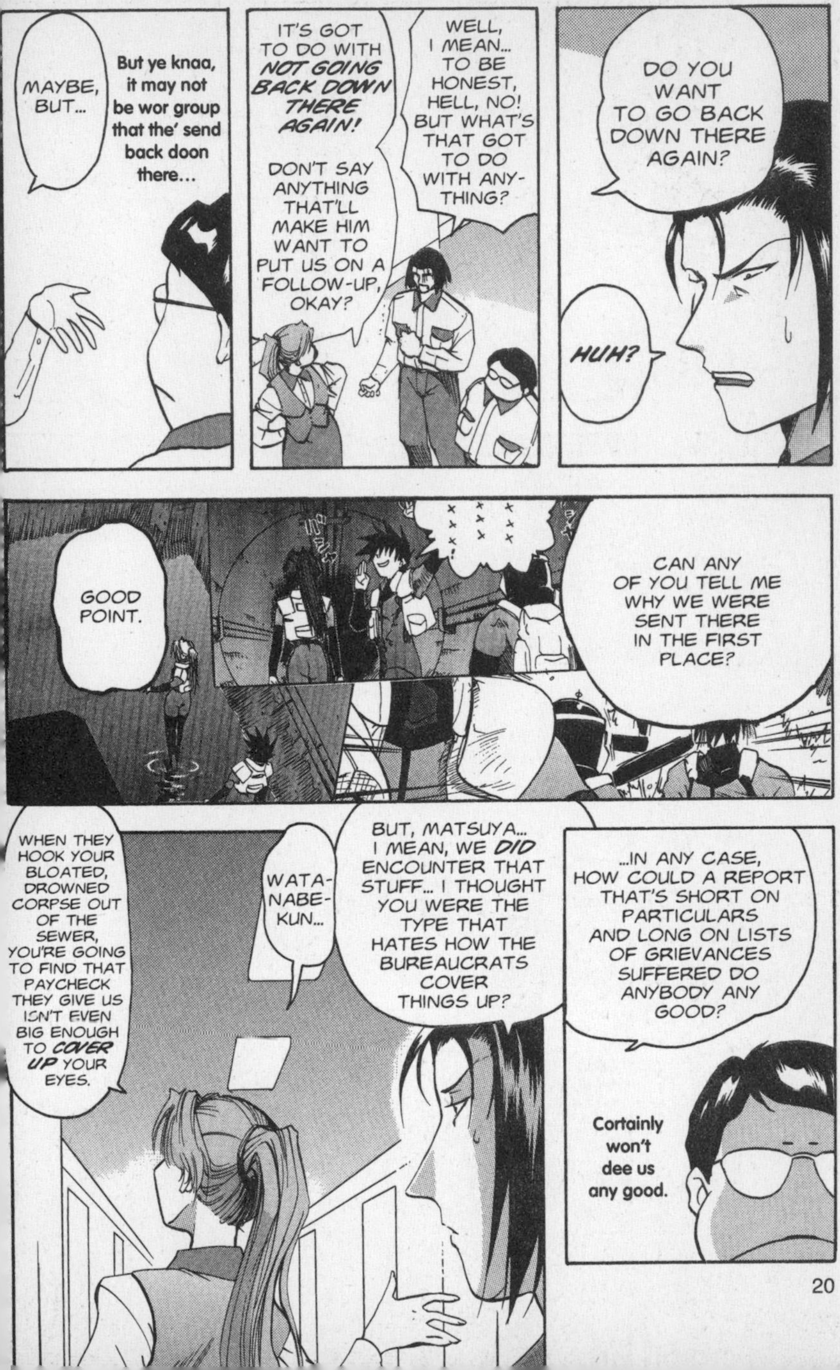
DO YOU WANT TO GO BACK DOWN THERE AGAIN?
HUH?
WELL, I MEAN... TO BE HONEST, HELL, NO! BUT WHAT'S THAT GOT TO DO WITH ANY-THING?
IT'S GOT TO DO WITH NOT GOING BACK DOWN THERE AGAIN!
DON'T SAY ANYTHING THAT'LL MAKE HIM WANT TO PUT US ON A FOLLOW-UP, OKAY?
MAYBE, BUT...
But ye knaa, it may not be wor group that the' send back doon there...
CAN ANY OF YOU TELL ME WHY WE WERE SENT THERE IN THE FIRST PLACE?
GOOD POINT.
...IN ANY CASE, HOW COULD A REPORT THAT'S SHORT ON PARTICULARS AND LONG ON LISTS OF GRIEVANCES SUFFERED DO ANYBODY ANY GOOD?
Cortainly won't dee us any good.
BUT, MATSUYA... I MEAN, WE DID ENCOUNTER THAT STUFF... I THOUGHT YOU WERE THE TYPE THAT HATES HOW THE BUREAUCRATS COVER THINGS UP?
WATA-NABE-KUN...
WHEN THEY HOOK YOUR BLOATED, DROWNED CORPSE OUT OF THE SEWER, YOU'RE GOING TO FIND THAT PAYCHECK THEY GIVE US ISN'T EVEN BIG ENOUGH TO COVER UP YOUR EYES.

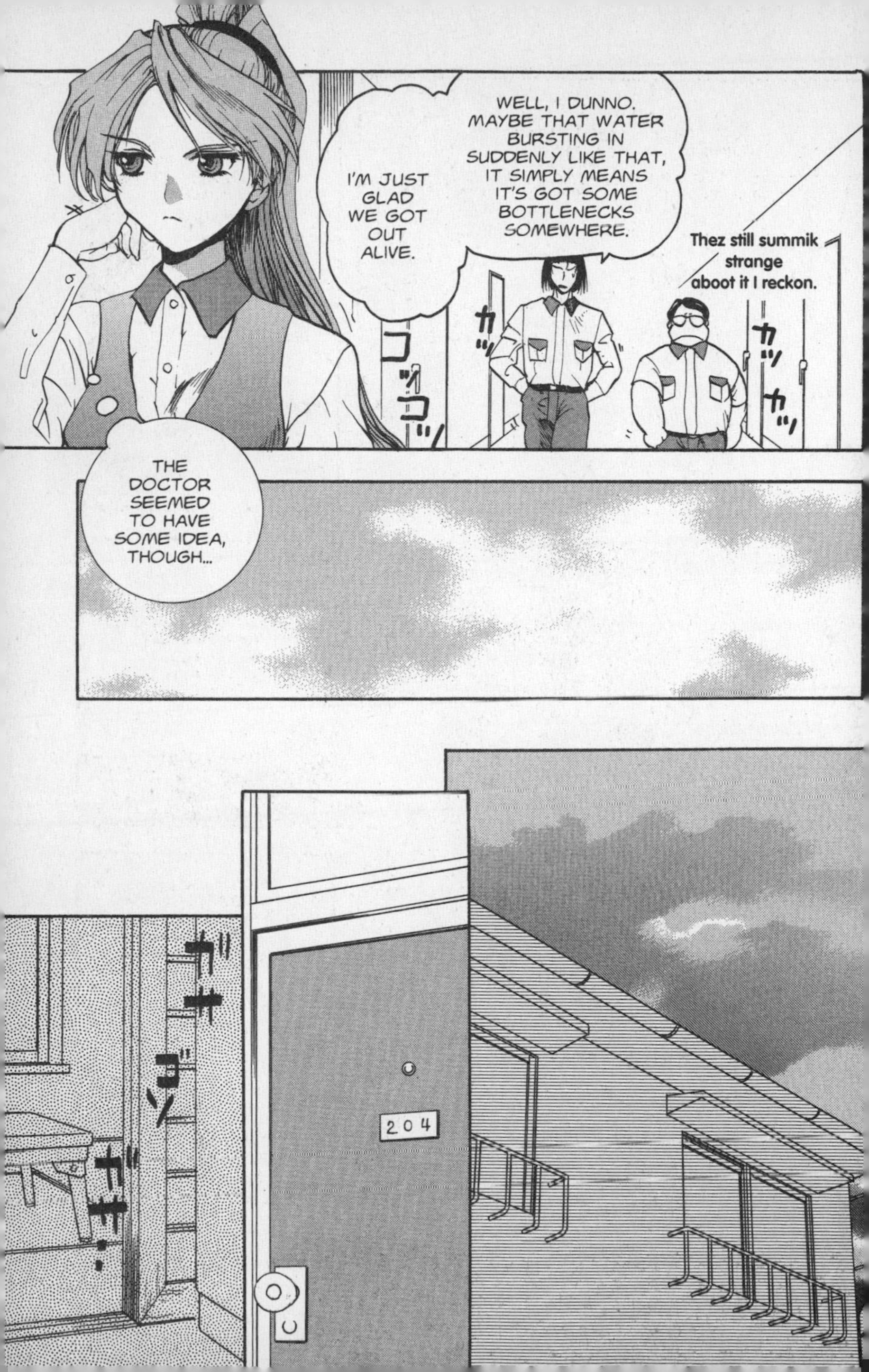
Thez still summik strange aboot it I reckon.
WELL, I DUNNO. MAYBE THAT WATER BURSTING IN SUDDENLY LIKE THAT, IT SIMPLY MEANS IT'S GOT SOME BOTTLENECKS SOMEWHERE.
I'M JUST GLAD WE GOT OUT ALIVE.
THE DOCTOR SEEMED TO HAVE SOME IDEA, THOUGH...
204

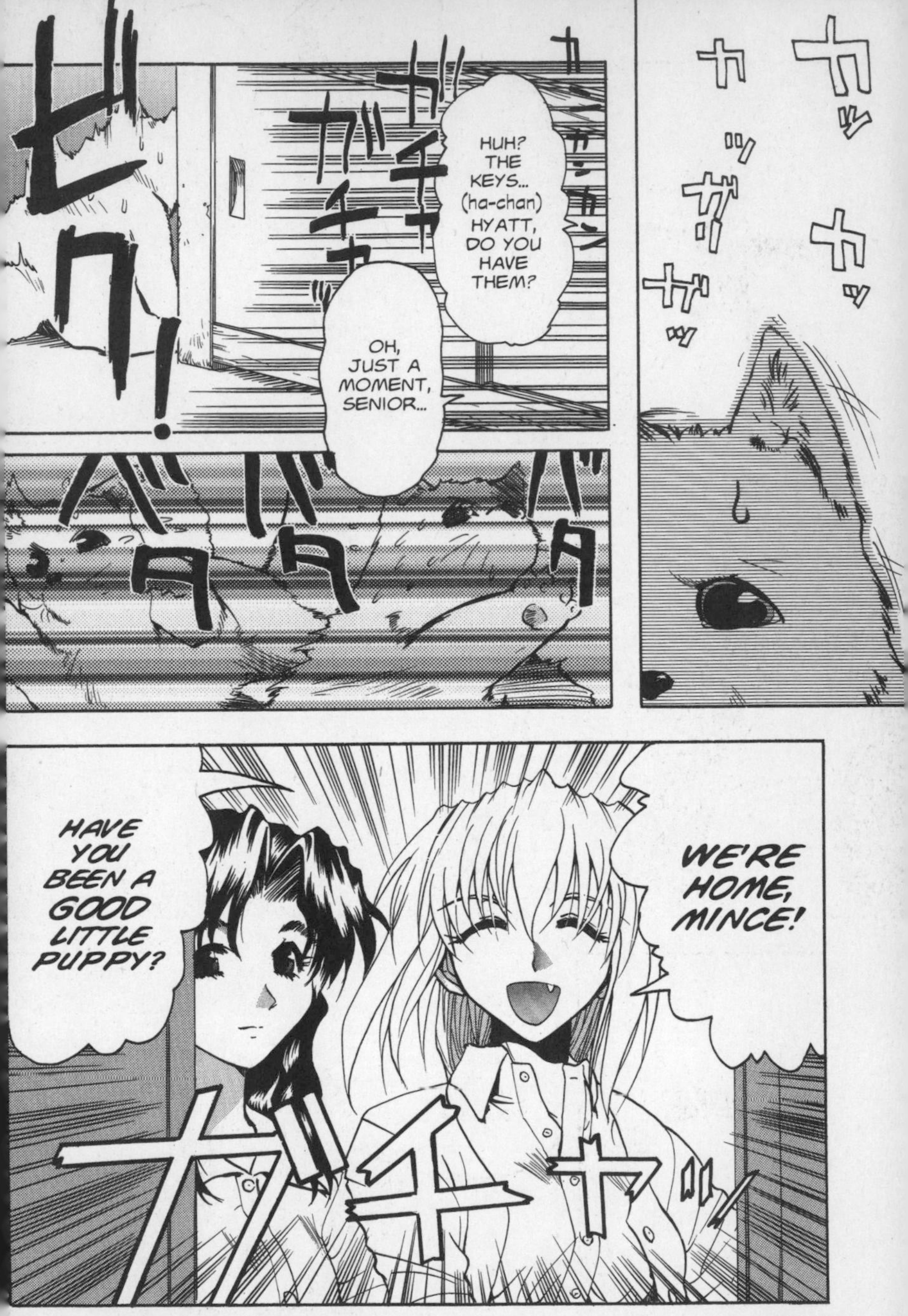
HUH? THE KEYS... (ha-chan) HYATT, DO YOU HAVE THEM?
OH, JUST A MOMENT, SENIOR...
WE'RE HOME, MINCE!
HAVE YOU BEEN A GOOD LITTLE PUPPY?

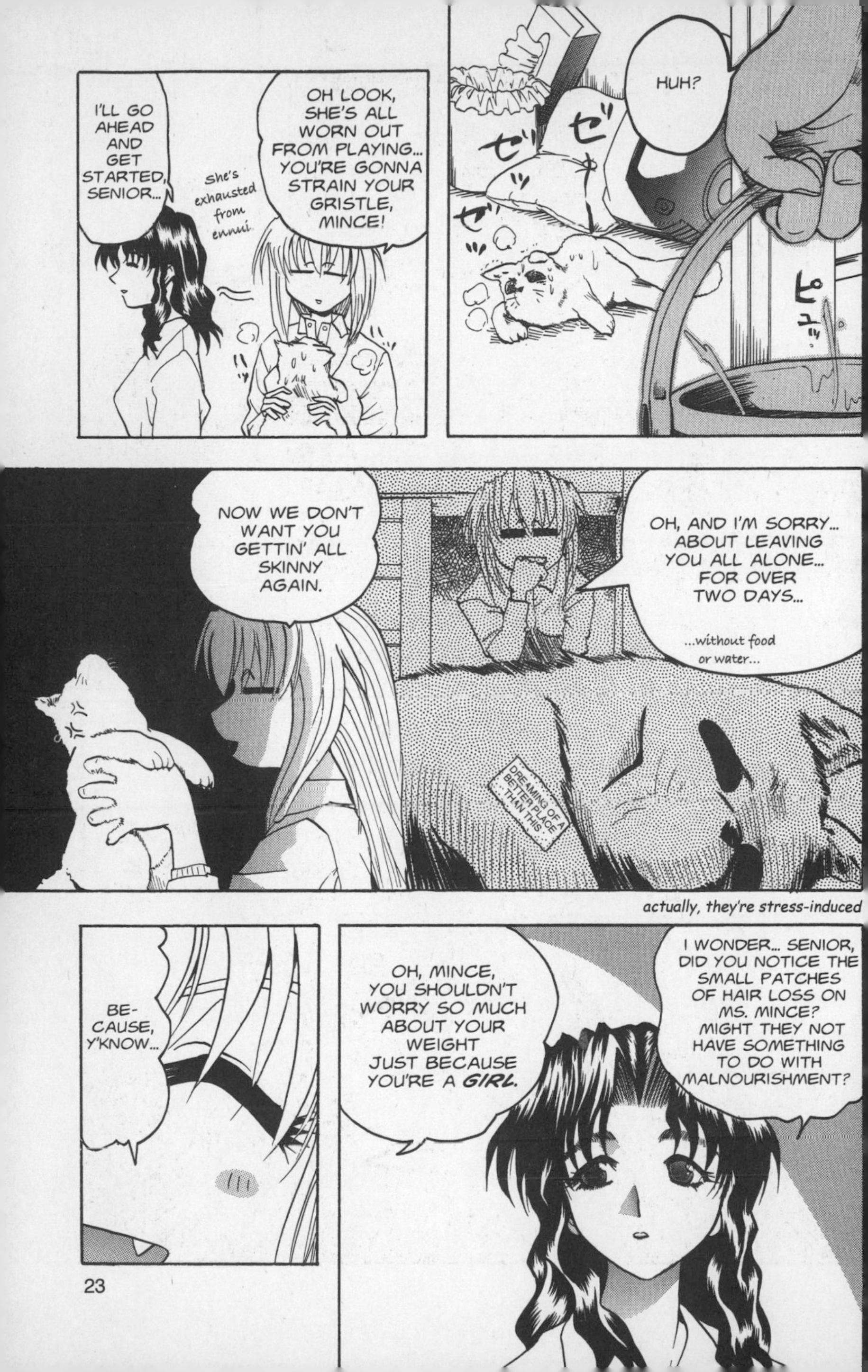
HUH?
ゼ
ゼ
ゼ
ピュッ
OH LOOK, SHE'S ALL WORN OUT FROM PLAYING... YOU'RE GONNA STRAIN YOUR GRISTLE, MINCE!
she's exhausted from ennui
I'LL GO AHEAD AND GET STARTED, SENIOR...
OH, AND I'M SORRY... ABOUT LEAVING YOU ALL ALONE... FOR OVER TWO DAYS...
...without food or water...
DREAMING OF A BETTER PLACE THAN THIS...
NOW WE DON'T WANT YOU GETTIN' ALL SKINNY AGAIN.
actually, they're stress-induced
I WONDER... SENIOR, DID YOU NOTICE THE SMALL PATCHES OF HAIR LOSS ON MS. MINCE? MIGHT THEY NOT HAVE SOMETHING TO DO WITH MALNOURISHMENT?
OH, MINCE, YOU SHOULDN'T WORRY SO MUCH ABOUT YOUR WEIGHT JUST BECAUSE YOU'RE A GIRL.
BE-CAUSE, Y'KNOW...

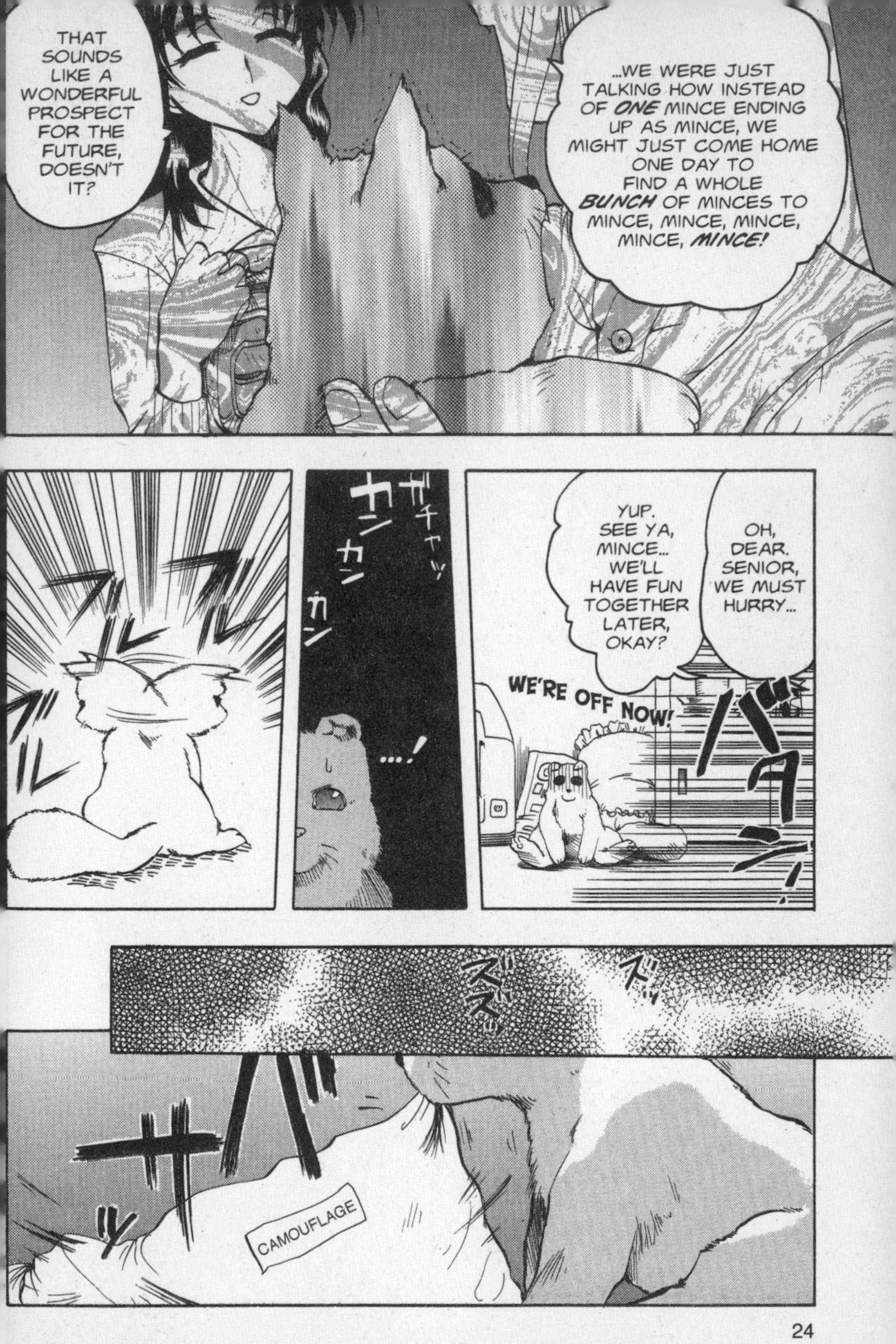
...WE WERE JUST TALKING HOW INSTEAD OF ONE MINCE ENDING UP AS MINCE, WE MIGHT JUST COME HOME ONE DAY TO FIND A WHOLE BUNCH OF MINCES TO MINCE, MINCE, MINCE, MINCE, MINCE!
THAT SOUNDS LIKE A WONDERFUL PROSPECT FOR THE FUTURE, DOESN'T IT?
OH, DEAR. SENIOR, WE MUST HURRY...
YUP. SEE YA, MINCE... WE'LL HAVE FUN TOGETHER LATER, OKAY?
WE'RE OFF NOW!
ガチャッ
カン
カン
カン
....!
CAMOUFLAGE

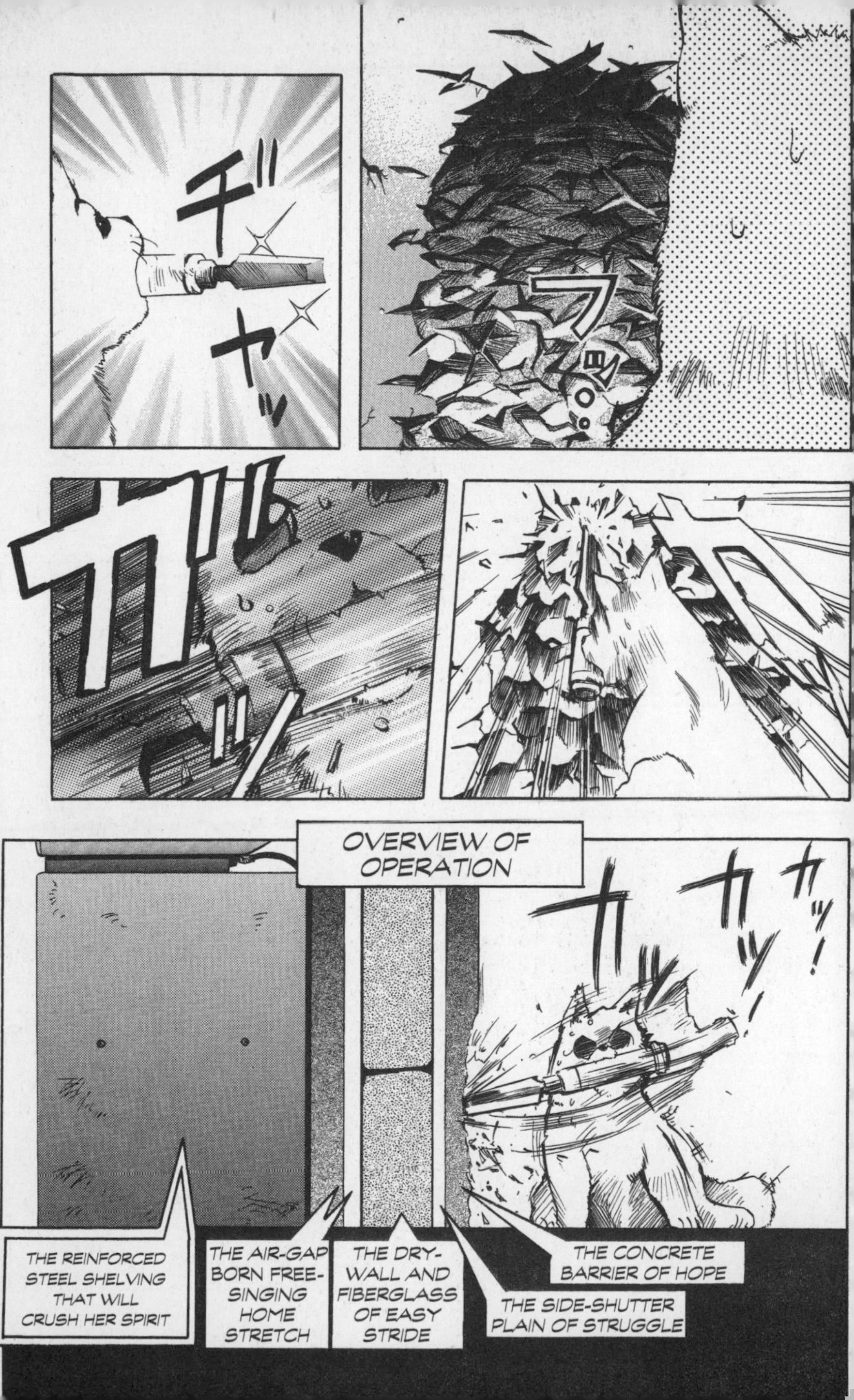
OVERVIEW OF OPERATION
THE CONCRETE BARRIER OF HOPE
THE SIDE-SHUTTER PLAIN OF STRUGGLE
THE DRY-WALL AND FIBERGLASS OF EASY STRIDE
THE AIR-GAP BORN FREE-SINGING HOME STRETCH
THE REINFORCED STEEL SHELVING THAT WILL CRUSH HER SPIRIT

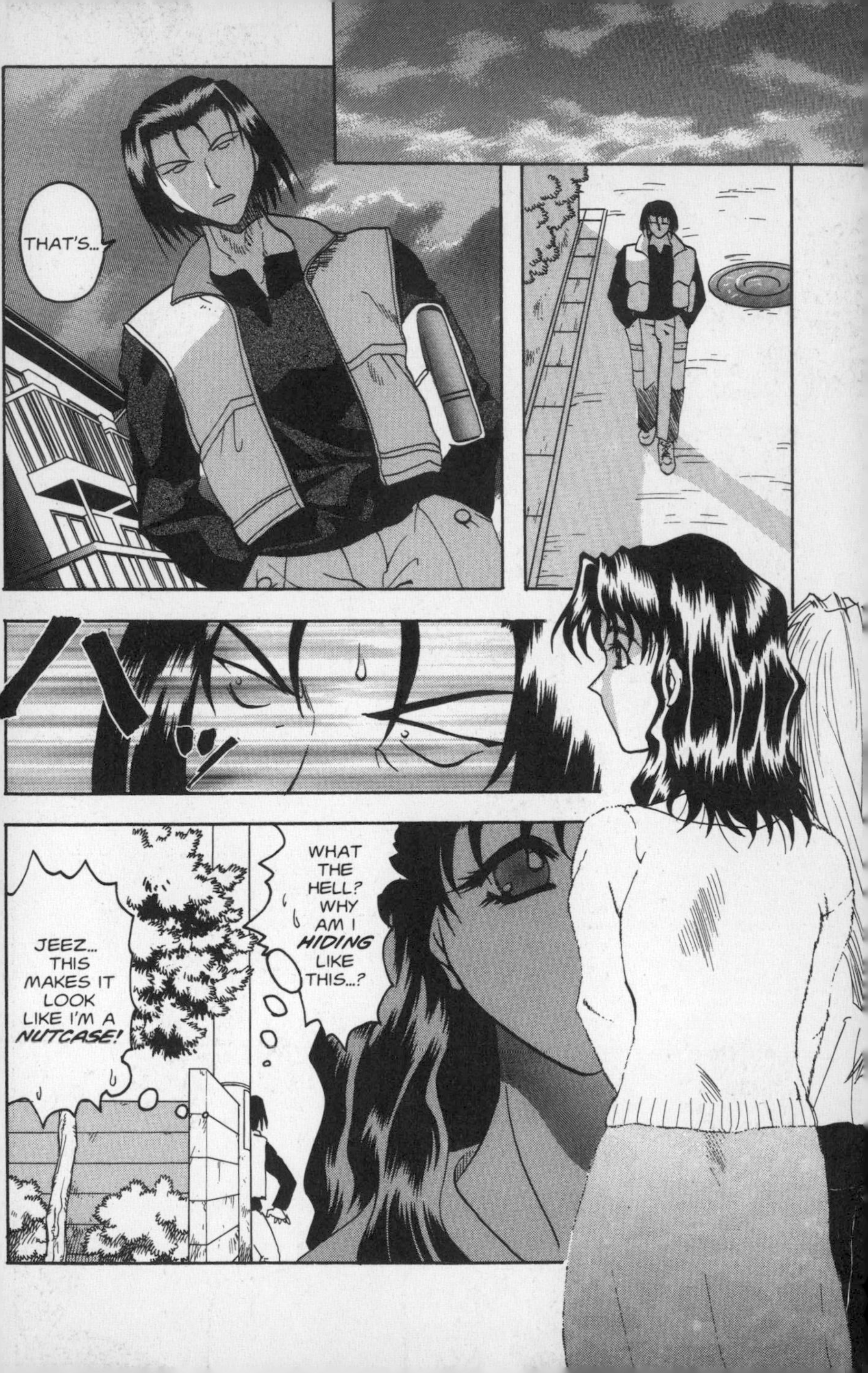
THAT'S...
WHAT THE HELL? WHY AM I *HIDING* LIKE THIS...?
JEEZ... THIS MAKES IT LOOK LIKE I'M A *NUTCASE!*

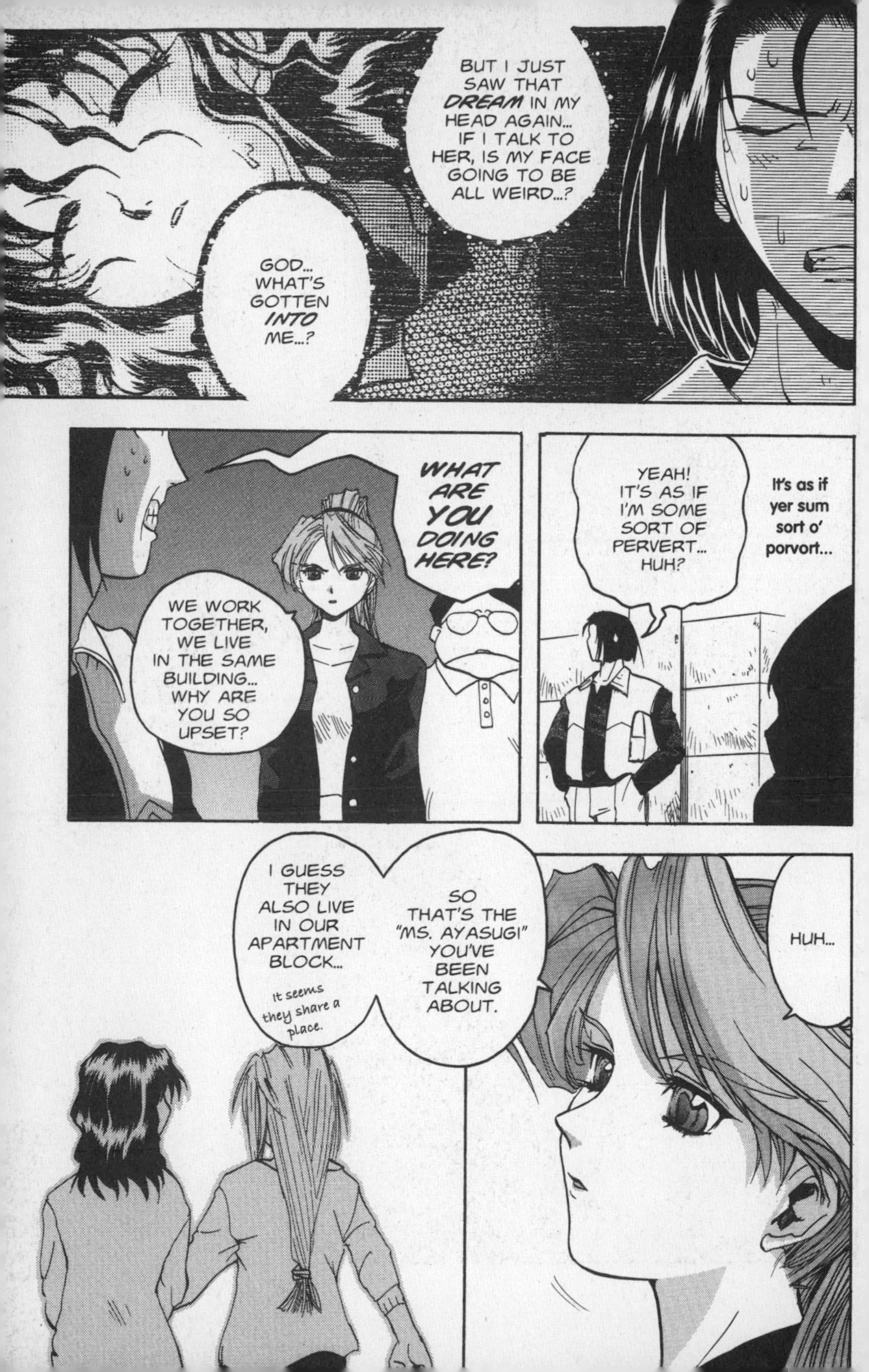
BUT I JUST SAW THAT *DREAM* IN MY HEAD AGAIN... IF I TALK TO HER, IS MY FACE GOING TO BE ALL WEIRD...?
GOD... WHAT'S GOTTEN *INTO* ME...?
It's as if yer sum sort o' porvort...
YEAH! IT'S AS IF I'M SOME SORT OF PERVERT... HUH?
WHAT ARE YOU DOING HERE?
WE WORK TOGETHER, WE LIVE IN THE SAME BUILDING... WHY ARE YOU SO UPSET?
HUH...
SO THAT'S THE "MS. AYASUGI" YOU'VE BEEN TALKING ABOUT.
I GUESS THEY ALSO LIVE IN OUR APARTMENT BLOCK...
It seems they share a place.

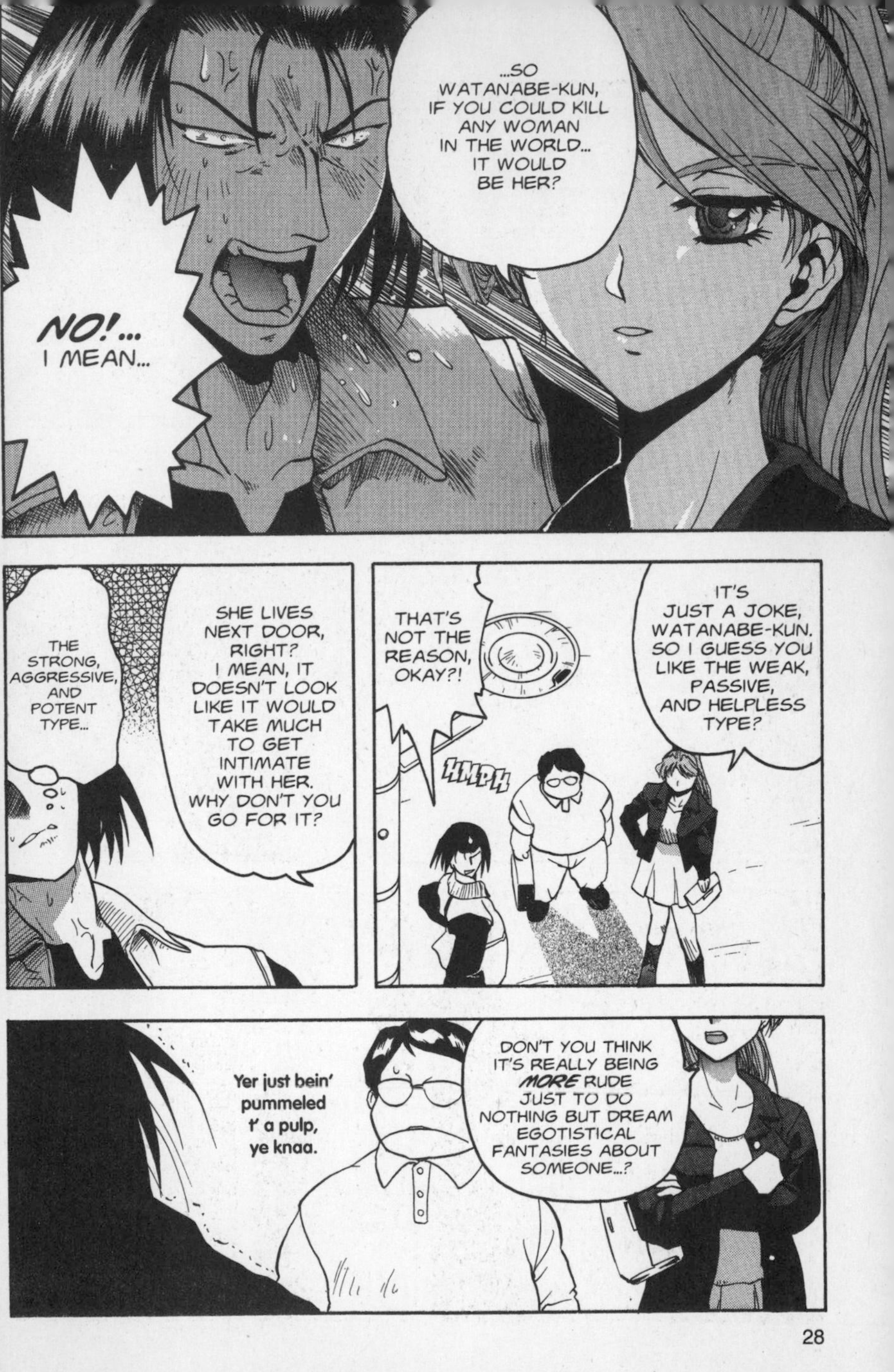
...SO WATANABE-KUN, IF YOU COULD KILL ANY WOMAN IN THE WORLD... IT WOULD BE HER?
NO!... I MEAN...
IT'S JUST A JOKE, WATANABE-KUN. SO I GUESS YOU LIKE THE WEAK, PASSIVE, AND HELPLESS TYPE?
THAT'S NOT THE REASON, OKAY?!
HMPH
SHE LIVES NEXT DOOR, RIGHT? I MEAN, IT DOESN'T LOOK LIKE IT WOULD TAKE MUCH TO GET INTIMATE WITH HER. WHY DON'T YOU GO FOR IT?
THE STRONG, AGGRESSIVE, AND POTENT TYPE...
DON'T YOU THINK IT'S REALLY BEING MORE RUDE JUST TO DO NOTHING BUT DREAM EGOTISTICAL FANTASIES ABOUT SOMEONE...?
Yer just bein' pummeled t' a pulp, ye knaa.

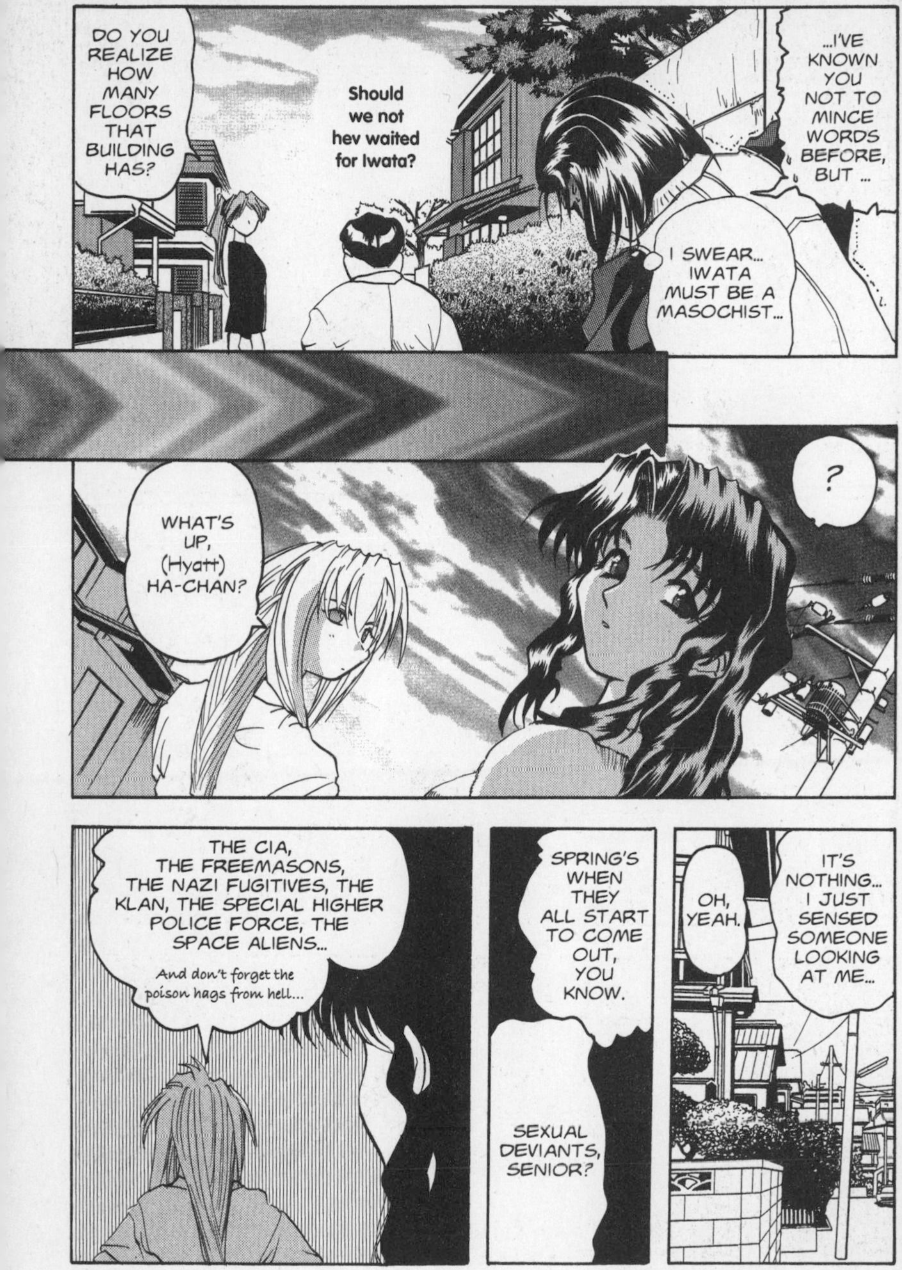
...I'VE KNOWN YOU NOT TO MINCE WORDS BEFORE, BUT ...
I SWEAR... IWATA MUST BE A MASOCHIST...
Should we not hev waited for Iwata?
DO YOU REALIZE HOW MANY FLOORS THAT BUILDING HAS?
?
WHAT'S UP, (Hyatt) HA-CHAN?
IT'S NOTHING... I JUST SENSED SOMEONE LOOKING AT ME...
OH, YEAH.
SPRING'S WHEN THEY ALL START TO COME OUT, YOU KNOW.
SEXUAL DEVIANTS, SENIOR?
THE CIA, THE FREEMASONS, THE NAZI FUGITIVES, THE KLAN, THE SPECIAL HIGHER POLICE FORCE, THE SPACE ALIENS...
And don't forget the poison hags from hell...

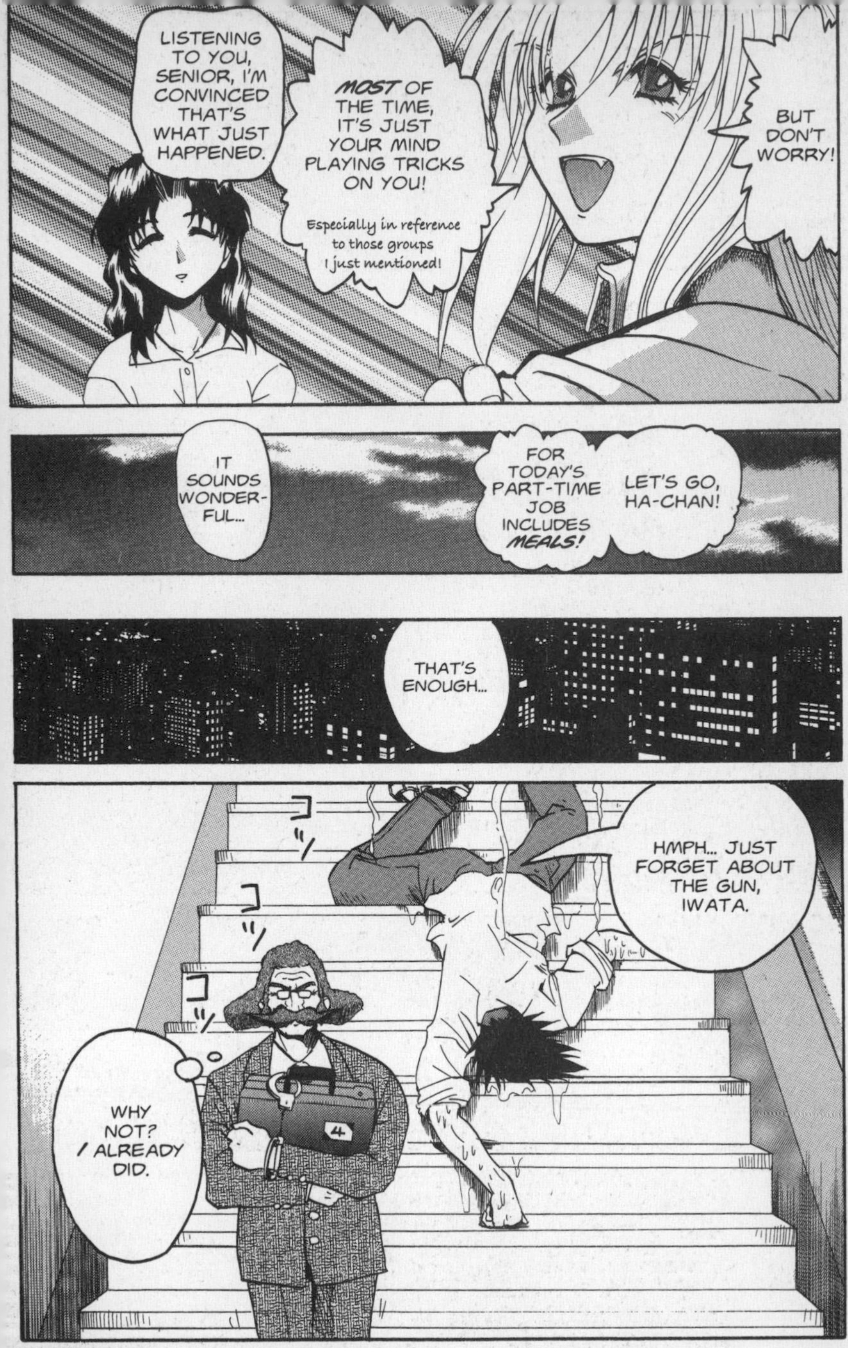
BUT DON'T WORRY!
MOST OF THE TIME, IT'S JUST YOUR MIND PLAYING TRICKS ON YOU!
Especially in reference to those groups I just mentioned!
LISTENING TO YOU, SENIOR, I'M CONVINCED THAT'S WHAT JUST HAPPENED.
LET'S GO, HA-CHAN!
FOR TODAY'S PART-TIME JOB INCLUDES *MEALS!*
IT SOUNDS WONDERFUL...
THAT'S ENOUGH...
HMPH... JUST FORGET ABOUT THE GUN, IWATA.
WHY NOT? *I* ALREADY DID.

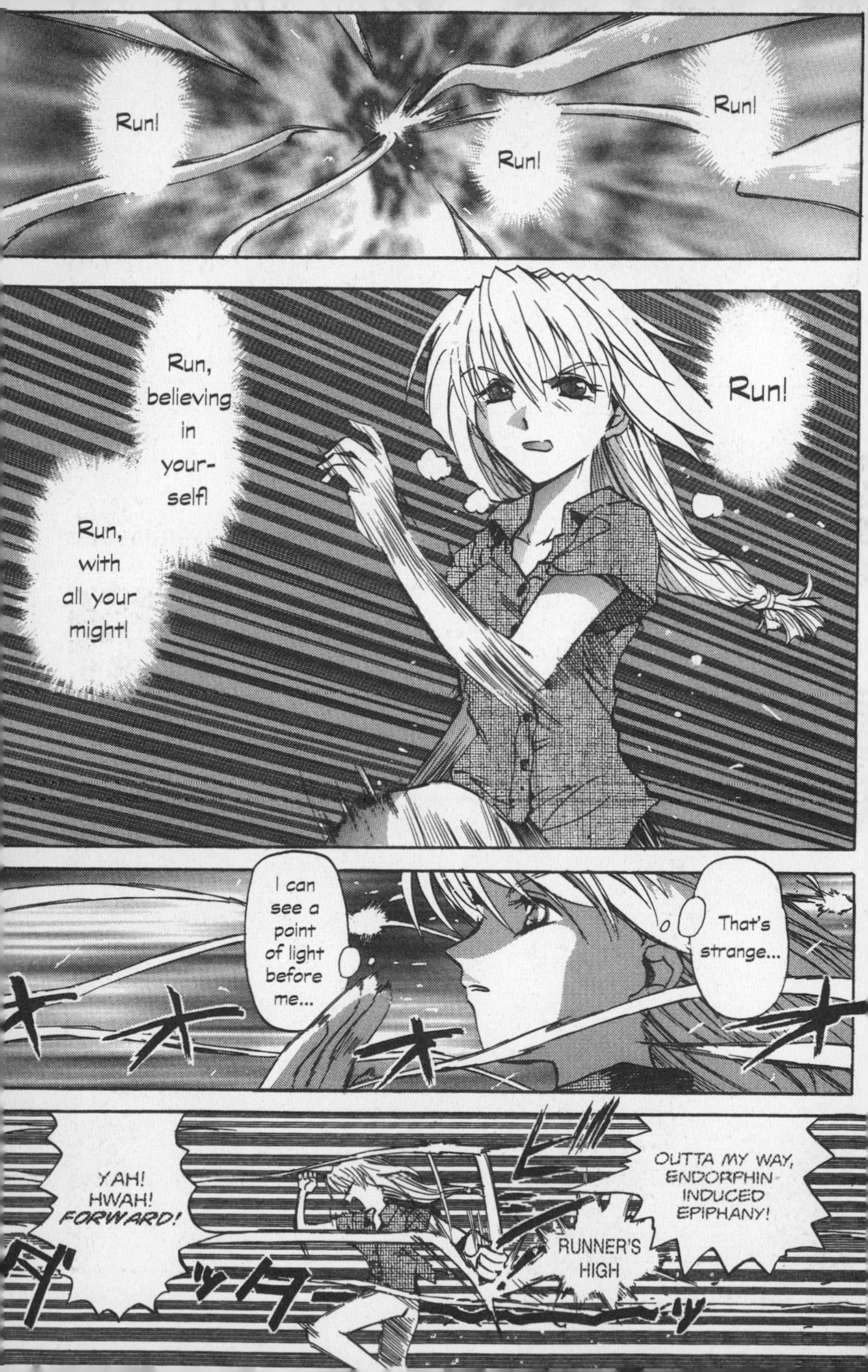
Run!
Run!
Run!
Run!
Run, believing in your-self!
Run, with all your might!
That's strange...
I can see a point of light before me...
OUTTA MY WAY, ENDORPHIN INDUCED EPIPHANY!
RUNNER'S HIGH
YAH! HWAH! *FORWARD!*

MISSION 2
HOW TO CONSUME OXYGEN

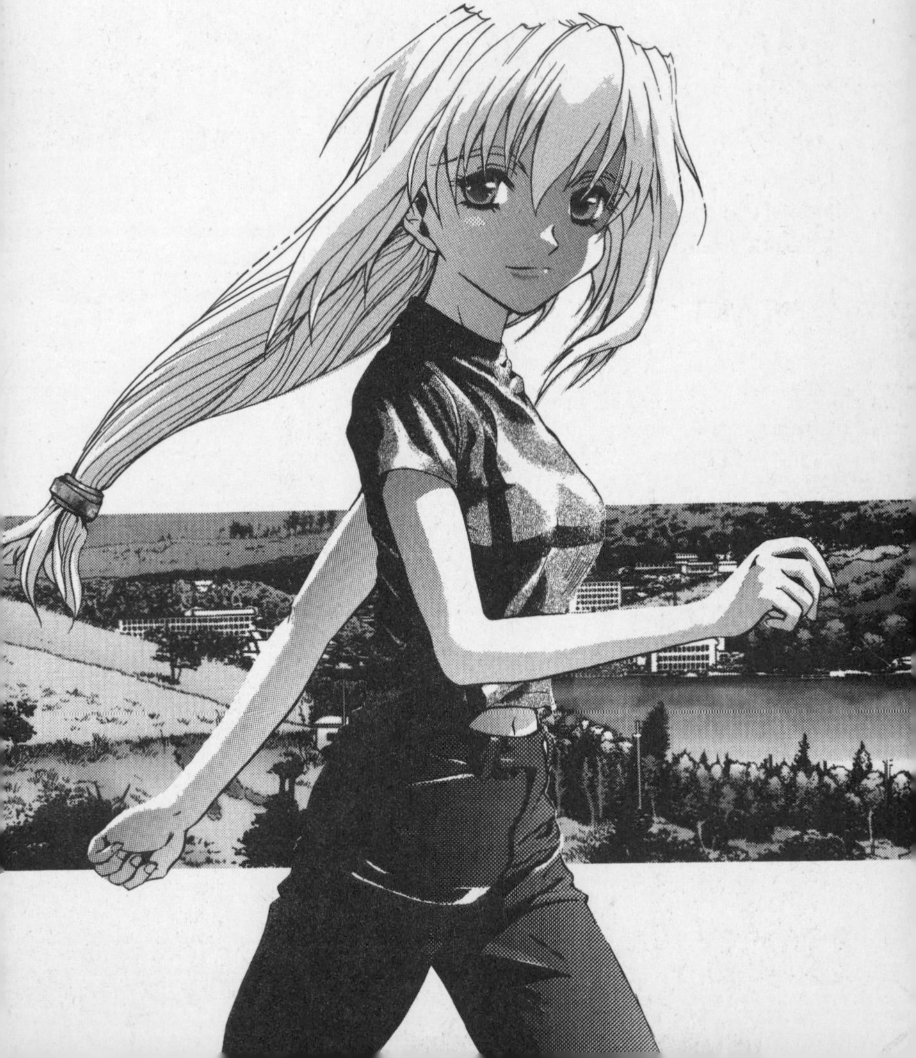

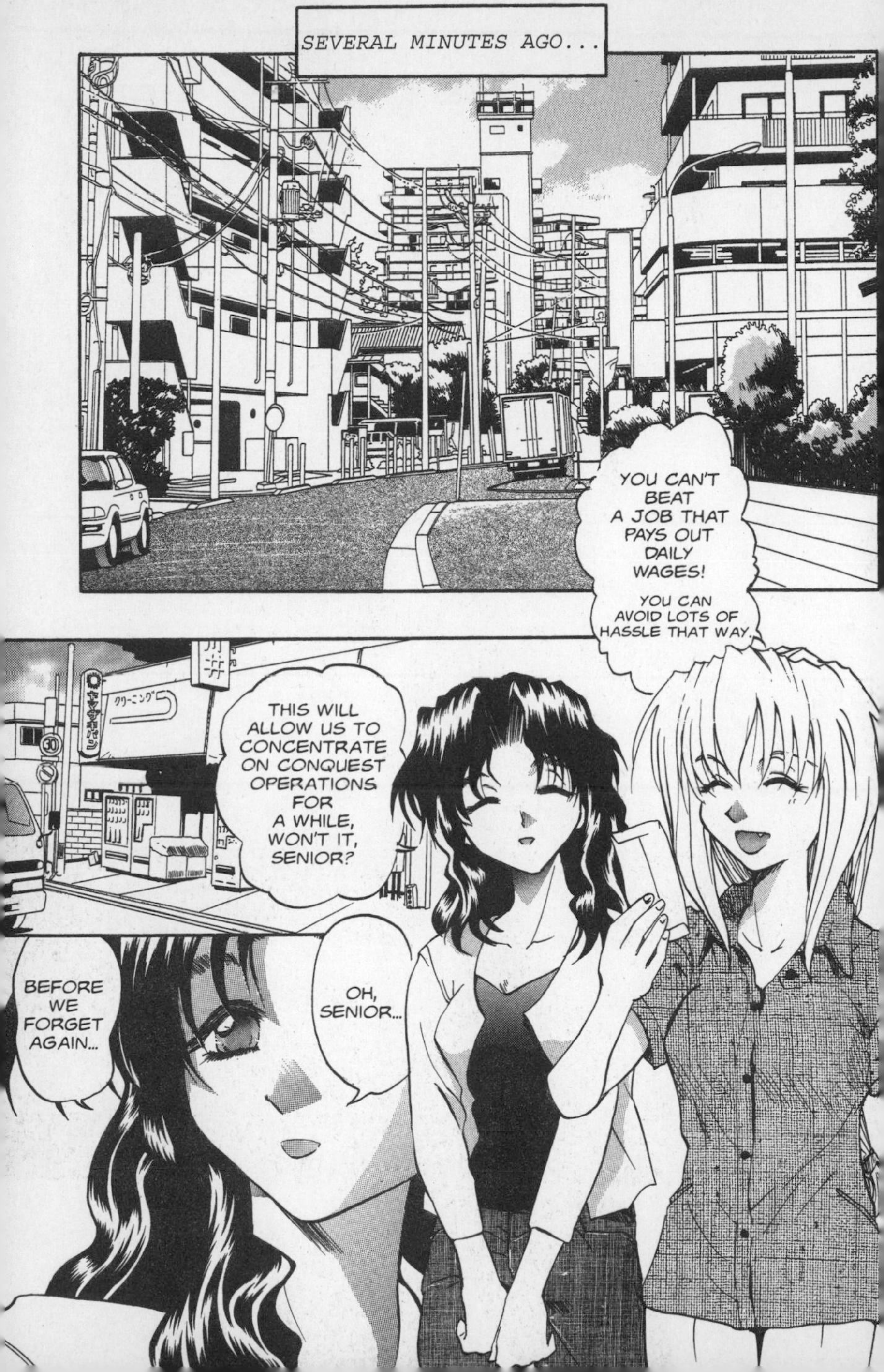
SEVERAL MINUTES AGO...
YOU CAN'T BEAT A JOB THAT PAYS OUT DAILY WAGES!
YOU CAN AVOID LOTS OF HASSLE THAT WAY.
THIS WILL ALLOW US TO CONCENTRATE ON CONQUEST OPERATIONS FOR A WHILE, WON'T IT, SENIOR?
OH, SENIOR...
BEFORE WE FORGET AGAIN...

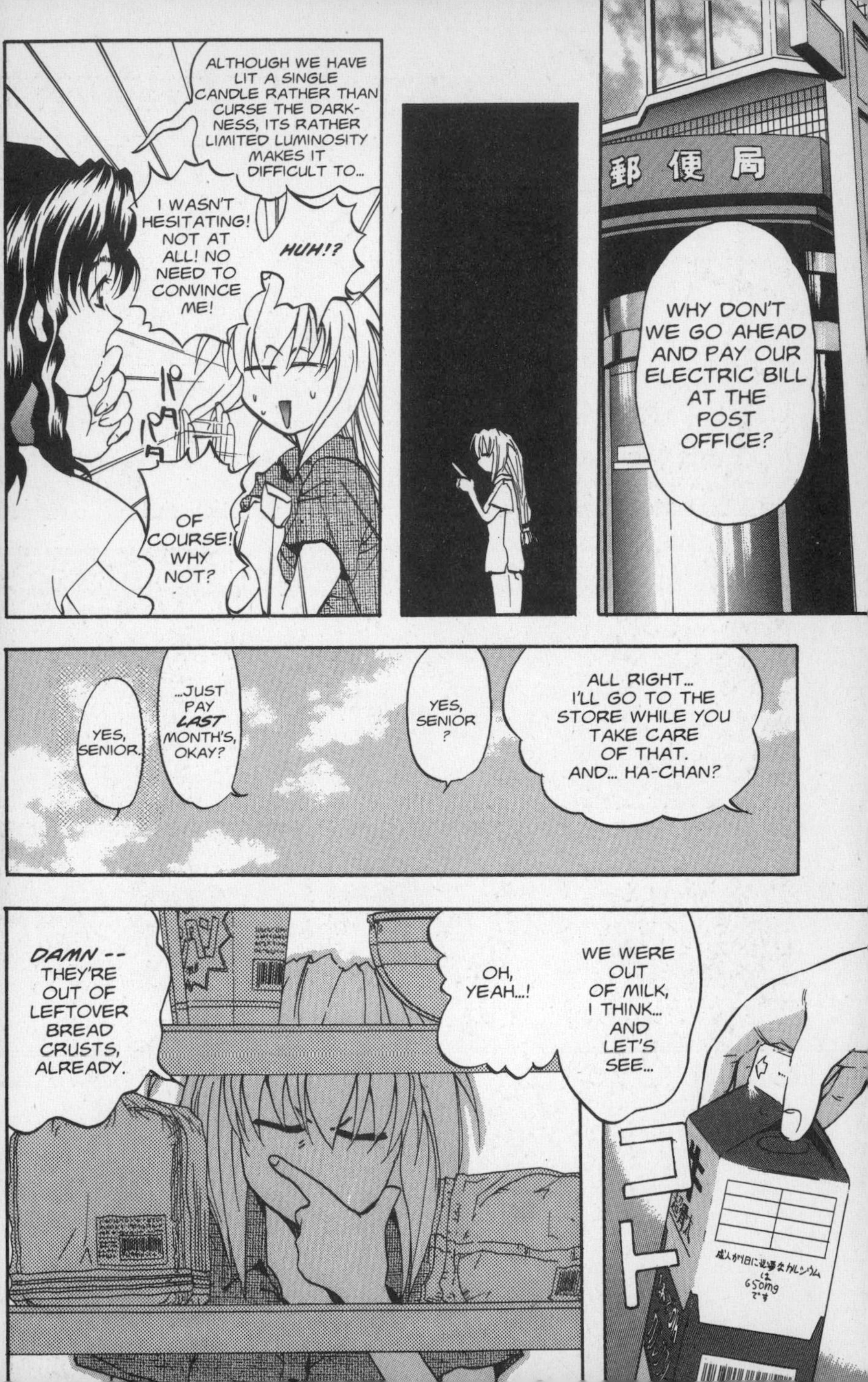
郵便局
WHY DON'T WE GO AHEAD AND PAY OUR ELECTRIC BILL AT THE POST OFFICE?
ALTHOUGH WE HAVE LIT A SINGLE CANDLE RATHER THAN CURSE THE DARKNESS, ITS RATHER LIMITED LUMINOSITY MAKES IT DIFFICULT TO...
HUH!?
I WASN'T HESITATING! NOT AT ALL! NO NEED TO CONVINCE ME!
OF COURSE! WHY NOT?
ALL RIGHT... I'LL GO TO THE STORE WHILE YOU TAKE CARE OF THAT. AND... HA-CHAN?
YES, SENIOR ?
...JUST PAY LAST MONTH'S, OKAY?
YES, SENIOR.
WE WERE OUT OF MILK, I THINK... AND LET'S SEE...
OH, YEAH...!
コト
成人が1日に必要なカルシウムは650mgです
DAMN -- THEY'RE OUT OF LEFTOVER BREAD CRUSTS, ALREADY.

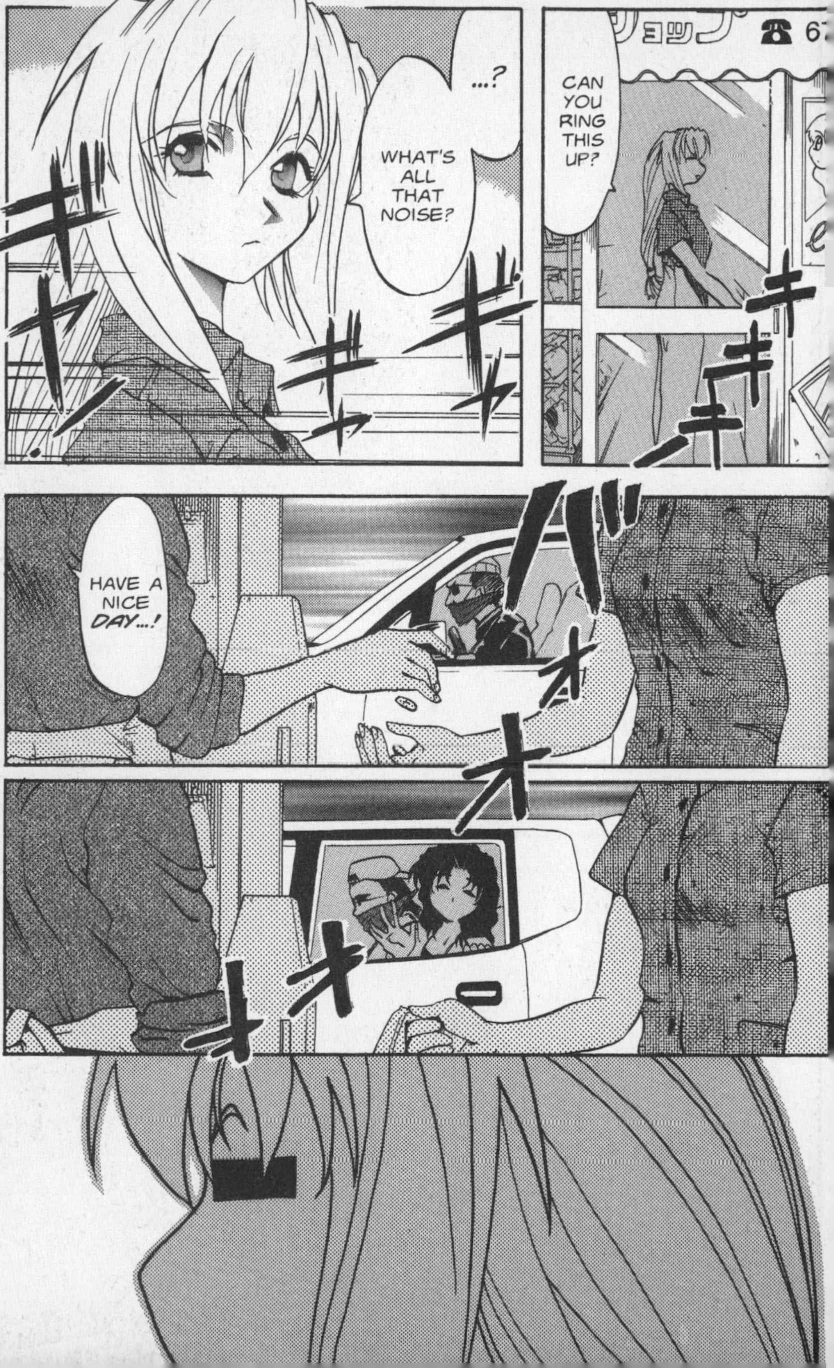
CAN YOU RING THIS UP?
...?
WHAT'S ALL THAT NOISE?
HAVE A NICE *DAY*...!

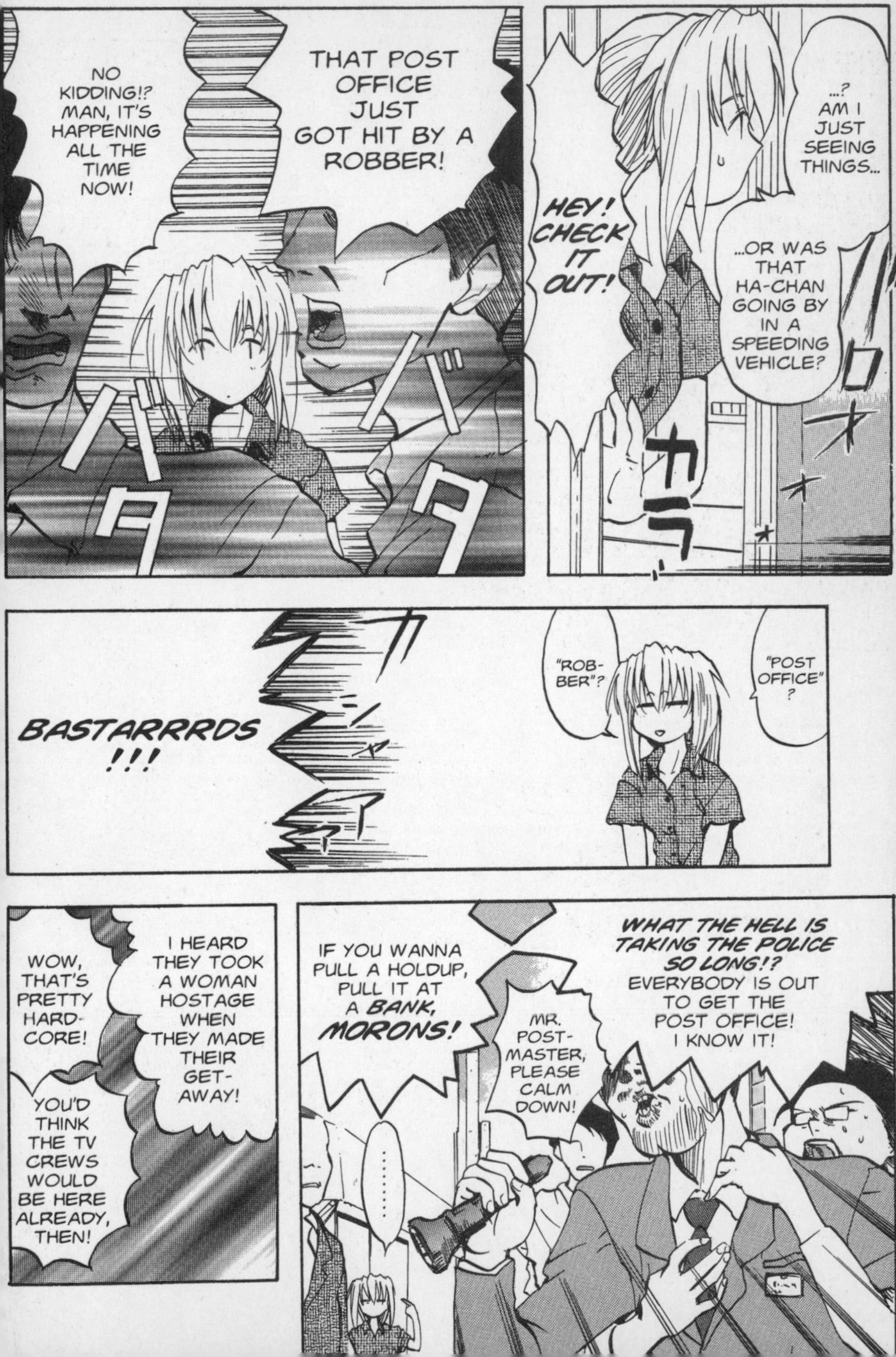
...? AM I JUST SEEING THINGS...
...OR WAS THAT HA-CHAN GOING BY IN A SPEEDING VEHICLE?
HEY! CHECK IT OUT!
THAT POST OFFICE JUST GOT HIT BY A ROBBER!
NO KIDDING!? MAN, IT'S HAPPENING ALL THE TIME NOW!
"POST OFFICE"?
"ROB-BER"?
BASTARRRDS!!!
WHAT THE HELL IS TAKING THE POLICE SO LONG!? EVERYBODY IS OUT TO GET THE POST OFFICE! I KNOW IT!
IF YOU WANNA PULL A HOLDUP, PULL IT AT A BANK, MORONS!
MR. POST-MASTER, PLEASE CALM DOWN!
......
I HEARD THEY TOOK A WOMAN HOSTAGE WHEN THEY MADE THEIR GET-AWAY!
WOW, THAT'S PRETTY HARD-CORE!
YOU'D THINK THE TV CREWS WOULD BE HERE ALREADY, THEN!

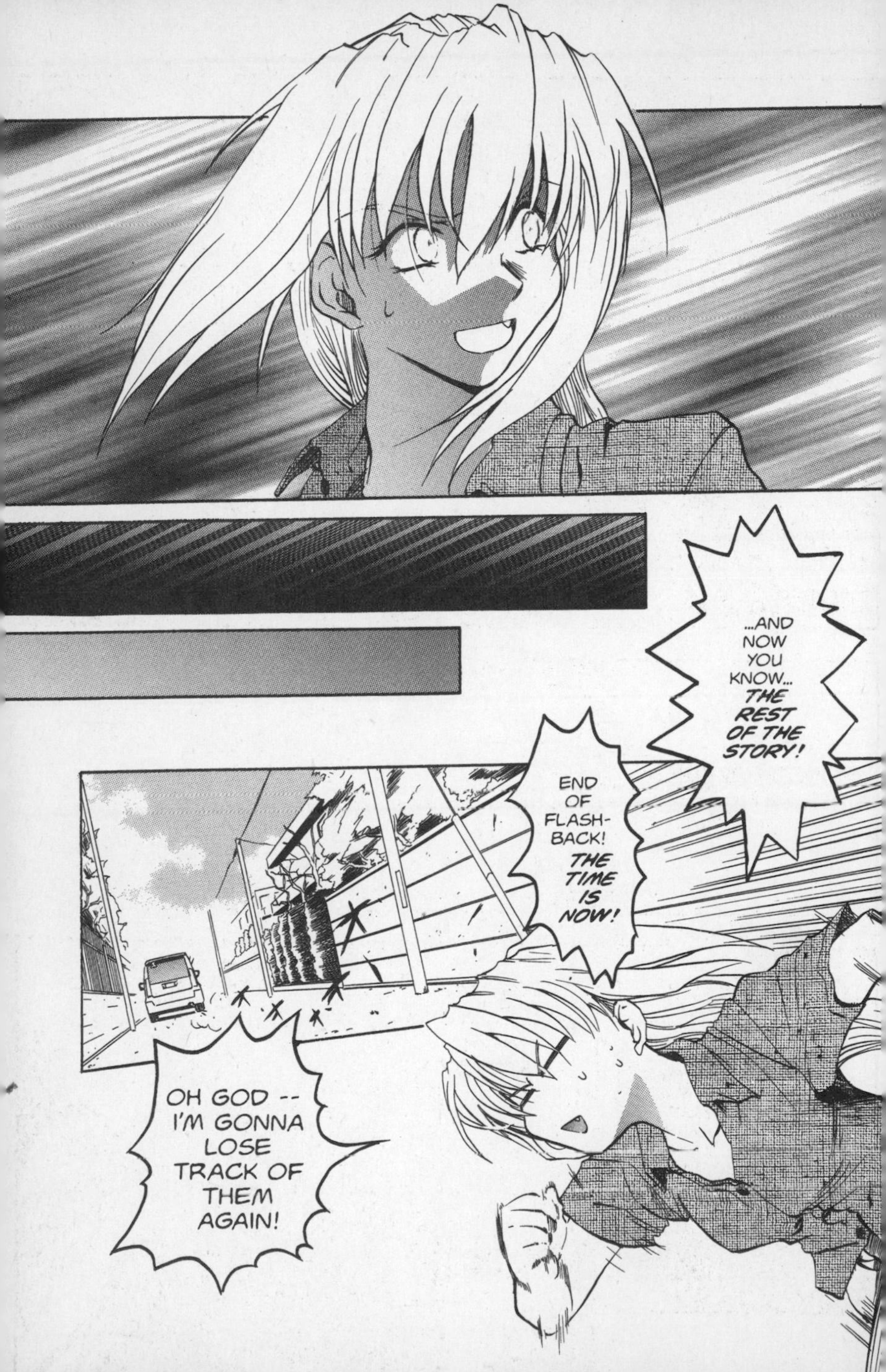
...AND NOW YOU KNOW... THE REST OF THE STORY!
END OF FLASH-BACK! THE TIME IS NOW!
OH GOD -- I'M GONNA LOSE TRACK OF THEM AGAIN!

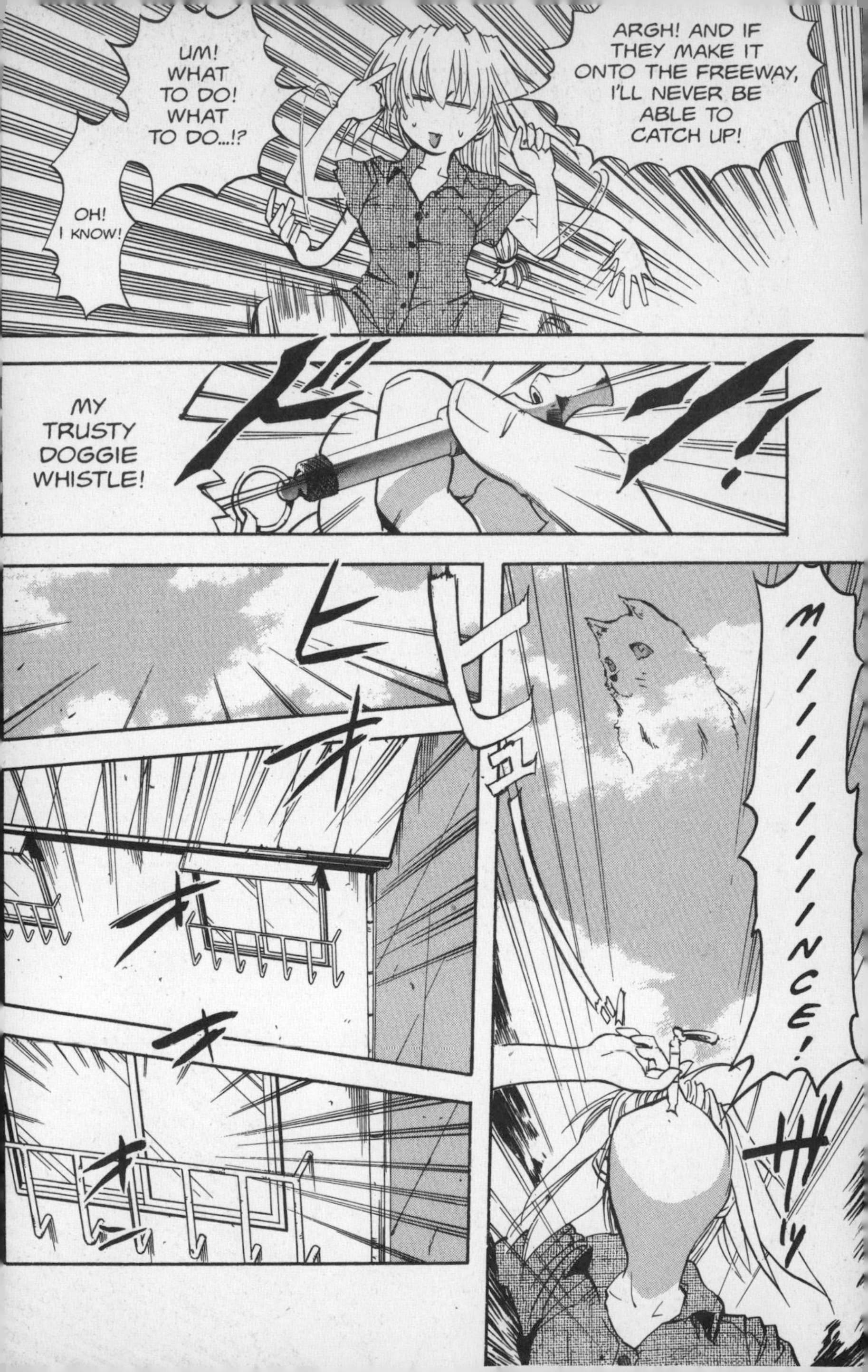
ARGH! AND IF THEY MAKE IT ONTO THE FREEWAY, I'LL NEVER BE ABLE TO CATCH UP!
UM! WHAT TO DO! WHAT TO DO...!?
OH! I KNOW!
MY TRUSTY DOGGIE WHISTLE!
MIIIIIIIIIINCE!

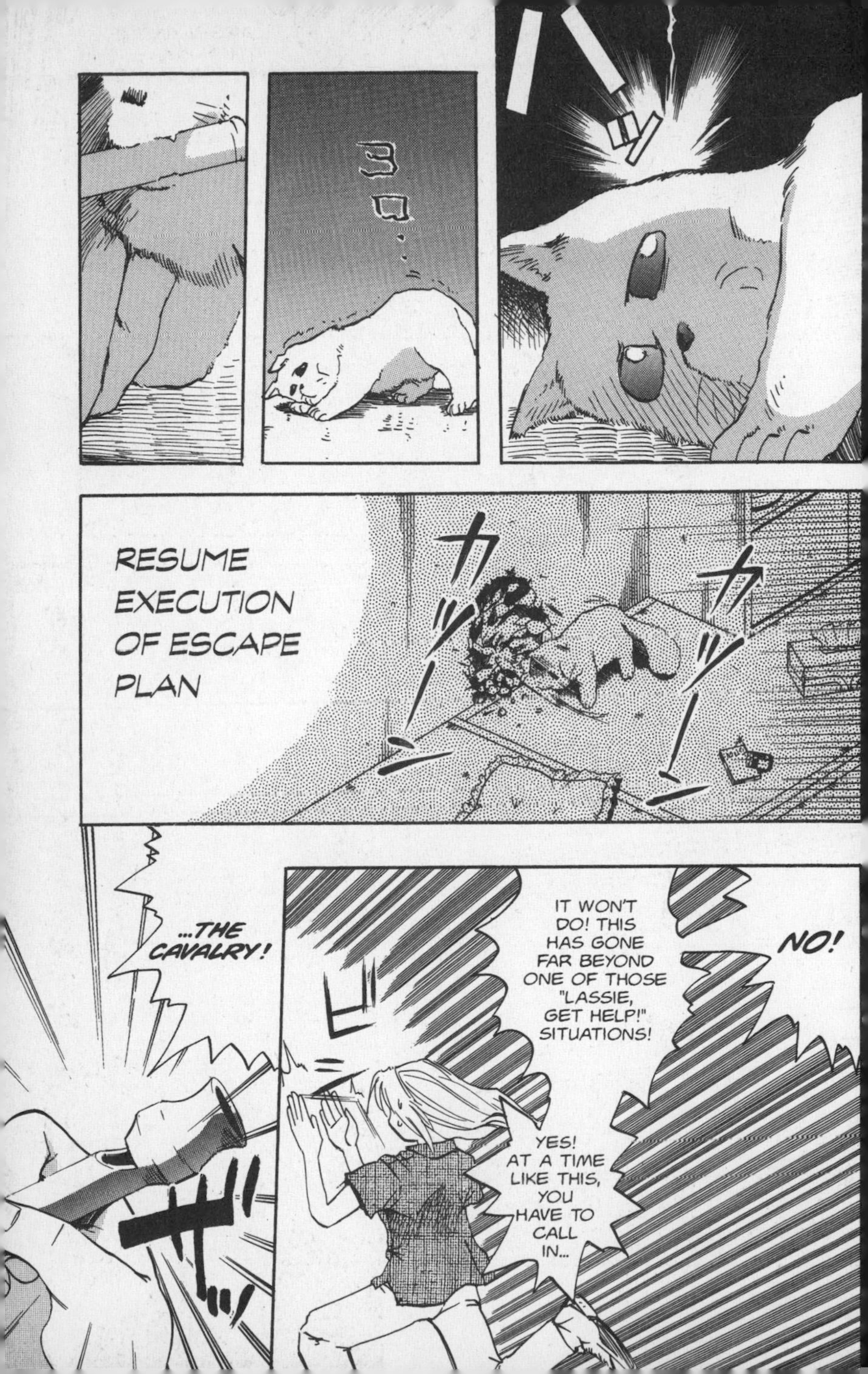
RESUME EXECUTION OF ESCAPE PLAN
NO!
IT WON'T DO! THIS HAS GONE FAR BEYOND ONE OF THOSE "LASSIE, GET HELP!" SITUATIONS!
YES! AT A TIME LIKE THIS, YOU HAVE TO CALL IN...
...THE CAVALRY!

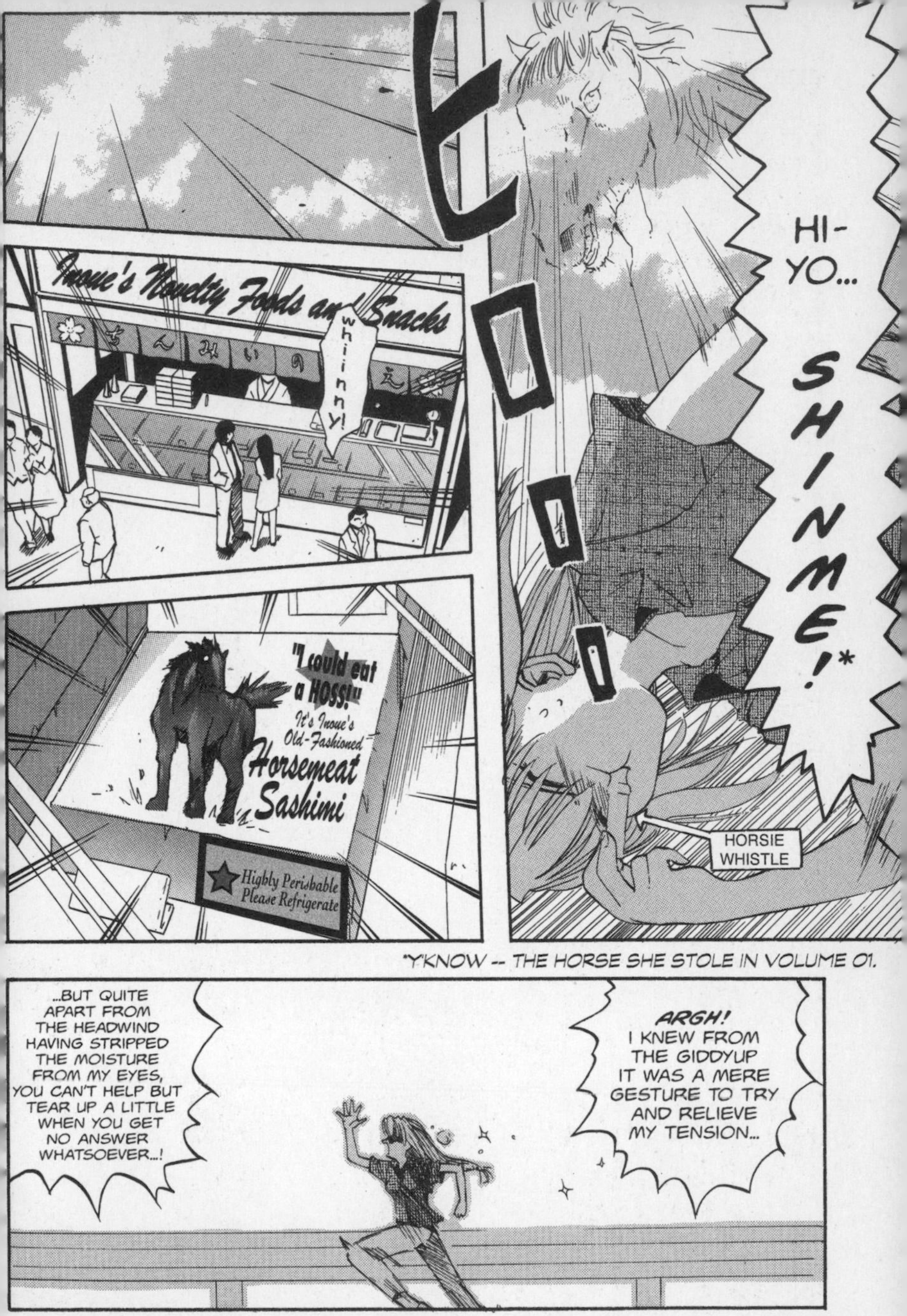
HI-YO... SHINME!*
HORSIE WHISTLE
Inoue's Novelty Foods and Snacks
whiinny!
"I could eat a HOSS!"
It's Inoue's Old-Fashioned Horsemeat Sashimi
Highly Perishable Please Refrigerate
*Y'KNOW -- THE HORSE SHE STOLE IN VOLUME 01.
ARGH! I KNEW FROM THE GIDDYUP IT WAS A MERE GESTURE TO TRY AND RELIEVE MY TENSION...
...BUT QUITE APART FROM THE HEADWIND HAVING STRIPPED THE MOISTURE FROM MY EYES, YOU CAN'T HELP BUT TEAR UP A LITTLE WHEN YOU GET NO ANSWER WHATSOEVER...!

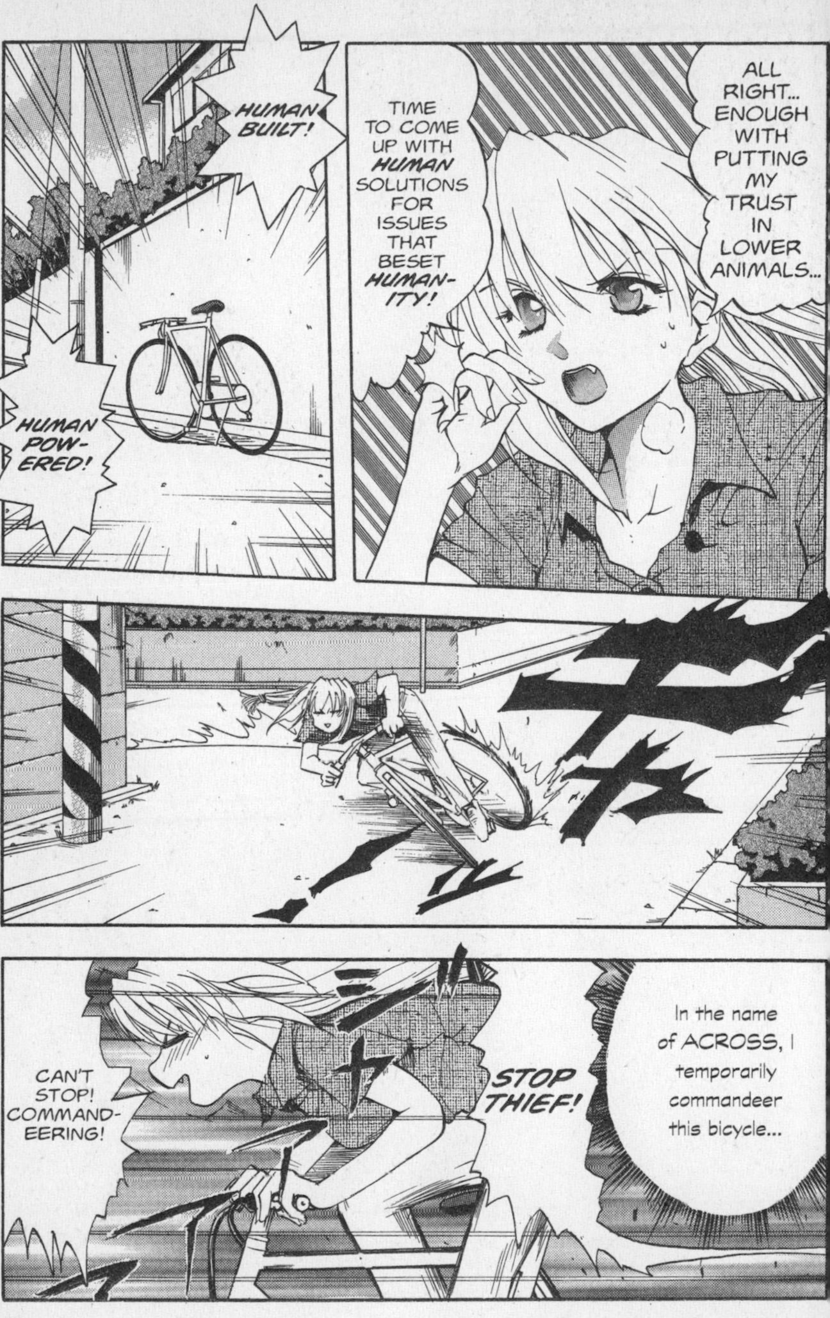
ALL RIGHT... ENOUGH WITH PUTTING MY TRUST IN LOWER ANIMALS...
TIME TO COME UP WITH HUMAN SOLUTIONS FOR ISSUES THAT BESET HUMAN-ITY!
HUMAN BUILT!
HUMAN POW-ERED!
In the name of ACROSS, I temporarily commandeer this bicycle...
STOP THIEF!
CAN'T STOP! COMMAND-EERING!

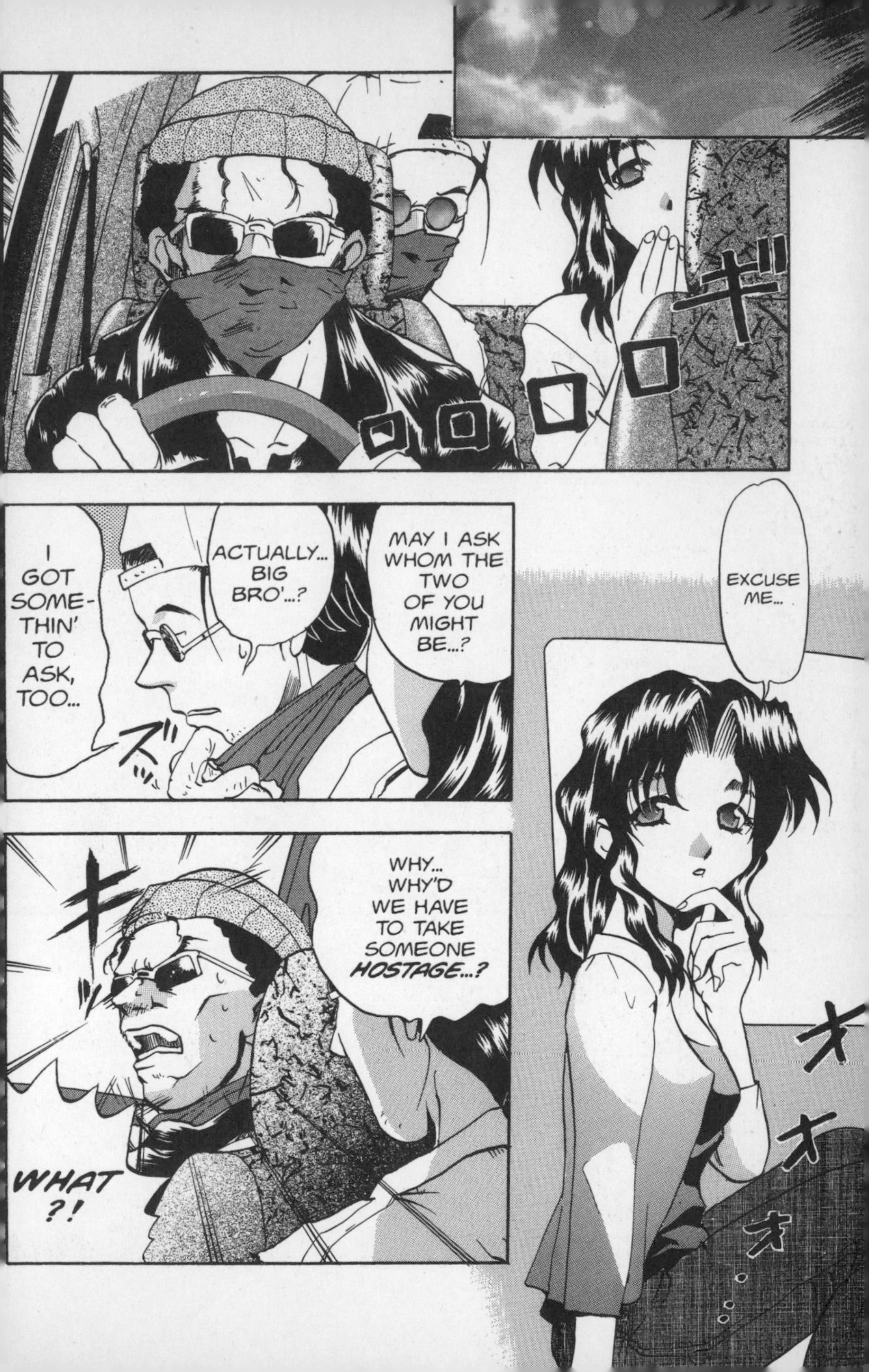
EXCUSE ME...
MAY I ASK WHOM THE TWO OF YOU MIGHT BE...?
ACTUALLY... BIG BRO'...?
I GOT SOME-THIN' TO ASK, TOO...
WHY... WHY'D WE HAVE TO TAKE SOMEONE *HOSTAGE*...?
WHAT?!

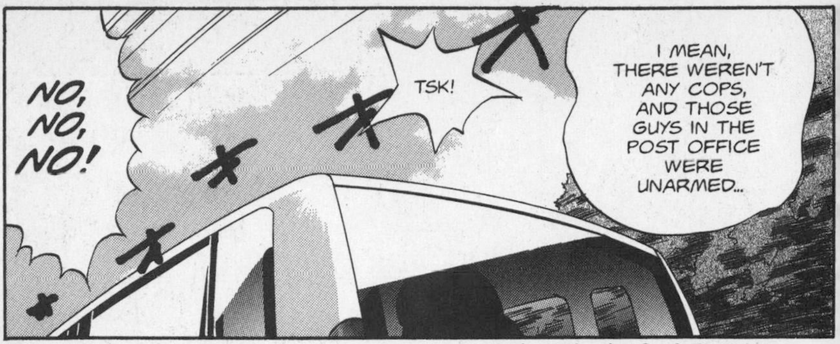
I MEAN, THERE WEREN'T ANY COPS, AND THOSE GUYS IN THE POST OFFICE WERE UNARMED...
TSK!
NO, NO, NO!

Muchos Thanks, Po & Jinnojyou.

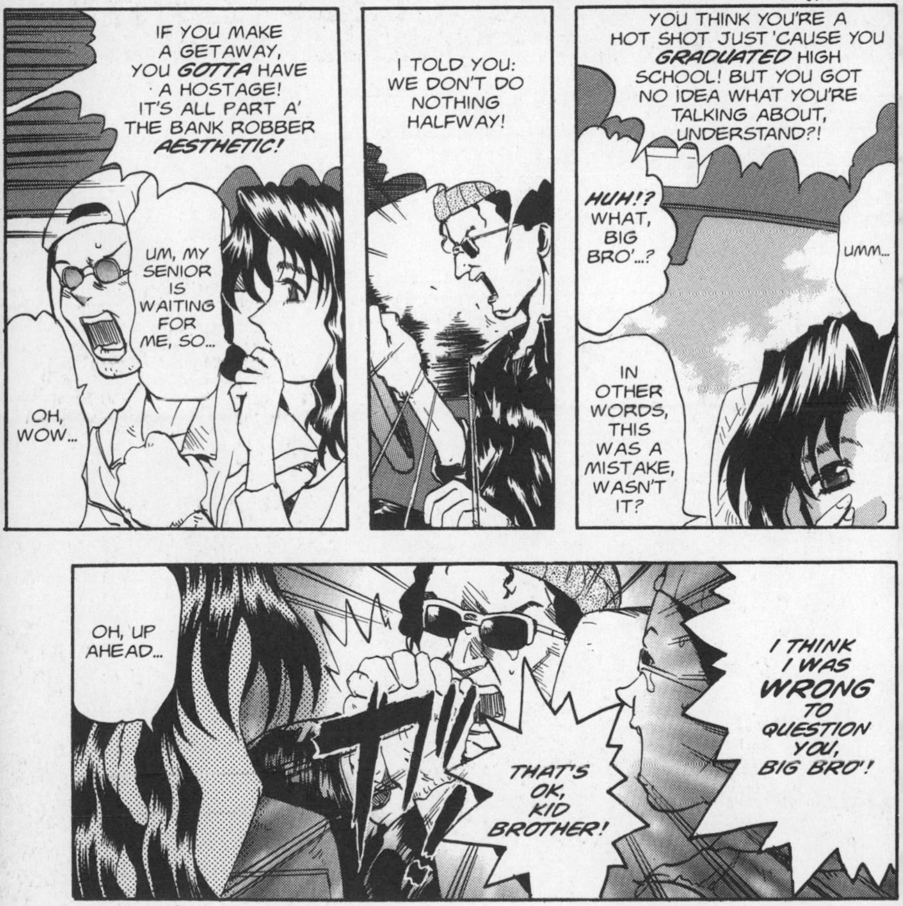
YOU THINK YOU'RE A HOT SHOT JUST 'CAUSE YOU GRADUATED HIGH SCHOOL! BUT YOU GOT NO IDEA WHAT YOU'RE TALKING ABOUT, UNDERSTAND?!
UMM...
HUH!? WHAT, BIG BRO'...?
IN OTHER WORDS, THIS WAS A MISTAKE, WASN'T IT?
I TOLD YOU: WE DON'T DO NOTHING HALFWAY!
IF YOU MAKE A GETAWAY, YOU GOTTA HAVE A HOSTAGE! IT'S ALL PART A' THE BANK ROBBER AESTHETIC!
UM, MY SENIOR IS WAITING FOR ME, SO...
OH, WOW...
I THINK I WAS WRONG TO QUESTION YOU, BIG BRO'!
THAT'S OK, KID BROTHER!
OH, UP AHEAD...

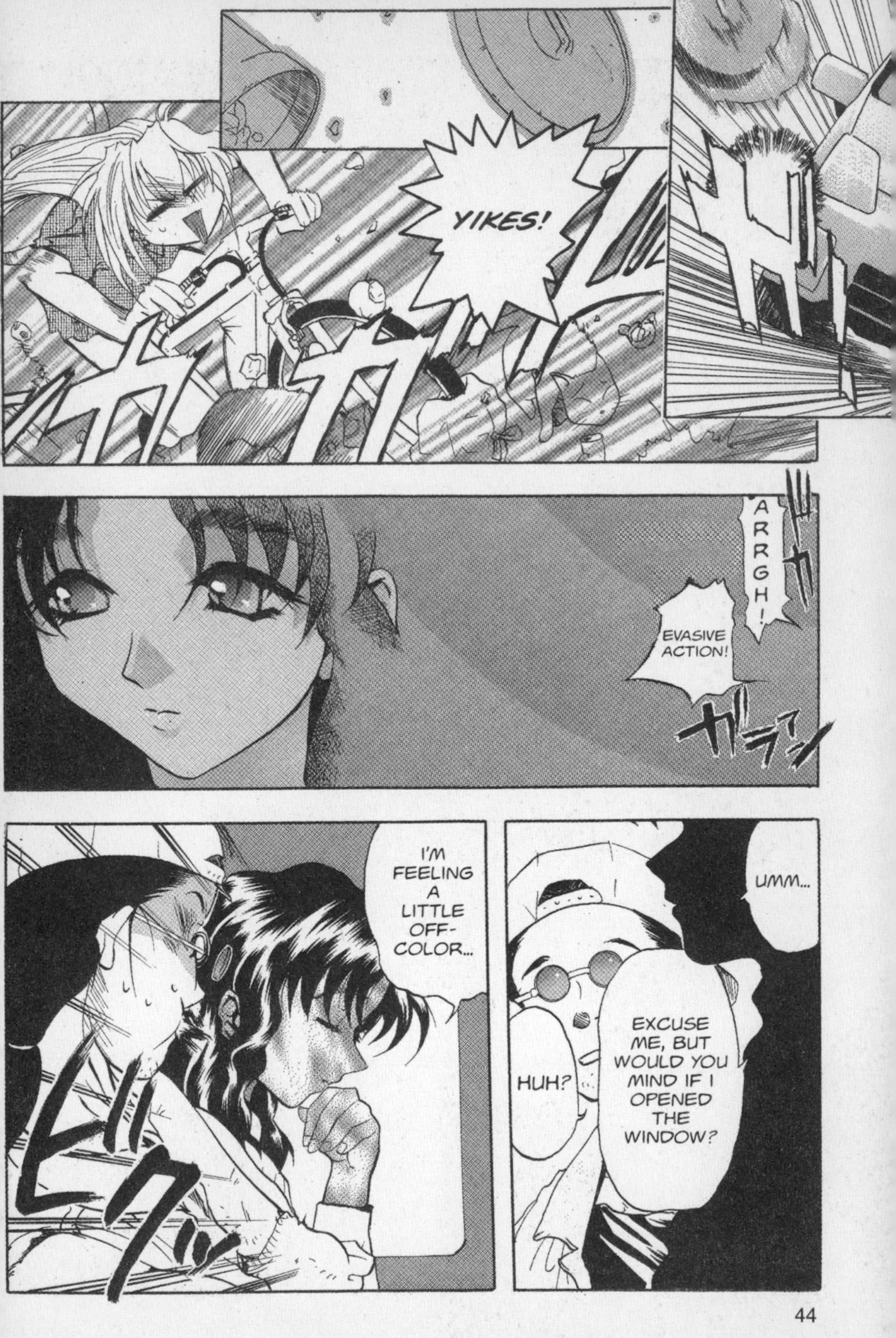
YIKES!
ARRGH!
EVASIVE ACTION!
UMM...
EXCUSE ME, BUT WOULD YOU MIND IF I OPENED THE WINDOW?
HUH?
I'M FEELING A LITTLE OFF-COLOR...

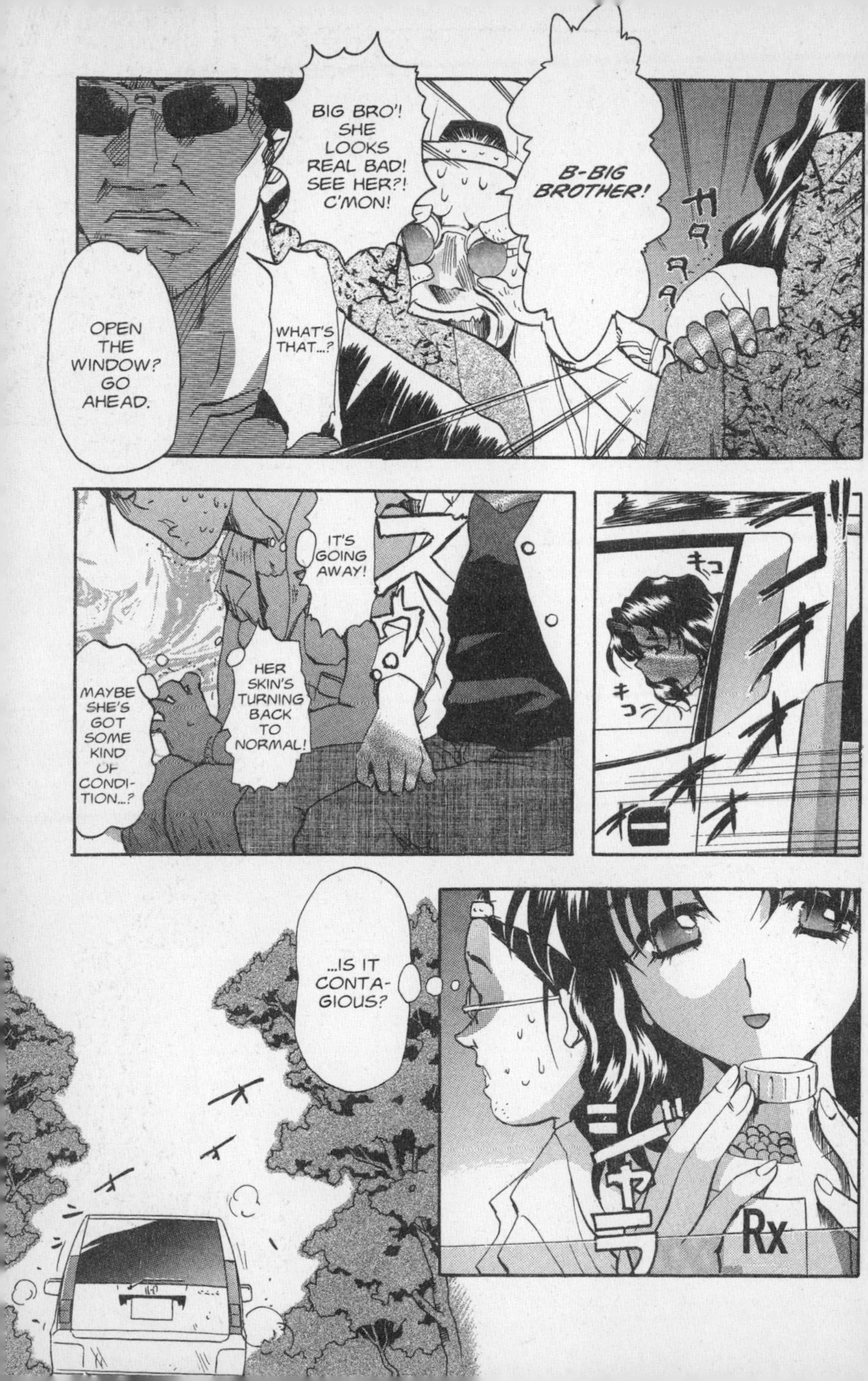
B-BIG BROTHER!
BIG BRO'! SHE LOOKS REAL BAD! SEE HER?! C'MON!
WHAT'S THAT...?
OPEN THE WINDOW? GO AHEAD.
IT'S GOING AWAY!
HER SKIN'S TURNING BACK TO NORMAL!
MAYBE SHE'S GOT SOME KIND OF CONDITION...?
Rx
...IS IT CONTAGIOUS?

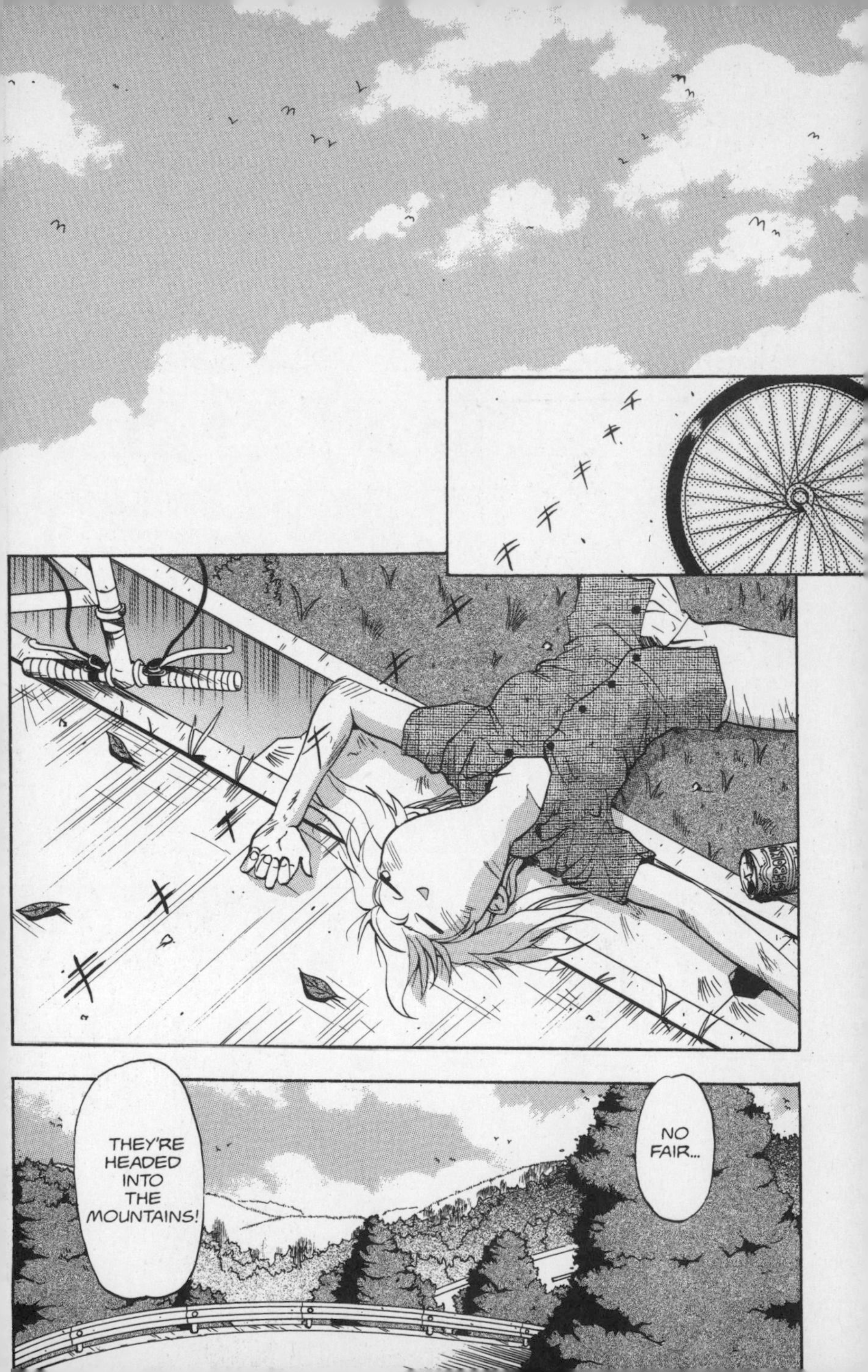
NO FAIR...
THEY'RE HEADED INTO THE MOUNTAINS!

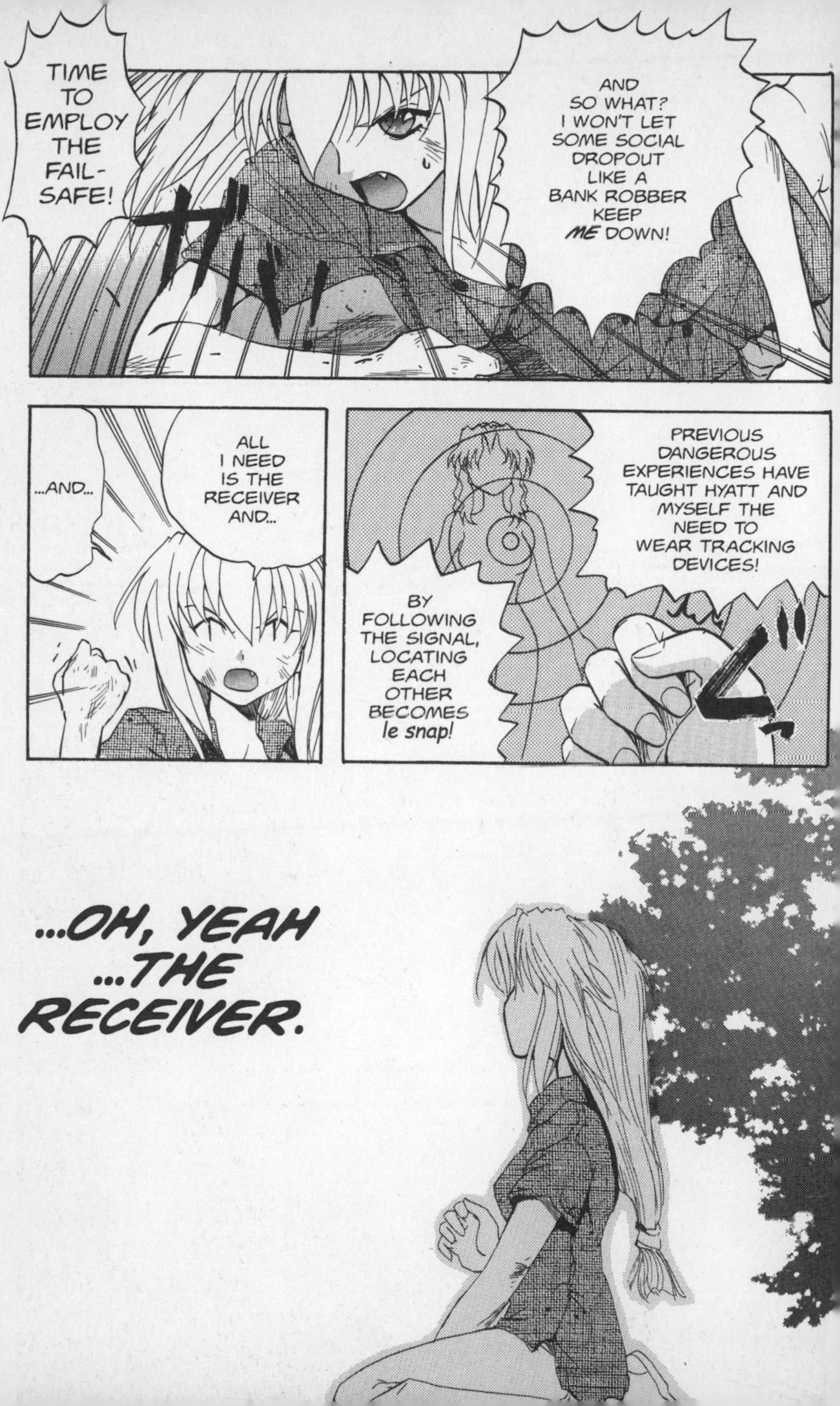
AND SO WHAT? I WON'T LET SOME SOCIAL DROPOUT LIKE A BANK ROBBER KEEP *ME* DOWN!
TIME TO EMPLOY THE FAIL-SAFE!
PREVIOUS DANGEROUS EXPERIENCES HAVE TAUGHT HYATT AND MYSELF THE NEED TO WEAR TRACKING DEVICES!
BY FOLLOWING THE SIGNAL, LOCATING EACH OTHER BECOMES *le snap!*
ALL I NEED IS THE RECEIVER AND...
...AND...
...OH, YEAH ...THE RECEIVER.

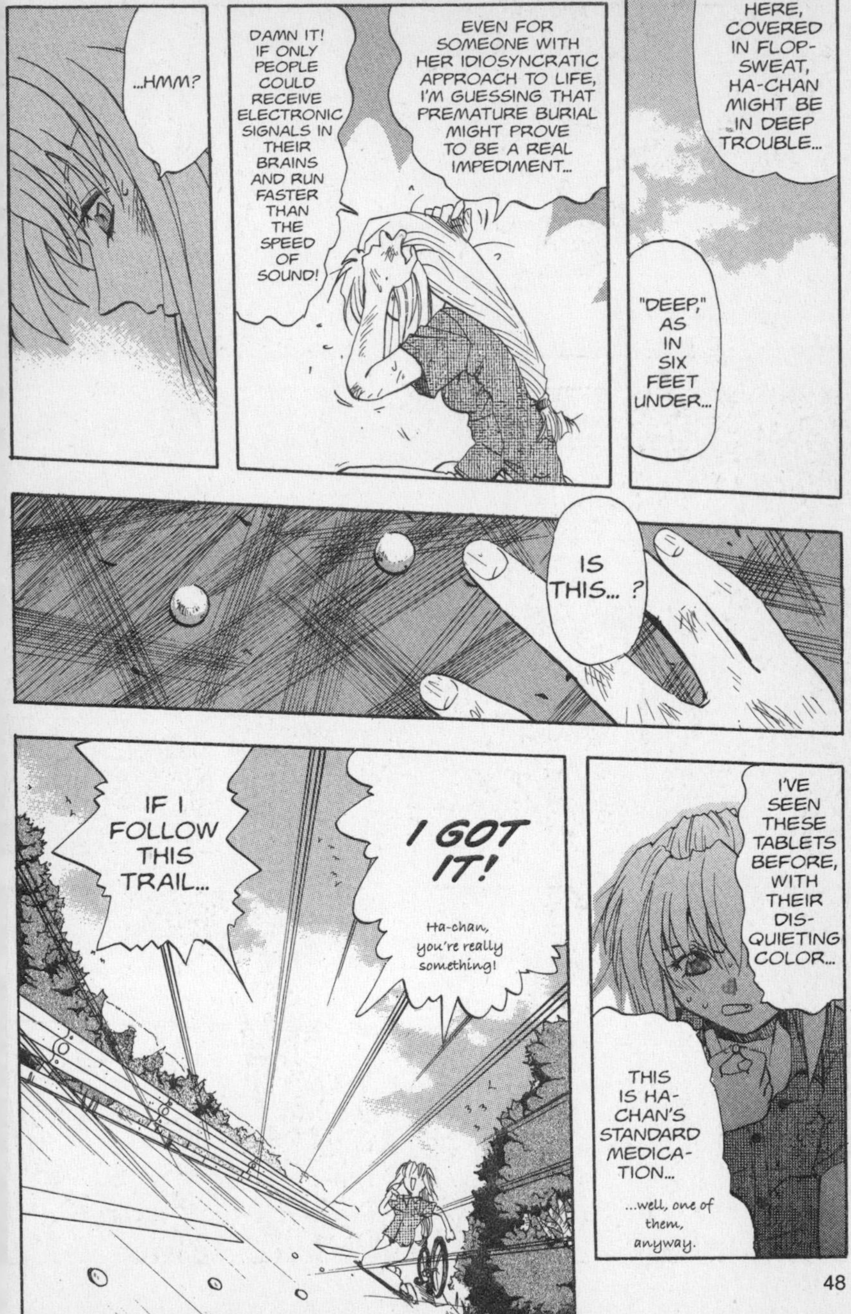
EVEN AS I SIT HERE, COVERED IN FLOP-SWEAT, HA-CHAN MIGHT BE IN DEEP TROUBLE...
"DEEP," AS IN SIX FEET UNDER...
EVEN FOR SOMEONE WITH HER IDIOSYNCRATIC APPROACH TO LIFE, I'M GUESSING THAT PREMATURE BURIAL MIGHT PROVE TO BE A REAL IMPEDIMENT...
DAMN IT! IF ONLY PEOPLE COULD RECEIVE ELECTRONIC SIGNALS IN THEIR BRAINS AND RUN FASTER THAN THE SPEED OF SOUND!
...HMM?
IS THIS... ?
I'VE SEEN THESE TABLETS BEFORE, WITH THEIR DIS-QUIETING COLOR...
THIS IS HA-CHAN'S STANDARD MEDICA-TION...
...well, one of them, anyway.
I GOT IT!
Ha-chan, you're really something!
IF I FOLLOW THIS TRAIL...

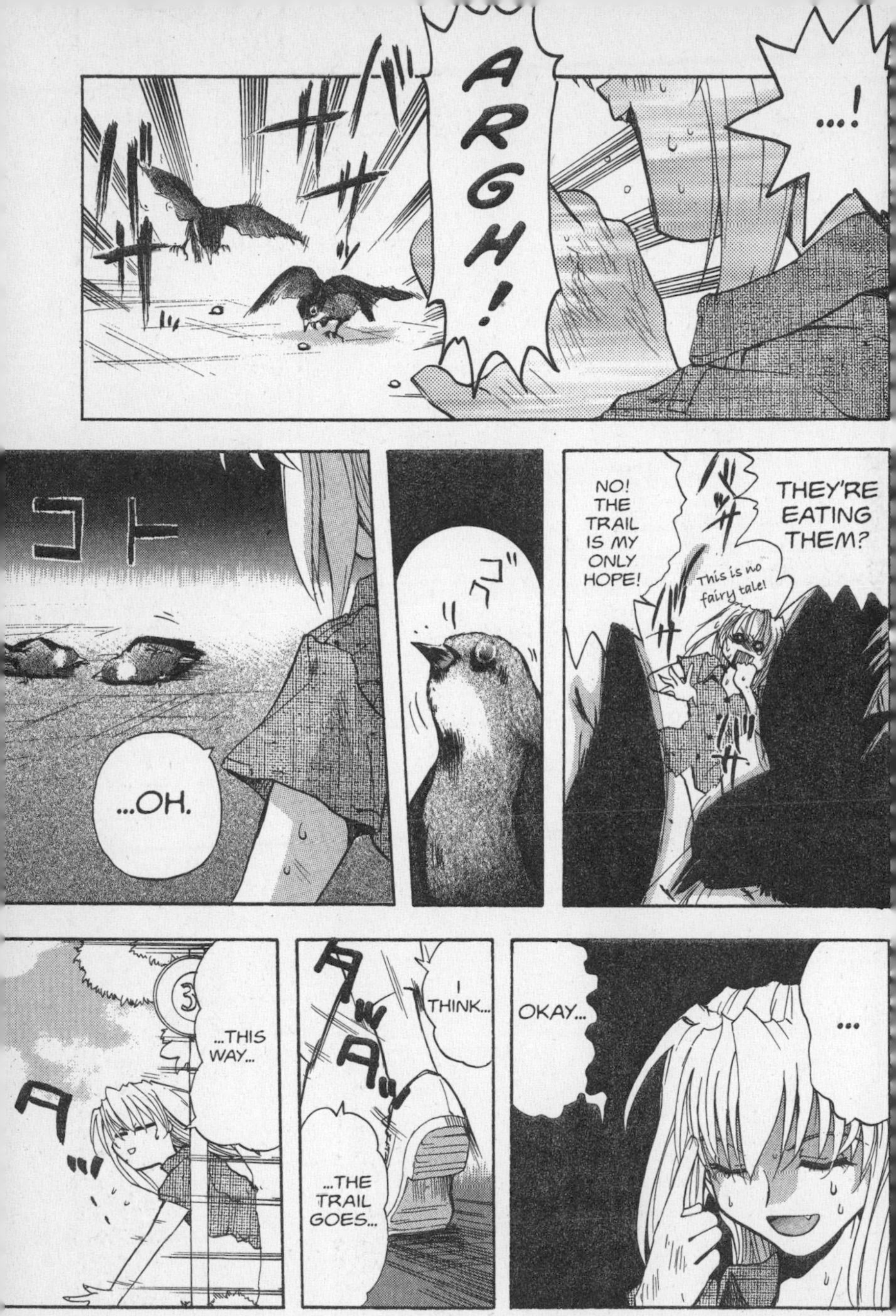
...!
ARGH!
THEY'RE EATING THEM?
NO! THE TRAIL IS MY ONLY HOPE!
This is no fairy tale!
コト
...OH.
...
OKAY...
I THINK...
...THE TRAIL GOES...
...THIS WAY...

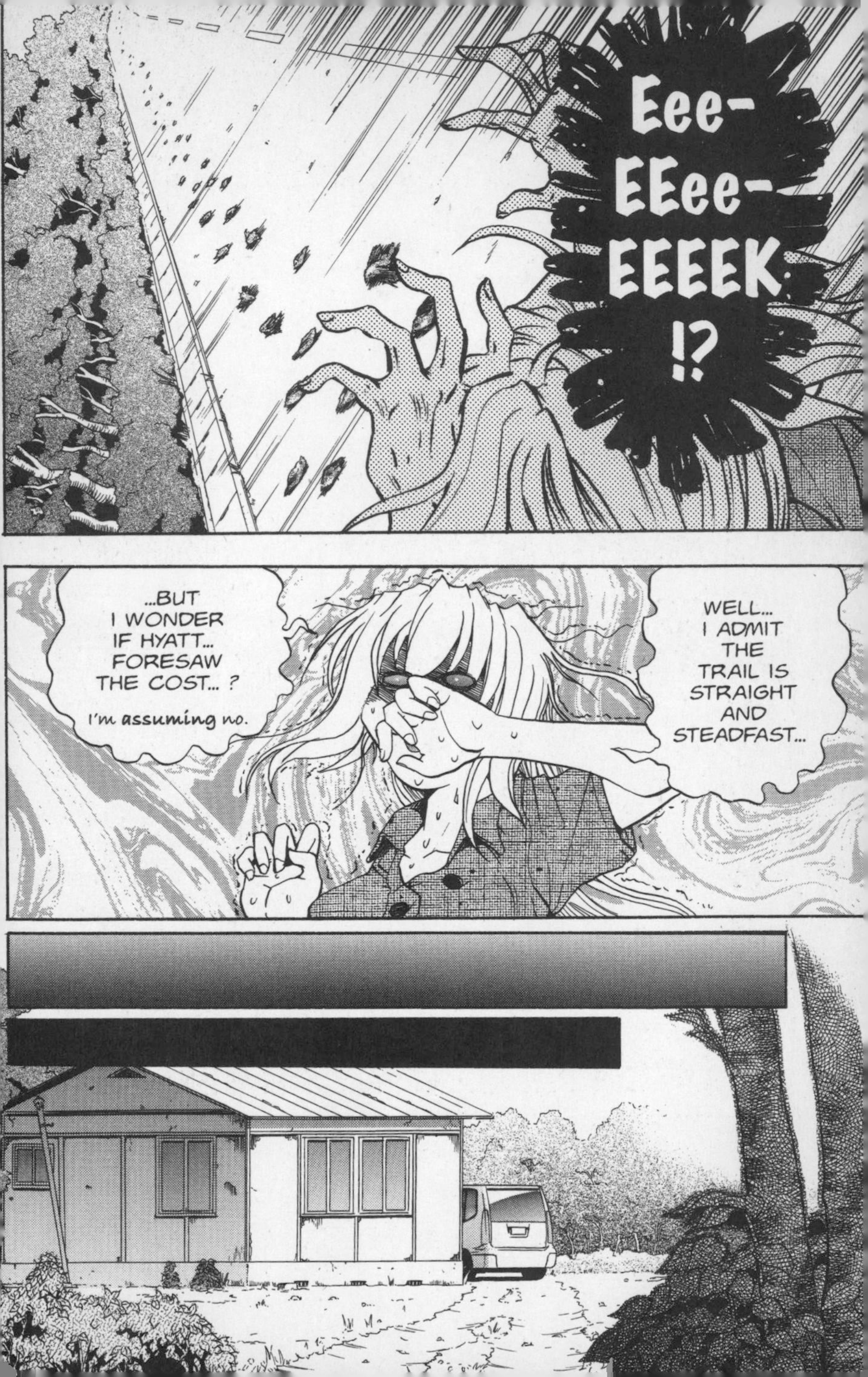
Eee-EEee-EEEEK!?
WELL... I ADMIT THE TRAIL IS STRAIGHT AND STEADFAST...
...BUT I WONDER IF HYATT... FORESAW THE COST... ?
I'm assuming no.

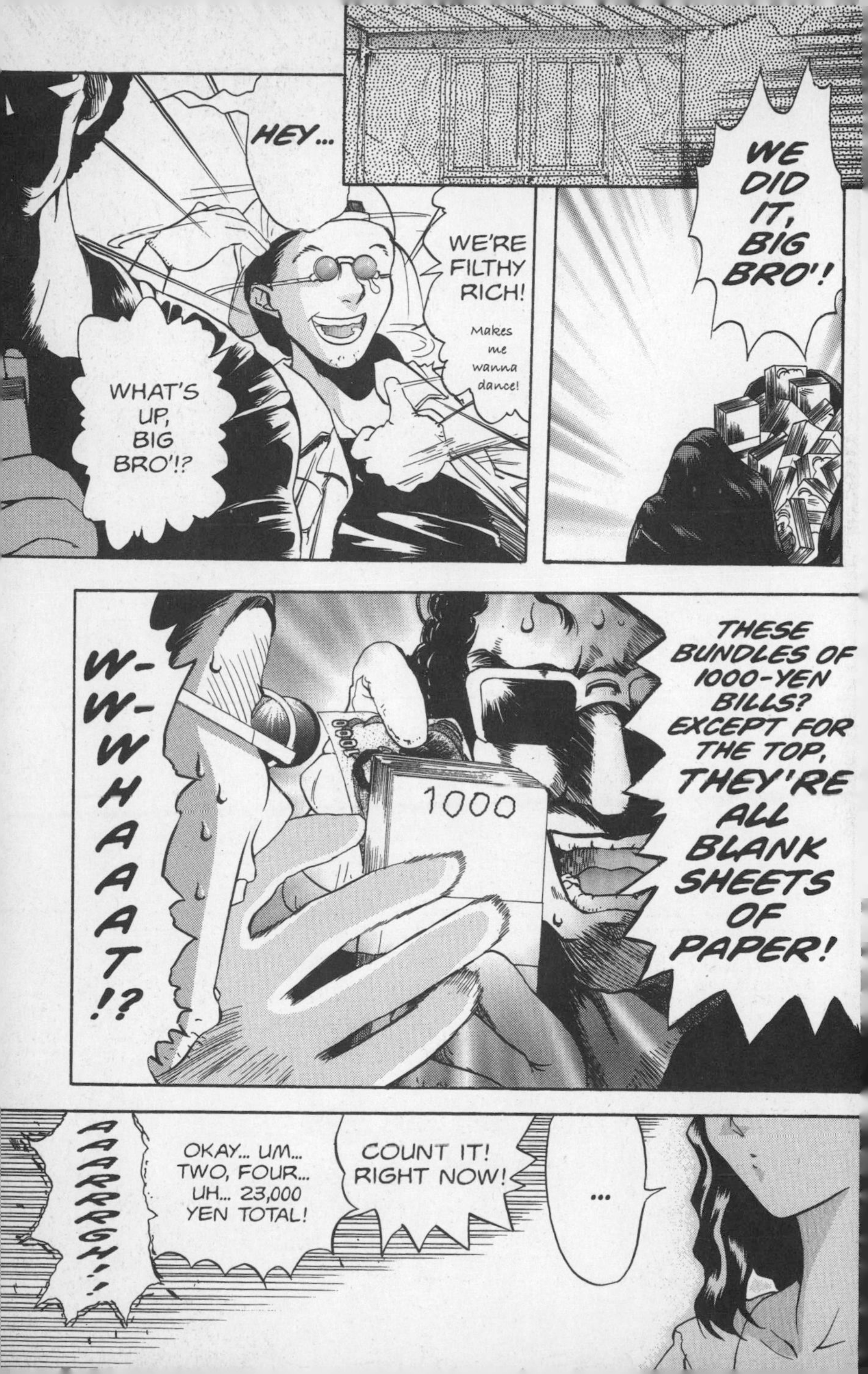
WE DID IT, BIG BRO'!
WE'RE FILTHY RICH!
Makes me wanna dance!
HEY...
WHAT'S UP, BIG BRO'!?
THESE BUNDLES OF 1000-YEN BILLS? EXCEPT FOR THE TOP, THEY'RE ALL BLANK SHEETS OF PAPER!
1000
W-W-WHAAAAT!?
...
COUNT IT! RIGHT NOW!
OKAY... UM... TWO, FOUR... UH... 23,000 YEN TOTAL!
AAARRRGH!!

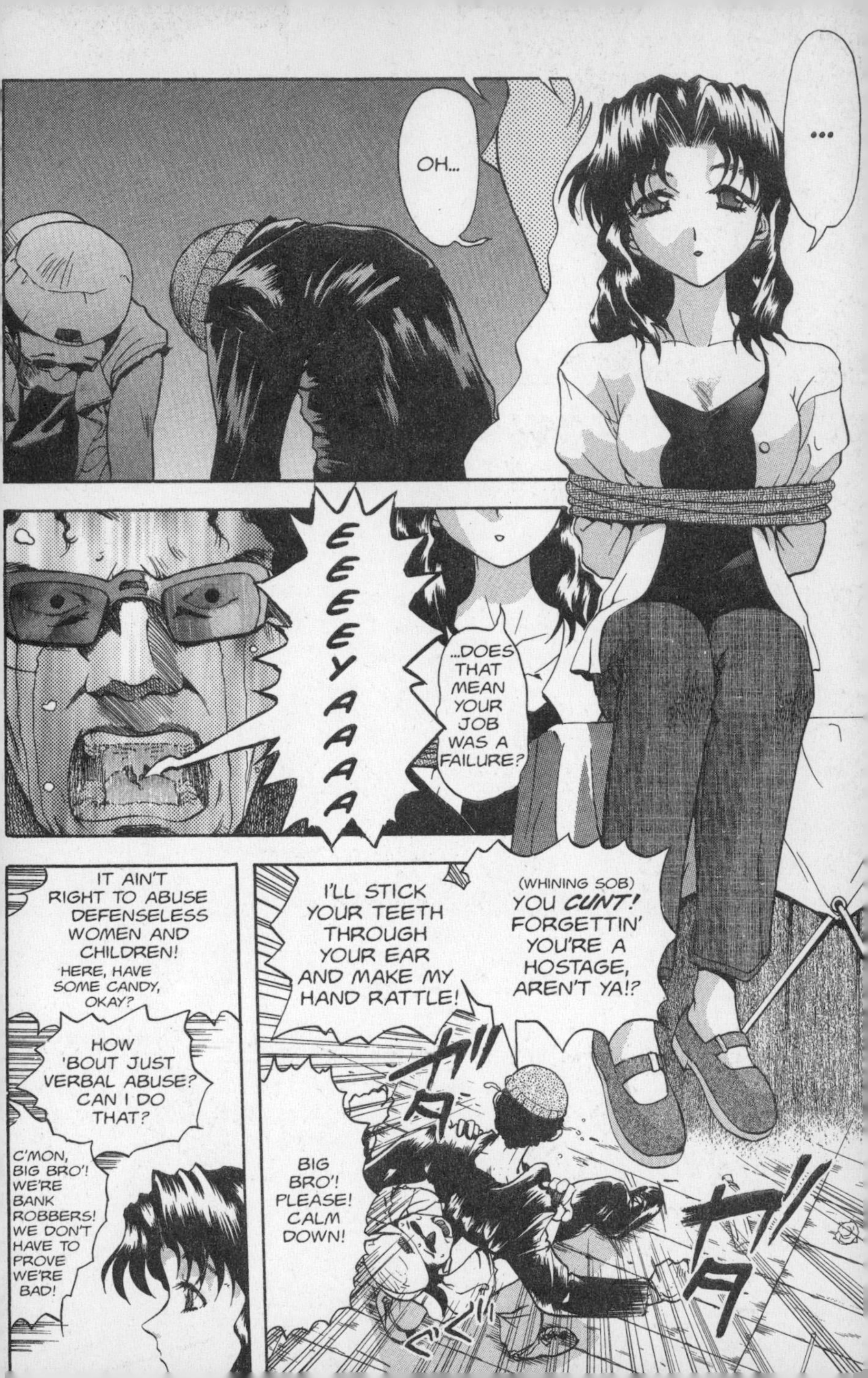
...
OH...
...DOES THAT MEAN YOUR JOB WAS A FAILURE?
EEEEEYAAAAA
(WHINING SOB) YOU ***CUNT!*** FORGETTIN' YOU'RE A HOSTAGE, AREN'T YA!?
I'LL STICK YOUR TEETH THROUGH YOUR EAR AND MAKE MY HAND RATTLE!
ガタ
ガタ
BIG BRO'! PLEASE! CALM DOWN!
IT AIN'T RIGHT TO ABUSE DEFENSELESS WOMEN AND CHILDREN!
HERE, HAVE SOME CANDY, OKAY?
HOW 'BOUT JUST VERBAL ABUSE? CAN I DO THAT?
C'MON, BIG BRO'! WE'RE BANK ROBBERS! WE DON'T HAVE TO PROVE WE'RE BAD!

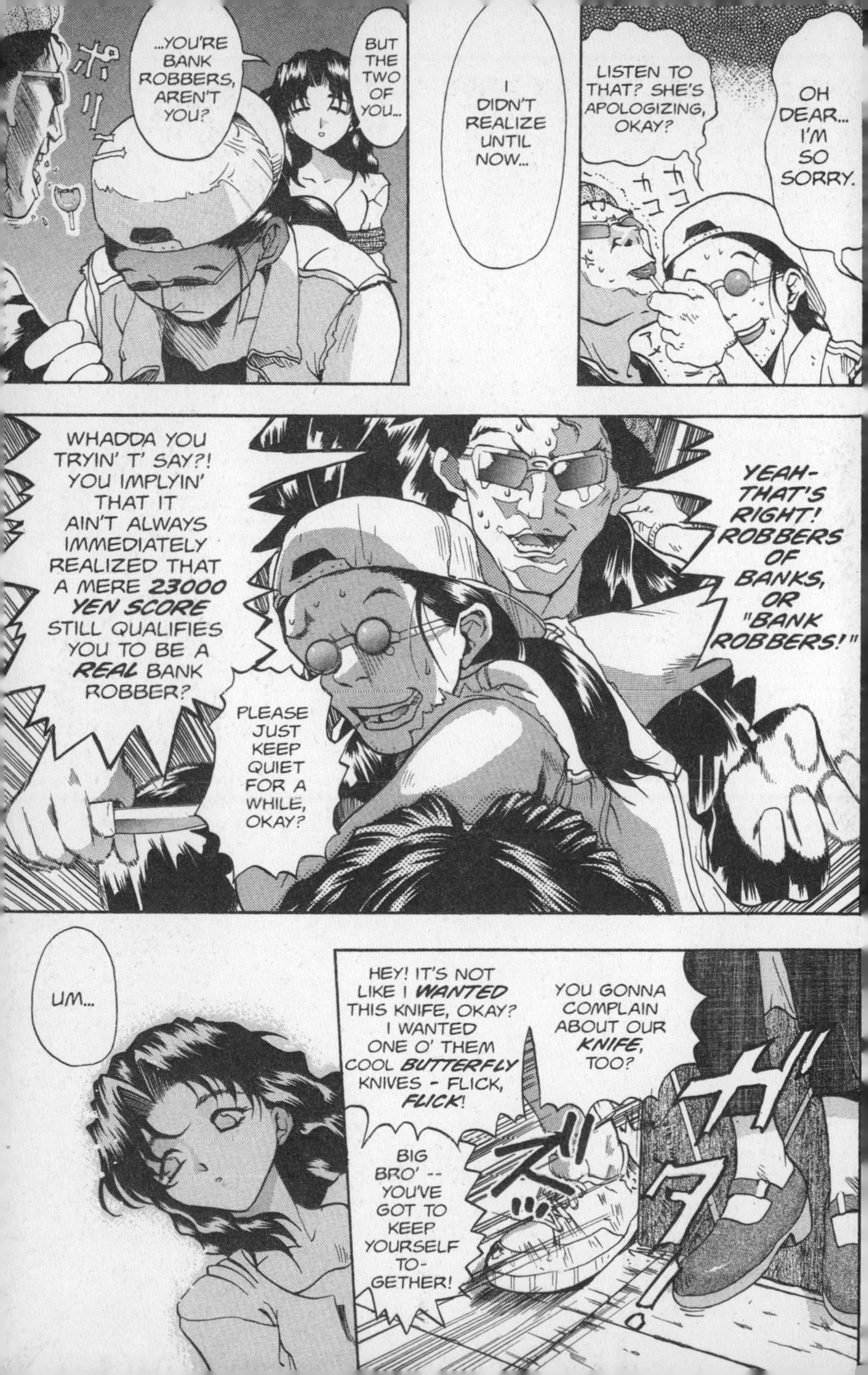
OH DEAR... I'M SO SORRY.
LISTEN TO THAT? SHE'S APOLOGIZING, OKAY?
I DIDN'T REALIZE UNTIL NOW...
BUT THE TWO OF YOU...
...YOU'RE BANK ROBBERS, AREN'T YOU?
YEAH-THAT'S RIGHT! ROBBERS OF BANKS, OR "BANK ROBBERS!"
WHADDA YOU TRYIN' T' SAY?! YOU IMPLYIN' THAT IT AIN'T ALWAYS IMMEDIATELY REALIZED THAT A MERE *23000 YEN SCORE* STILL QUALIFIES YOU TO BE A *REAL* BANK ROBBER?
PLEASE JUST KEEP QUIET FOR A WHILE, OKAY?
YOU GONNA COMPLAIN ABOUT OUR *KNIFE*, TOO?
HEY! IT'S NOT LIKE I *WANTED* THIS KNIFE, OKAY? I WANTED ONE O' THEM COOL *BUTTERFLY* KNIVES - FLICK, *FLICK*!
BIG BRO' -- YOU'VE GOT TO KEEP YOURSELF TO-GETHER!
UM...

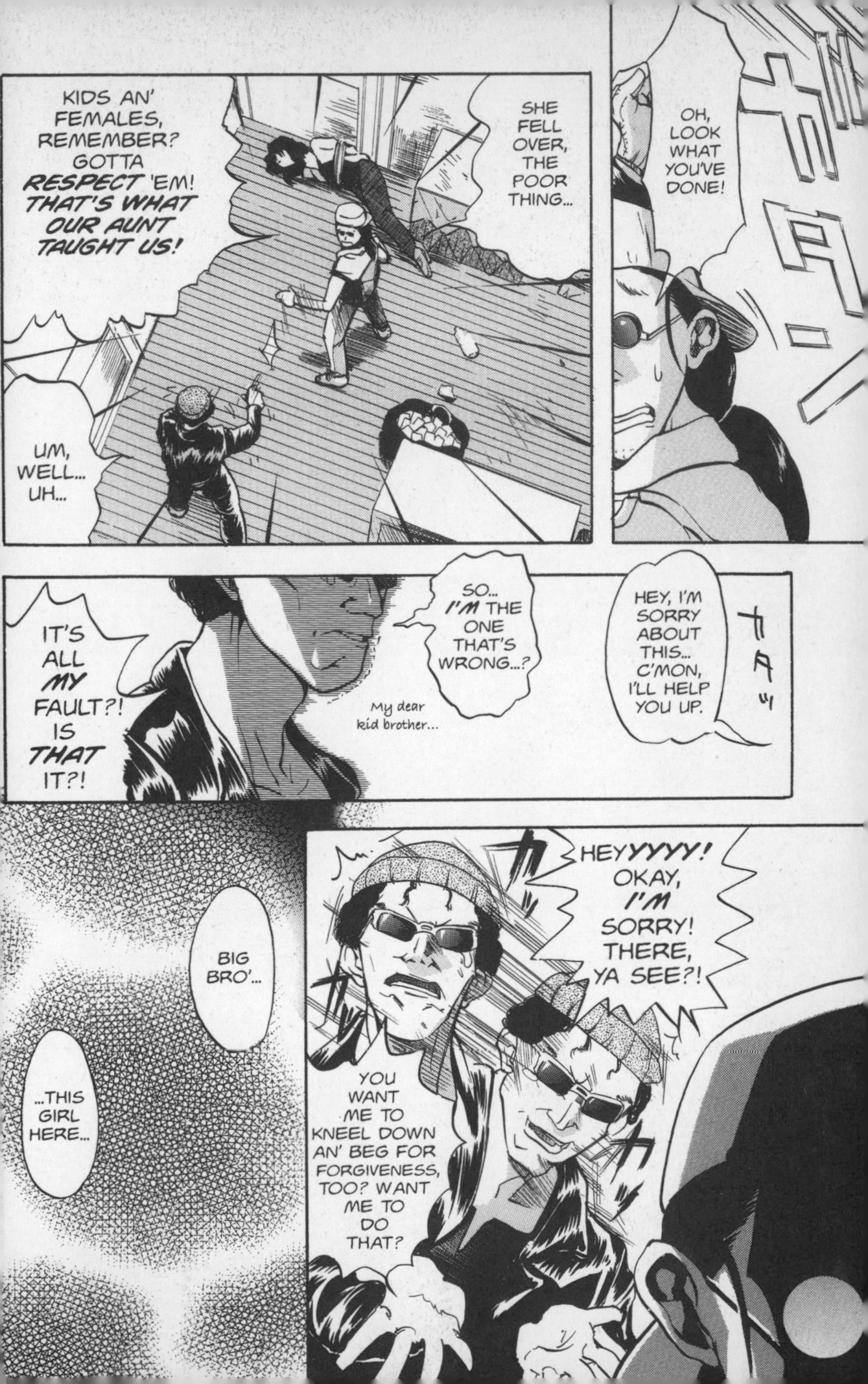
OH, LOOK WHAT YOU'VE DONE!
SHE FELL OVER, THE POOR THING...
KIDS AN' FEMALES, REMEMBER? GOTTA RESPECT 'EM! THAT'S WHAT OUR AUNT TAUGHT US!
UM, WELL... UH...
HEY, I'M SORRY ABOUT THIS... C'MON, I'LL HELP YOU UP.
SO... I'M THE ONE THAT'S WRONG...?
My dear kid brother...
IT'S ALL MY FAULT?! IS THAT IT?!
HEYYYYY! OKAY, I'M SORRY! THERE, YA SEE?!
YOU WANT ME TO KNEEL DOWN AN' BEG FOR FORGIVENESS, TOO? WANT ME TO DO THAT?
BIG BRO'...
...THIS GIRL HERE...

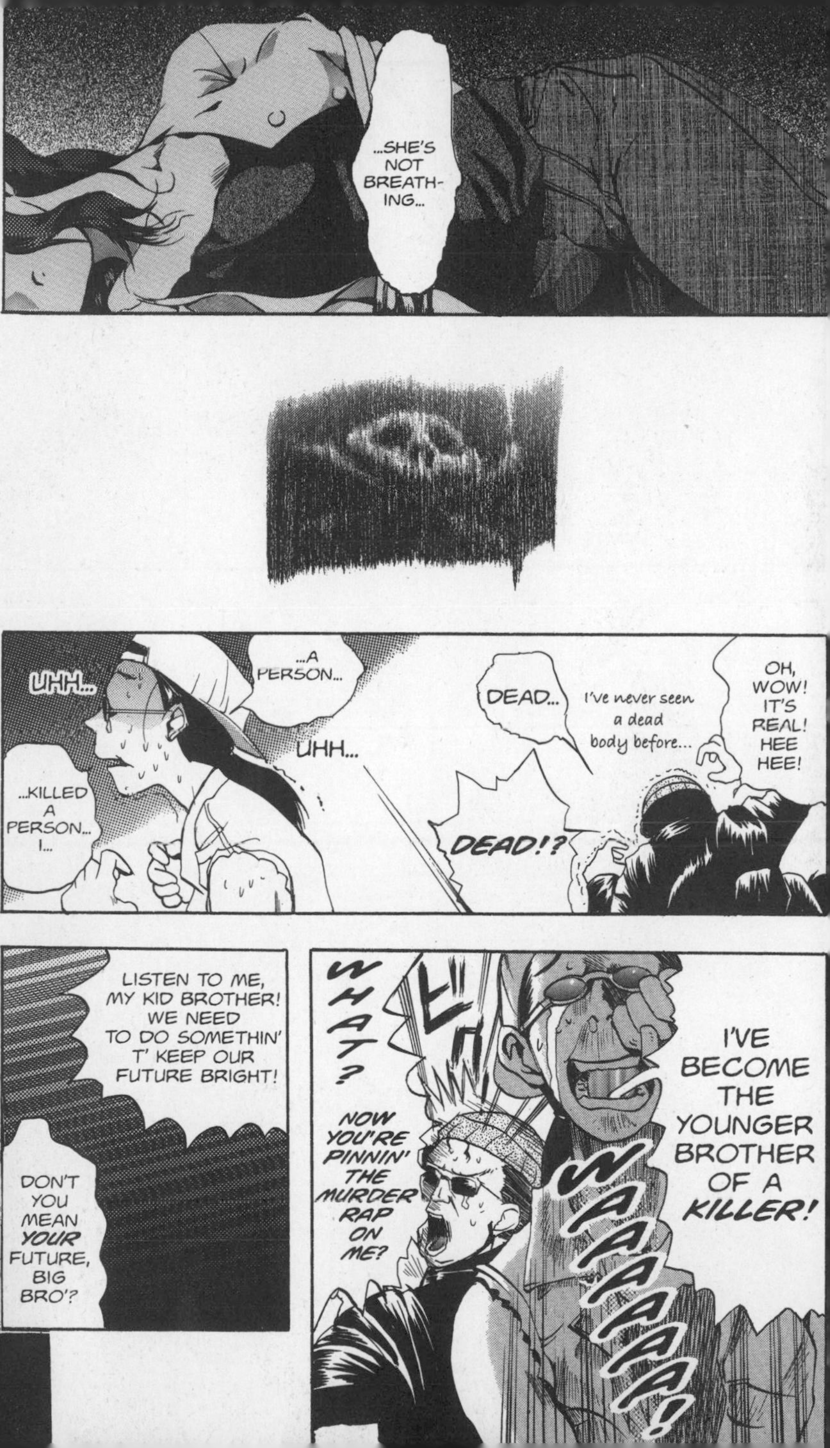
...SHE'S NOT BREATHING...
OH, WOW! IT'S REAL! HEE HEE!
I've never seen a dead body before...
DEAD...
DEAD!?
...A PERSON...
UHH...
UHH...
...KILLED A PERSON... I...
WHAT?
I'VE BECOME THE YOUNGER BROTHER OF A KILLER!
WAAAAAAA!
NOW YOU'RE PINNIN' THE MURDER RAP ON ME?
LISTEN TO ME, MY KID BROTHER! WE NEED TO DO SOMETHIN' T' KEEP OUR FUTURE BRIGHT!
DON'T YOU MEAN YOUR FUTURE, BIG BRO'?

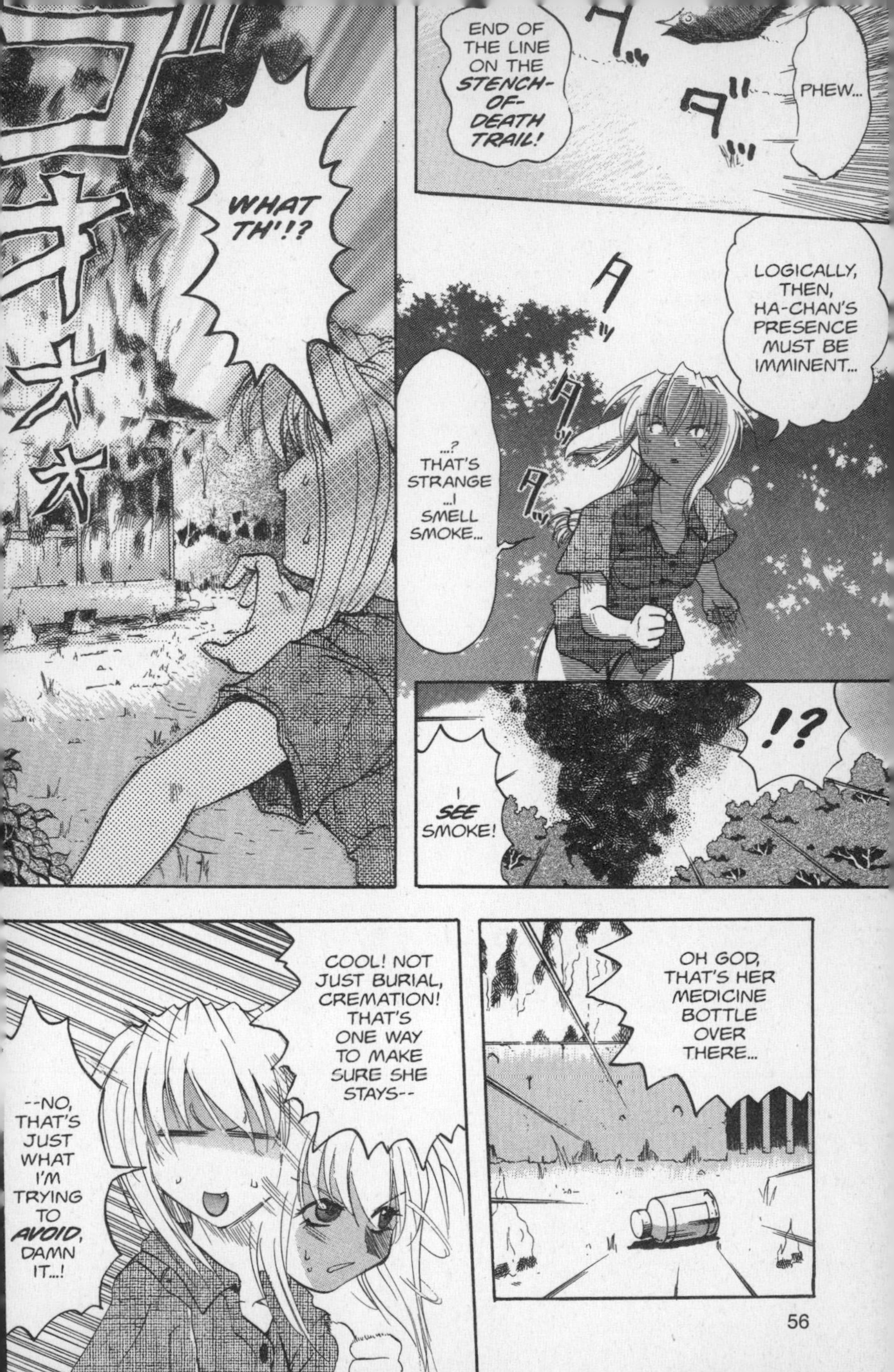
PHEW...
END OF THE LINE ON THE *STENCH-OF-DEATH TRAIL!*
LOGICALLY, THEN, HA-CHAN'S PRESENCE MUST BE IMMINENT...
...? THAT'S STRANGE ...I SMELL SMOKE...
!?
I *SEE* SMOKE!
WHAT TH'!?
OH GOD, THAT'S HER MEDICINE BOTTLE OVER THERE...
COOL! NOT JUST BURIAL, CREMATION! THAT'S ONE WAY TO MAKE SURE SHE STAYS--
--NO, THAT'S JUST WHAT I'M TRYING TO *AVOID*, DAMN IT...!

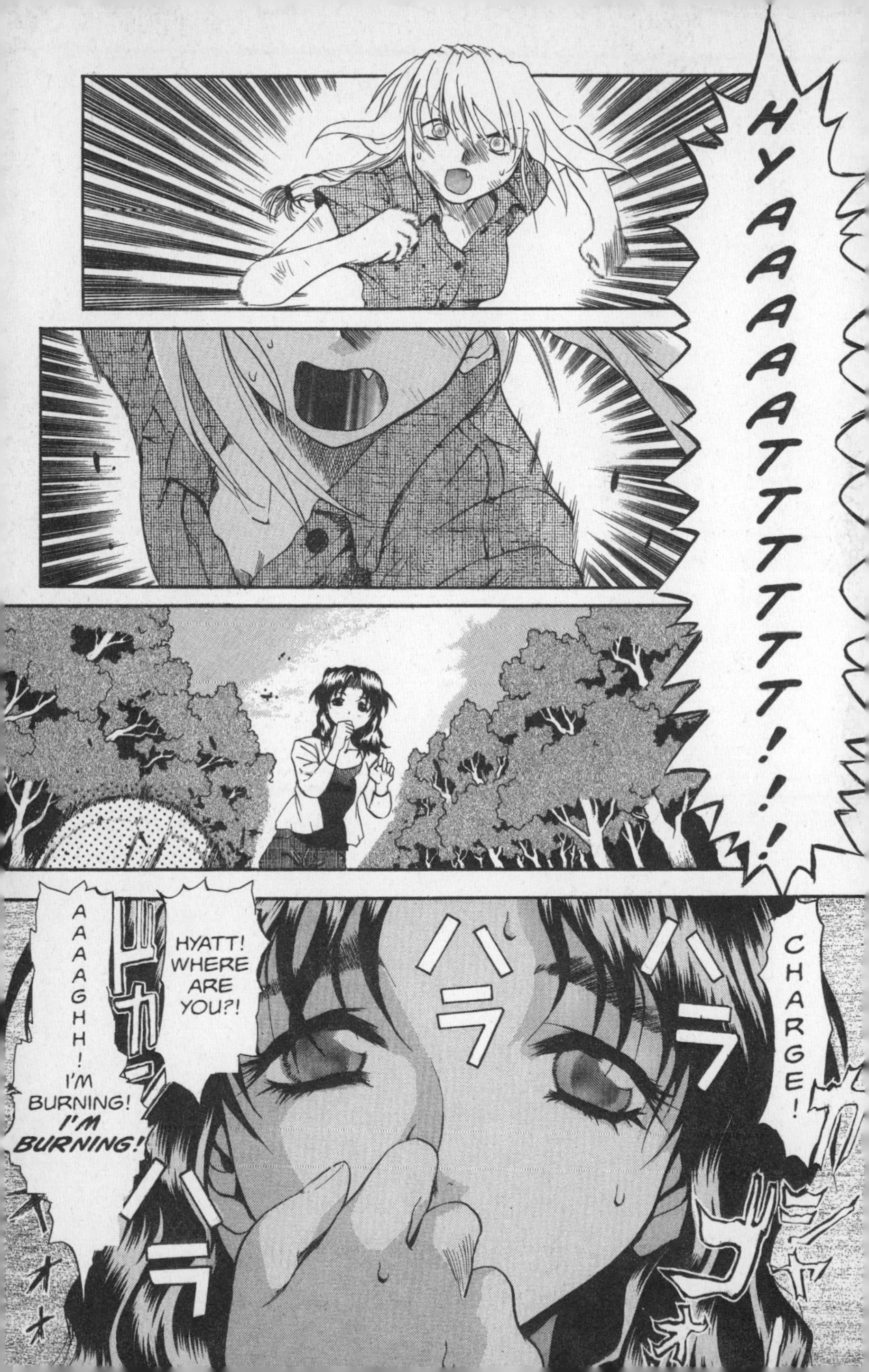
HYAAAAATTTTTT!!!!
CHARGE!
HYATT! WHERE ARE YOU?!
AAAAAGHH! I'M BURNING! *I'M BURNING!*

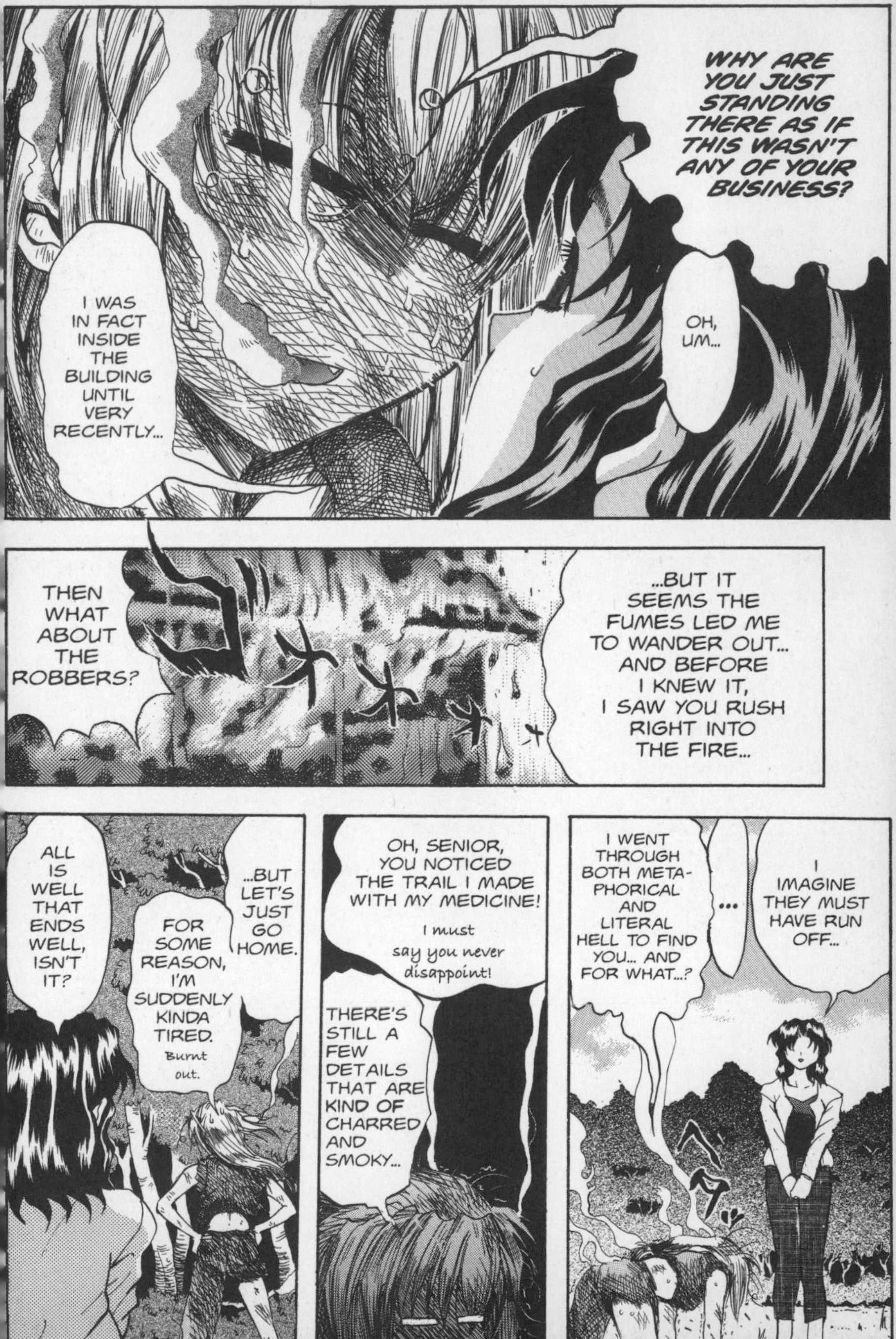
WHY ARE YOU JUST STANDING THERE AS IF THIS WASN'T ANY OF YOUR BUSINESS?
OH, UM...
I WAS IN FACT INSIDE THE BUILDING UNTIL VERY RECENTLY...
...BUT IT SEEMS THE FUMES LED ME TO WANDER OUT... AND BEFORE I KNEW IT, I SAW YOU RUSH RIGHT INTO THE FIRE...
THEN WHAT ABOUT THE ROBBERS?
I IMAGINE THEY MUST HAVE RUN OFF...
...
I WENT THROUGH BOTH META-PHORICAL AND LITERAL HELL TO FIND YOU... AND FOR WHAT...?
OH, SENIOR, YOU NOTICED THE TRAIL I MADE WITH MY MEDICINE!
I must say you never disappoint!
THERE'S STILL A FEW DETAILS THAT ARE KIND OF CHARRED AND SMOKY...
ALL IS WELL THAT ENDS WELL, ISN'T IT?
...BUT LET'S JUST GO HOME.
FOR SOME REASON, I'M SUDDENLY KINDA TIRED.
Burnt out.

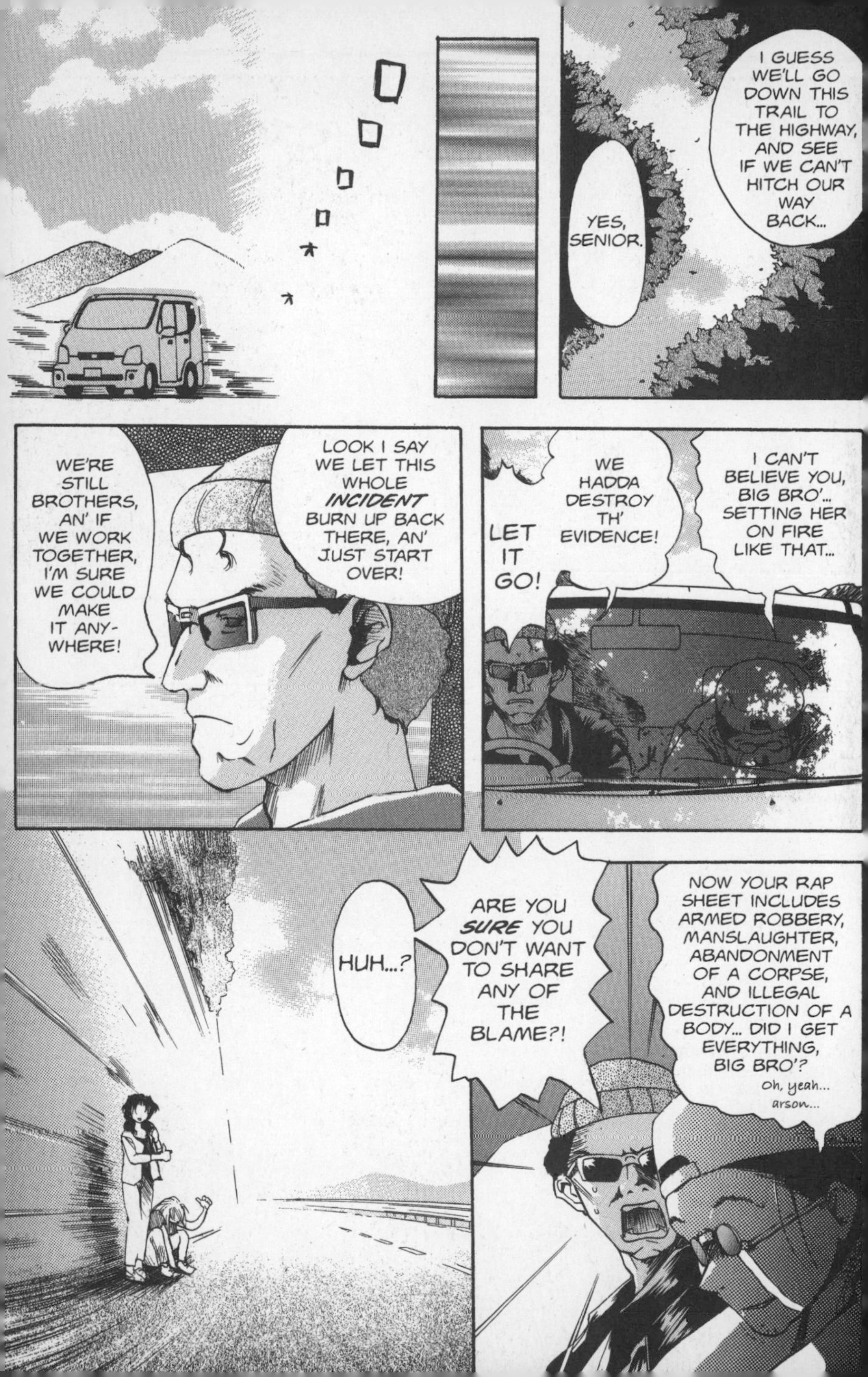
I GUESS WE'LL GO DOWN THIS TRAIL TO THE HIGHWAY, AND SEE IF WE CAN'T HITCH OUR WAY BACK...
YES, SENIOR.
I CAN'T BELIEVE YOU, BIG BRO'... SETTING HER ON FIRE LIKE THAT...
WE HADDA DESTROY TH' EVIDENCE!
LET IT GO!
LOOK I SAY WE LET THIS WHOLE *INCIDENT* BURN UP BACK THERE, AN' JUST START OVER!
WE'RE STILL BROTHERS, AN' IF WE WORK TOGETHER, I'M SURE WE COULD MAKE IT ANY-WHERE!
NOW YOUR RAP SHEET INCLUDES ARMED ROBBERY, MANSLAUGHTER, ABANDONMENT OF A CORPSE, AND ILLEGAL DESTRUCTION OF A BODY... DID I GET EVERYTHING, BIG BRO'?
Oh, yeah... arson...
ARE YOU *SURE* YOU DON'T WANT TO SHARE ANY OF THE BLAME?!
HUH...?

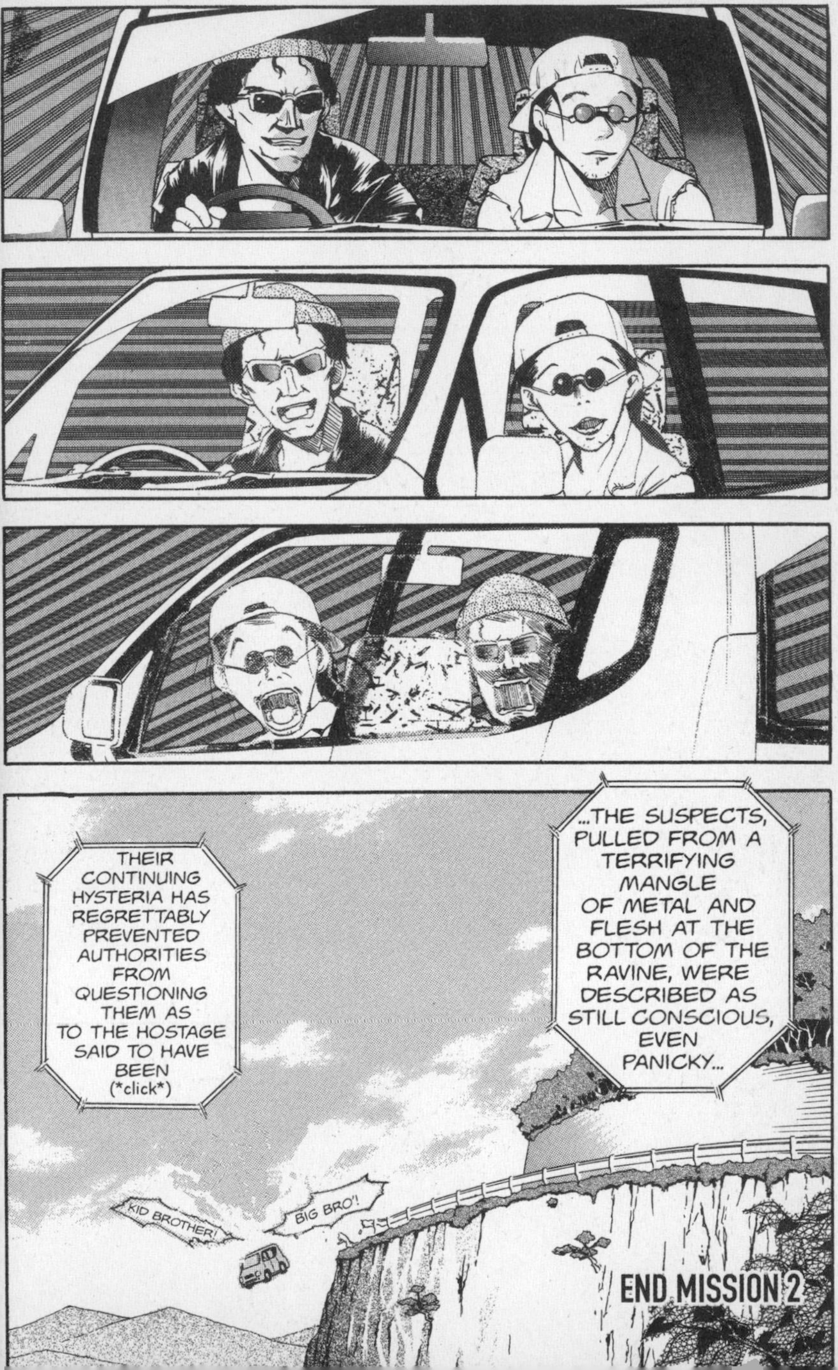
...THE SUSPECTS, PULLED FROM A TERRIFYING MANGLE OF METAL AND FLESH AT THE BOTTOM OF THE RAVINE, WERE DESCRIBED AS STILL CONSCIOUS, EVEN PANICKY...
THEIR CONTINUING HYSTERIA HAS REGRETTABLY PREVENTED AUTHORITIES FROM QUESTIONING THEM AS TO THE HOSTAGE SAID TO HAVE BEEN (*click*)
BIG BRO'!
KID BROTHER!
END MISSION 2

MISSION 3

"THE SMEARING BUG'S..."

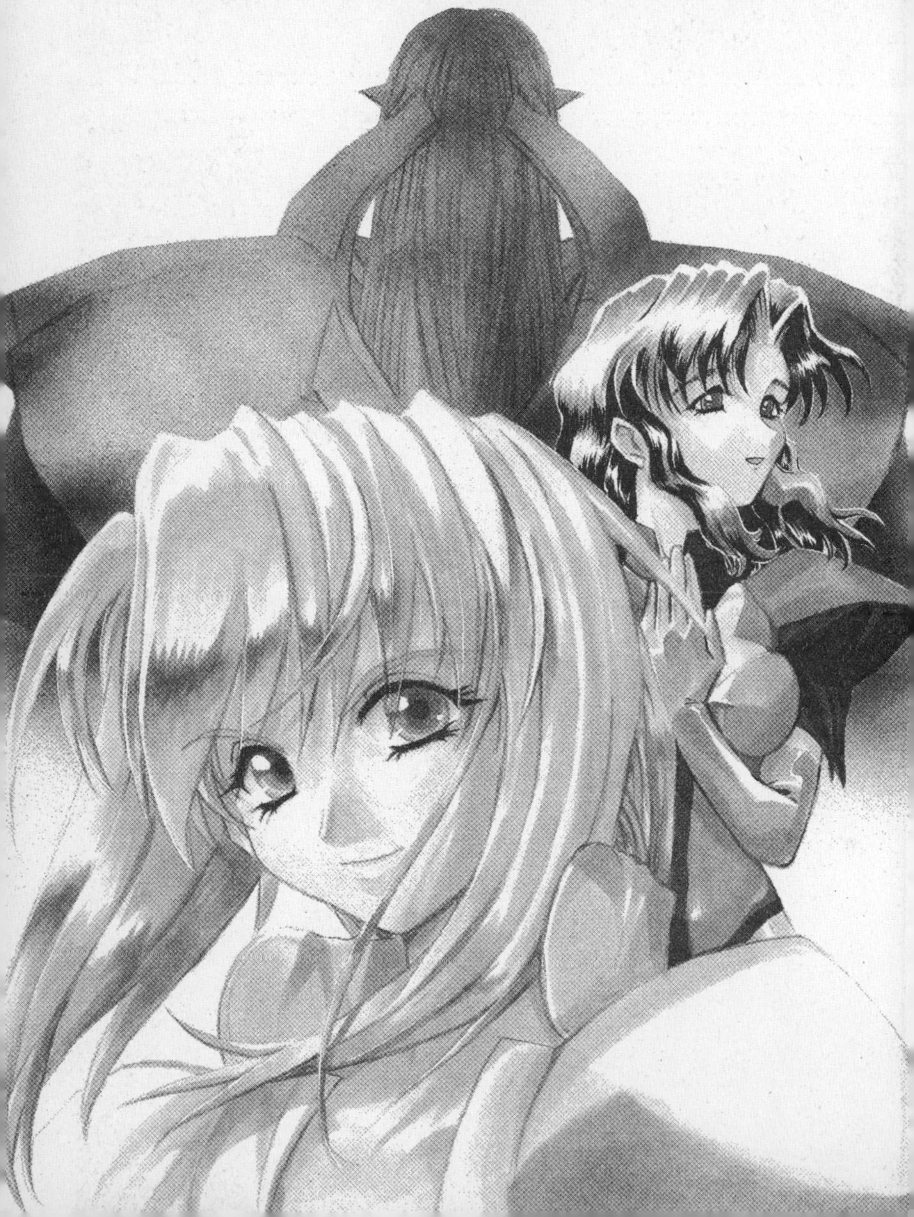

EXCEL SAGA

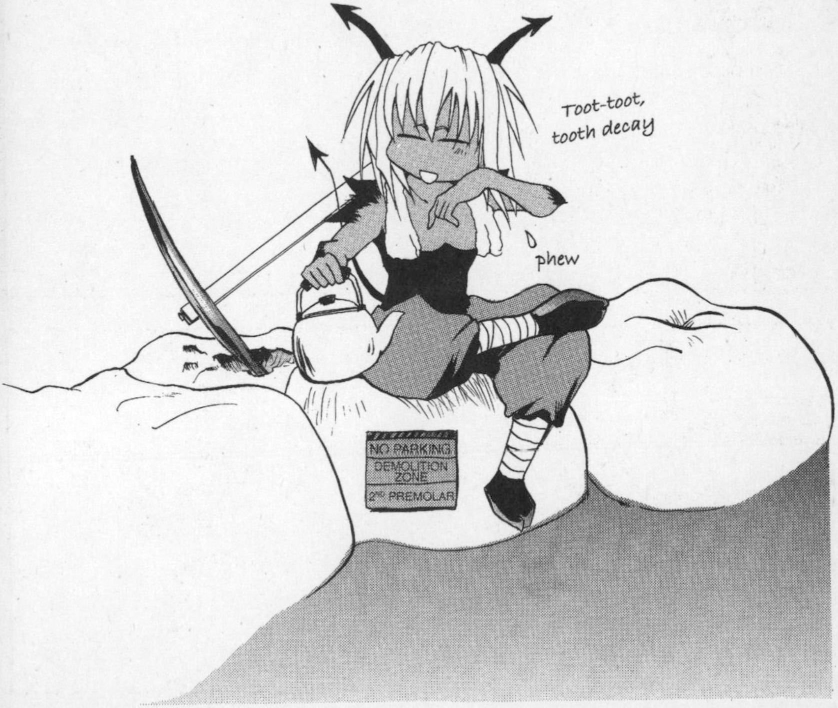
Toot-toot, tooth decay
phew
NO PARKING
DEMOLITION ZONE
2ND PREMOLAR

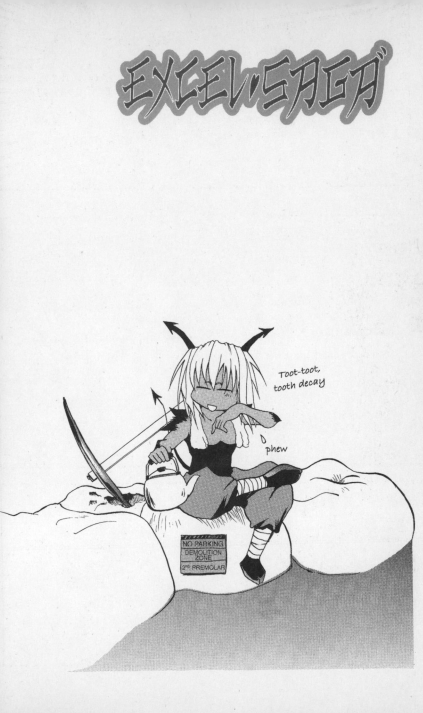

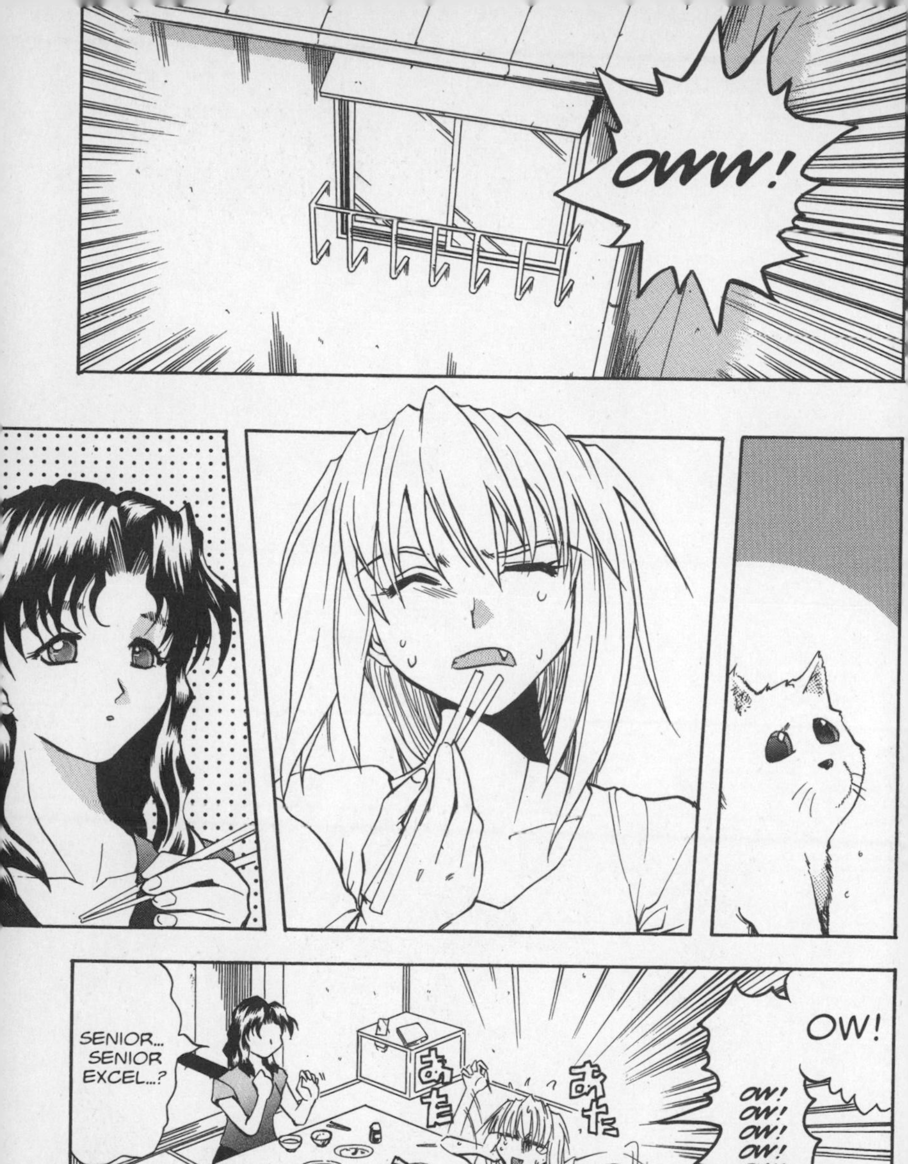
OWW!
OW!
OW! OW! OW! OW! OW!
SENIOR... SENIOR EXCEL...?

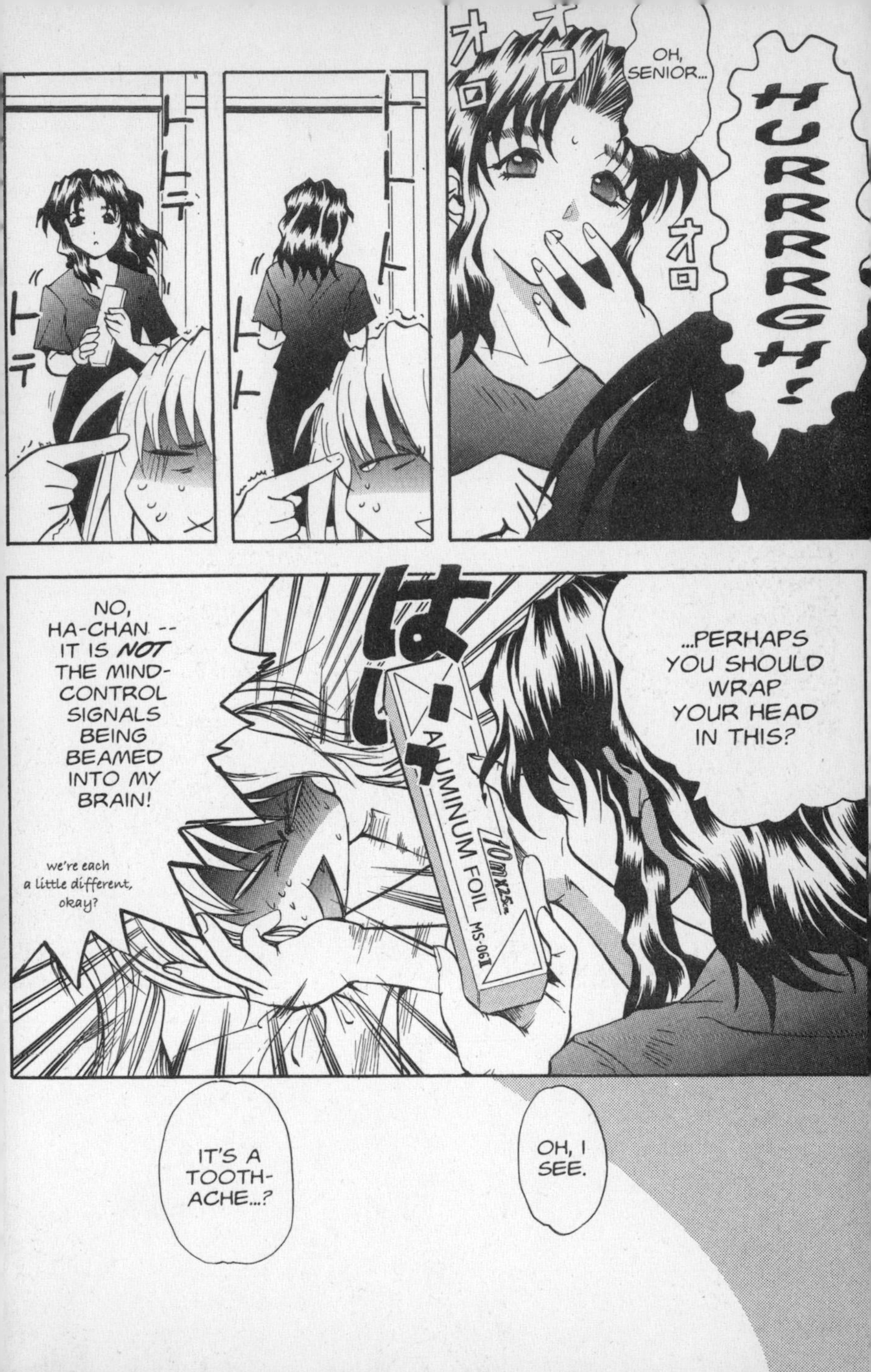
HURRRRGH!
OH, SENIOR...
オロオロ
オロ
トトト
トテトテ
...PERHAPS YOU SHOULD WRAP YOUR HEAD IN THIS?
はいっ
ALUMINUM FOIL
10m x 25cm
MS-06II
NO, HA-CHAN -- IT IS *NOT* THE MIND-CONTROL SIGNALS BEING BEAMED INTO MY BRAIN!
we're each a little different, okay?
OH, I SEE.
IT'S A TOOTH-ACHE...?

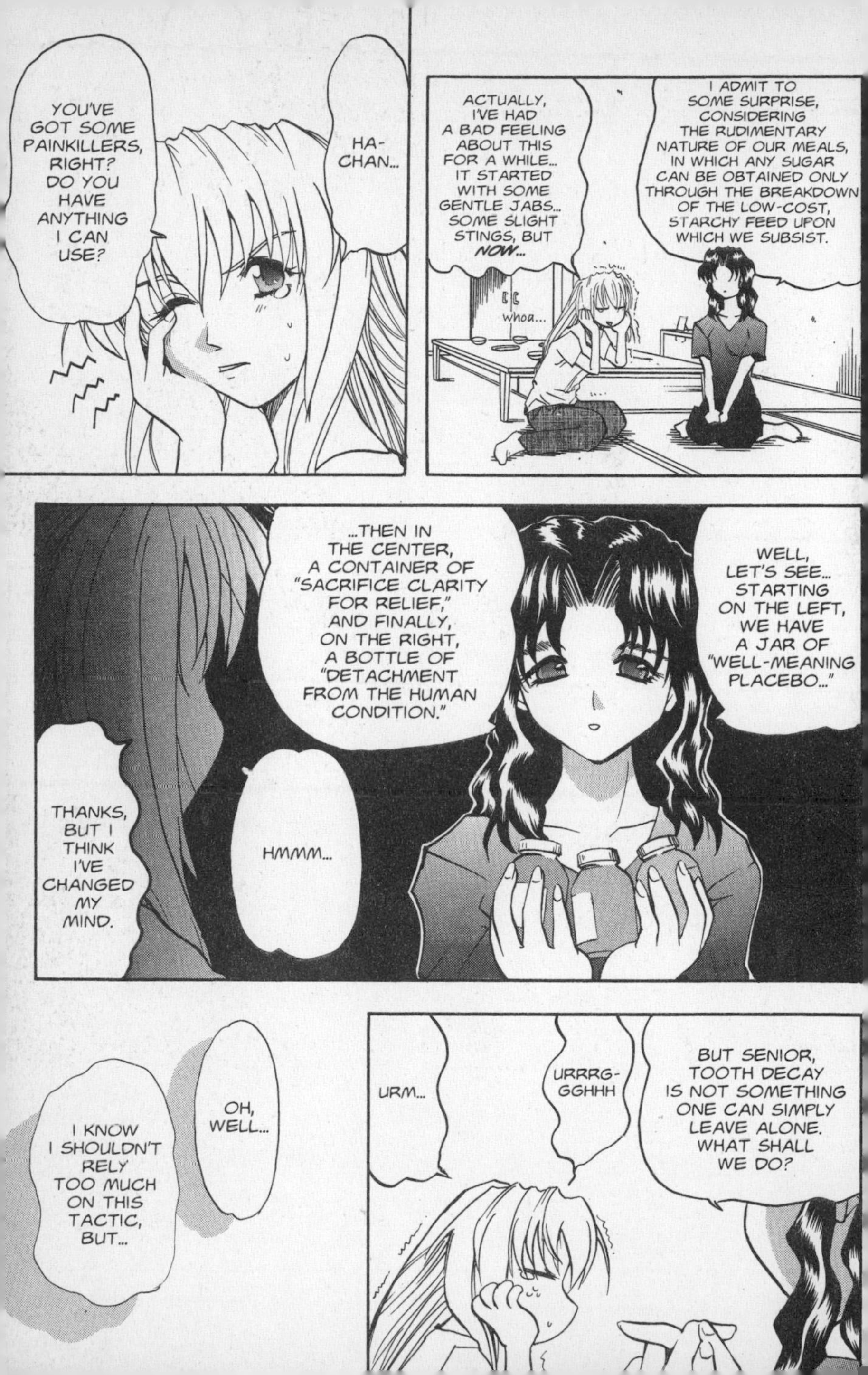
I ADMIT TO SOME SURPRISE, CONSIDERING THE RUDIMENTARY NATURE OF OUR MEALS, IN WHICH ANY SUGAR CAN BE OBTAINED ONLY THROUGH THE BREAKDOWN OF THE LOW-COST, STARCHY FEED UPON WHICH WE SUBSIST.
ACTUALLY, I'VE HAD A BAD FEELING ABOUT THIS FOR A WHILE... IT STARTED WITH SOME GENTLE JABS... SOME SLIGHT STINGS, BUT *NOW*...
whoa...
HA-CHAN...
YOU'VE GOT SOME PAINKILLERS, RIGHT? DO YOU HAVE ANYTHING I CAN USE?
WELL, LET'S SEE... STARTING ON THE LEFT, WE HAVE A JAR OF "WELL-MEANING PLACEBO..."
...THEN IN THE CENTER, A CONTAINER OF "SACRIFICE CLARITY FOR RELIEF," AND FINALLY, ON THE RIGHT, A BOTTLE OF "DETACHMENT FROM THE HUMAN CONDITION."
HMMM...
THANKS, BUT I THINK I'VE CHANGED MY MIND.
BUT SENIOR, TOOTH DECAY IS NOT SOMETHING ONE CAN SIMPLY LEAVE ALONE. WHAT SHALL WE DO?
URRRG-GGHHH
URM...
OH, WELL...
I KNOW I SHOULDN'T RELY TOO MUCH ON THIS TACTIC, BUT...

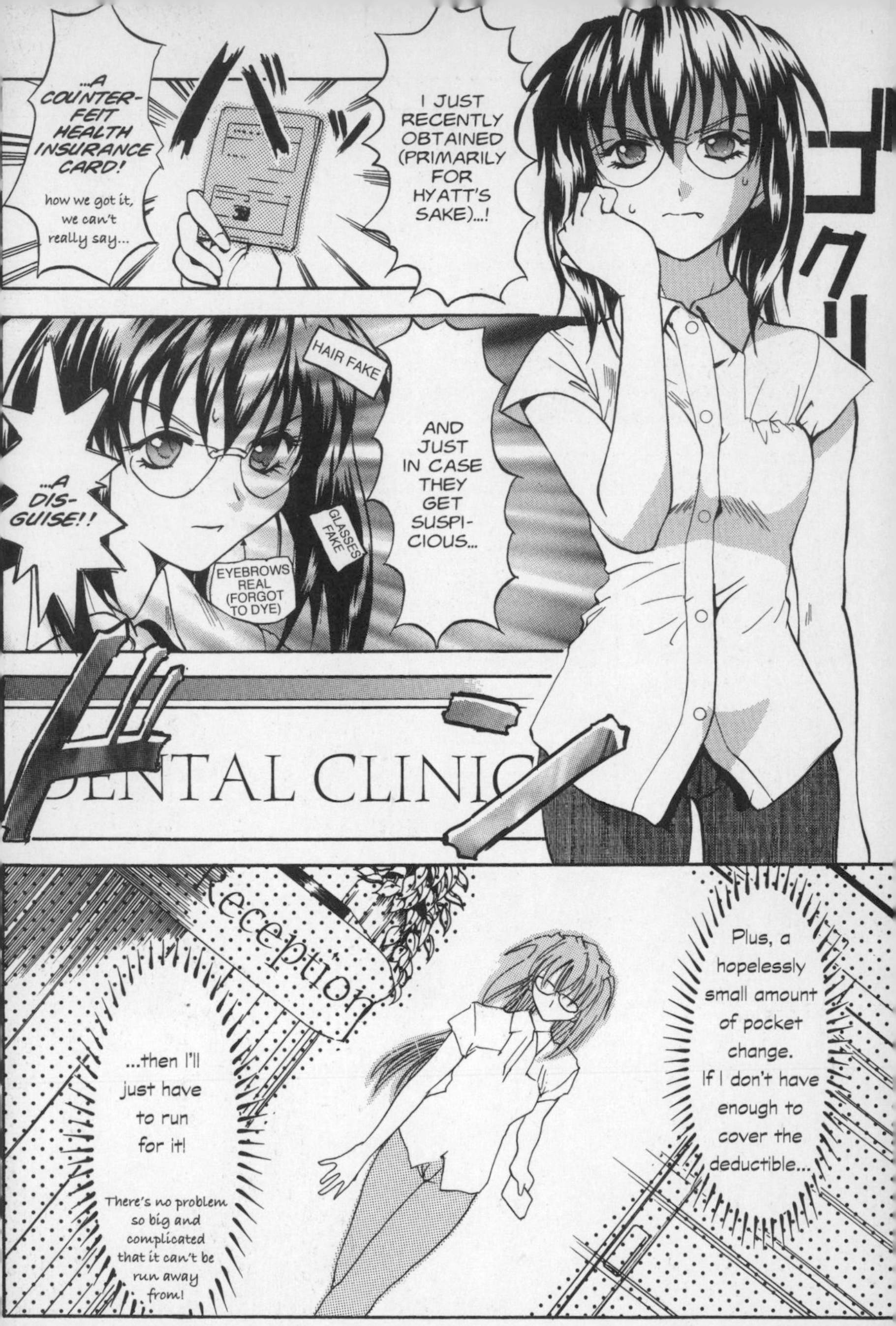
I JUST RECENTLY OBTAINED (PRIMARILY FOR HYATT'S SAKE)...!
...A COUNTERFEIT HEALTH INSURANCE CARD!
how we got it, we can't really say...
AND JUST IN CASE THEY GET SUSPICIOUS...
...A DISGUISE!!
HAIR FAKE
GLASSES FAKE
EYEBROWS REAL (FORGOT TO DYE)
DENTAL CLINIC
Reception
Plus, a hopelessly small amount of pocket change. If I don't have enough to cover the deductible...
...then I'll just have to run for it!
There's no problem so big and complicated that it can't be run away from!

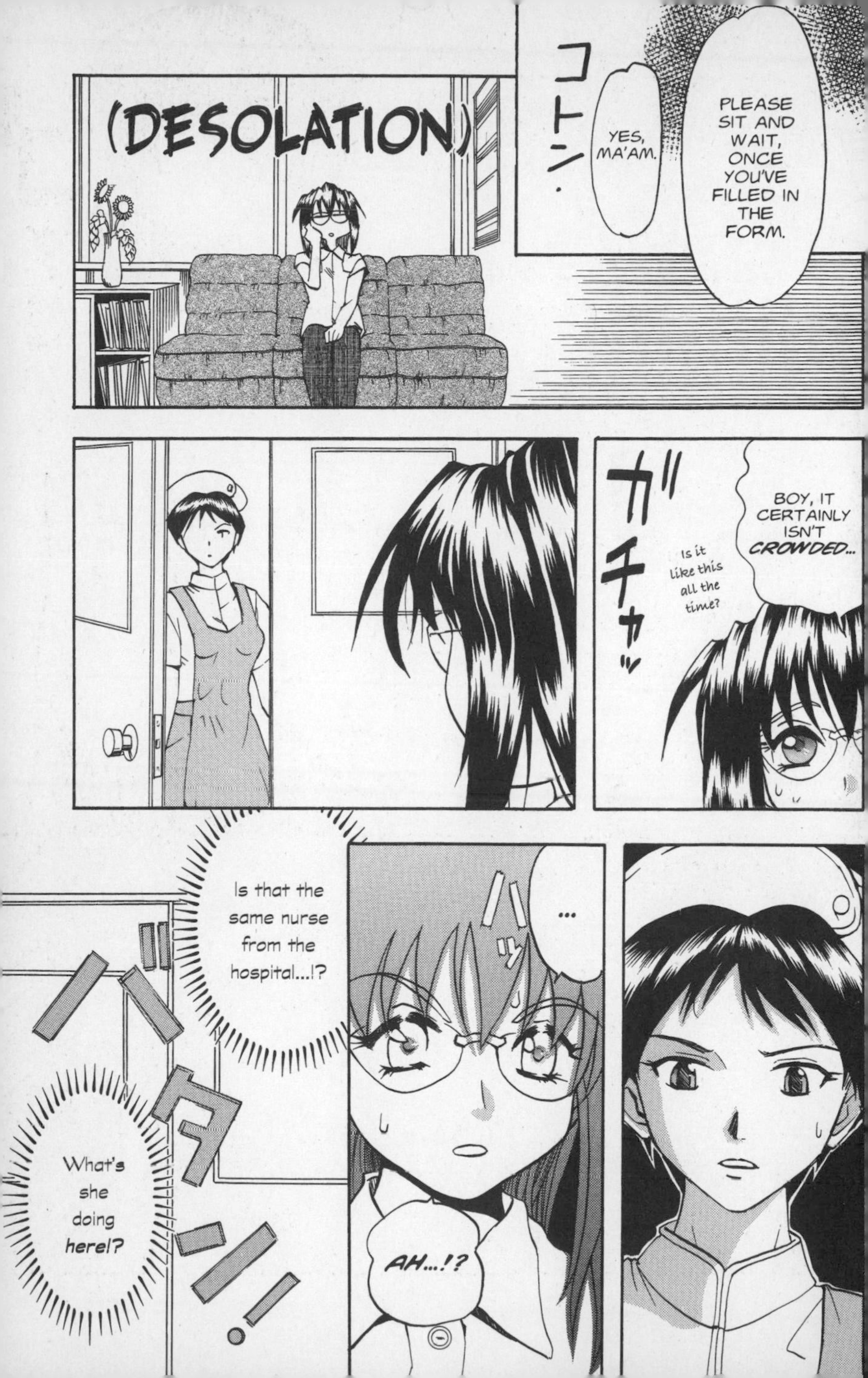
PLEASE SIT AND WAIT, ONCE YOU'VE FILLED IN THE FORM.
YES, MA'AM.
コトン・
(DESOLATION)
ガチャッ
BOY, IT CERTAINLY ISN'T CROWDED...
Is it like this all the time?
...
ハッ
AH...!?
Is that the same nurse from the hospital...!?
What's she doing here!?
バタン!

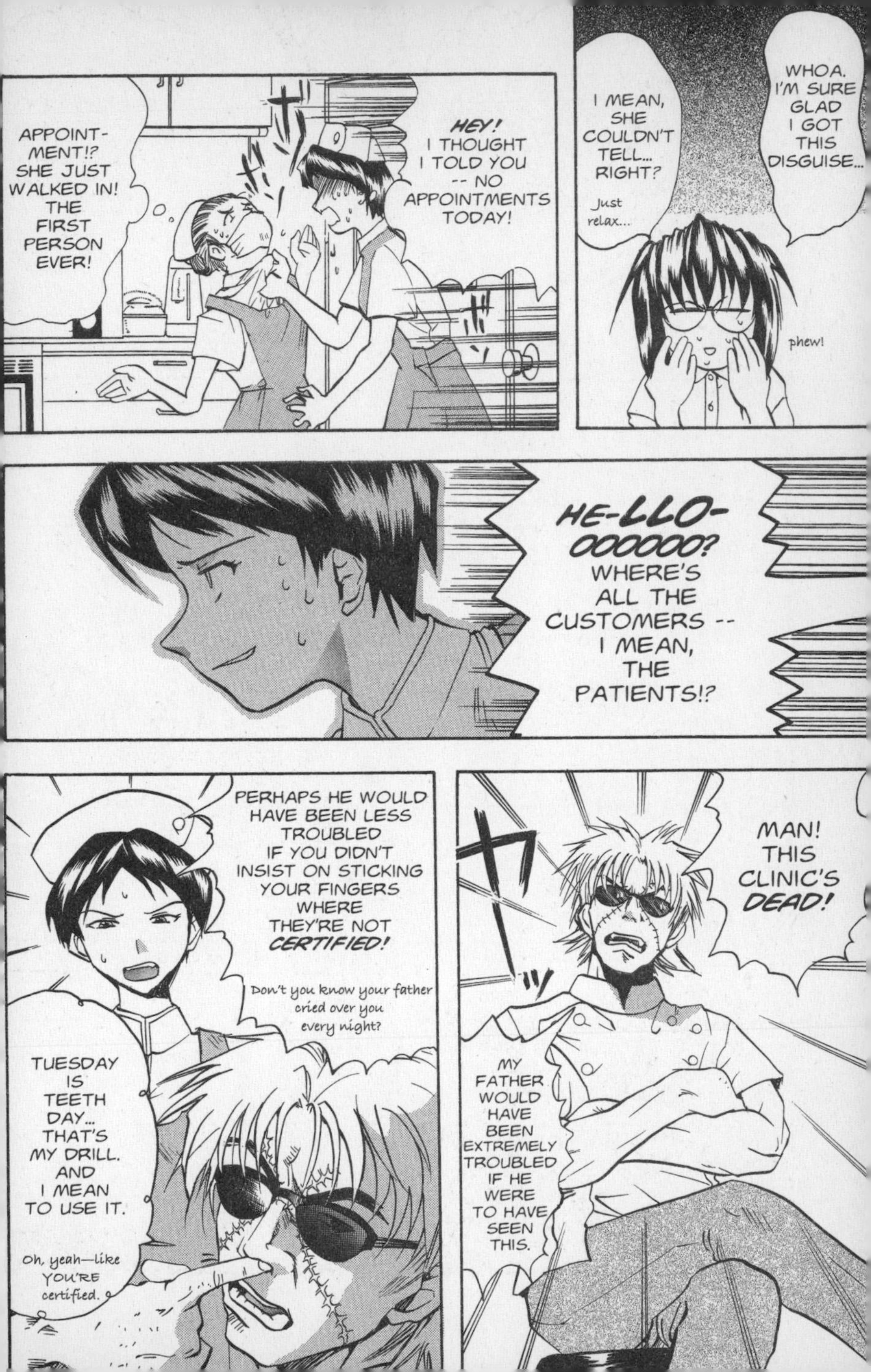
WHOA. I'M SURE GLAD I GOT THIS DISGUISE...
I MEAN, SHE COULDN'T TELL... RIGHT?
Just relax...
phew!
HEY! I THOUGHT I TOLD YOU -- NO APPOINTMENTS TODAY!
APPOINT-MENT!? SHE JUST WALKED IN! THE FIRST PERSON EVER!
HE-LLO-OOOOOO? WHERE'S ALL THE CUSTOMERS -- I MEAN, THE PATIENTS!?
MAN! THIS CLINIC'S DEAD!
MY FATHER WOULD HAVE BEEN EXTREMELY TROUBLED IF HE WERE TO HAVE SEEN THIS.
PERHAPS HE WOULD HAVE BEEN LESS TROUBLED IF YOU DIDN'T INSIST ON STICKING YOUR FINGERS WHERE THEY'RE NOT CERTIFIED!
Don't you know your father cried over you every night?
TUESDAY IS TEETH DAY... THAT'S MY DRILL. AND I MEAN TO USE IT.
Oh, yeah—like YOU'RE certified.

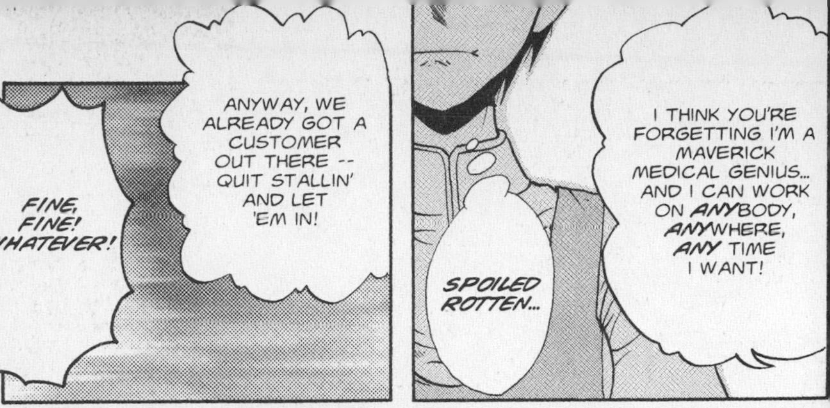
I THINK YOU'RE FORGETTING I'M A MAVERICK MEDICAL GENIUS... AND I CAN WORK ON ANYBODY, ANYWHERE, ANY TIME I WANT!
SPOILED ROTTEN...
ANYWAY, WE ALREADY GOT A CUSTOMER OUT THERE -- QUIT STALLIN' AND LET 'EM IN!
FINE, FINE! WHATEVER!

THE STORIES, CHARACTERS, AND INCIDENTS MENTIONED IN THIS PUBLICATION ARE ENTIRELY FICTIONAL...

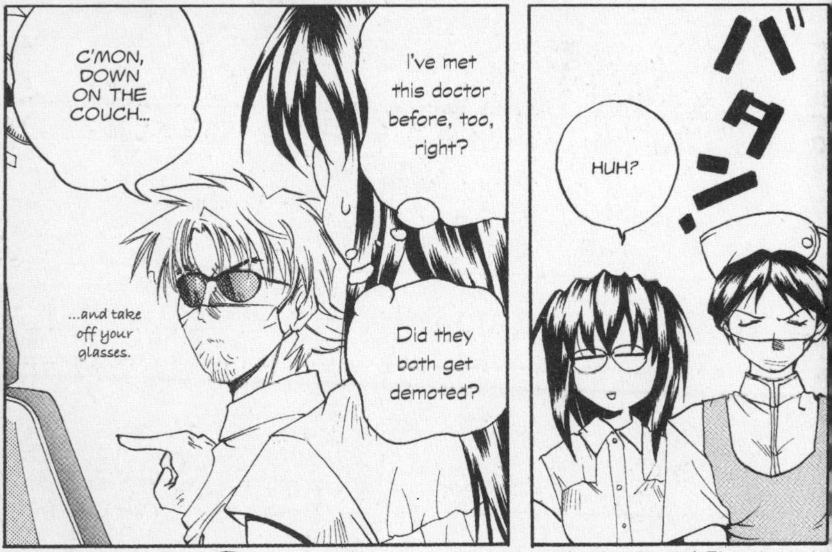
バタン
HUH?
I've met this doctor before, too, right?
C'MON, DOWN ON THE COUCH...
Did they both get demoted?
...and take off your glasses.

Thanks: Po and Jinnojyou.

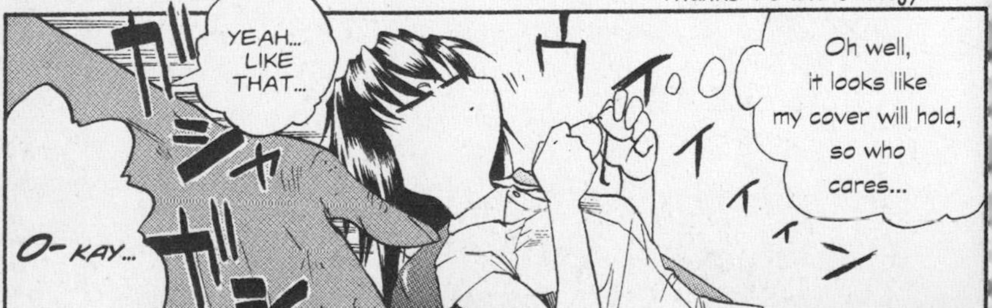
Oh well, it looks like my cover will hold, so who cares...
ウイイイン
YEAH... LIKE THAT...
ガシャガシャ
O-KAY...

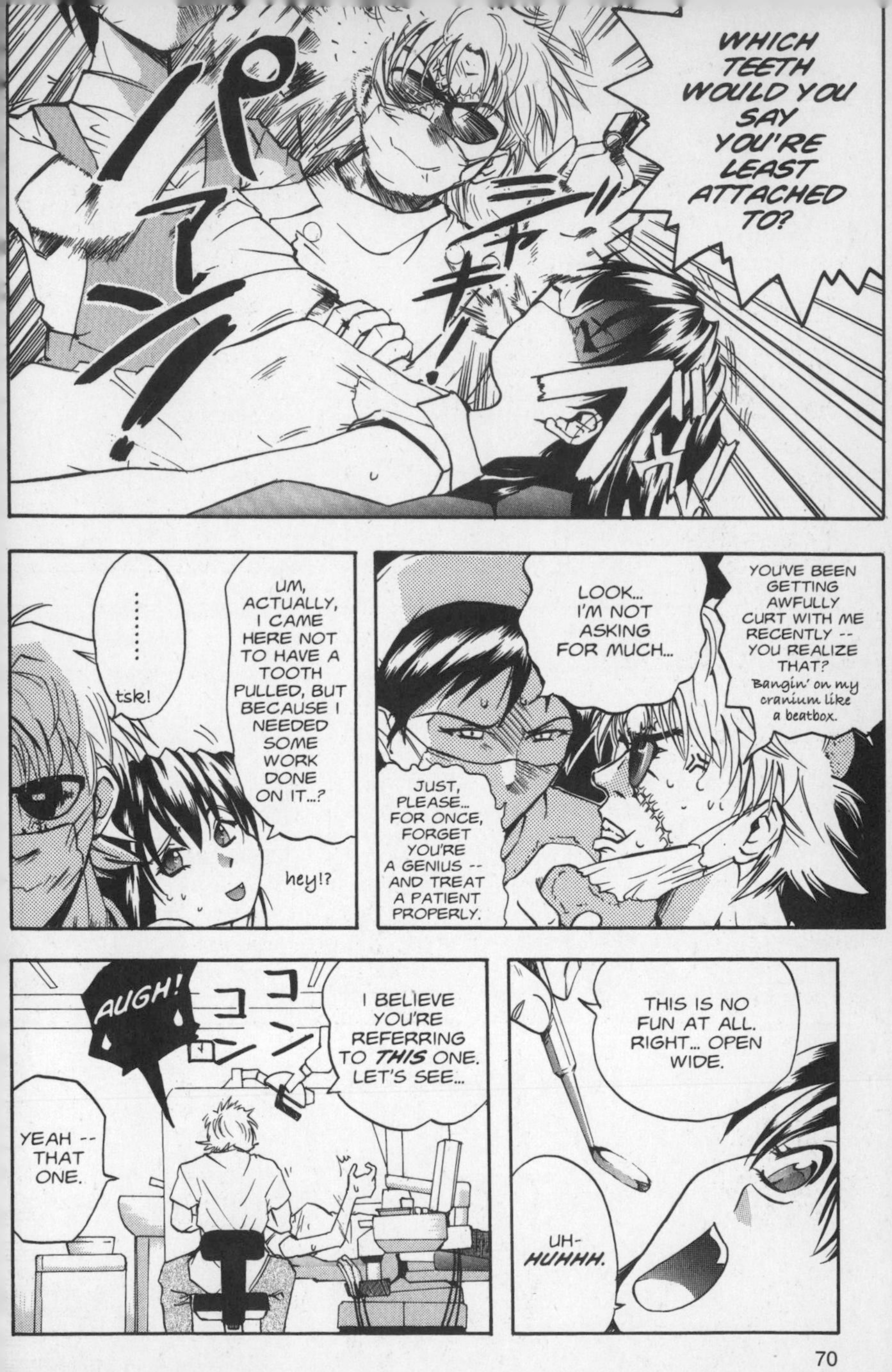
WHICH TEETH WOULD YOU SAY YOU'RE LEAST ATTACHED TO?
YOU'VE BEEN GETTING AWFULLY CURT WITH ME RECENTLY -- YOU REALIZE THAT?
Bangin' on my cranium like a beatbox.
LOOK... I'M NOT ASKING FOR MUCH...
JUST, PLEASE... FOR ONCE, FORGET YOU'RE A GENIUS -- AND TREAT A PATIENT PROPERLY.
UM, ACTUALLY, I CAME HERE NOT TO HAVE A TOOTH PULLED, BUT BECAUSE I NEEDED SOME WORK DONE ON IT...?
hey!?
....
tsk!
THIS IS NO FUN AT ALL. RIGHT... OPEN WIDE.
UH-HUHHH.
I BELIEVE YOU'RE REFERRING TO THIS ONE. LET'S SEE...
AUGH!
YEAH -- THAT ONE.

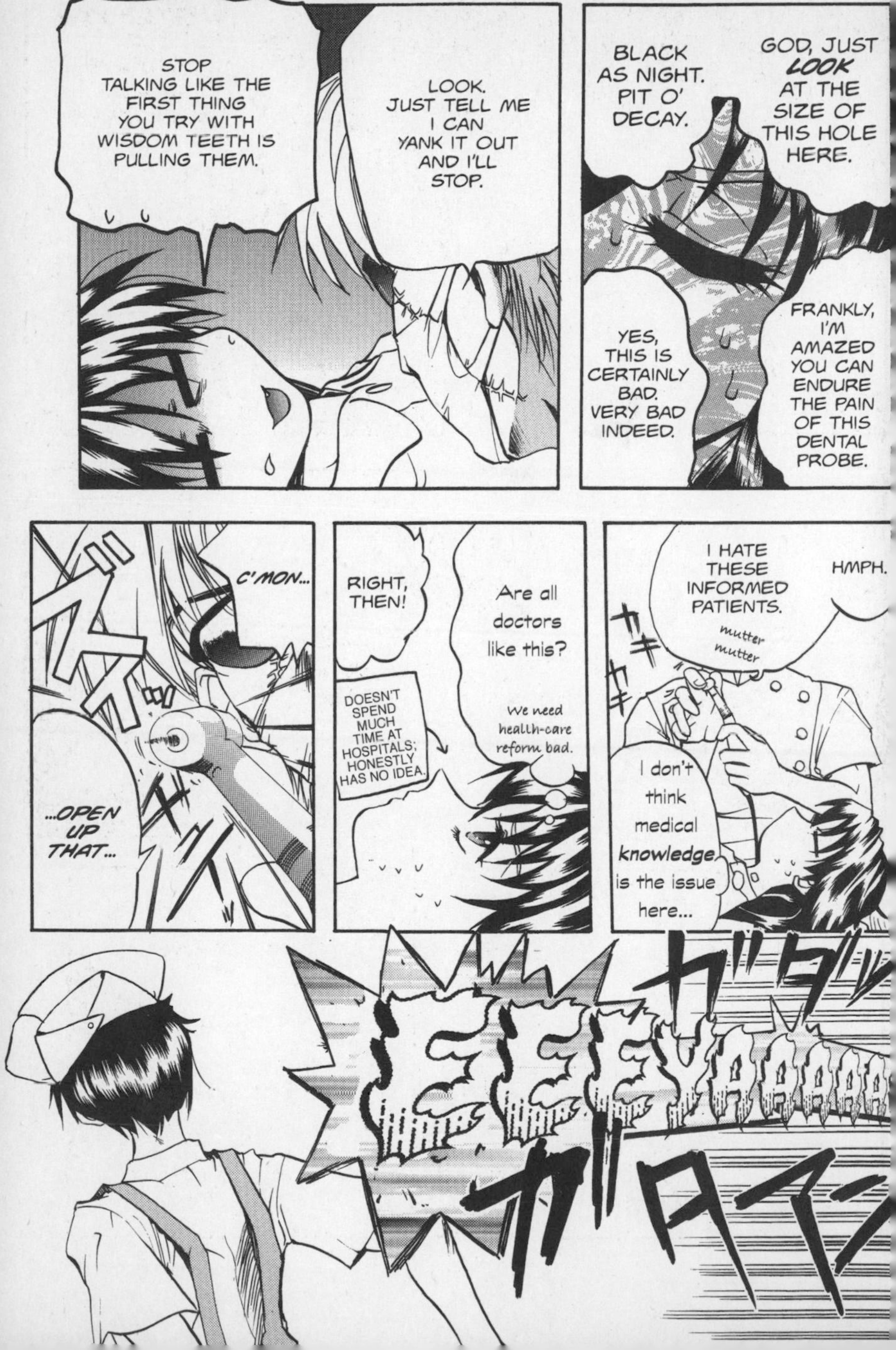
GOD, JUST LOOK AT THE SIZE OF THIS HOLE HERE.
BLACK AS NIGHT. PIT O' DECAY.
FRANKLY, I'M AMAZED YOU CAN ENDURE THE PAIN OF THIS DENTAL PROBE.
YES, THIS IS CERTAINLY BAD. VERY BAD INDEED.
LOOK. JUST TELL ME I CAN YANK IT OUT AND I'LL STOP.
STOP TALKING LIKE THE FIRST THING YOU TRY WITH WISDOM TEETH IS PULLING THEM.
HMPH.
I HATE THESE INFORMED PATIENTS.
mutter mutter
I don't think medical knowledge is the issue here...
Are all doctors like this?
We need health-care reform bad.
RIGHT, THEN!
DOESN'T SPEND MUCH TIME AT HOSPITALS; HONESTLY HAS NO IDEA.
C'MON...
...OPEN UP THAT...
EEEYAAAAA

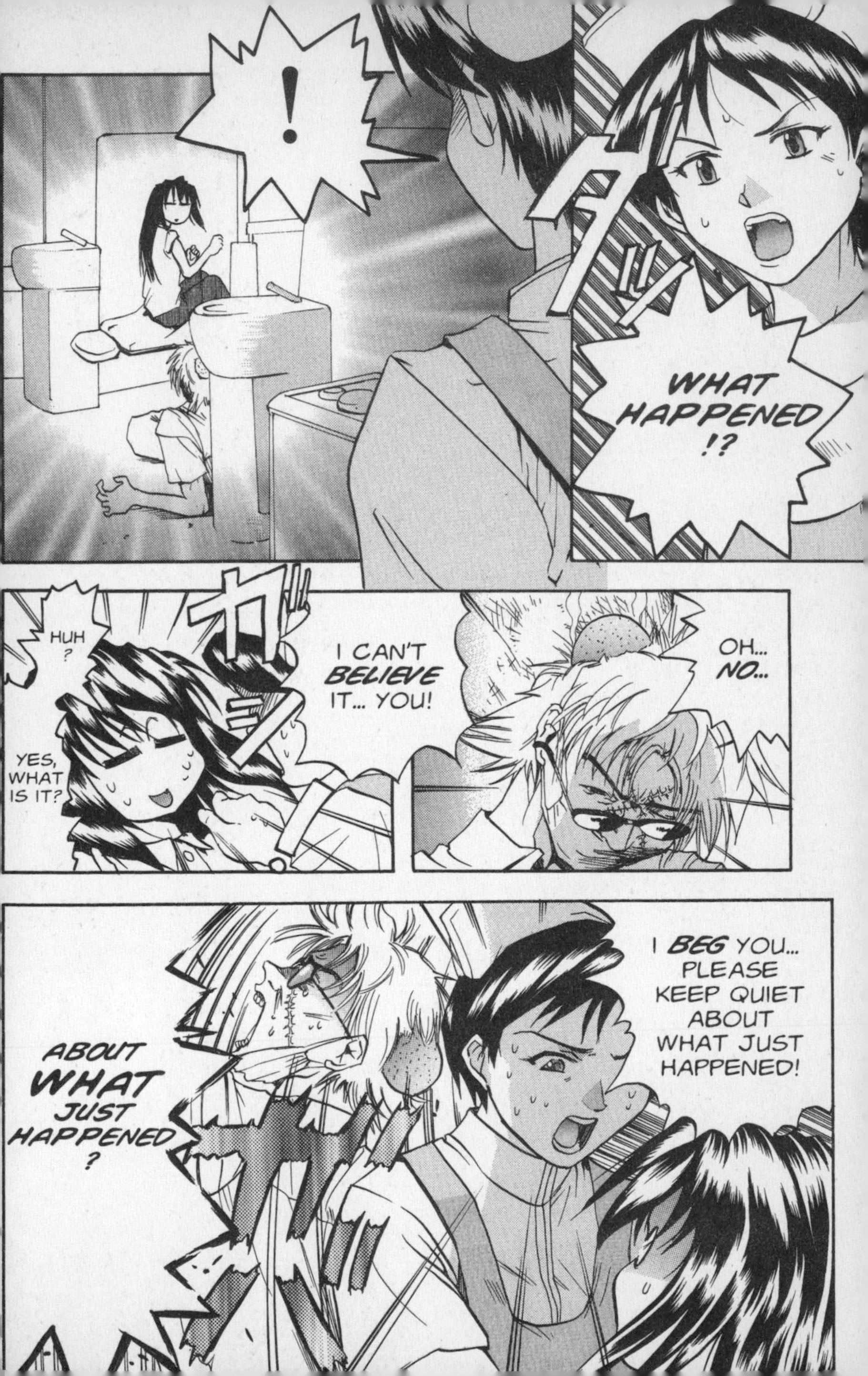
WHAT HAPPENED!?
!
OH... NO...
I CAN'T BELIEVE IT... YOU!
HUH?
YES, WHAT IS IT?
I BEG YOU... PLEASE KEEP QUIET ABOUT WHAT JUST HAPPENED!
ABOUT WHAT JUST HAPPENED?

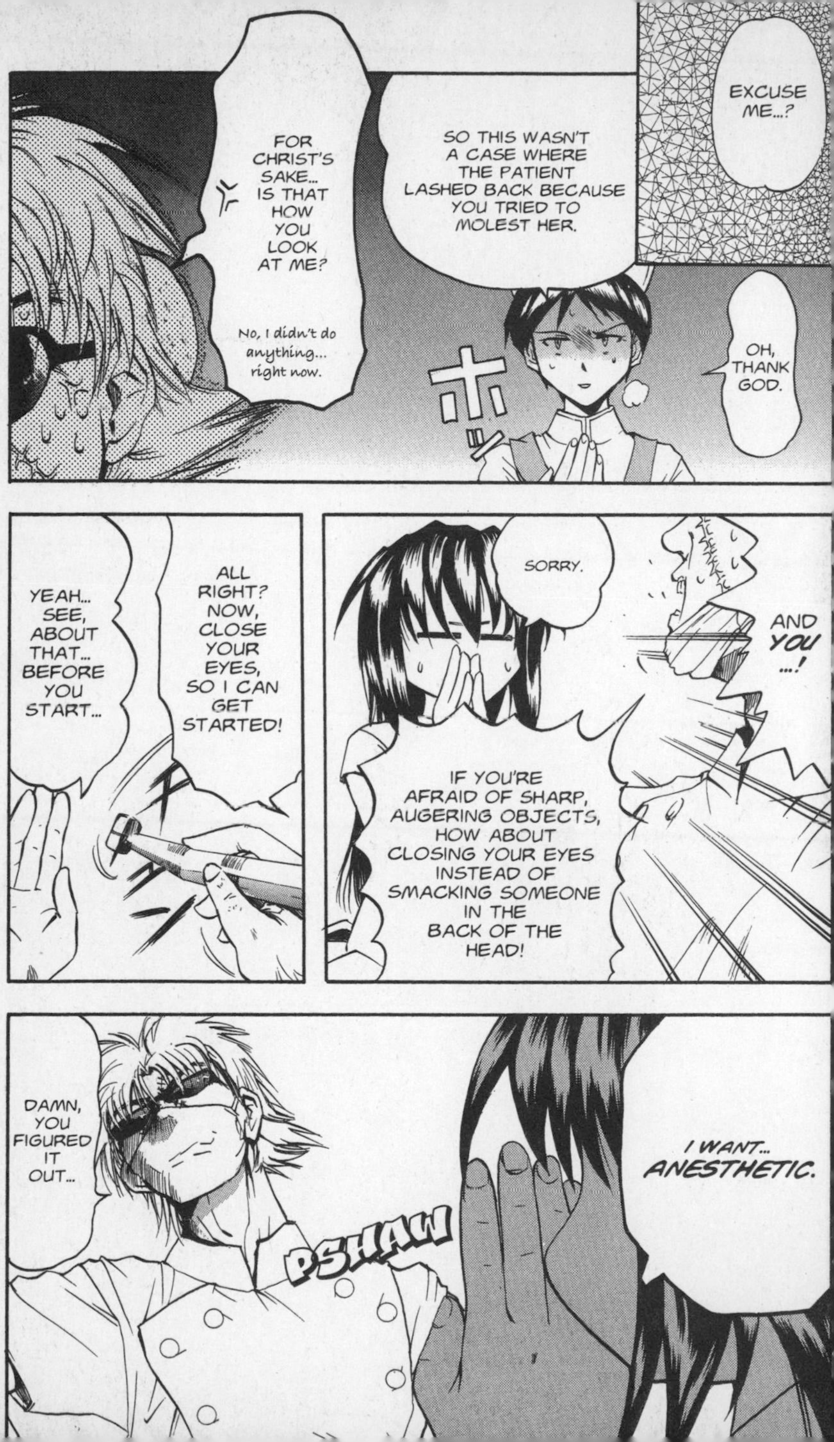
EXCUSE ME...?
SO THIS WASN'T A CASE WHERE THE PATIENT LASHED BACK BECAUSE YOU TRIED TO MOLEST HER.
FOR CHRIST'S SAKE... IS THAT HOW YOU LOOK AT ME?
No, I didn't do anything... right now.
OH, THANK GOD.
AND YOU ...!
IF YOU'RE AFRAID OF SHARP, AUGERING OBJECTS, HOW ABOUT CLOSING YOUR EYES INSTEAD OF SMACKING SOMEONE IN THE BACK OF THE HEAD!
SORRY.
ALL RIGHT? NOW, CLOSE YOUR EYES, SO I CAN GET STARTED!
YEAH... SEE, ABOUT THAT... BEFORE YOU START...
I WANT... ANESTHETIC.
PSHAW
DAMN, YOU FIGURED IT OUT...

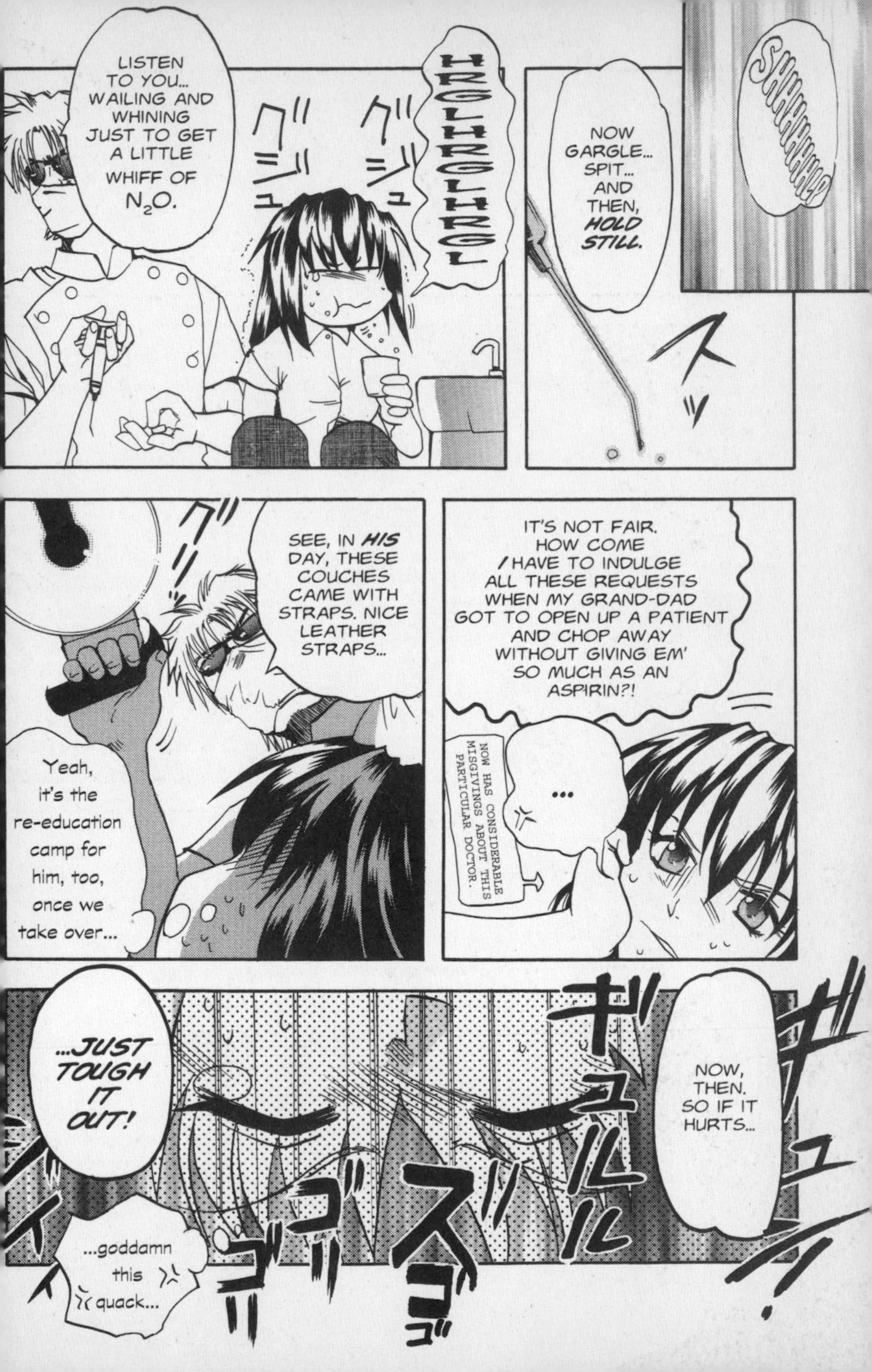
SHHHHHHH!
NOW GARGLE... SPIT... AND THEN, *HOLD STILL.*
HRGLHRGLHRGL
LISTEN TO YOU... WAILING AND WHINING JUST TO GET A LITTLE WHIFF OF N_2O.
IT'S NOT FAIR. HOW COME *I* HAVE TO INDULGE ALL THESE REQUESTS WHEN MY GRAND-DAD GOT TO OPEN UP A PATIENT AND CHOP AWAY WITHOUT GIVING EM' SO MUCH AS AN ASPIRIN?!
...
NOW HAS CONSIDERABLE MISGIVINGS ABOUT THIS PARTICULAR DOCTOR.
SEE, IN *HIS* DAY, THESE COUCHES CAME WITH STRAPS. NICE LEATHER STRAPS...
Yeah, it's the re-education camp for him, too, once we take over...
NOW, THEN. SO IF IT HURTS...
...JUST TOUGH IT OUT!
...goddamn this quack...

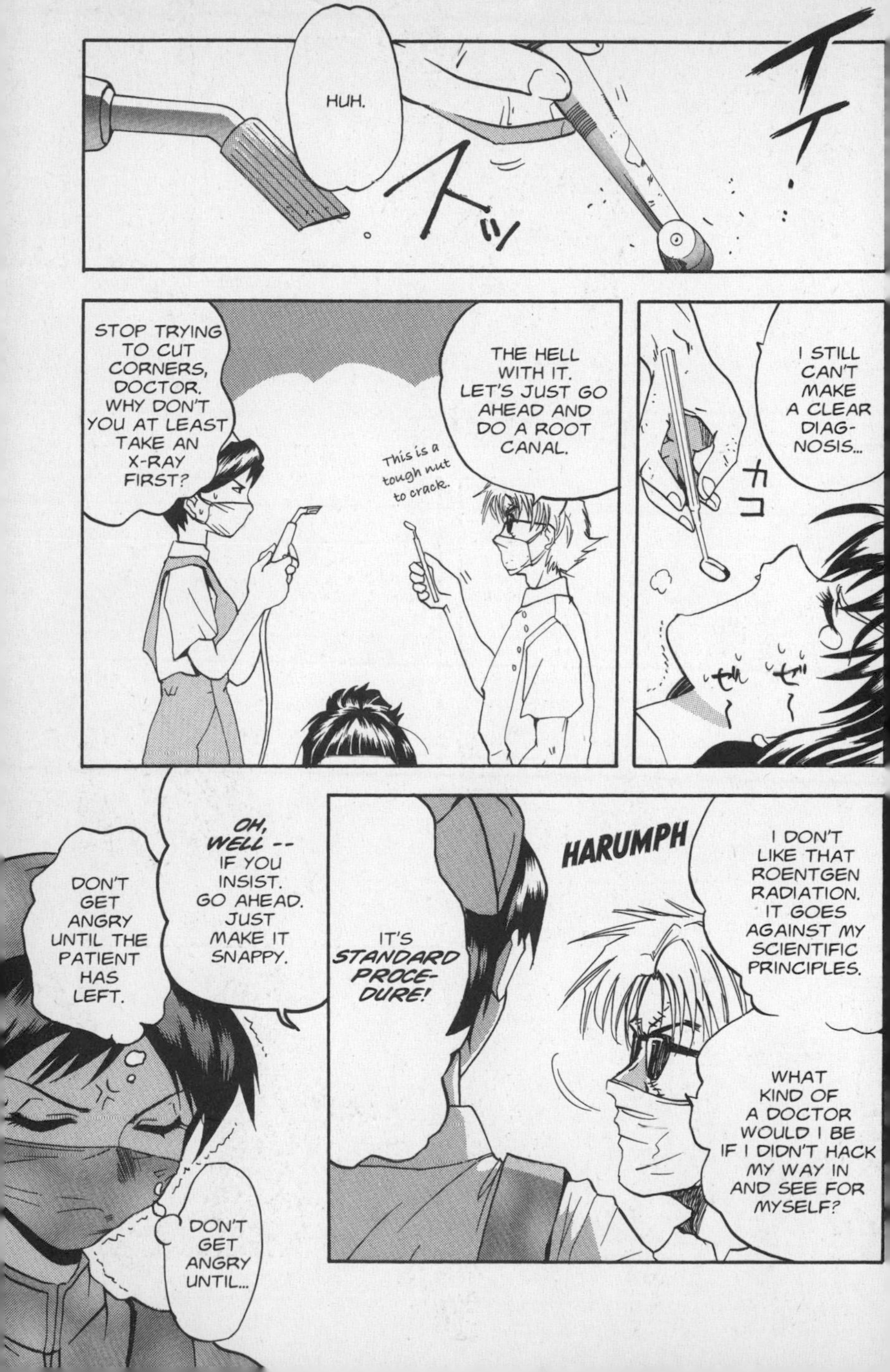
HUH.
I STILL CAN'T MAKE A CLEAR DIAG-NOSIS...
THE HELL WITH IT. LET'S JUST GO AHEAD AND DO A ROOT CANAL.
This is a tough nut to crack.
STOP TRYING TO CUT CORNERS, DOCTOR. WHY DON'T YOU AT LEAST TAKE AN X-RAY FIRST?
I DON'T LIKE THAT ROENTGEN RADIATION. IT GOES AGAINST MY SCIENTIFIC PRINCIPLES.
HARUMPH
WHAT KIND OF A DOCTOR WOULD I BE IF I DIDN'T HACK MY WAY IN AND SEE FOR MYSELF?
IT'S STANDARD PROCE-DURE!
OH, WELL -- IF YOU INSIST. GO AHEAD. JUST MAKE IT SNAPPY.
DON'T GET ANGRY UNTIL THE PATIENT HAS LEFT.
DON'T GET ANGRY UNTIL...

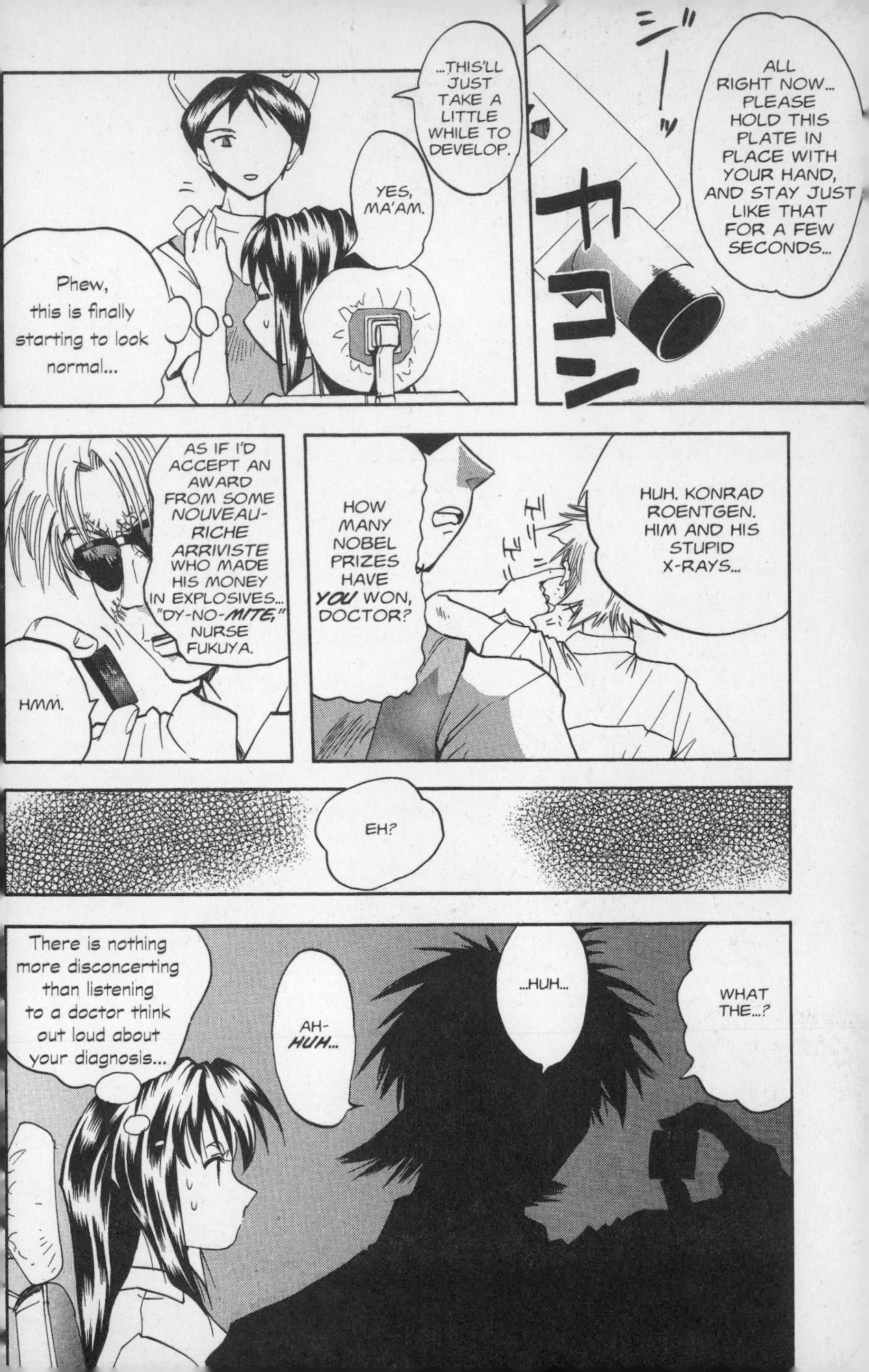
ALL RIGHT NOW... PLEASE HOLD THIS PLATE IN PLACE WITH YOUR HAND, AND STAY JUST LIKE THAT FOR A FEW SECONDS...
...THIS'LL JUST TAKE A LITTLE WHILE TO DEVELOP.
YES, MA'AM.
Phew, this is finally starting to look normal...
HUH. KONRAD ROENTGEN. HIM AND HIS STUPID X-RAYS...
HOW MANY NOBEL PRIZES HAVE YOU WON, DOCTOR?
AS IF I'D ACCEPT AN AWARD FROM SOME NOUVEAU-RICHE ARRIVISTE WHO MADE HIS MONEY IN EXPLOSIVES... "DY-NO-MITE," NURSE FUKUYA.
HMM.
EH?
WHAT THE...?
...HUH...
AH-HUH...
There is nothing more disconcerting than listening to a doctor think out loud about your diagnosis...

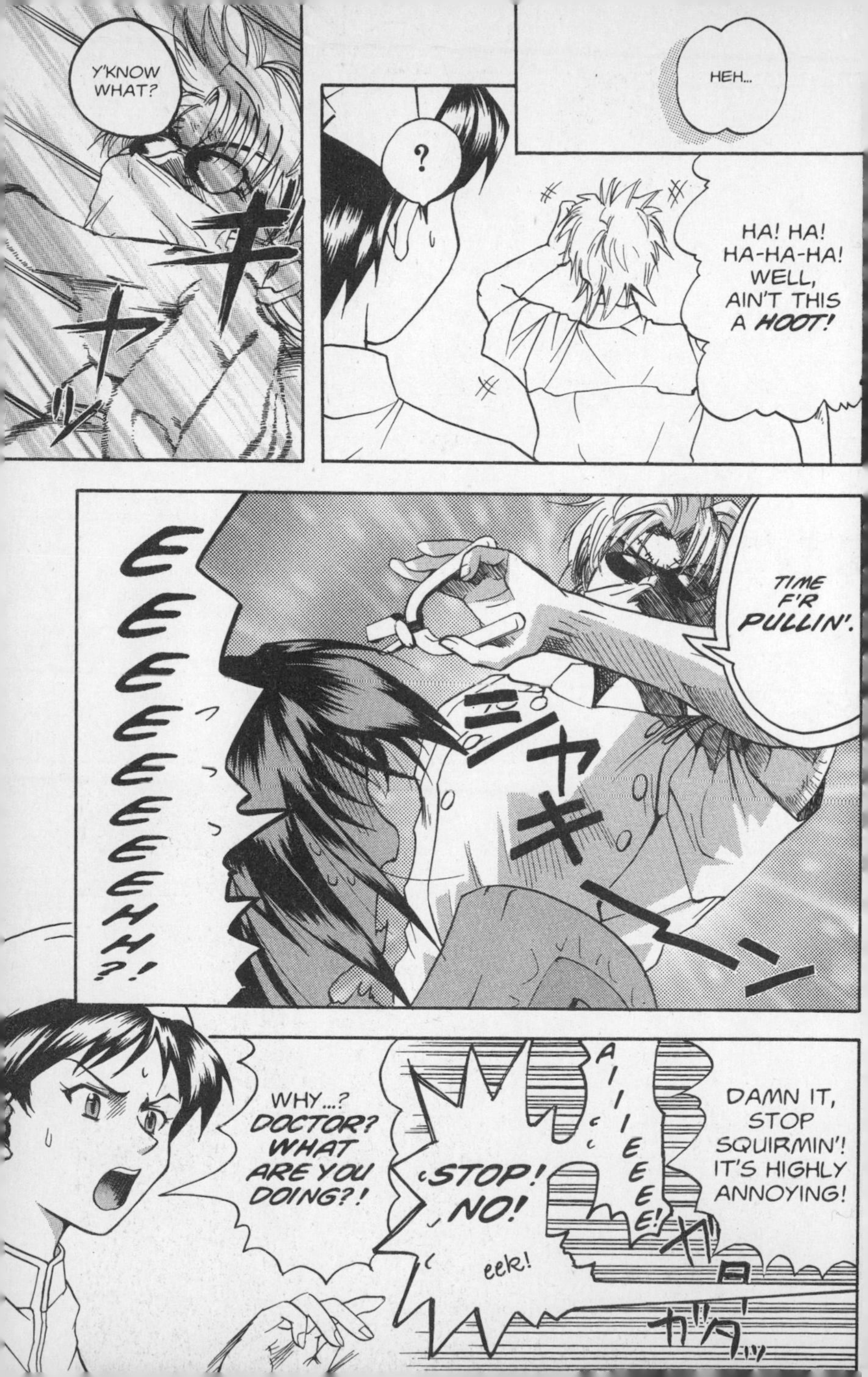
HEH...
HA! HA! HA-HA-HA! WELL, AIN'T THIS A HOOT!
?
Y'KNOW WHAT?
TIME F'R PULLIN'.
EEEEEEEEEEEHH?!
DAMN IT, STOP SQUIRMIN'! IT'S HIGHLY ANNOYING!
AIIIEEEEE!
STOP! NO!
eek!
WHY...? DOCTOR? WHAT ARE YOU DOING?!

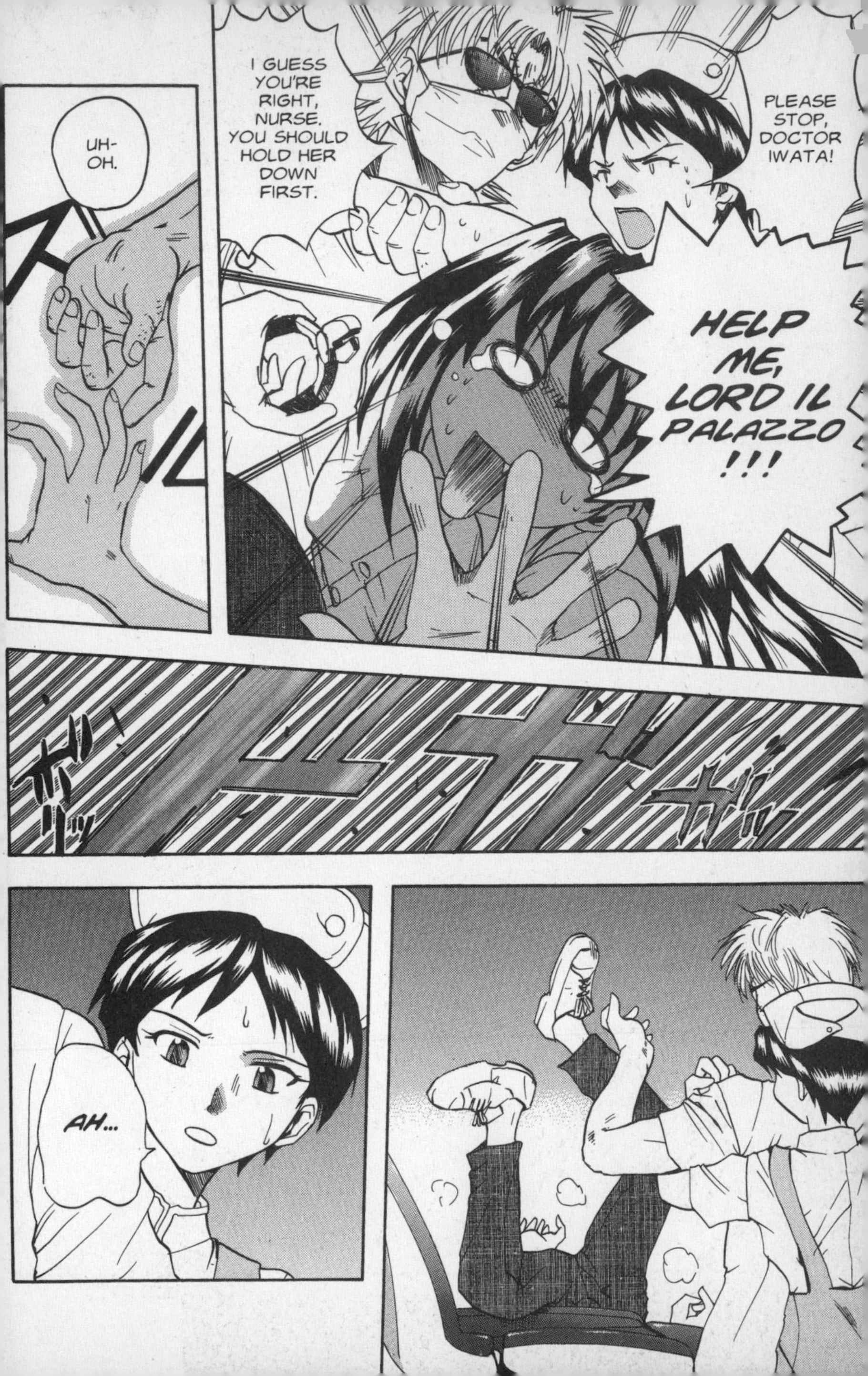
PLEASE STOP, DOCTOR IWATA!
I GUESS YOU'RE RIGHT, NURSE. YOU SHOULD HOLD HER DOWN FIRST.
HELP ME, LORD IL PALAZZO!!!
UH-OH.
AH...

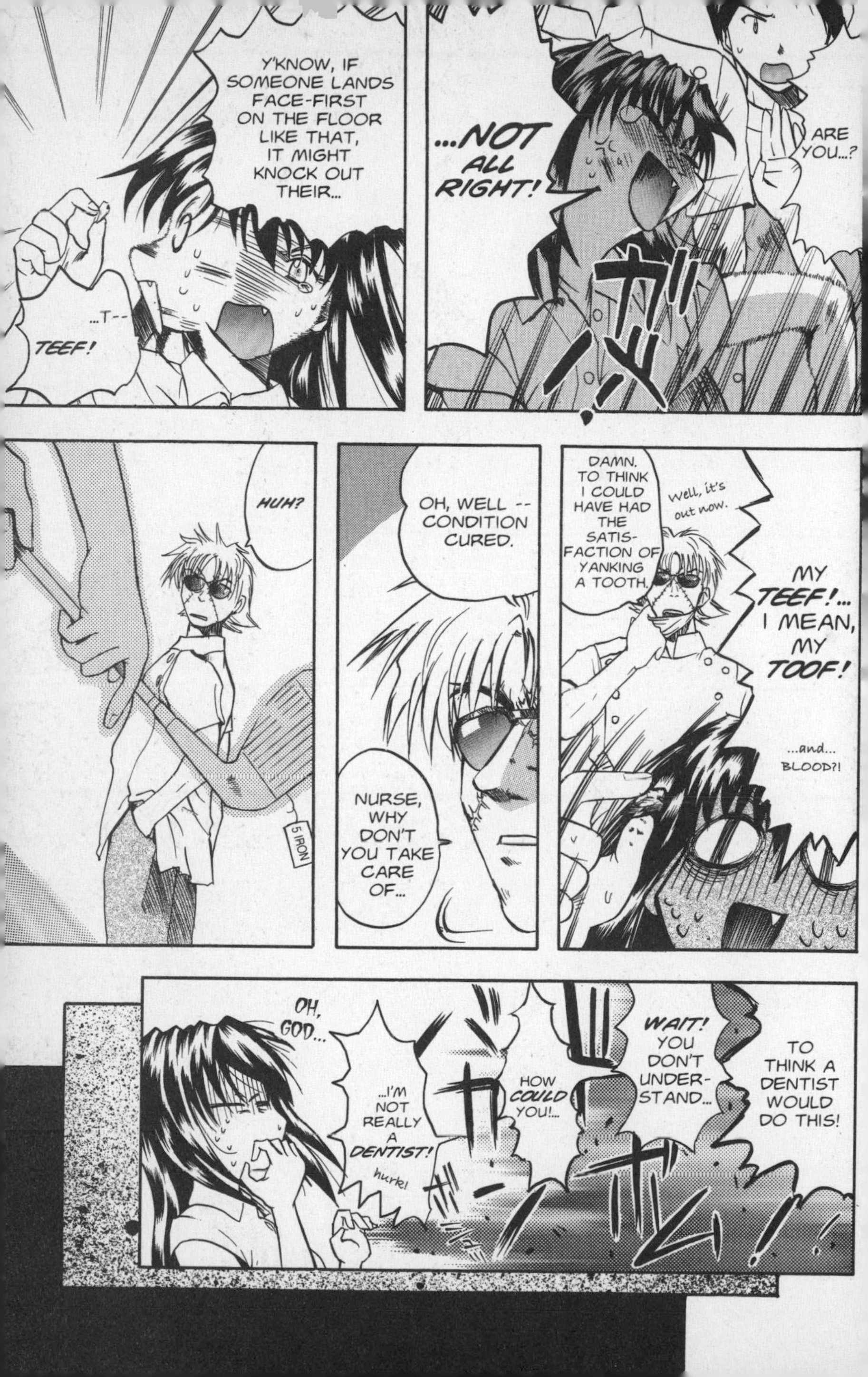
ARE YOU...?
...NOT ALL RIGHT!
Y'KNOW, IF SOMEONE LANDS FACE-FIRST ON THE FLOOR LIKE THAT, IT MIGHT KNOCK OUT THEIR...
...T-- TEEF!
Well, it's out now.
DAMN. TO THINK I COULD HAVE HAD THE SATIS-FACTION OF YANKING A TOOTH.
MY TEEF!... I MEAN, MY TOOF!
...and... BLOOD?!
OH, WELL -- CONDITION CURED.
NURSE, WHY DON'T YOU TAKE CARE OF...
HUH?
5 IRON
TO THINK A DENTIST WOULD DO THIS!
WAIT! YOU DON'T UNDER-STAND...
HOW COULD YOU!...
...I'M NOT REALLY A DENTIST!
hurk!
OH, GOD...

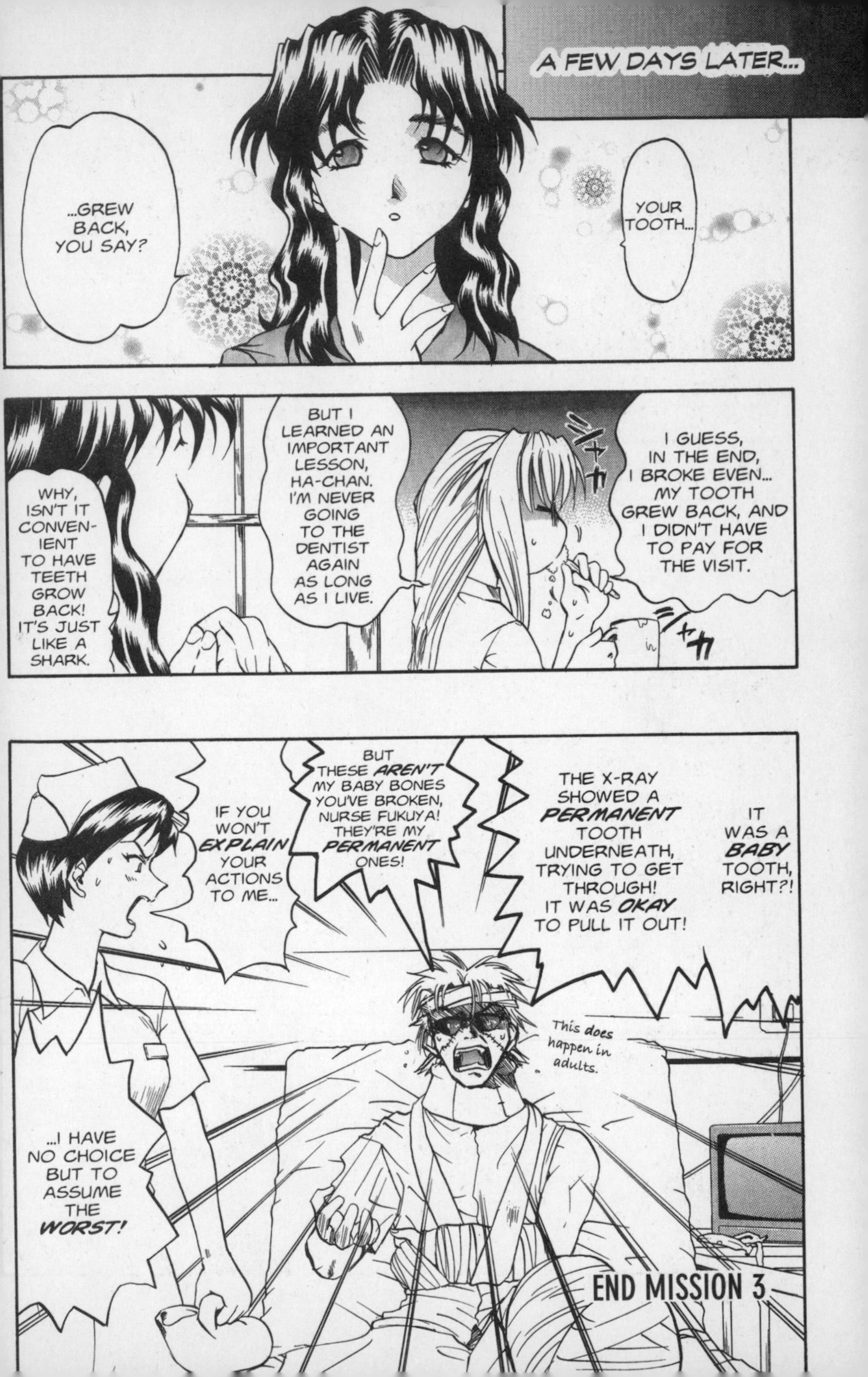
A FEW DAYS LATER...
YOUR TOOTH...
...GREW BACK, YOU SAY?
I GUESS, IN THE END, I BROKE EVEN... MY TOOTH GREW BACK, AND I DIDN'T HAVE TO PAY FOR THE VISIT.
BUT I LEARNED AN IMPORTANT LESSON, HA-CHAN. I'M NEVER GOING TO THE DENTIST AGAIN AS LONG AS I LIVE.
WHY, ISN'T IT CONVENIENT TO HAVE TEETH GROW BACK! IT'S JUST LIKE A SHARK.
IT WAS A *BABY* TOOTH, RIGHT?!
THE X-RAY SHOWED A *PERMANENT* TOOTH UNDERNEATH, TRYING TO GET THROUGH! IT WAS *OKAY* TO PULL IT OUT!
BUT THESE *AREN'T* MY BABY BONES YOU'VE BROKEN, NURSE FUKUYA! THEY'RE MY *PERMANENT* ONES!
IF YOU WON'T *EXPLAIN* YOUR ACTIONS TO ME...
This **does** happen in adults.
...I HAVE NO CHOICE BUT TO ASSUME THE *WORST!*
END MISSION 3

Scenes of the Personal Life of Rikdo Koshi Vol.④

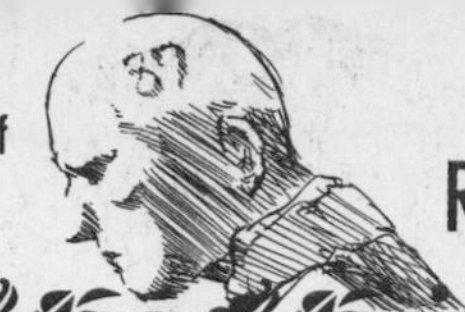
87

We, the Beloved

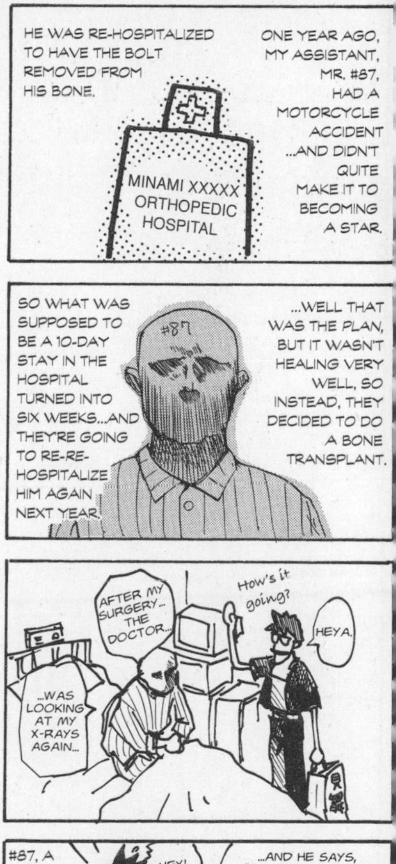
ONE YEAR AGO, MY ASSISTANT, MR. #87, HAD A MOTORCYCLE ACCIDENT ...AND DIDN'T QUITE MAKE IT TO BECOMING A STAR.
HE WAS RE-HOSPITALIZED TO HAVE THE BOLT REMOVED FROM HIS BONE.
MINAMI XXXXX ORTHOPEDIC HOSPITAL
...WELL THAT WAS THE *PLAN*, BUT IT WASN'T HEALING VERY WELL, SO INSTEAD, THEY DECIDED TO DO A BONE TRANSPLANT.
SO WHAT WAS SUPPOSED TO BE A 10-DAY STAY IN THE HOSPITAL TURNED INTO SIX WEEKS...AND THEY'RE GOING TO RE-RE-HOSPITALIZE HIM AGAIN NEXT YEAR.
#87
HEYA.
How's it going?
AFTER MY SURGERY... THE DOCTOR...
...WAS LOOKING AT MY X-RAYS AGAIN...
Thank you, Minami.
...AND HE SAYS, "OH, WOW, THERE'S A GAP IN THE BONE HERE! I DIDN'T NOTICE AT ALL!"
HEY! GOT-CHA GIFTS!
#87, A MAN BELOVED... BY QUACKS.
FWAP!
IT'S CHOCK-FULL OF CRAPPY PLAY-STATION GAMES!
C'mon, have a laugh!

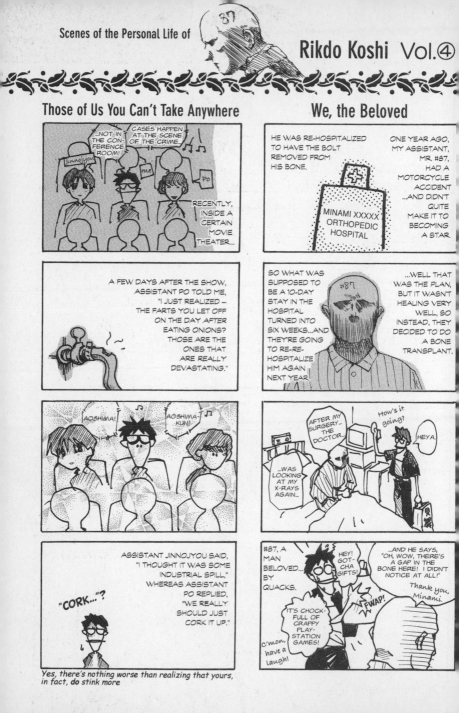

Those of Us You Can't Take Anywhere

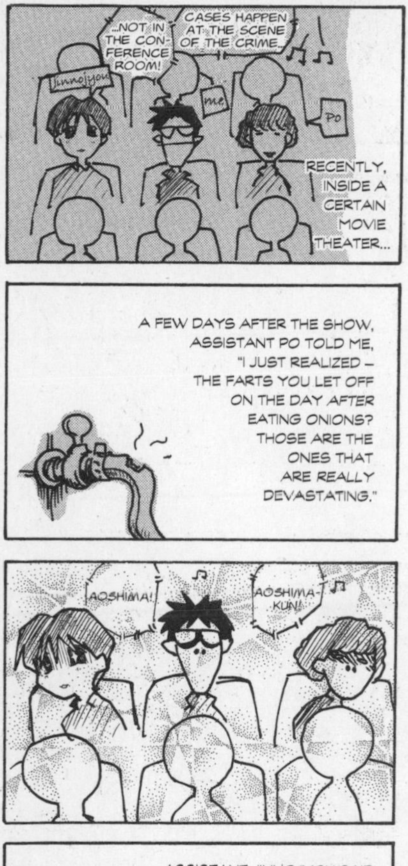
RECENTLY, INSIDE A CERTAIN MOVIE THEATER...
CASES HAPPEN AT THE SCENE OF THE CRIME.
...NOT IN THE CON-FERENCE ROOM!
Po
me
Jinnojyou
A FEW DAYS AFTER THE SHOW, ASSISTANT PO TOLD ME, "I JUST REALIZED – THE FARTS YOU LET OFF ON THE DAY *AFTER* EATING ONIONS? THOSE ARE THE ONES THAT ARE *REALLY* DEVASTATING."
AOSHIMA-KUN!
AOSHIMA!
ASSISTANT JINNOJYOU SAID, "I THOUGHT IT WAS SOME INDUSTRIAL SPILL," WHEREAS ASSISTANT PO REPLIED, "WE REALLY SHOULD JUST CORK IT UP."
"CORK..."?

Yes, there's nothing worse than realizing that yours, in fact, do stink more

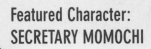

Featured Character:
SECRETARY MOMOCHI

Her full name:
her measurements:
her age:
her profile:
the type of men she's
attracted to:
and all that other stuff:

...ARE...

DETAILS ONLY I NEED TO KNOW.

heh!

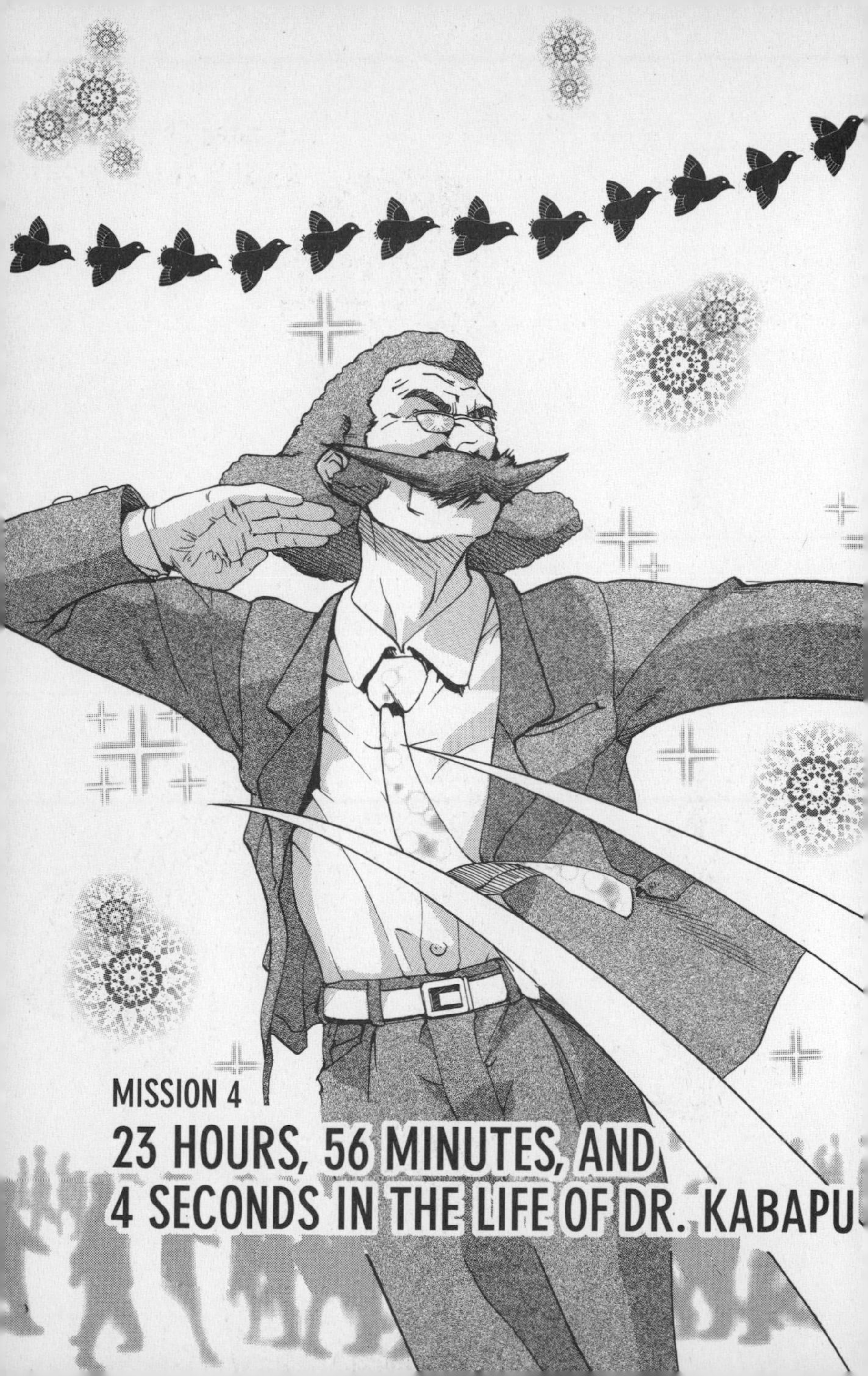
MISSION 4
23 HOURS, 56 MINUTES, AND
4 SECONDS IN THE LIFE OF DR. KABAPU

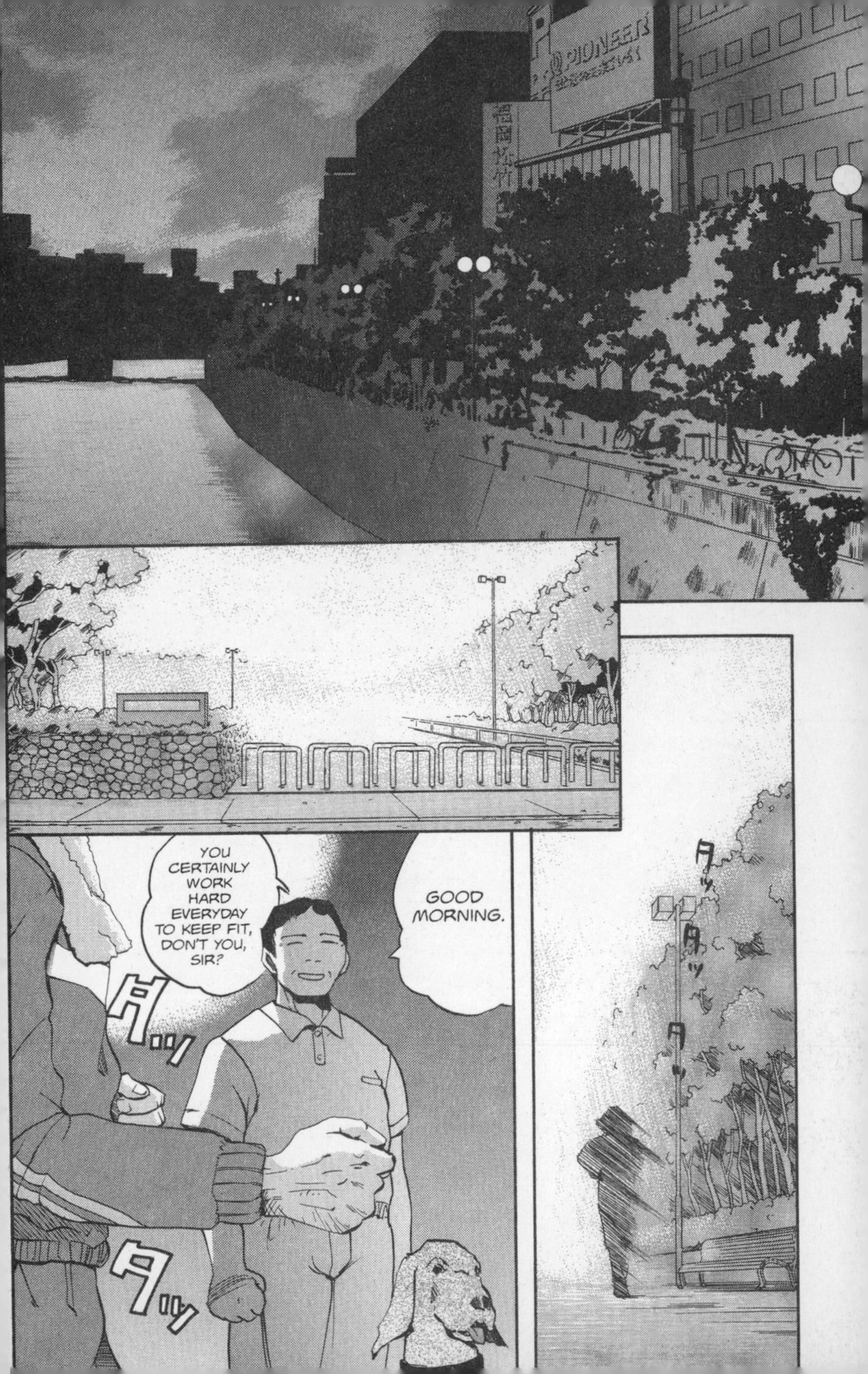
PIONEER
タッ
タッ
タッ
GOOD MORNING.
YOU CERTAINLY WORK HARD EVERYDAY TO KEEP FIT, DON'T YOU, SIR?
ダッ
タッ

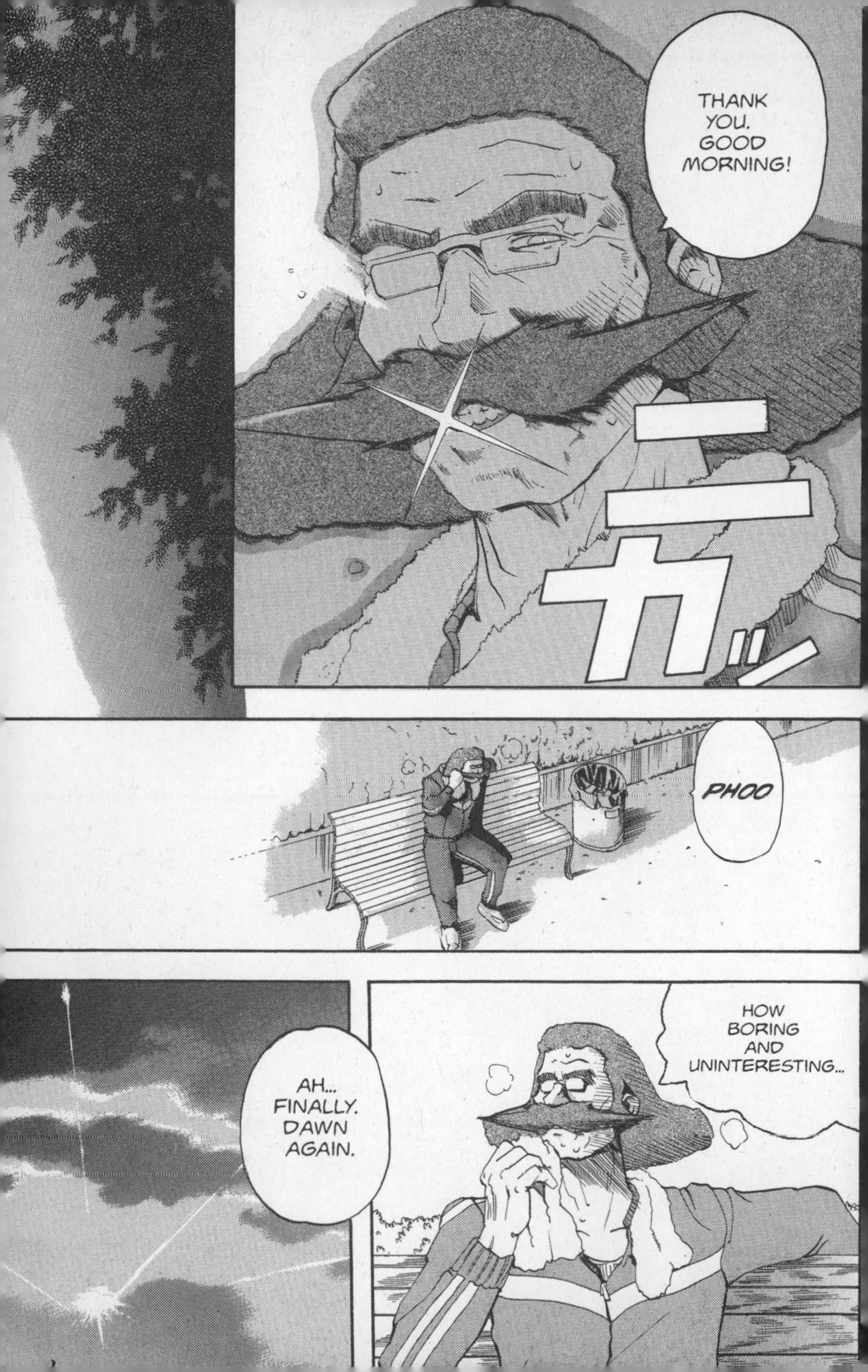
THANK YOU. GOOD MORNING!
PHOO
HOW BORING AND UNINTERESTING...
AH... FINALLY. DAWN AGAIN.

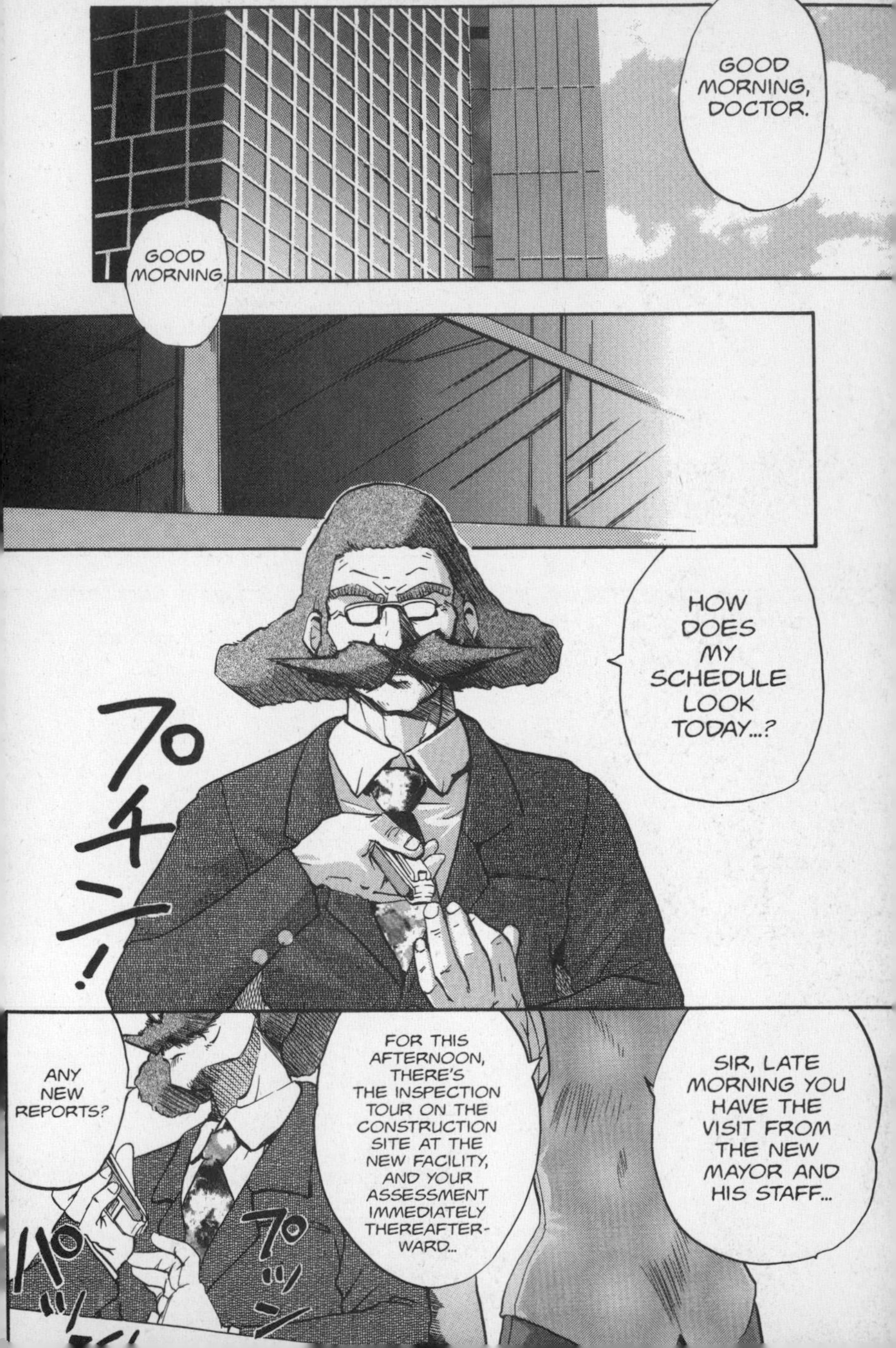
GOOD MORNING, DOCTOR.
GOOD MORNING.
HOW DOES MY SCHEDULE LOOK TODAY...?
プチン!
SIR, LATE MORNING YOU HAVE THE VISIT FROM THE NEW MAYOR AND HIS STAFF...
FOR THIS AFTERNOON, THERE'S THE INSPECTION TOUR ON THE CONSTRUCTION SITE AT THE NEW FACILITY, AND YOUR ASSESSMENT IMMEDIATELY THEREAFTER-WARD...
ANY NEW REPORTS?
プツン

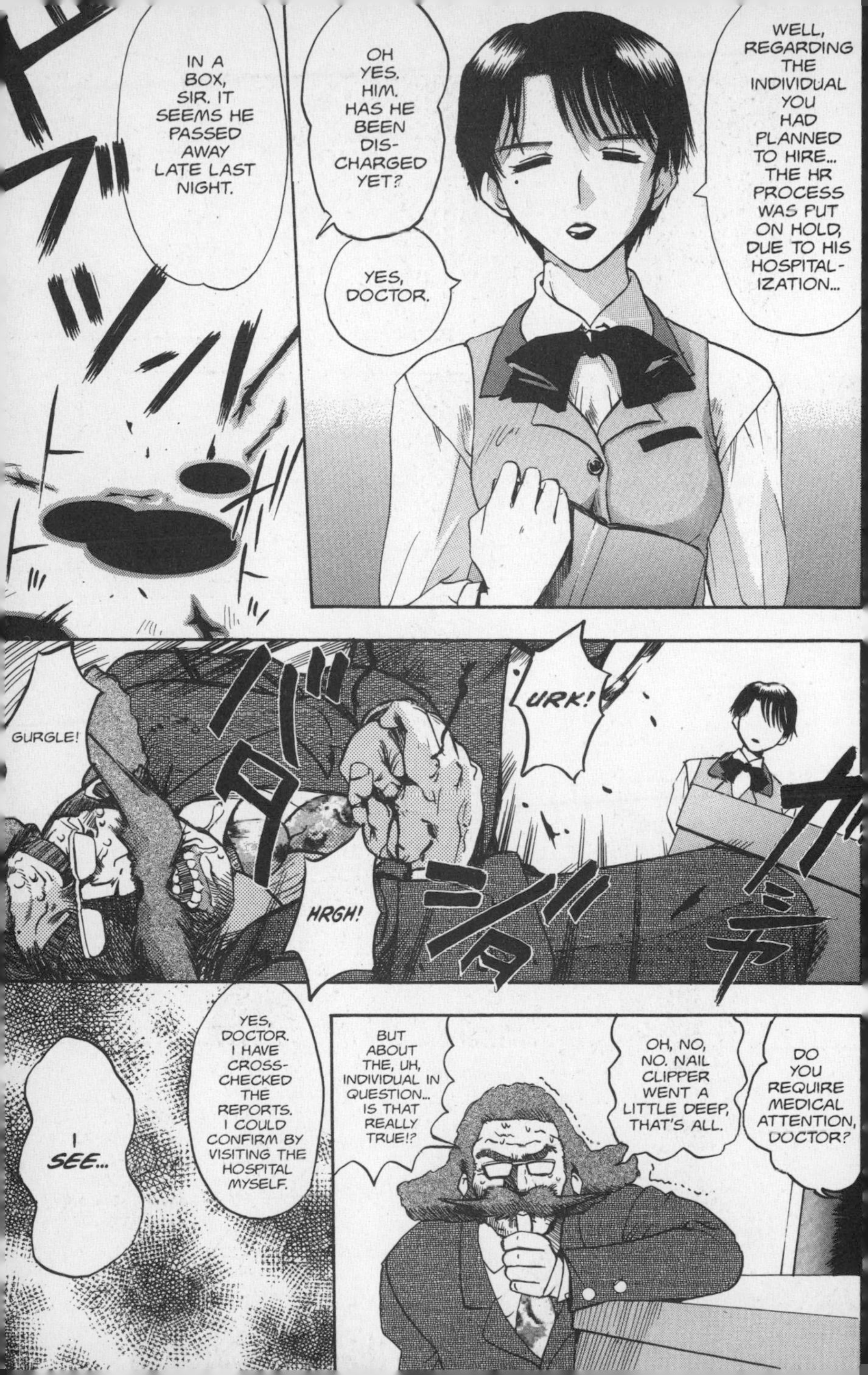
WELL, REGARDING THE INDIVIDUAL YOU HAD PLANNED TO HIRE... THE HR PROCESS WAS PUT ON HOLD, DUE TO HIS HOSPITALIZATION...
OH YES. HIM. HAS HE BEEN DISCHARGED YET?
YES, DOCTOR.
IN A BOX, SIR. IT SEEMS HE PASSED AWAY LATE LAST NIGHT.
URK!
GURGLE!
HRGH!
DO YOU REQUIRE MEDICAL ATTENTION, DOCTOR?
OH, NO, NO. NAIL CLIPPER WENT A LITTLE DEEP, THAT'S ALL.
BUT ABOUT THE, UH, INDIVIDUAL IN QUESTION... IS THAT REALLY TRUE!?
YES, DOCTOR. I HAVE CROSS-CHECKED THE REPORTS. I COULD CONFIRM BY VISITING THE HOSPITAL MYSELF.
I SEE...

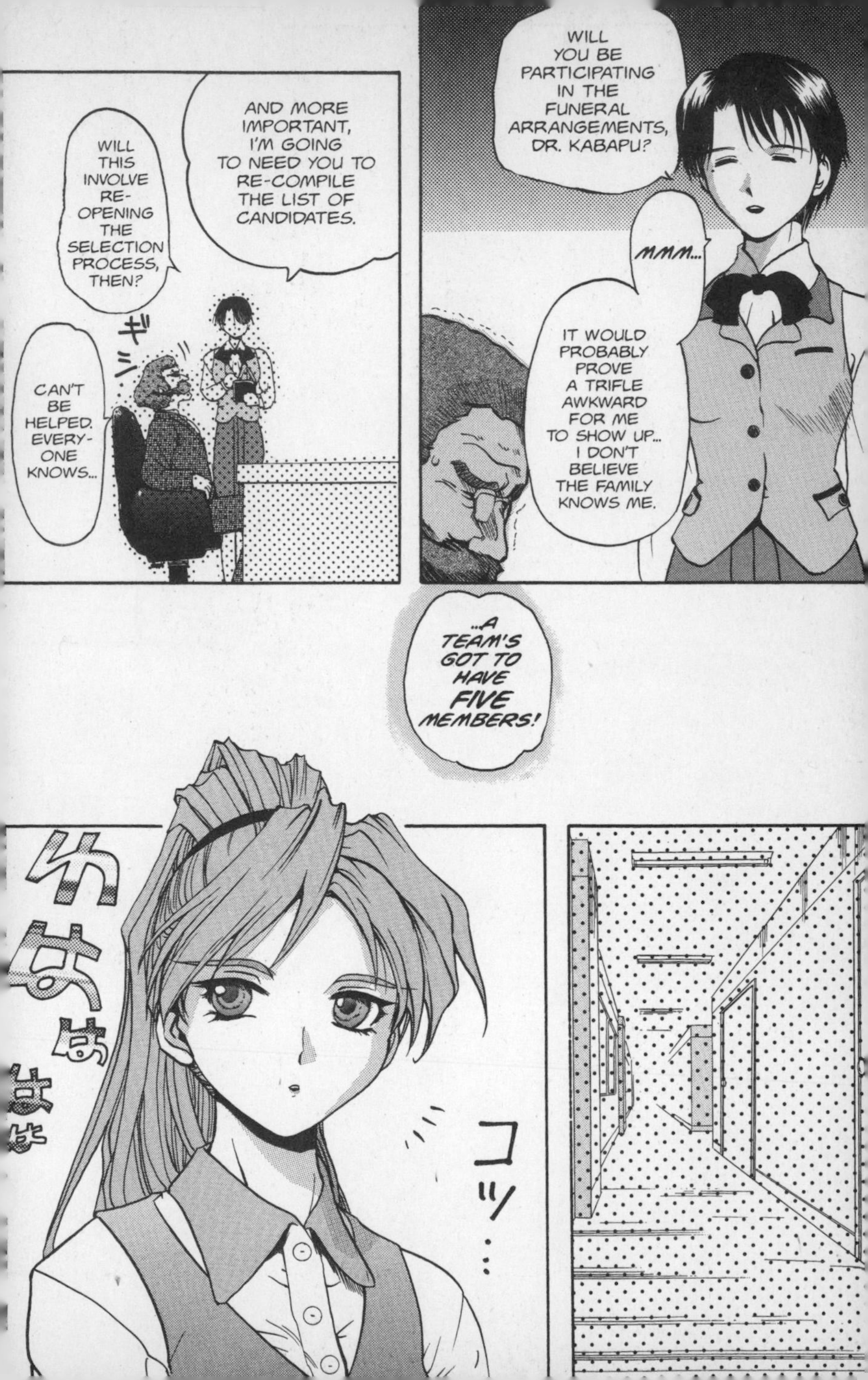
WILL YOU BE PARTICIPATING IN THE FUNERAL ARRANGEMENTS, DR. KABAPU?
MMM...
IT WOULD PROBABLY PROVE A TRIFLE AWKWARD FOR ME TO SHOW UP... I DON'T BELIEVE THE FAMILY KNOWS ME.
AND MORE IMPORTANT, I'M GOING TO NEED YOU TO RE-COMPILE THE LIST OF CANDIDATES.
WILL THIS INVOLVE RE-OPENING THE SELECTION PROCESS, THEN?
ギシ
CAN'T BE HELPED. EVERY-ONE KNOWS...
...A TEAM'S GOT TO HAVE FIVE MEMBERS!
コツ…

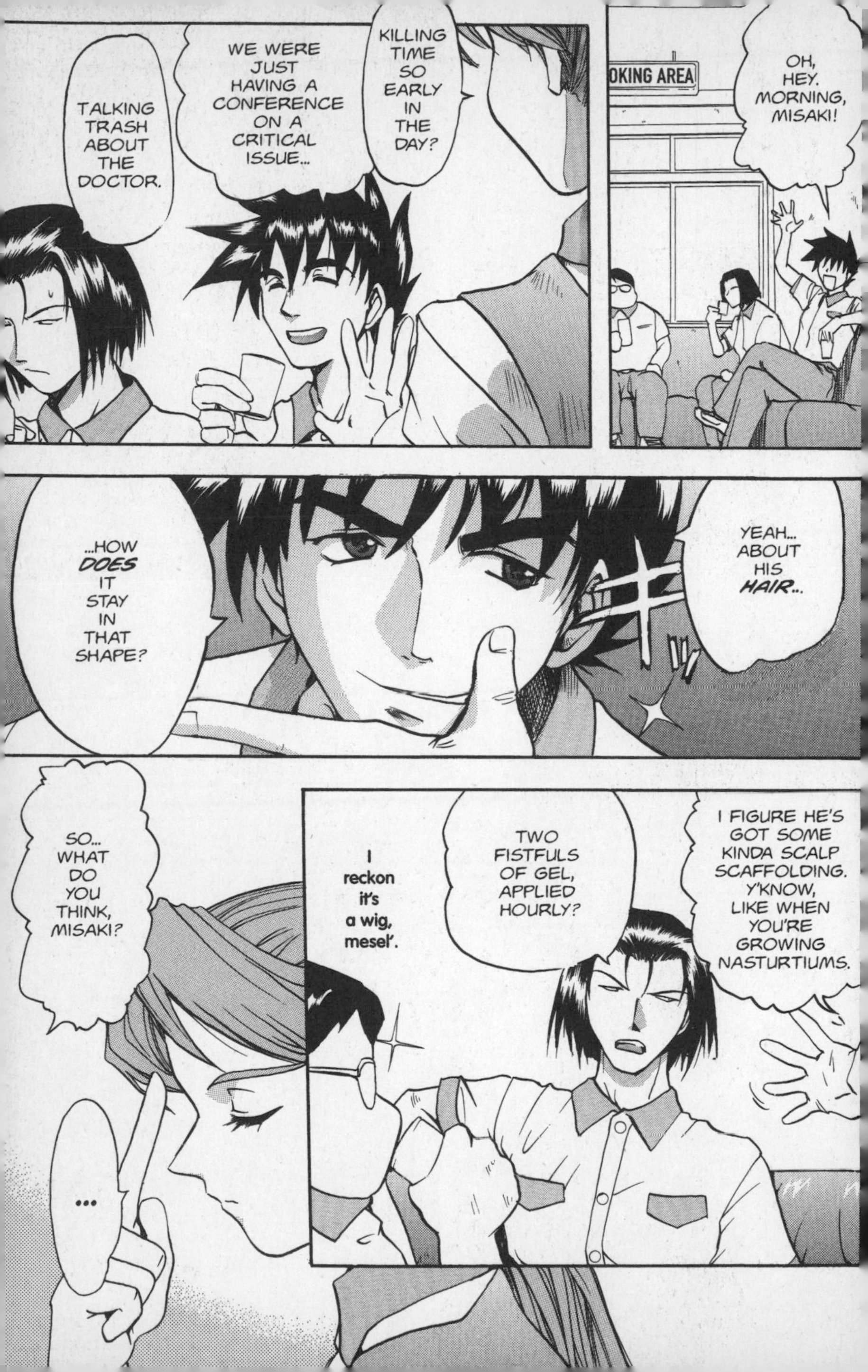
OH, HEY. MORNING, MISAKI!
OKING AREA
KILLING TIME SO EARLY IN THE DAY?
WE WERE JUST HAVING A CONFERENCE ON A CRITICAL ISSUE...
TALKING TRASH ABOUT THE DOCTOR.
YEAH... ABOUT HIS *HAIR*...
...HOW *DOES* IT STAY IN THAT SHAPE?
I FIGURE HE'S GOT SOME KINDA SCALP SCAFFOLDING. Y'KNOW, LIKE WHEN YOU'RE GROWING NASTURTIUMS.
TWO FISTFULS OF GEL, APPLIED HOURLY?
I reckon it's a wig, mesel'.
SO... WHAT DO YOU THINK, MISAKI?
...

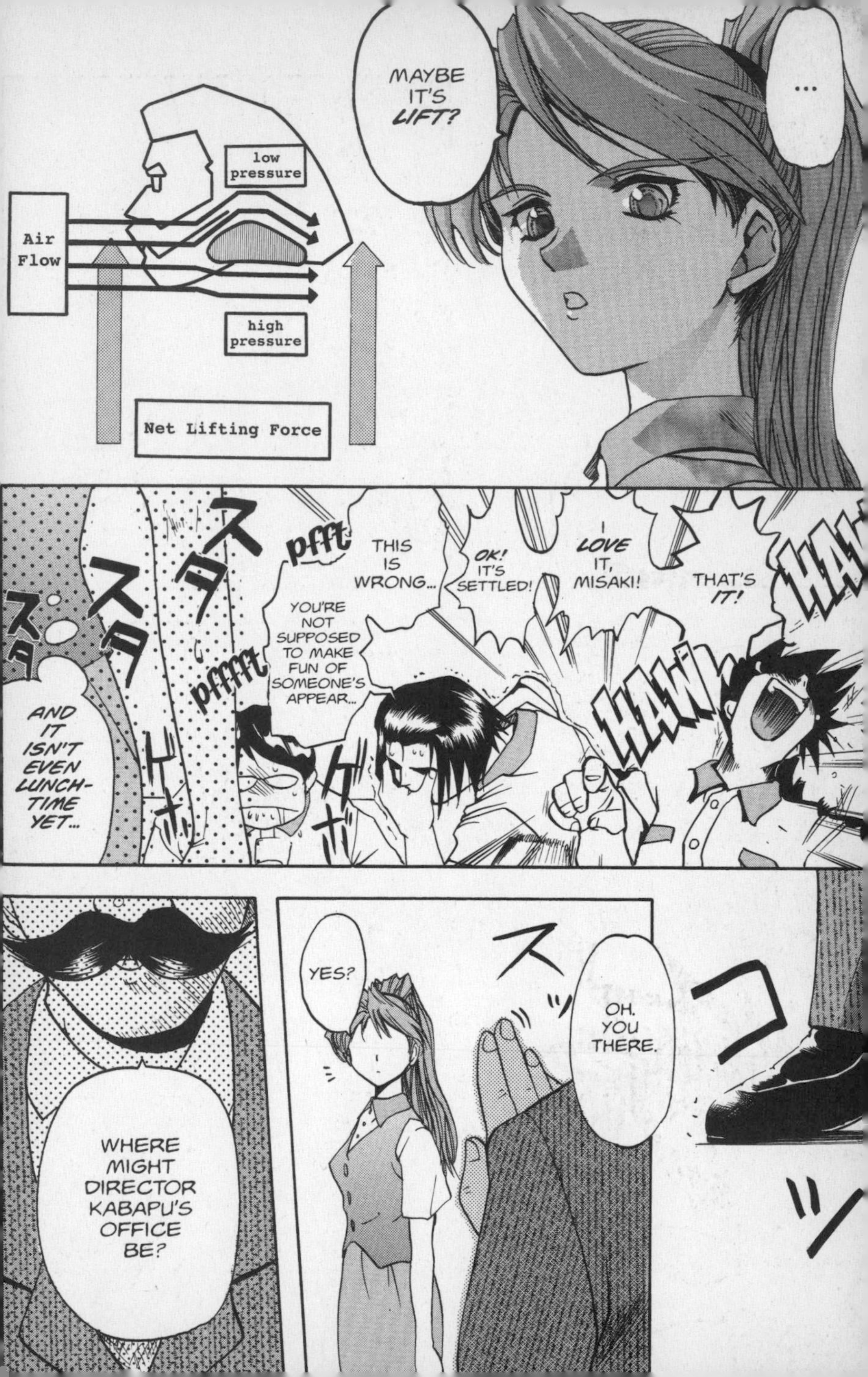
...
MAYBE IT'S *LIFT?*
low pressure
Air Flow
high pressure
Net Lifting Force
HA HA
THAT'S *IT!*
I *LOVE* IT, MISAKI!
OK! IT'S SETTLED!
THIS IS WRONG...
YOU'RE NOT SUPPOSED TO MAKE FUN OF SOMEONE'S APPEAR...
pfft
pfffft
スタ
スタ
スタ
AND IT ISN'T EVEN LUNCH-TIME YET...
ツ
コ
OH. YOU THERE.
ス
ツ
YES?
WHERE MIGHT DIRECTOR KABAPU'S OFFICE BE?

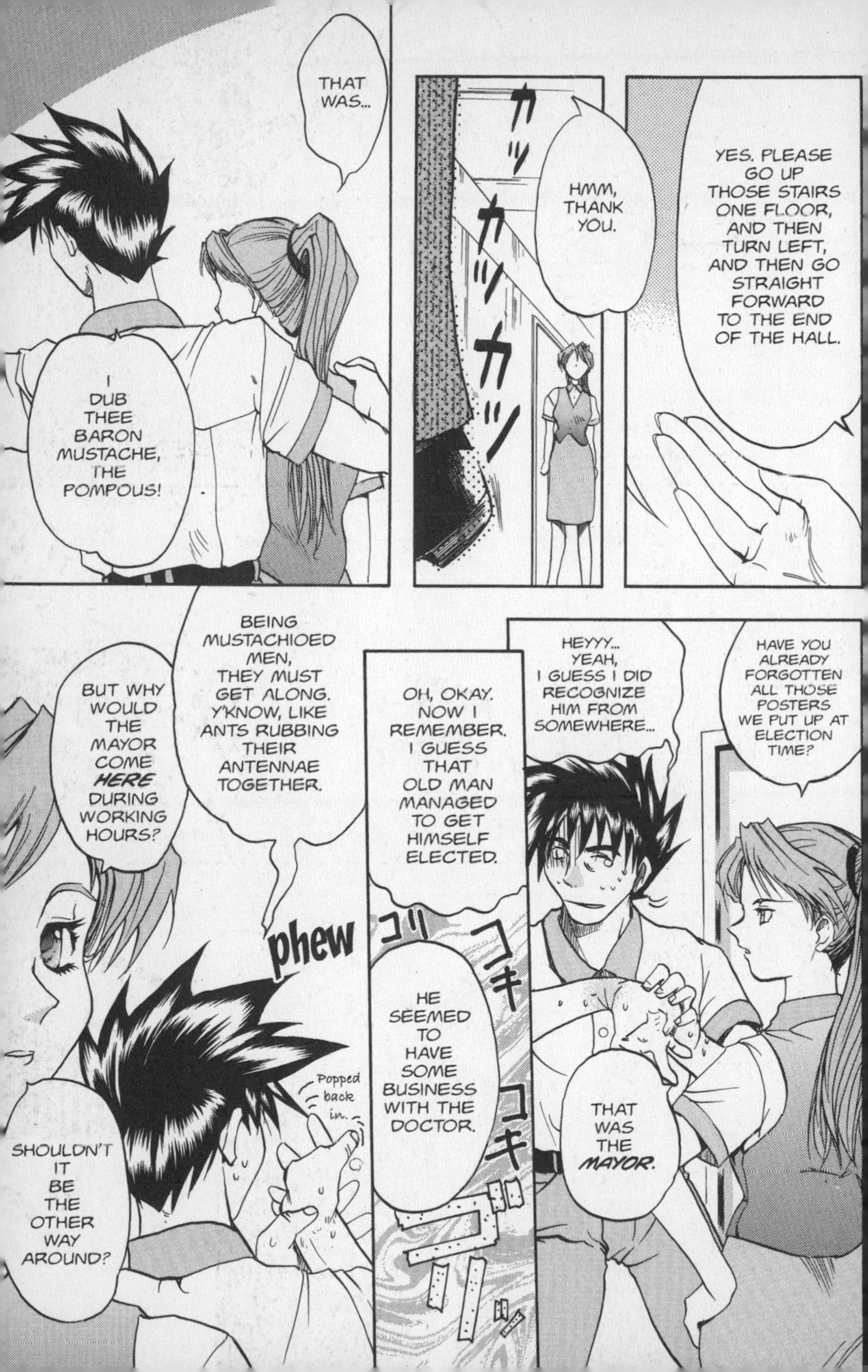

YES. PLEASE GO UP THOSE STAIRS ONE FLOOR, AND THEN TURN LEFT, AND THEN GO STRAIGHT FORWARD TO THE END OF THE HALL.
カッカッカツン
HMM, THANK YOU.
THAT WAS...
I DUB THEE BARON MUSTACHE, THE POMPOUS!
HAVE YOU ALREADY FORGOTTEN ALL THOSE POSTERS WE PUT UP AT ELECTION TIME?
HEYYY... YEAH, I GUESS I DID RECOGNIZE HIM FROM SOMEWHERE...
THAT WAS THE MAYOR.
OH, OKAY. NOW I REMEMBER. I GUESS THAT OLD MAN MANAGED TO GET HIMSELF ELECTED.
ゴリ
ゴキ
ゴキ
HE SEEMED TO HAVE SOME BUSINESS WITH THE DOCTOR.
BEING MUSTACHIOED MEN, THEY MUST GET ALONG. Y'KNOW, LIKE ANTS RUBBING THEIR ANTENNAE TOGETHER.
BUT WHY WOULD THE MAYOR COME HERE DURING WORKING HOURS?
phew
Popped back in.
SHOULDN'T IT BE THE OTHER WAY AROUND?

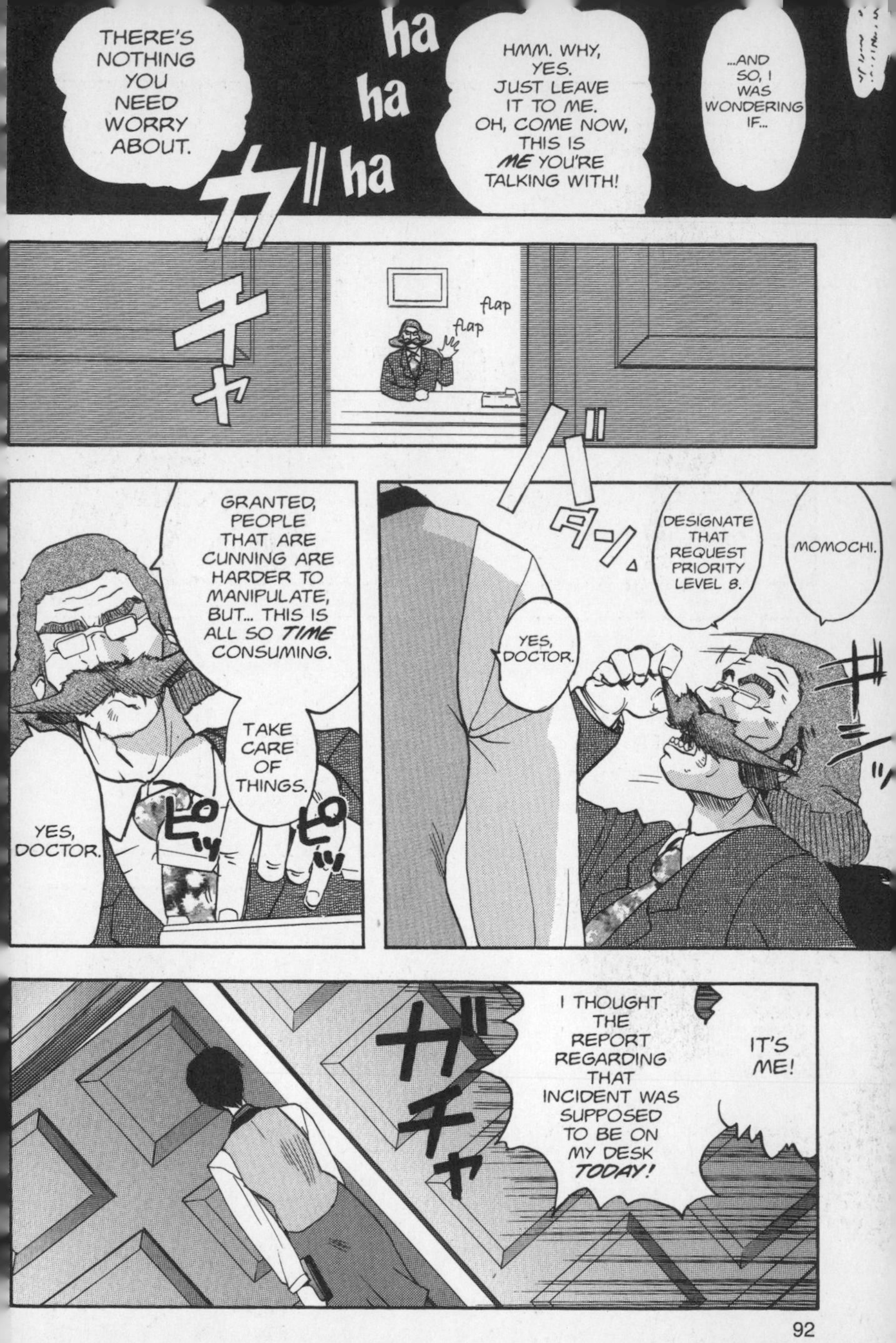
...AND SO, I WAS WONDERING IF...
HMM. WHY, YES. JUST LEAVE IT TO ME. OH, COME NOW, THIS IS *ME* YOU'RE TALKING WITH!
ha ha ha
THERE'S NOTHING YOU NEED WORRY ABOUT.
flap flap
MOMOCHI.
DESIGNATE THAT REQUEST PRIORITY LEVEL 8.
YES, DOCTOR.
GRANTED, PEOPLE THAT ARE CUNNING ARE HARDER TO MANIPULATE, BUT... THIS IS ALL SO *TIME* CONSUMING.
TAKE CARE OF THINGS.
YES, DOCTOR.
IT'S ME!
I THOUGHT THE REPORT REGARDING THAT INCIDENT WAS SUPPOSED TO BE ON MY DESK *TODAY!*

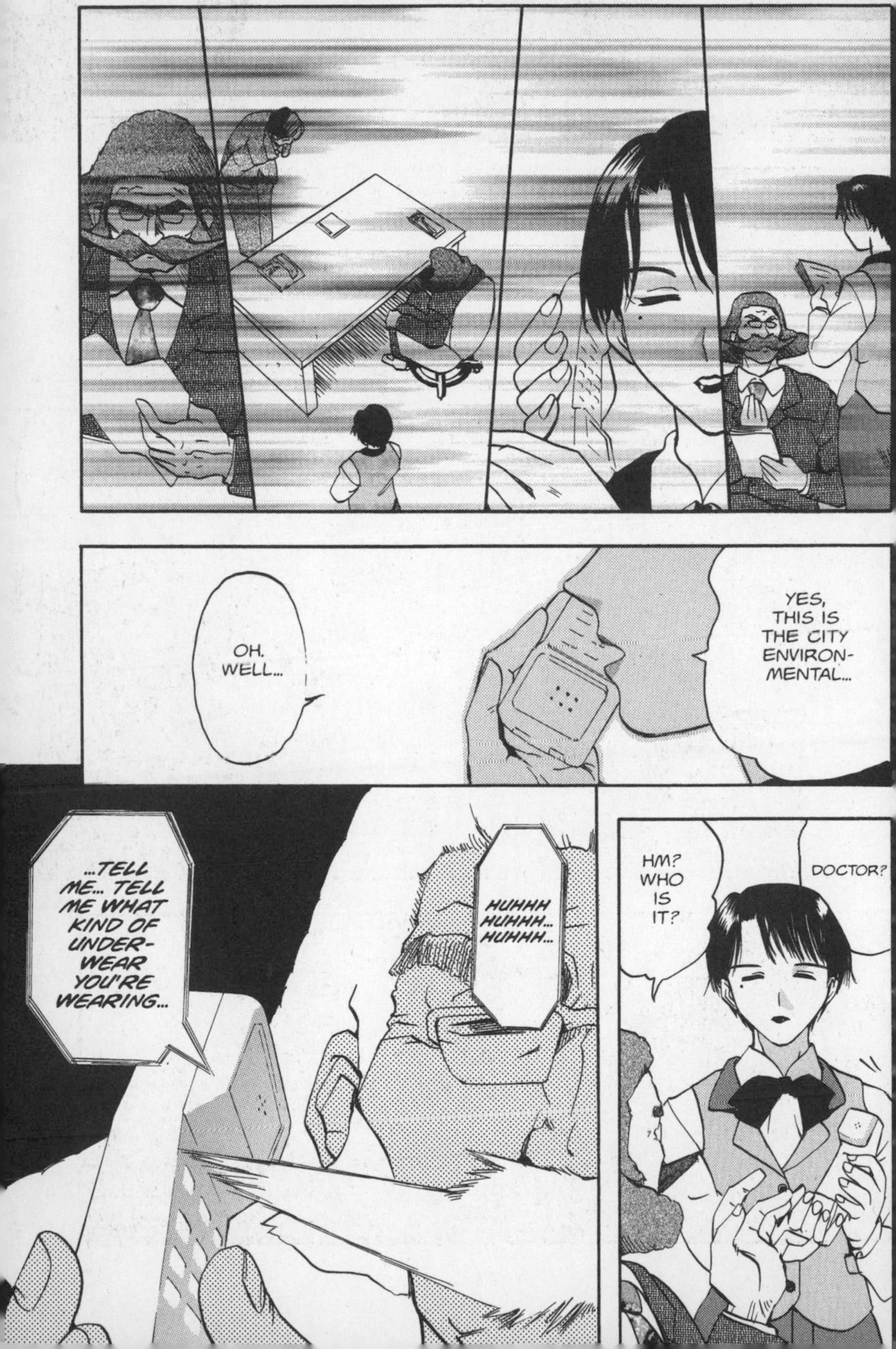
YES, THIS IS THE CITY ENVIRONMENTAL...
OH. WELL...
DOCTOR?
HM? WHO IS IT?
HUHHH HUHHH... HUHHH...
...TELL ME... TELL ME WHAT KIND OF UNDERWEAR YOU'RE WEARING...

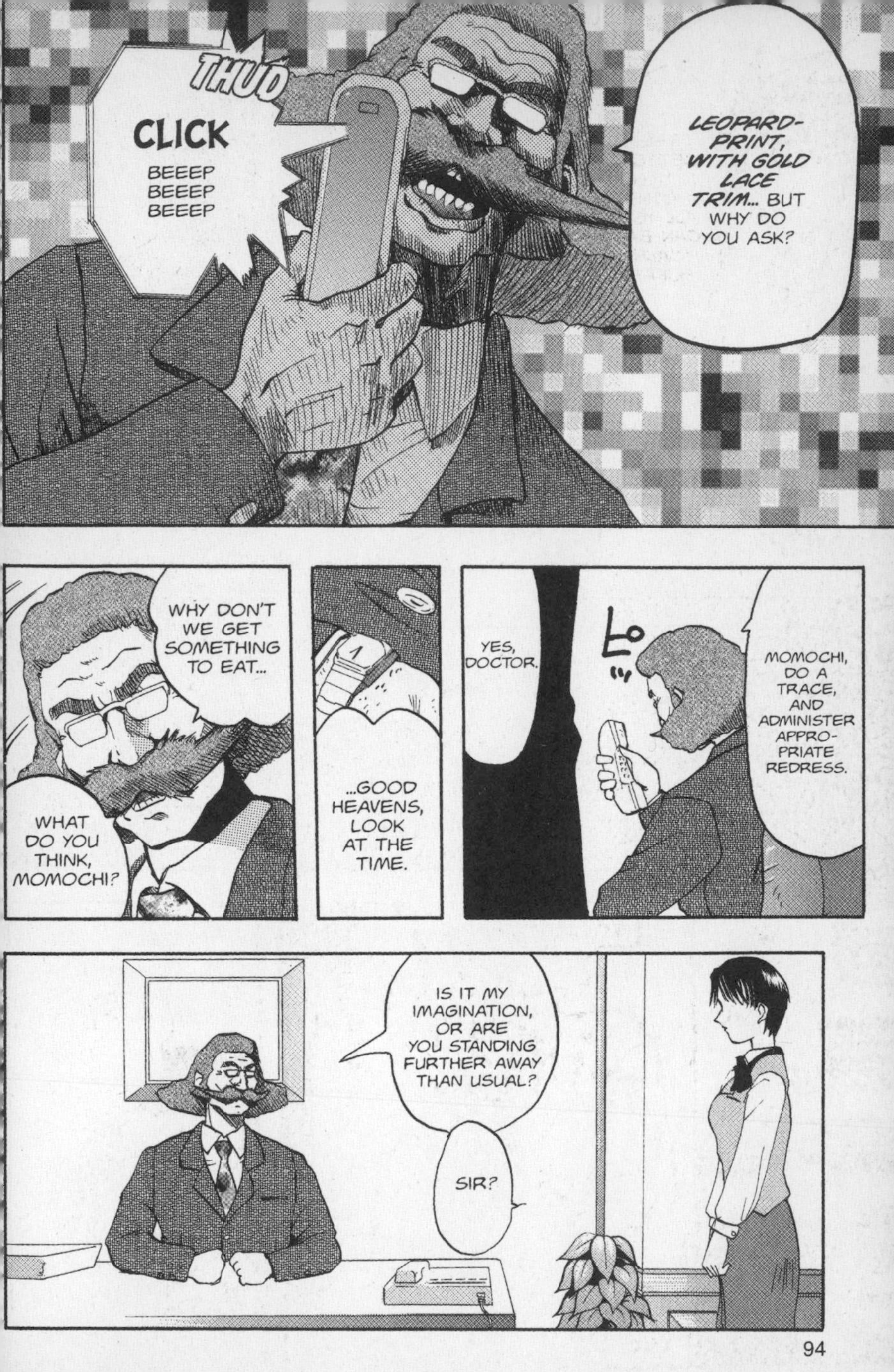
LEOPARD-PRINT, WITH GOLD LACE TRIM... BUT WHY DO YOU ASK?
THUD
CLICK
BEEEP BEEEP BEEEP
MOMOCHI, DO A TRACE, AND ADMINISTER APPROPRIATE REDRESS.
ピッ
YES, DOCTOR.
...GOOD HEAVENS, LOOK AT THE TIME.
WHY DON'T WE GET SOMETHING TO EAT...
WHAT DO YOU THINK, MOMOCHI?
IS IT MY IMAGINATION, OR ARE YOU STANDING FURTHER AWAY THAN USUAL?
SIR?

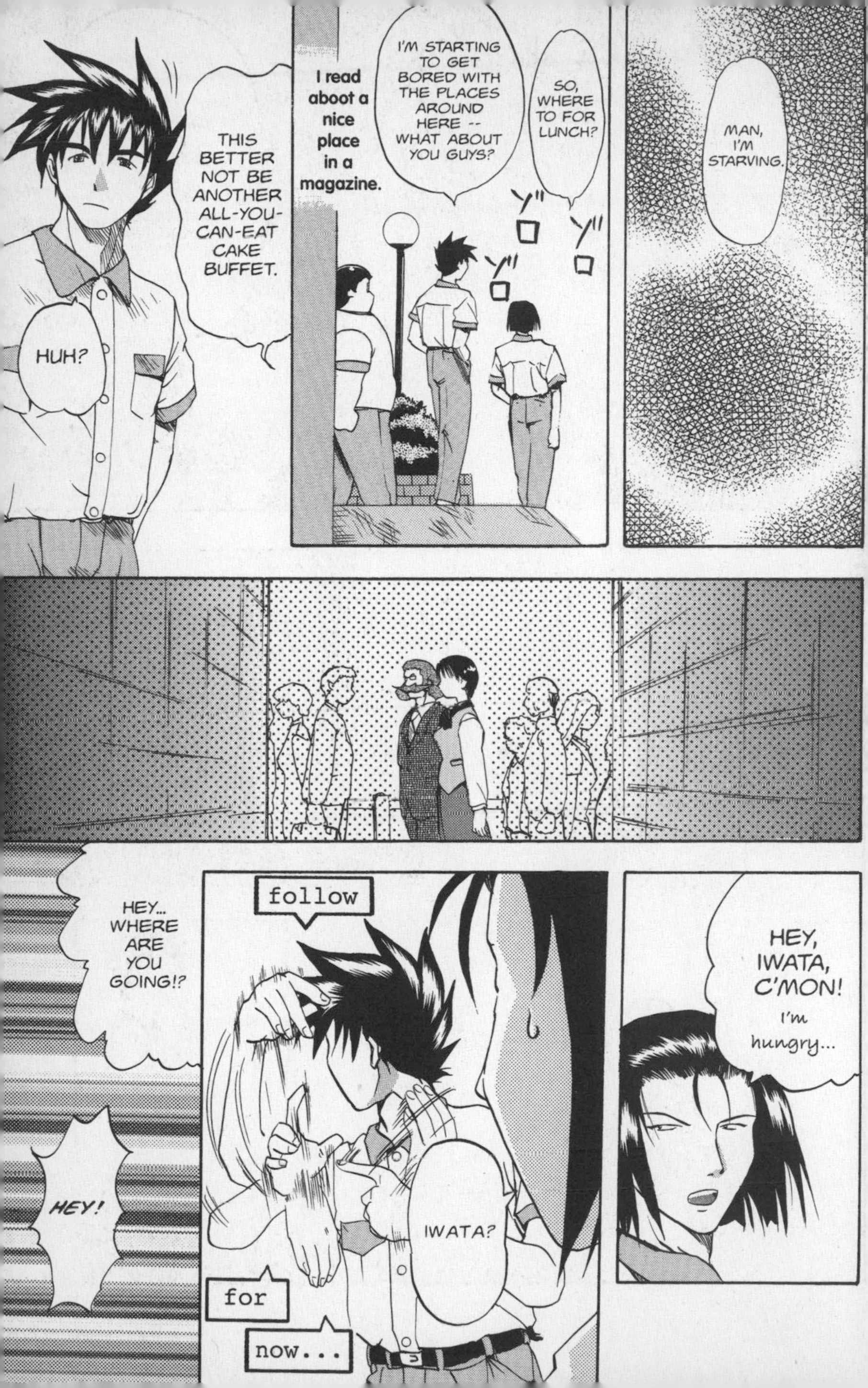
MAN, I'M STARVING.
SO, WHERE TO FOR LUNCH?
I'M STARTING TO GET BORED WITH THE PLACES AROUND HERE -- WHAT ABOUT YOU GUYS?
I read aboot a nice place in a magazine.
THIS BETTER NOT BE ANOTHER ALL-YOU-CAN-EAT CAKE BUFFET.
HUH?
HEY, IWATA, C'MON!
I'm hungry...
follow
IWATA?
for
now...
HEY... WHERE ARE YOU GOING!?
HEY!

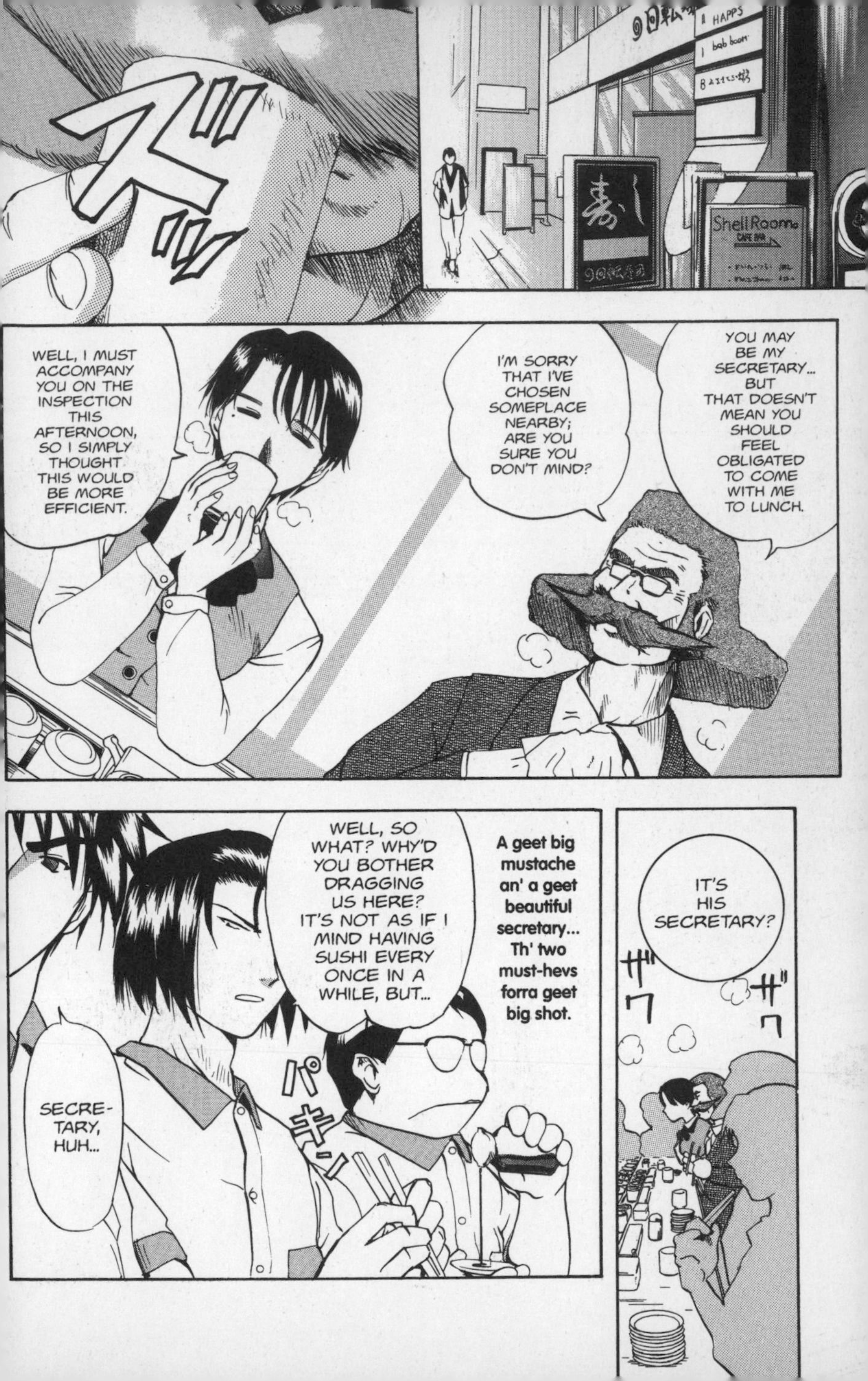
HAPPS
bab boom
すし
Shell Room
CAFE BAR
ズ
YOU MAY BE MY SECRETARY... BUT THAT DOESN'T MEAN YOU SHOULD FEEL OBLIGATED TO COME WITH ME TO LUNCH.
I'M SORRY THAT I'VE CHOSEN SOMEPLACE NEARBY; ARE YOU SURE YOU DON'T MIND?
WELL, I MUST ACCOMPANY YOU ON THE INSPECTION THIS AFTERNOON, SO I SIMPLY THOUGHT THIS WOULD BE MORE EFFICIENT.
IT'S HIS SECRETARY?
ザワ
ザワ
A geet big mustache an' a geet beautiful secretary... Th' two must-hevs forra geet big shot.
WELL, SO WHAT? WHY'D YOU BOTHER DRAGGING US HERE? IT'S NOT AS IF I MIND HAVING SUSHI EVERY ONCE IN A WHILE, BUT...
パキーン
SECRETARY, HUH...

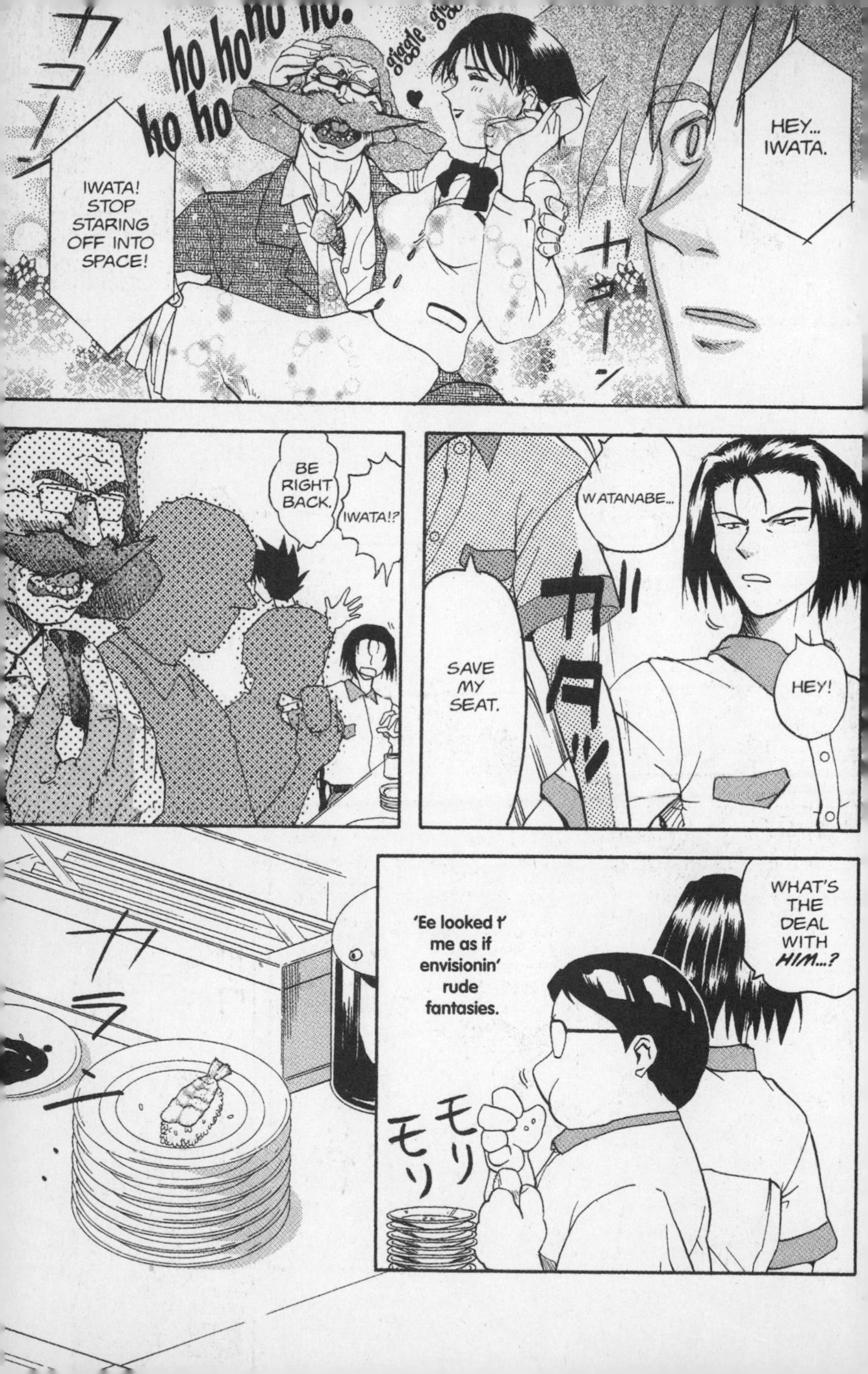
HEY... IWATA.
カターン
giggle giggle
ho ho ho ho ho ho.
IWATA! STOP STARING OFF INTO SPACE!
WATANABE...
HEY!
ガタッ
SAVE MY SEAT.
BE RIGHT BACK.
IWATA!?
WHAT'S THE DEAL WITH *HIM*...?
'Ee looked t' me as if envisionin' rude fantasies.
モリ モリ

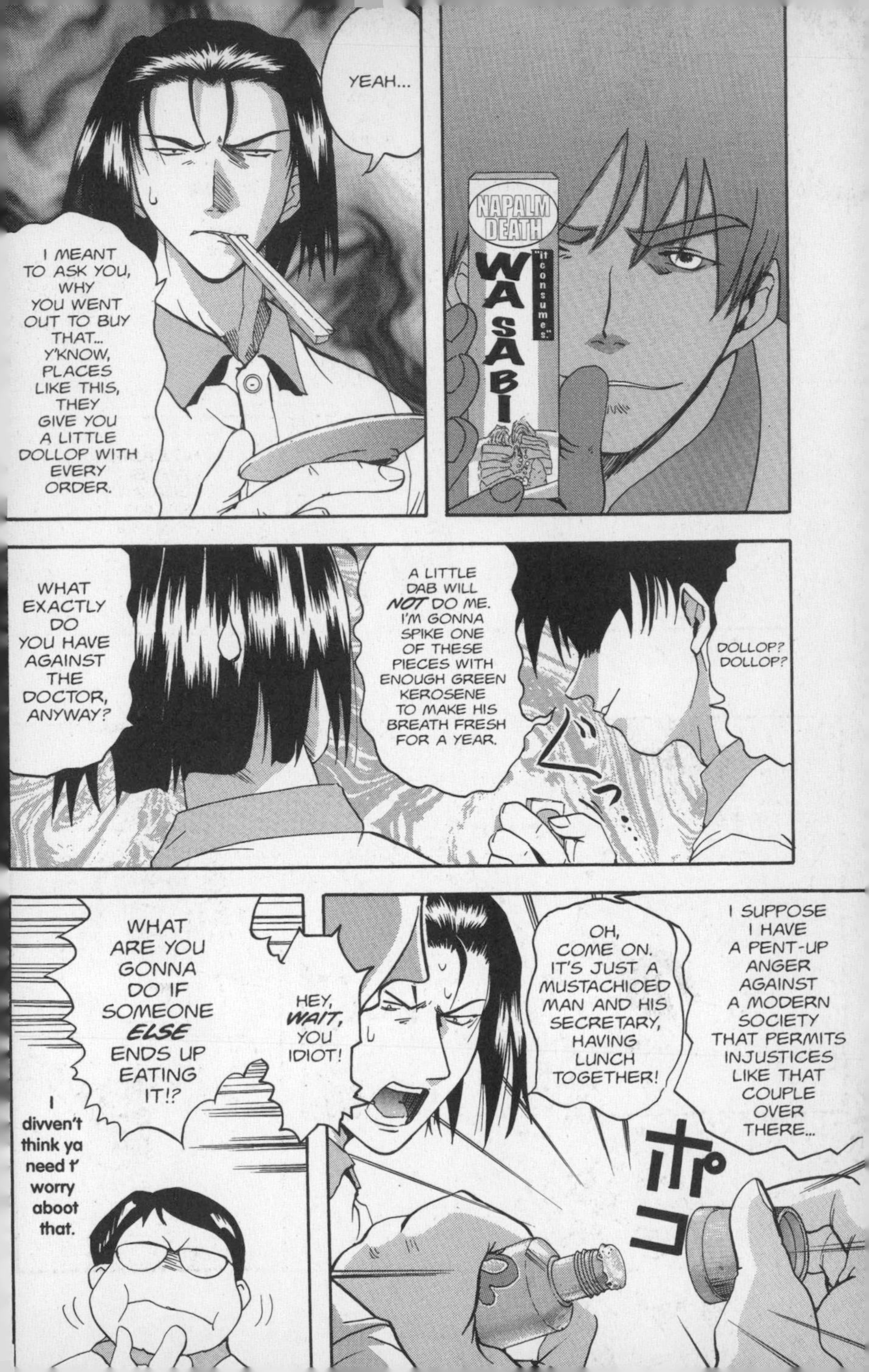
NAPALM DEATH
WASABI
"it consumes"
YEAH...
I MEANT TO ASK YOU, WHY YOU WENT OUT TO BUY THAT... Y'KNOW, PLACES LIKE THIS, THEY GIVE YOU A LITTLE DOLLOP WITH EVERY ORDER.
DOLLOP? DOLLOP?
A LITTLE DAB WILL NOT DO ME. I'M GONNA SPIKE ONE OF THESE PIECES WITH ENOUGH GREEN KEROSENE TO MAKE HIS BREATH FRESH FOR A YEAR.
WHAT EXACTLY DO YOU HAVE AGAINST THE DOCTOR, ANYWAY?
I SUPPOSE I HAVE A PENT-UP ANGER AGAINST A MODERN SOCIETY THAT PERMITS INJUSTICES LIKE THAT COUPLE OVER THERE...
ポコ
OH, COME ON. IT'S JUST A MUSTACHIOED MAN AND HIS SECRETARY, HAVING LUNCH TOGETHER!
HEY, WAIT, YOU IDIOT!
WHAT ARE YOU GONNA DO IF SOMEONE ELSE ENDS UP EATING IT!?
I divven't think ya need t' worry aboot that.

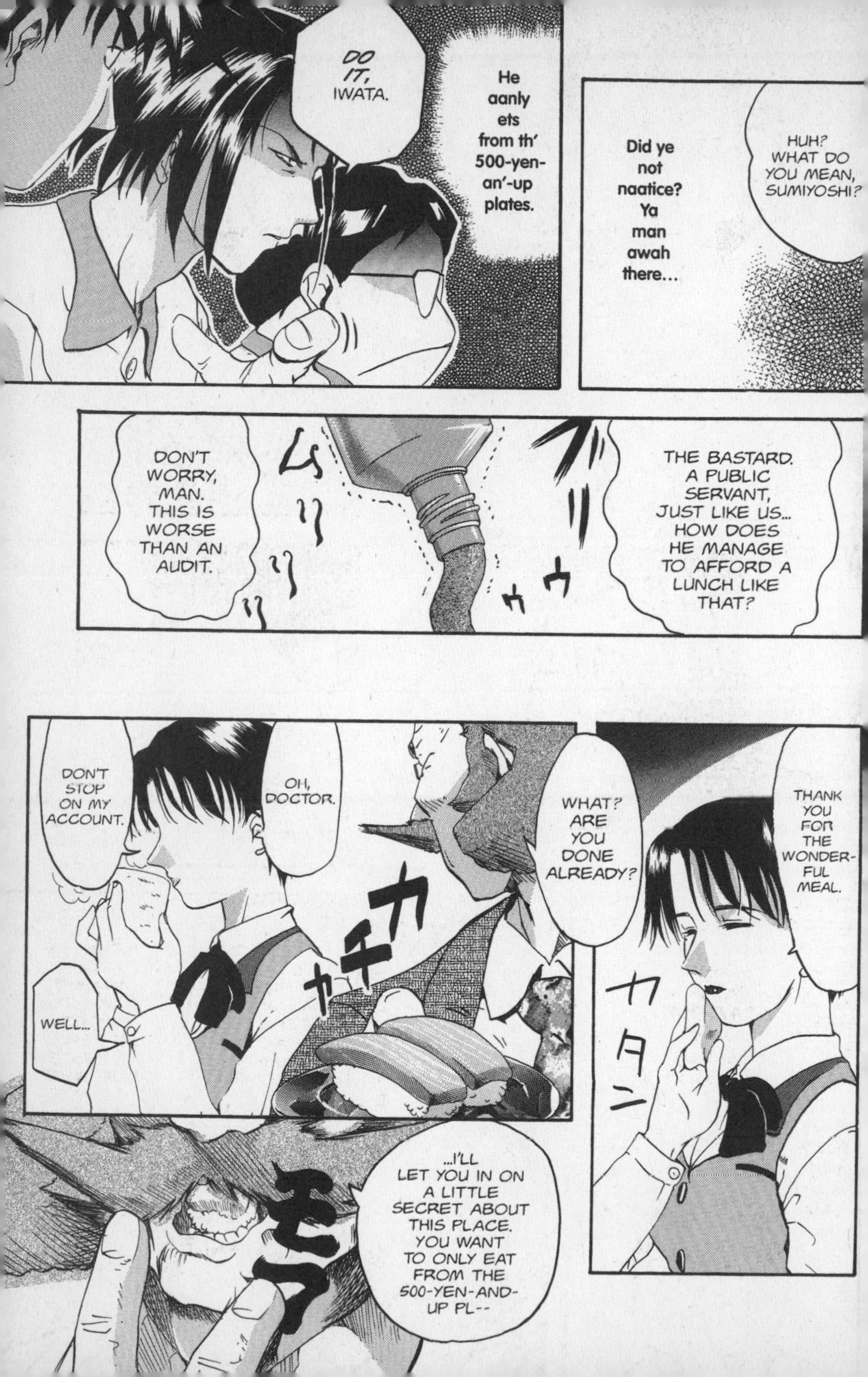
HUH? WHAT DO YOU MEAN, SUMIYOSHI?
Did ye not naatice? Ya man awah there…
He aanly ets from th' 500-yen-an'-up plates.
DO IT, IWATA.
THE BASTARD. A PUBLIC SERVANT, JUST LIKE US... HOW DOES HE MANAGE TO AFFORD A LUNCH LIKE THAT?
DON'T WORRY, MAN. THIS IS WORSE THAN AN AUDIT.
THANK YOU FOR THE WONDERFUL MEAL.
カタン
WHAT? ARE YOU DONE ALREADY?
OH, DOCTOR.
DON'T STOP ON MY ACCOUNT.
カチャ
WELL...
...I'LL LET YOU IN ON A LITTLE SECRET ABOUT THIS PLACE. YOU WANT TO ONLY EAT FROM THE 500-YEN-AND-UP PL--

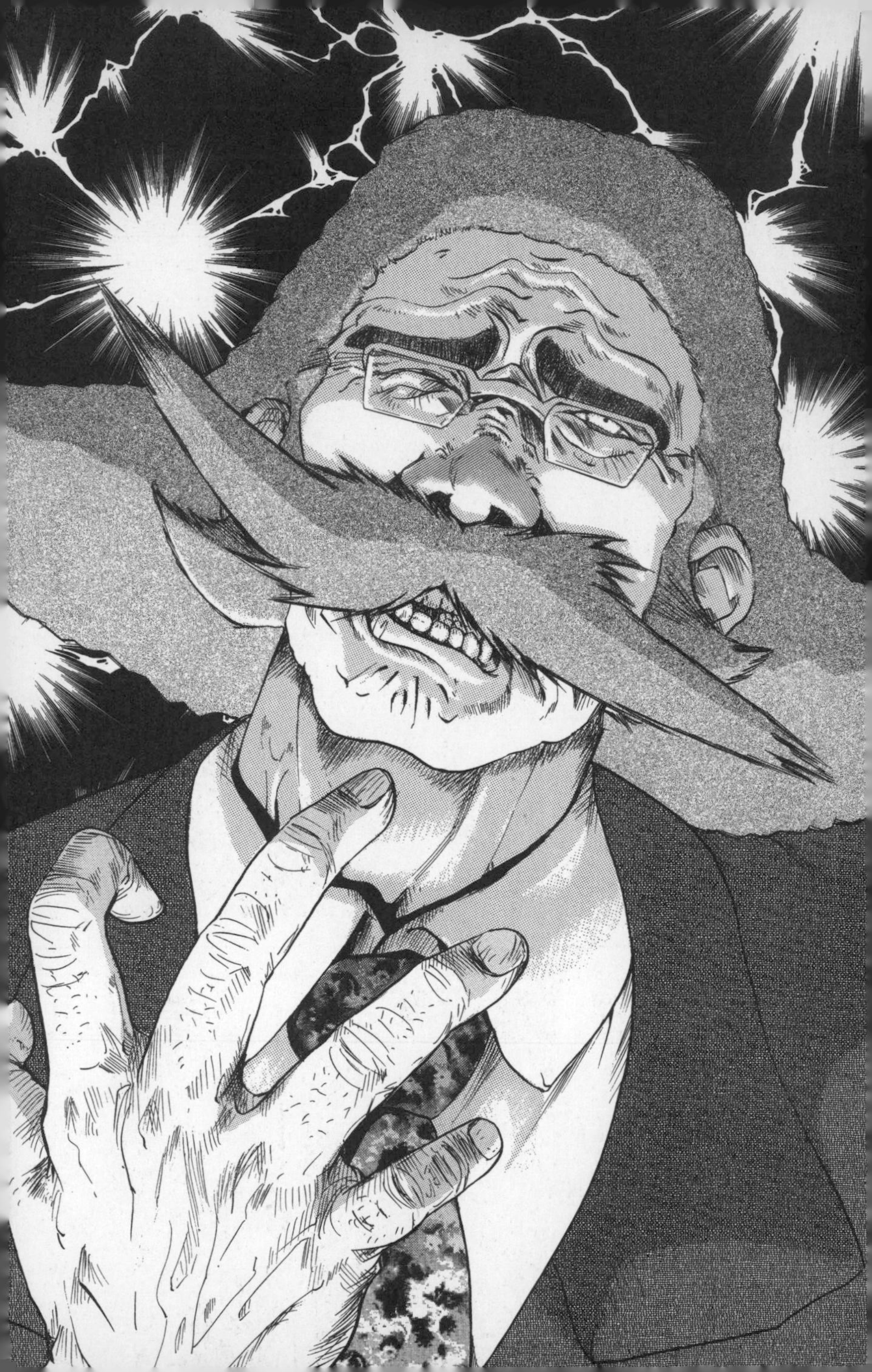

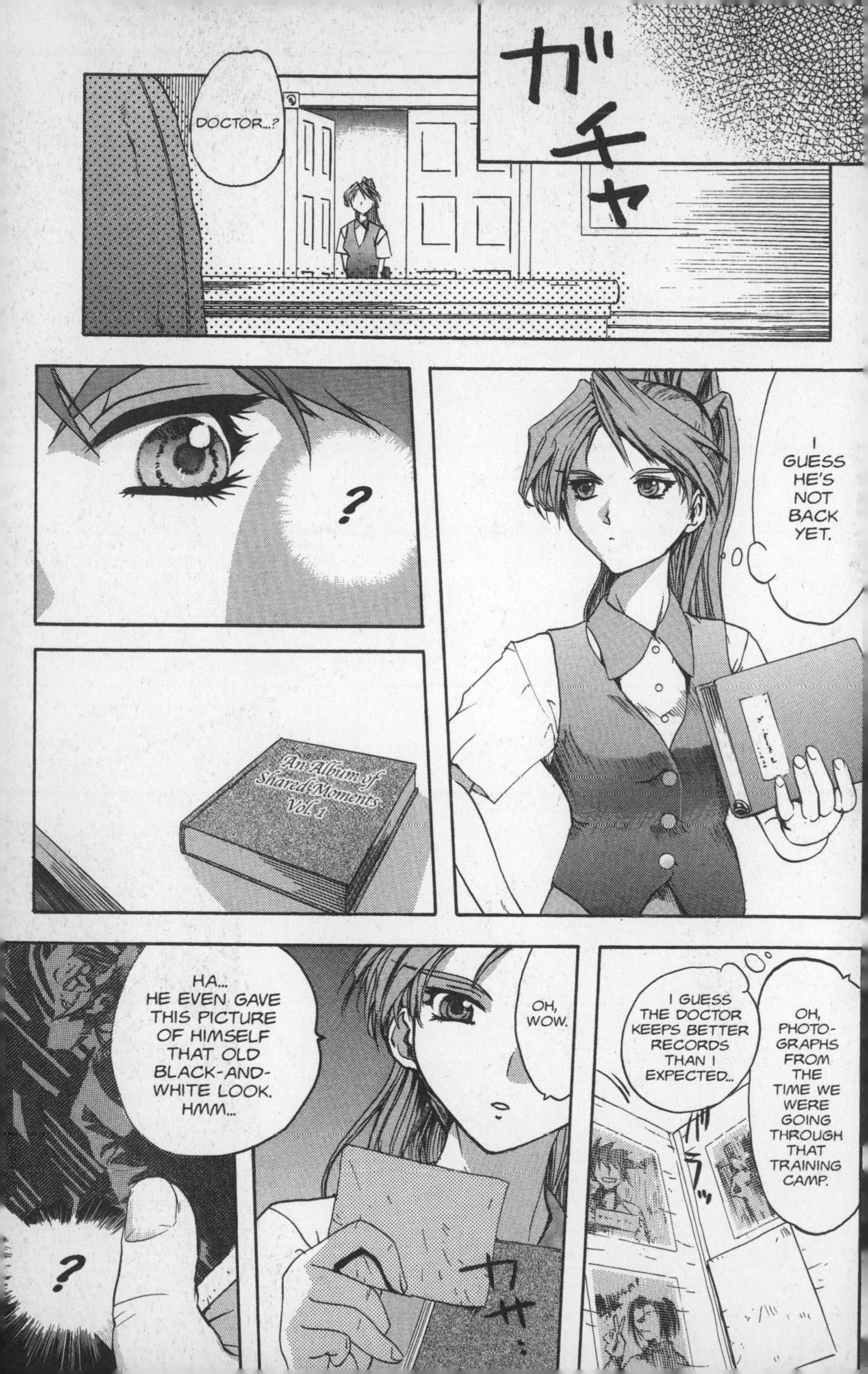
ガチャ
DOCTOR...?
I GUESS HE'S NOT BACK YET.
?
An Album of Shared Moments Vol. 1
OH, PHOTOGRAPHS FROM THE TIME WE WERE GOING THROUGH THAT TRAINING CAMP.
I GUESS THE DOCTOR KEEPS BETTER RECORDS THAN I EXPECTED...
OH, WOW.
HA... HE EVEN GAVE THIS PICTURE OF HIMSELF THAT OLD BLACK-AND-WHITE LOOK. HMM...
カサ
?

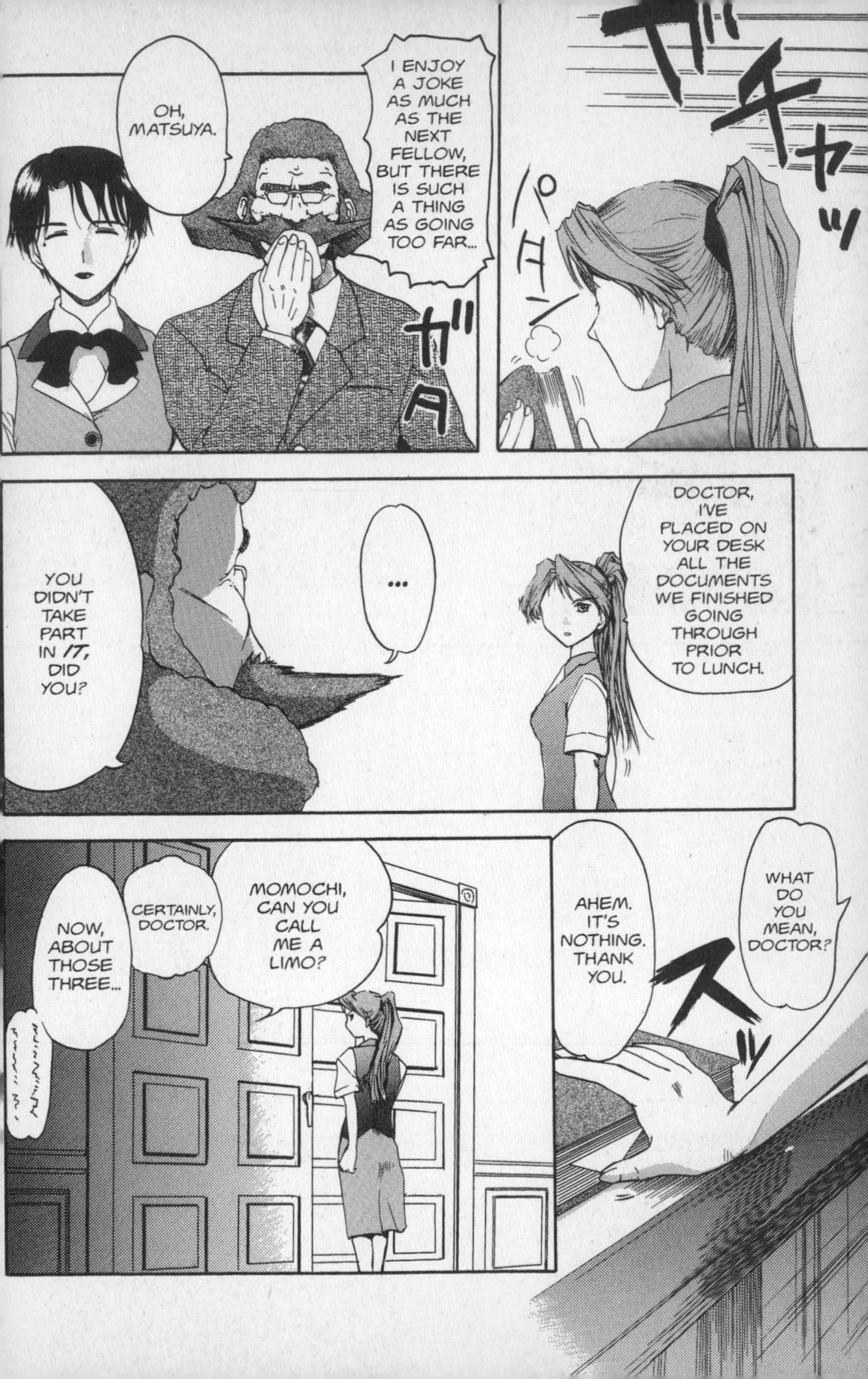
ガチャッ
パタン
I ENJOY A JOKE AS MUCH AS THE NEXT FELLOW, BUT THERE IS SUCH A THING AS GOING TOO FAR...
OH, MATSUYA.
ガタ
DOCTOR, I'VE PLACED ON YOUR DESK ALL THE DOCUMENTS WE FINISHED GOING THROUGH PRIOR TO LUNCH.
...
YOU DIDN'T TAKE PART IN *IT*, DID YOU?
WHAT DO YOU MEAN, DOCTOR?
AHEM. IT'S NOTHING. THANK YOU.
スッ
MOMOCHI, CAN YOU CALL ME A LIMO?
CERTAINLY, DOCTOR.
NOW, ABOUT THOSE THREE...

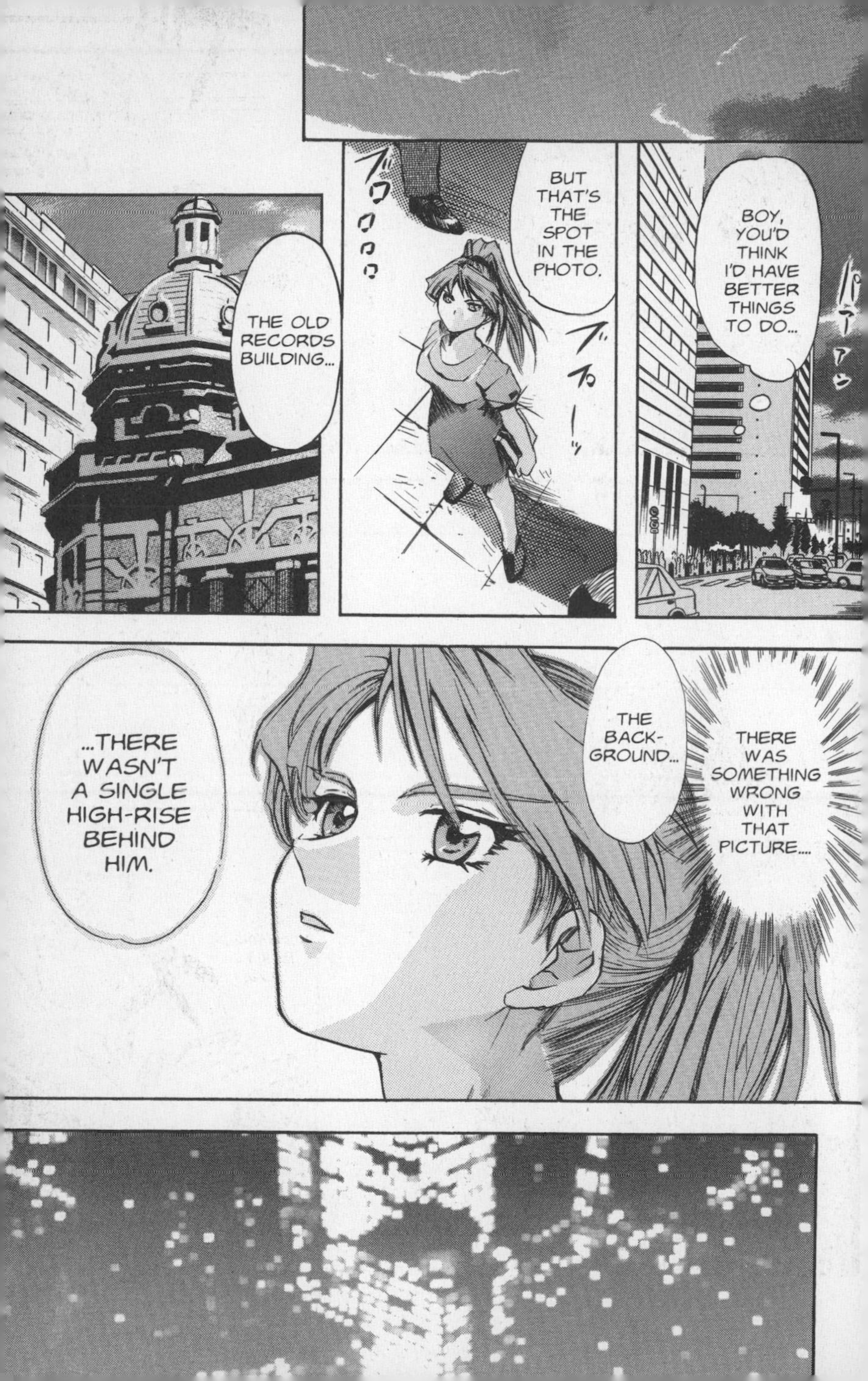
BOY, YOU'D THINK I'D HAVE BETTER THINGS TO DO...
BUT THAT'S THE SPOT IN THE PHOTO.
THE OLD RECORDS BUILDING...
THERE WAS SOMETHING WRONG WITH THAT PICTURE....
THE BACK-GROUND...
...THERE WASN'T A SINGLE HIGH-RISE BEHIND HIM.

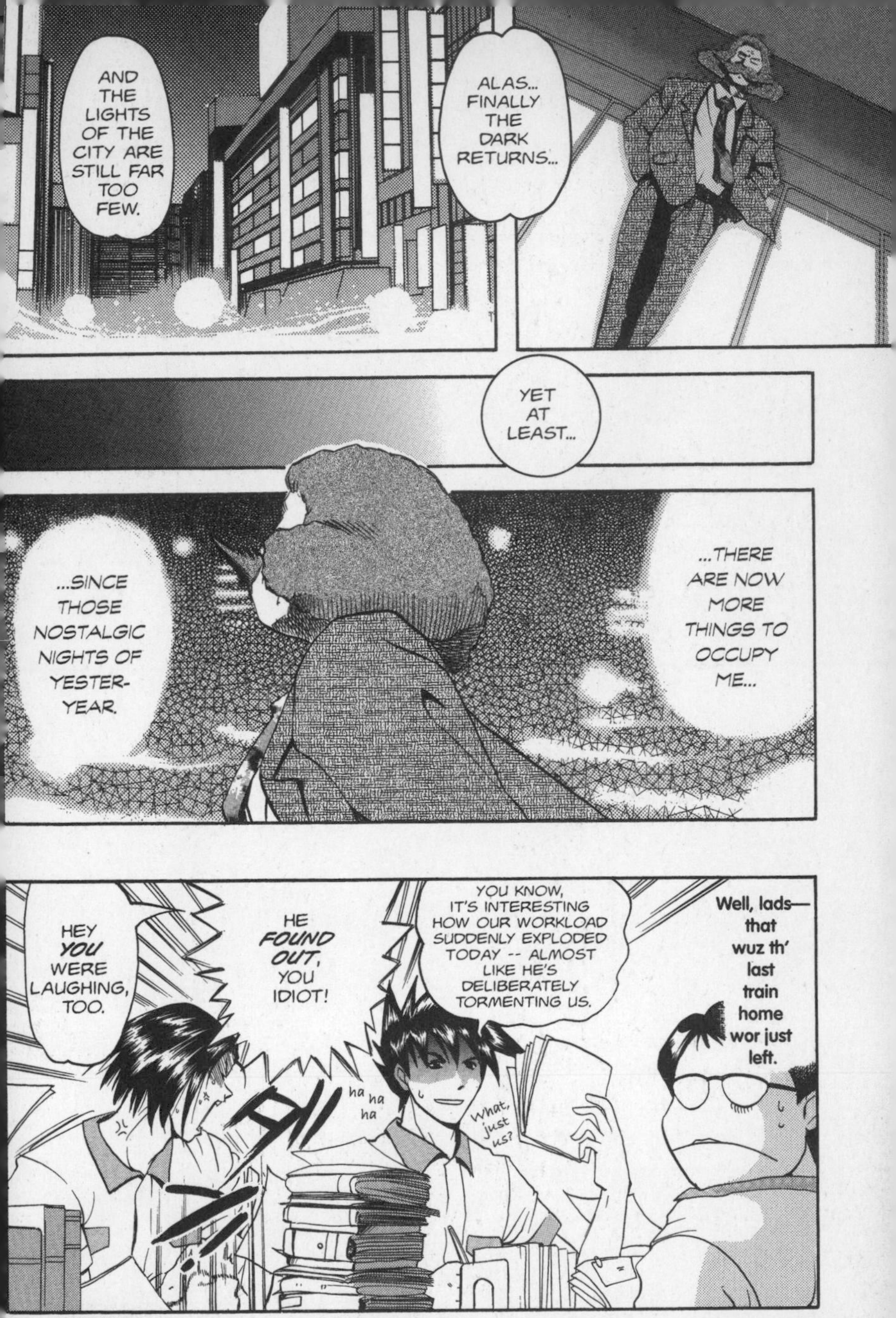
ALAS... FINALLY THE DARK RETURNS...
AND THE LIGHTS OF THE CITY ARE STILL FAR TOO FEW.
YET AT LEAST...
...THERE ARE NOW MORE THINGS TO OCCUPY ME...
...SINCE THOSE NOSTALGIC NIGHTS OF YESTER-YEAR.
Well, lads— that wuz th' last train home wor just left.
YOU KNOW, IT'S INTERESTING HOW OUR WORKLOAD SUDDENLY EXPLODED TODAY -- ALMOST LIKE HE'S DELIBERATELY TORMENTING US.
What, just us?
ha ha ha
HE FOUND OUT, YOU IDIOT!
HEY YOU WERE LAUGHING, TOO.

END MISSION 4

MISSION 5

THE SEASON FARAWAY FROM THE SUN

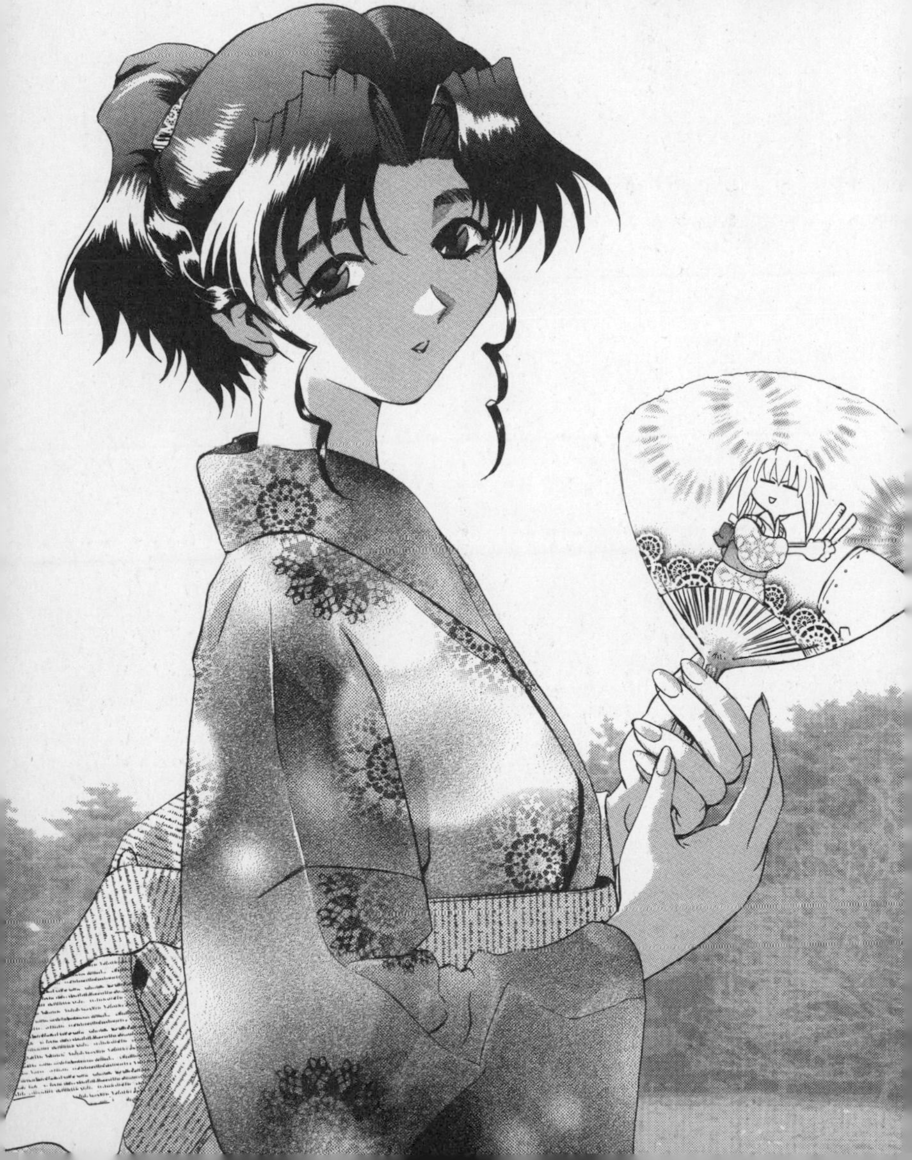

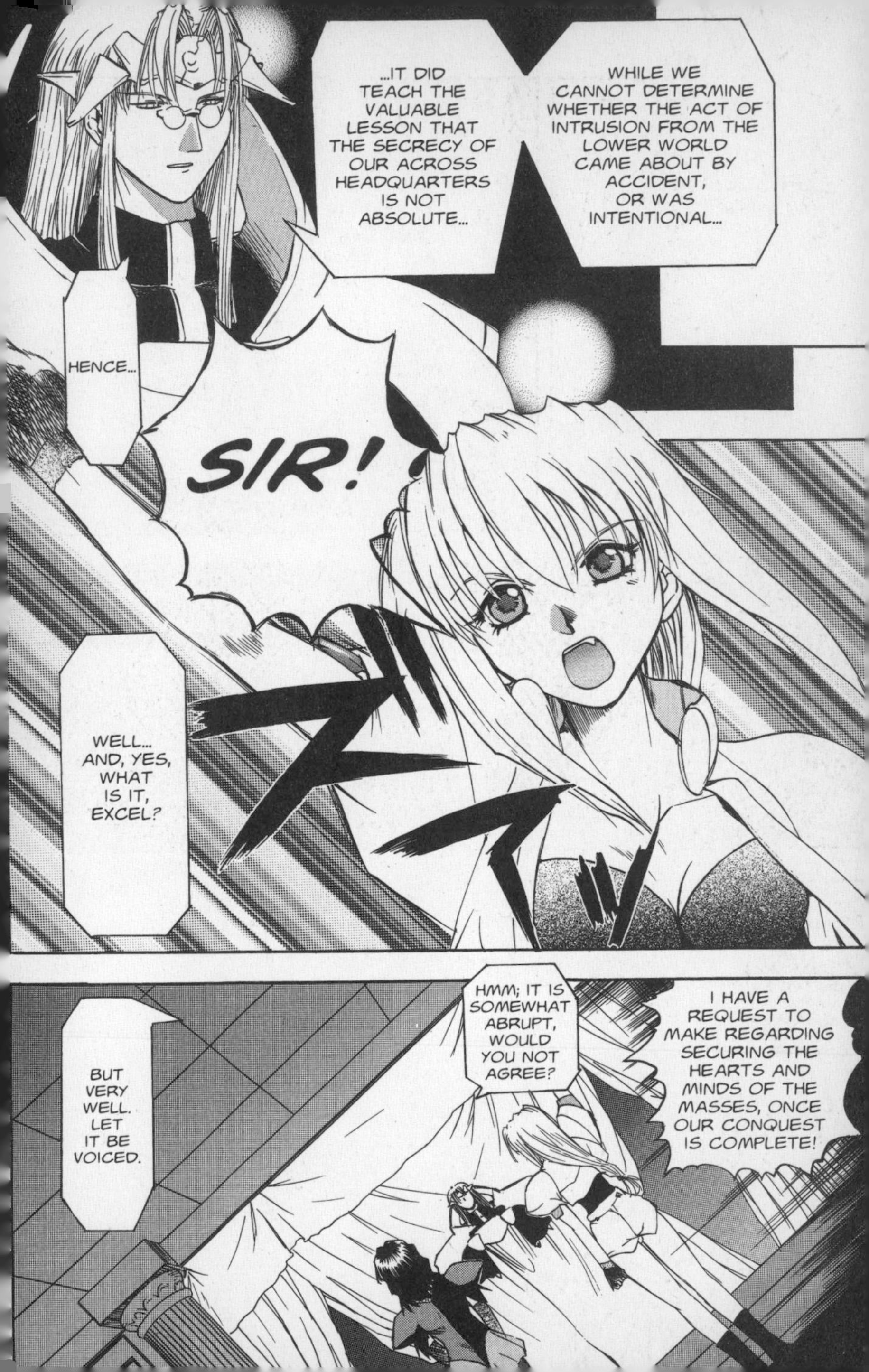
WHILE WE CANNOT DETERMINE WHETHER THE ACT OF INTRUSION FROM THE LOWER WORLD CAME ABOUT BY ACCIDENT, OR WAS INTENTIONAL...
...IT DID TEACH THE VALUABLE LESSON THAT THE SECRECY OF OUR ACROSS HEADQUARTERS IS NOT ABSOLUTE...
HENCE...
SIR!
WELL... AND, YES, WHAT IS IT, EXCEL?
I HAVE A REQUEST TO MAKE REGARDING SECURING THE HEARTS AND MINDS OF THE MASSES, ONCE OUR CONQUEST IS COMPLETE!
HMM; IT IS SOMEWHAT ABRUPT, WOULD YOU NOT AGREE?
BUT VERY WELL. LET IT BE VOICED.

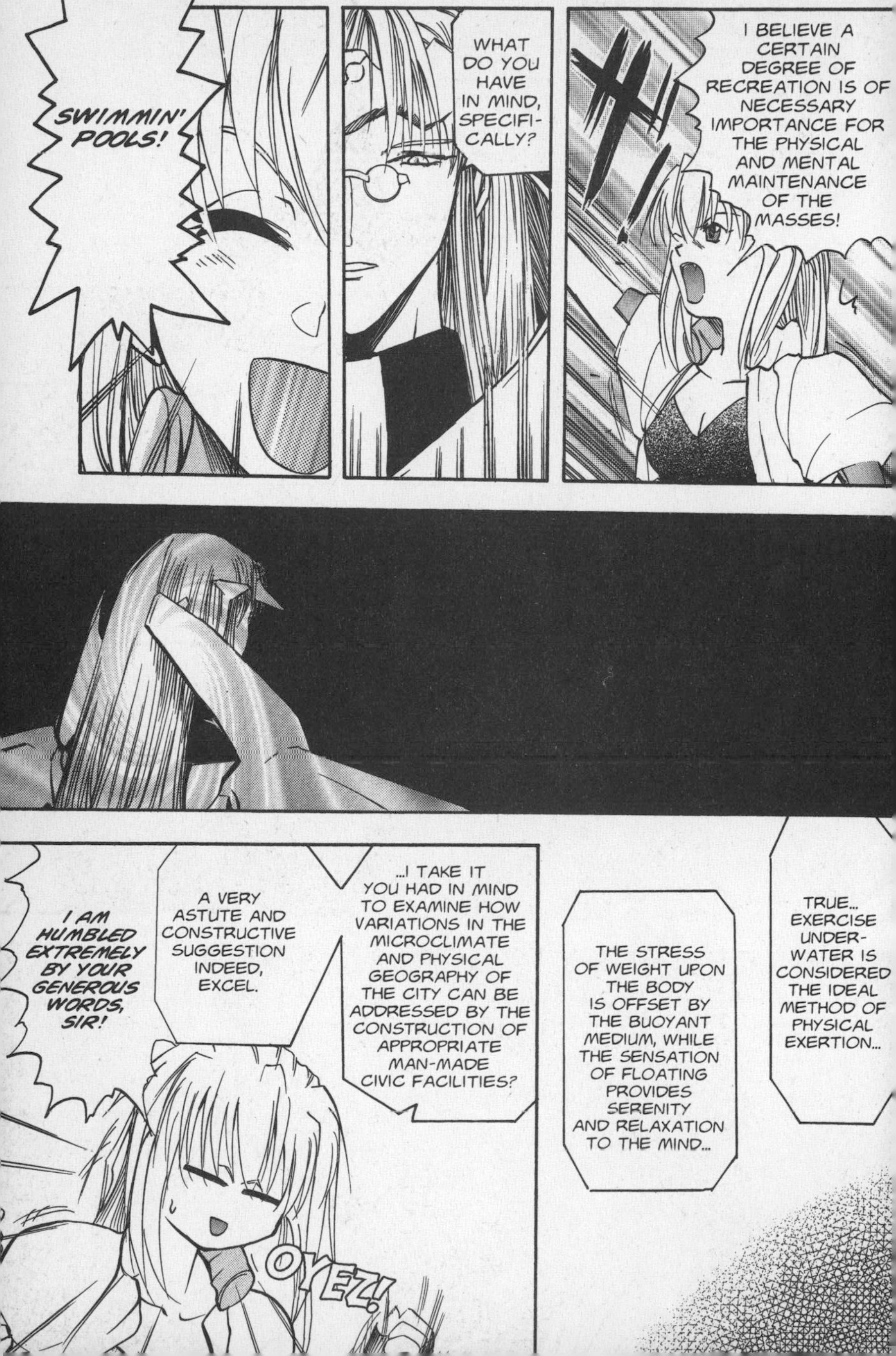
I BELIEVE A CERTAIN DEGREE OF RECREATION IS OF NECESSARY IMPORTANCE FOR THE PHYSICAL AND MENTAL MAINTENANCE OF THE MASSES!
WHAT DO YOU HAVE IN MIND, SPECIFICALLY?
SWIMMIN' POOLS!
TRUE... EXERCISE UNDERWATER IS CONSIDERED THE IDEAL METHOD OF PHYSICAL EXERTION...
THE STRESS OF WEIGHT UPON THE BODY IS OFFSET BY THE BUOYANT MEDIUM, WHILE THE SENSATION OF FLOATING PROVIDES SERENITY AND RELAXATION TO THE MIND...
...I TAKE IT YOU HAD IN MIND TO EXAMINE HOW VARIATIONS IN THE MICROCLIMATE AND PHYSICAL GEOGRAPHY OF THE CITY CAN BE ADDRESSED BY THE CONSTRUCTION OF APPROPRIATE MAN-MADE CIVIC FACILITIES?
A VERY ASTUTE AND CONSTRUCTIVE SUGGESTION INDEED, EXCEL.
I AM HUMBLED EXTREMELY BY YOUR GENEROUS WORDS, SIR!
OYEZ!

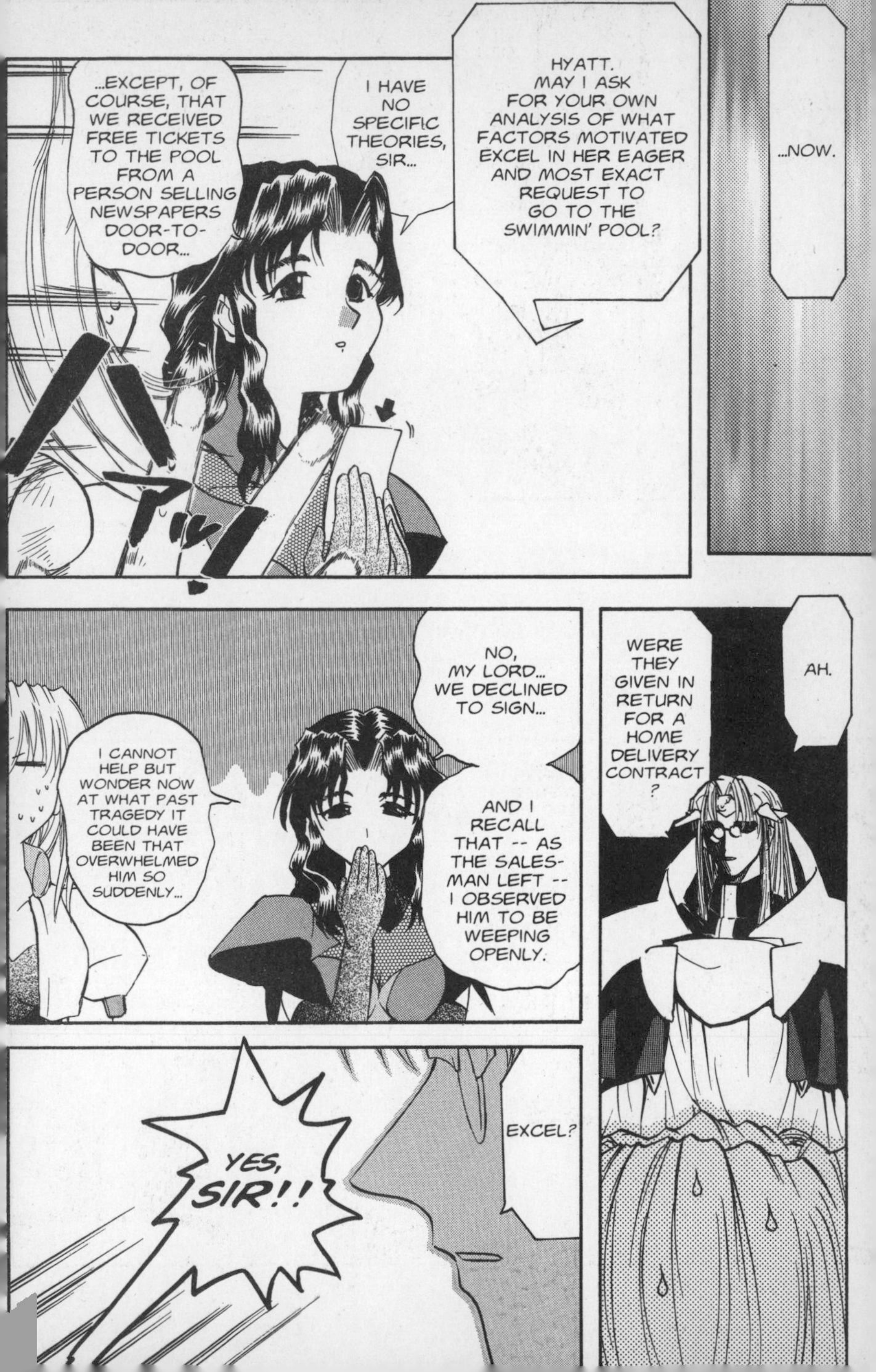
...NOW.
HYATT. MAY I ASK FOR YOUR OWN ANALYSIS OF WHAT FACTORS MOTIVATED EXCEL IN HER EAGER AND MOST EXACT REQUEST TO GO TO THE SWIMMIN' POOL?
I HAVE NO SPECIFIC THEORIES, SIR...
...EXCEPT, OF COURSE, THAT WE RECEIVED FREE TICKETS TO THE POOL FROM A PERSON SELLING NEWSPAPERS DOOR-TO-DOOR...
AH.
WERE THEY GIVEN IN RETURN FOR A HOME DELIVERY CONTRACT ?
NO, MY LORD... WE DECLINED TO SIGN...
AND I RECALL THAT -- AS THE SALES-MAN LEFT -- I OBSERVED HIM TO BE WEEPING OPENLY.
I CANNOT HELP BUT WONDER NOW AT WHAT PAST TRAGEDY IT COULD HAVE BEEN THAT OVERWHELMED HIM SO SUDDENLY...
EXCEL?
YES, SIR!!

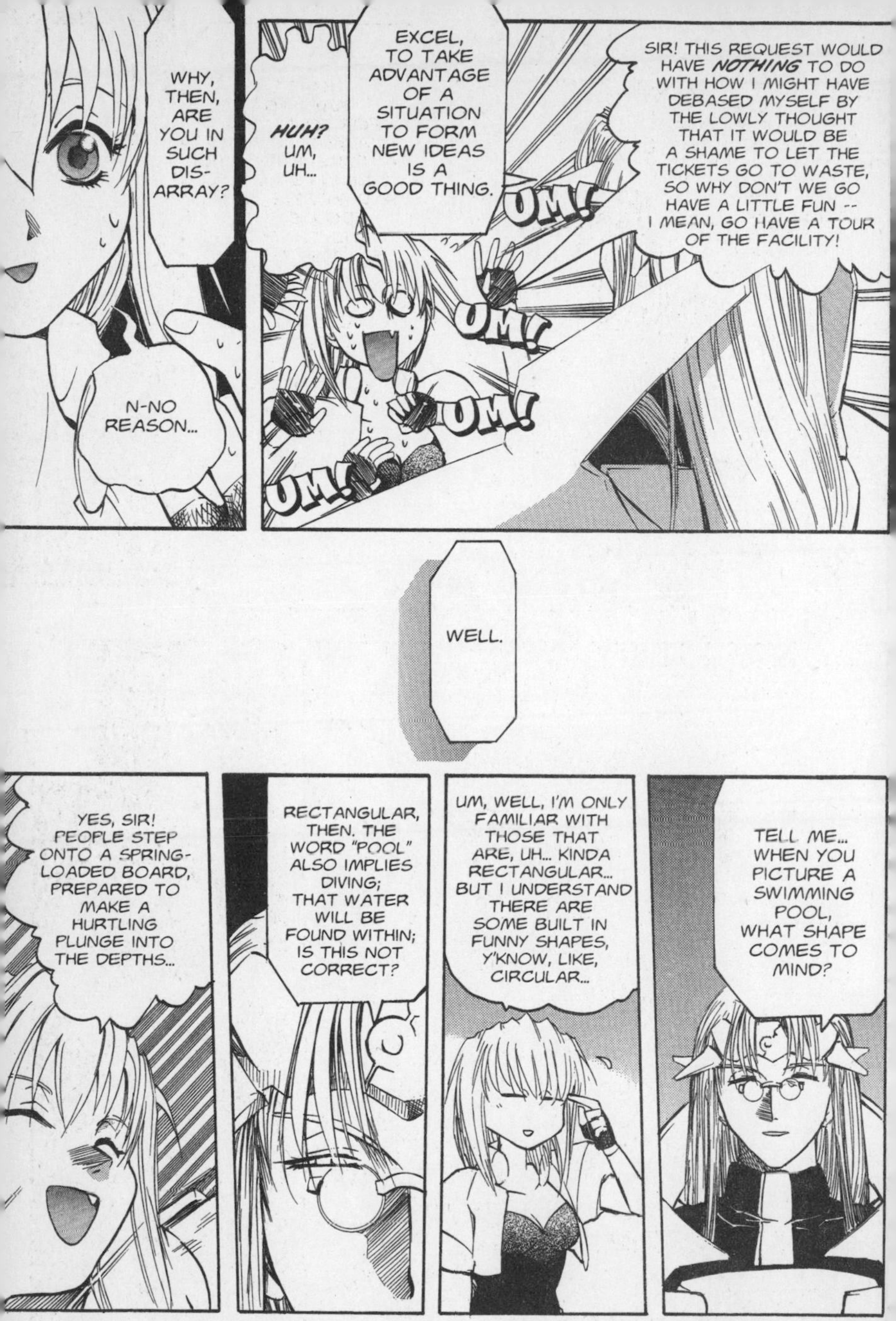
SIR! THIS REQUEST WOULD HAVE *NOTHING* TO DO WITH HOW I MIGHT HAVE DEBASED MYSELF BY THE LOWLY THOUGHT THAT IT WOULD BE A SHAME TO LET THE TICKETS GO TO WASTE, SO WHY DON'T WE GO HAVE A LITTLE FUN -- I MEAN, GO HAVE A TOUR OF THE FACILITY!
EXCEL, TO TAKE ADVANTAGE OF A SITUATION TO FORM NEW IDEAS IS A GOOD THING.
UM!
HUH? UM, UH...
UM!
UM!
UM!
WHY, THEN, ARE YOU IN SUCH DIS-ARRAY?
N-NO REASON...
WELL.
TELL ME... WHEN YOU PICTURE A SWIMMING POOL, WHAT SHAPE COMES TO MIND?
UM, WELL, I'M ONLY FAMILIAR WITH THOSE THAT ARE, UH... KINDA RECTANGULAR... BUT I UNDERSTAND THERE ARE SOME BUILT IN FUNNY SHAPES, Y'KNOW, LIKE, CIRCULAR...
RECTANGULAR, THEN. THE WORD "POOL" ALSO IMPLIES DIVING; THAT WATER WILL BE FOUND WITHIN; IS THIS NOT CORRECT?
YES, SIR! PEOPLE STEP ONTO A SPRING-LOADED BOARD, PREPARED TO MAKE A HURTLING PLUNGE INTO THE DEPTHS...

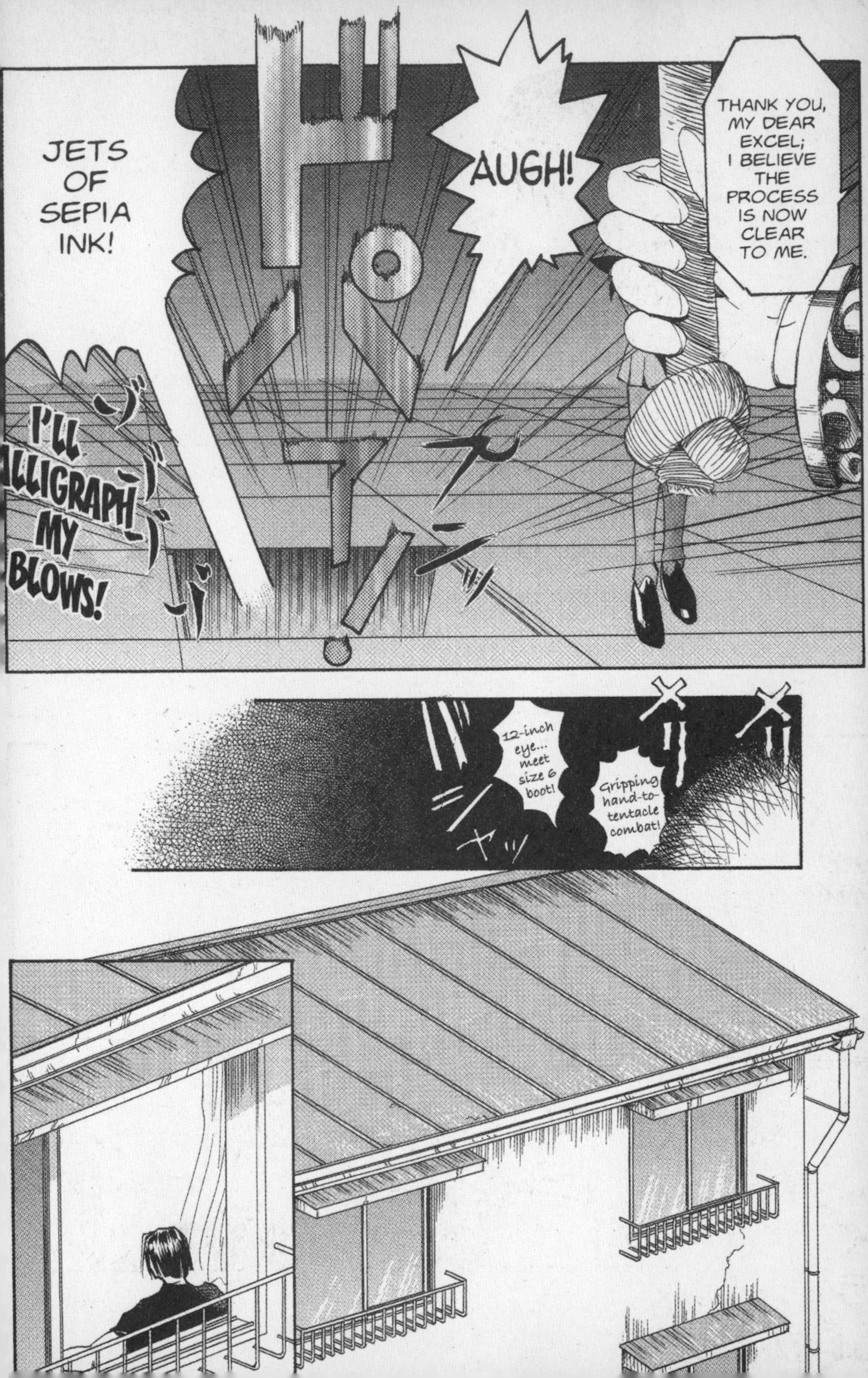
THANK YOU, MY DEAR EXCEL; I BELIEVE THE PROCESS IS NOW CLEAR TO ME.
AUGH!
JETS OF SEPIA INK!
I'LL ALLIGRAPH MY BLOWS!
Gripping hand-to-tentacle combat!
12-inch eye... meet size 6 boot!

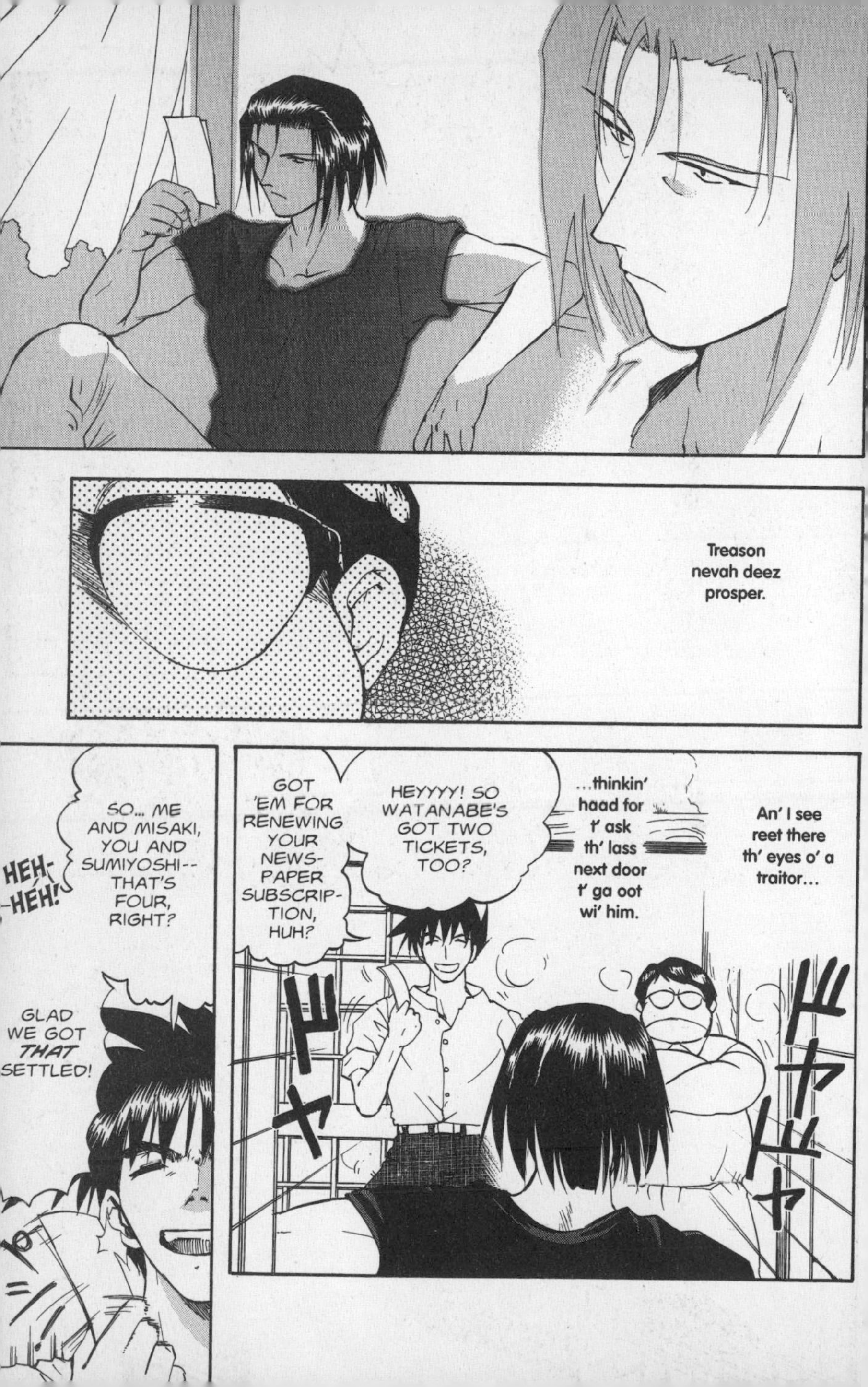
Treason nevah deez prosper.
An' I see reet there th' eyes o' a traitor…
…thinkin' haad for t' ask th' lass next door t' ga oot wi' him.
HEYYYY! SO WATANABE'S GOT TWO TICKETS, TOO?
GOT 'EM FOR RENEWING YOUR NEWSPAPER SUBSCRIPTION, HUH?
SO... ME AND MISAKI, YOU AND SUMIYOSHI-- THAT'S FOUR, RIGHT?
HEH-HÉH!
GLAD WE GOT *THAT* SETTLED!

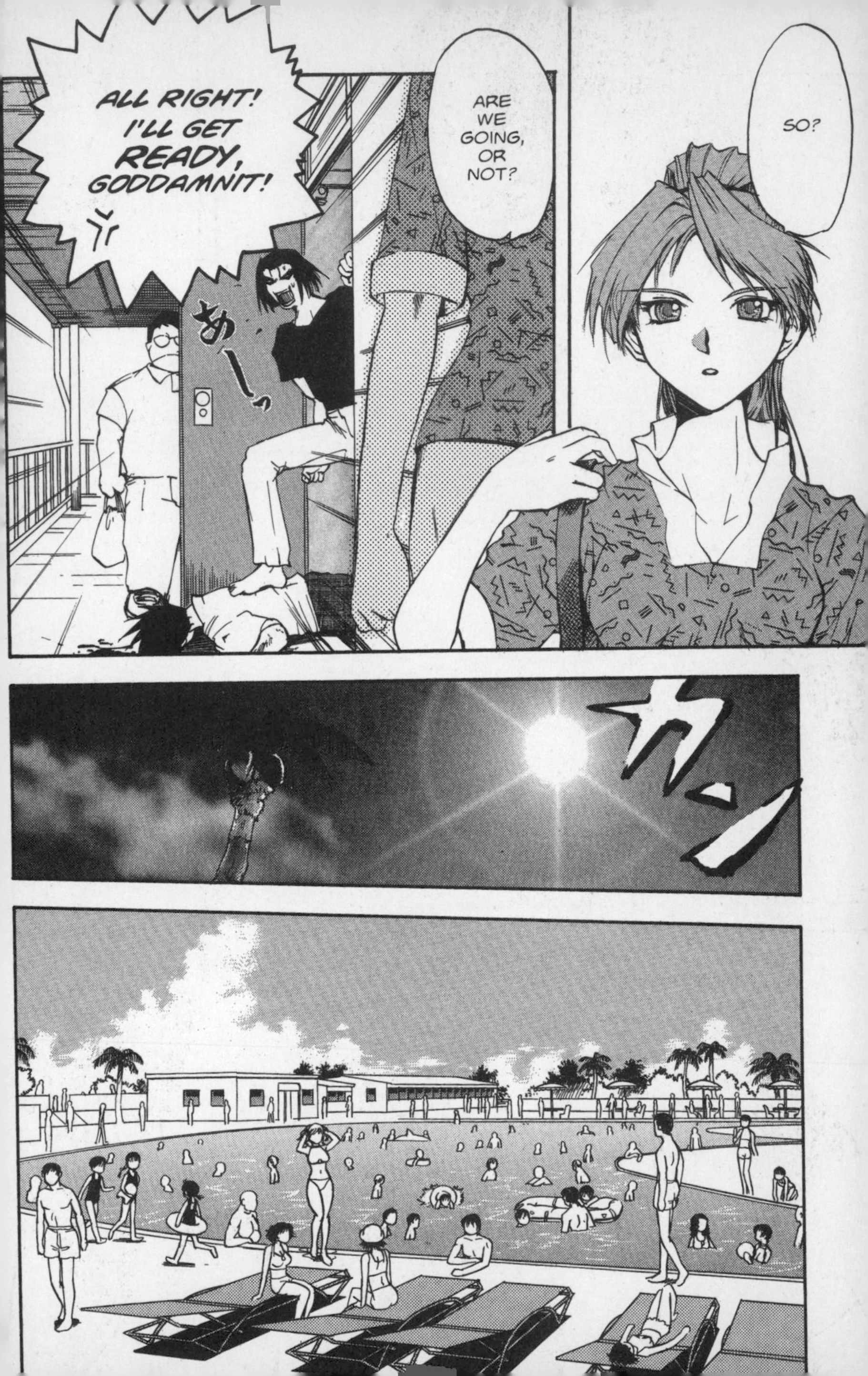
SO?
ARE WE GOING, OR NOT?
ALL RIGHT! I'LL GET READY, GODDAMNIT!

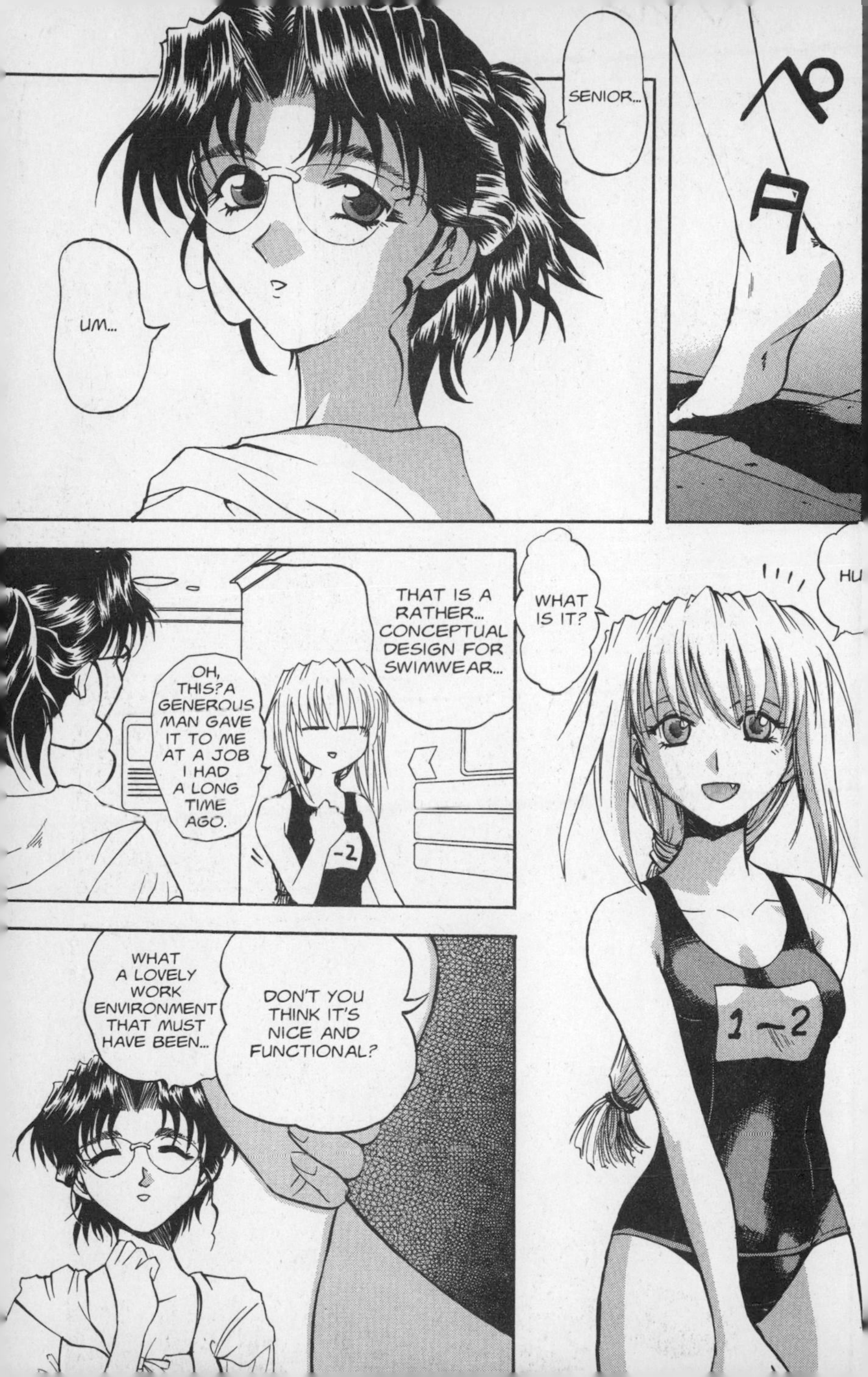
ペタ
SENIOR...
UM...
HU
WHAT IS IT?
THAT IS A RATHER... CONCEPTUAL DESIGN FOR SWIMWEAR...
OH, THIS? A GENEROUS MAN GAVE IT TO ME AT A JOB I HAD A LONG TIME AGO.
DON'T YOU THINK IT'S NICE AND FUNCTIONAL?
WHAT A LOVELY WORK ENVIRONMENT THAT MUST HAVE BEEN...

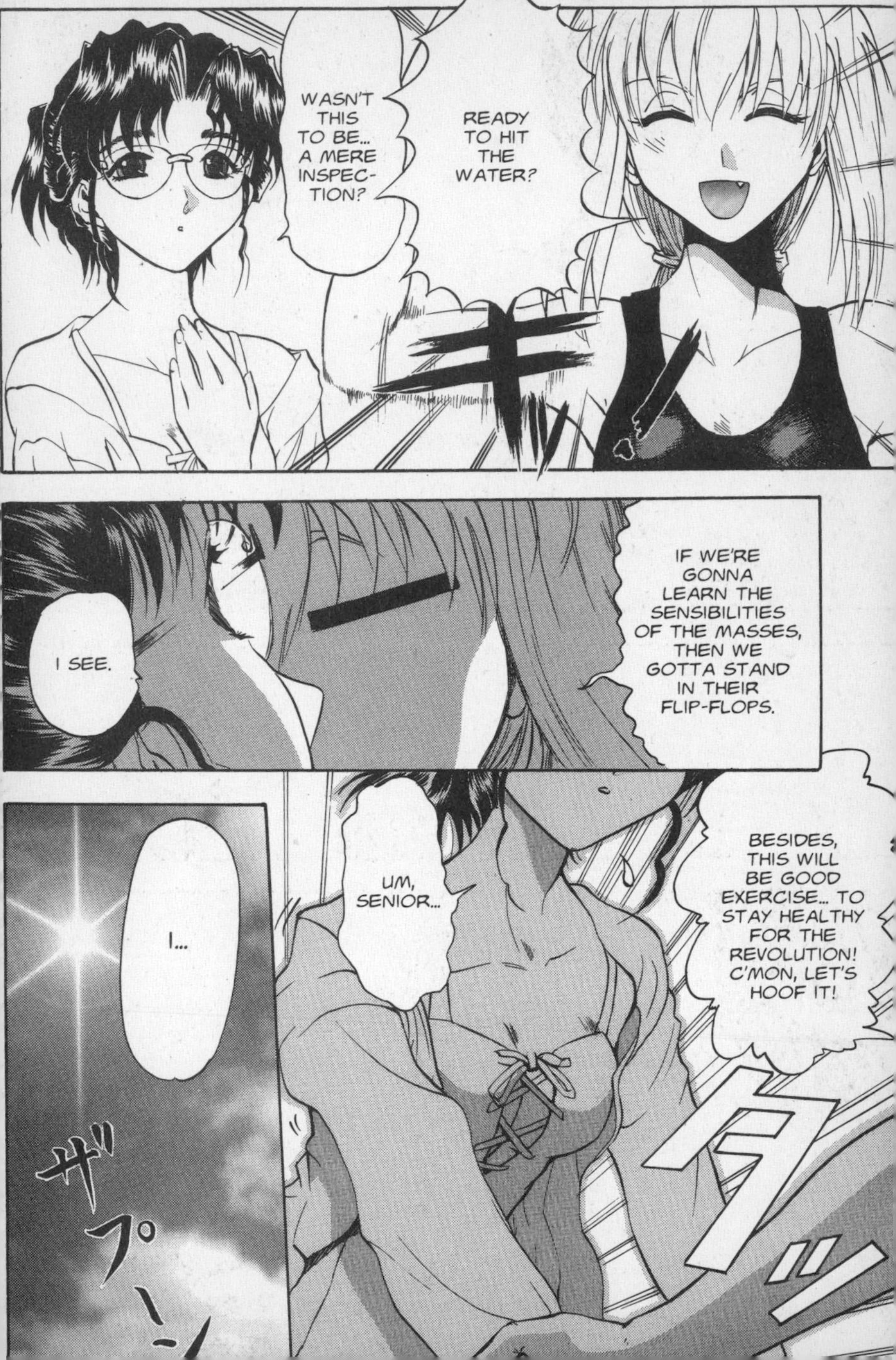
READY TO HIT THE WATER?
WASN'T THIS TO BE... A MERE INSPECTION?
IF WE'RE GONNA LEARN THE SENSIBILITIES OF THE MASSES, THEN WE GOTTA STAND IN THEIR FLIP-FLOPS.
I SEE.
BESIDES, THIS WILL BE GOOD EXERCISE... TO STAY HEALTHY FOR THE REVOLUTION! C'MON, LET'S HOOF IT!
UM, SENIOR...
I...

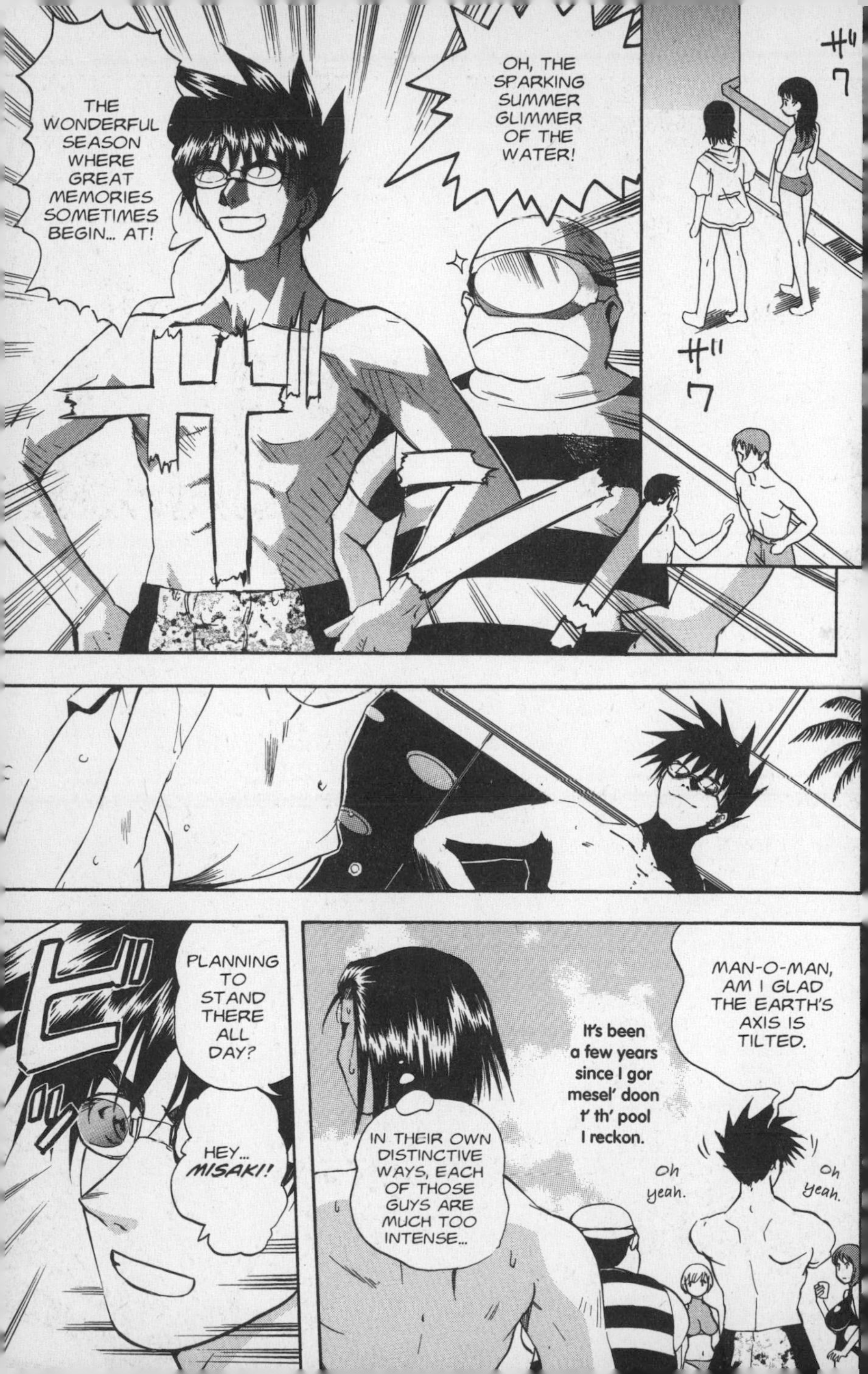
ザワ
ザワ
OH, THE SPARKING SUMMER GLIMMER OF THE WATER!
THE WONDERFUL SEASON WHERE GREAT MEMORIES SOMETIMES BEGIN... AT!
MAN-O-MAN, AM I GLAD THE EARTH'S AXIS IS TILTED.
Oh yeah.
It's been a few years since I gor mesel' doon t' th' pool I reckon.
Oh yeah.
IN THEIR OWN DISTINCTIVE WAYS, EACH OF THOSE GUYS ARE MUCH TOO INTENSE...
PLANNING TO STAND THERE ALL DAY?
HEY... MISAKI!

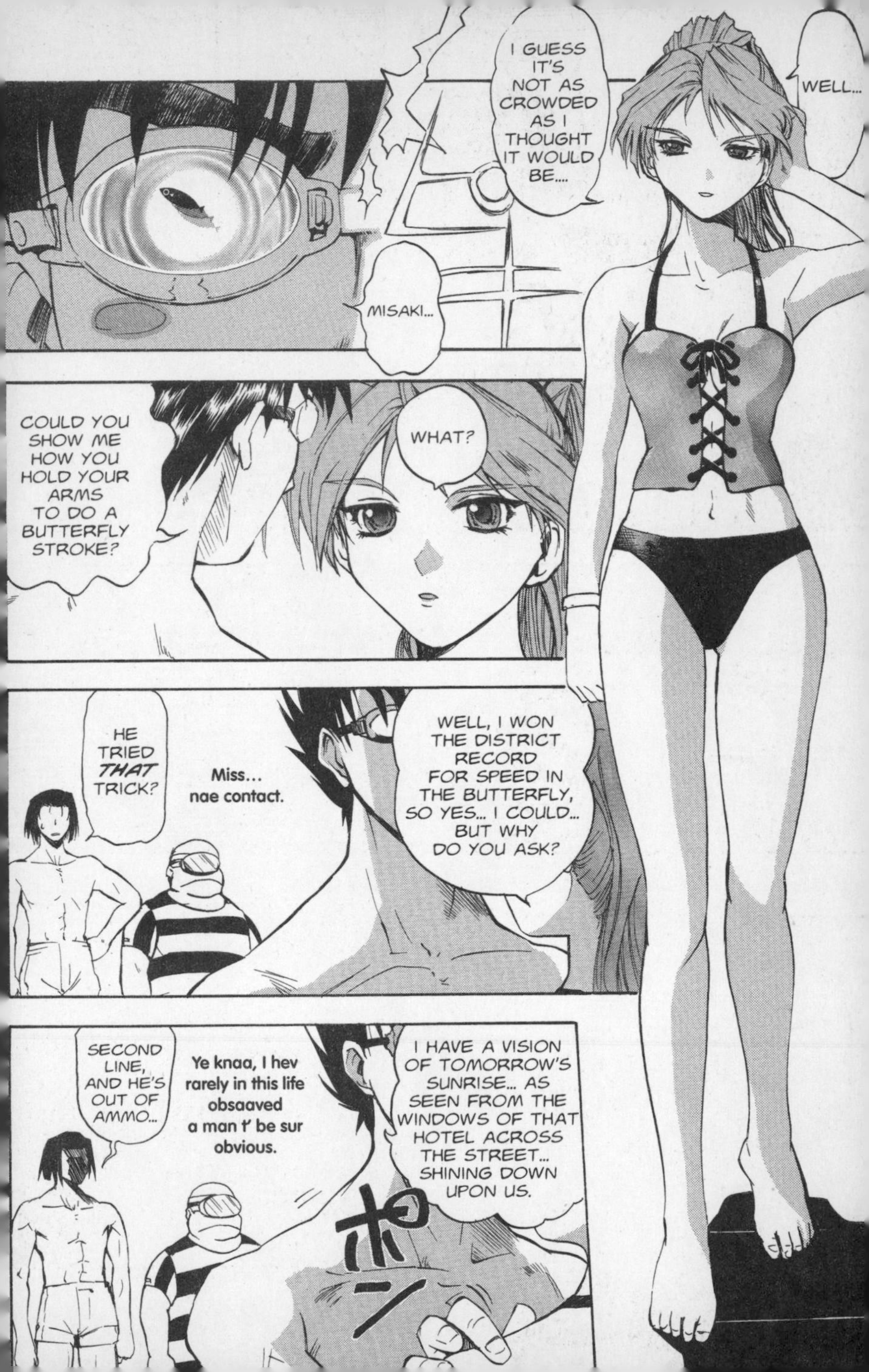
WELL...
I GUESS IT'S NOT AS CROWDED AS I THOUGHT IT WOULD BE....
MISAKI...
COULD YOU SHOW ME HOW YOU HOLD YOUR ARMS TO DO A BUTTERFLY STROKE?
WHAT?
WELL, I WON THE DISTRICT RECORD FOR SPEED IN THE BUTTERFLY, SO YES... I COULD... BUT WHY DO YOU ASK?
HE TRIED *THAT* TRICK?
Miss... nae contact.
I HAVE A VISION OF TOMORROW'S SUNRISE... AS SEEN FROM THE WINDOWS OF THAT HOTEL ACROSS THE STREET... SHINING DOWN UPON US.
SECOND LINE, AND HE'S OUT OF AMMO...
Ye knaa, I hev rarely in this life obsaaved a man t' be sur obvious.
ポン

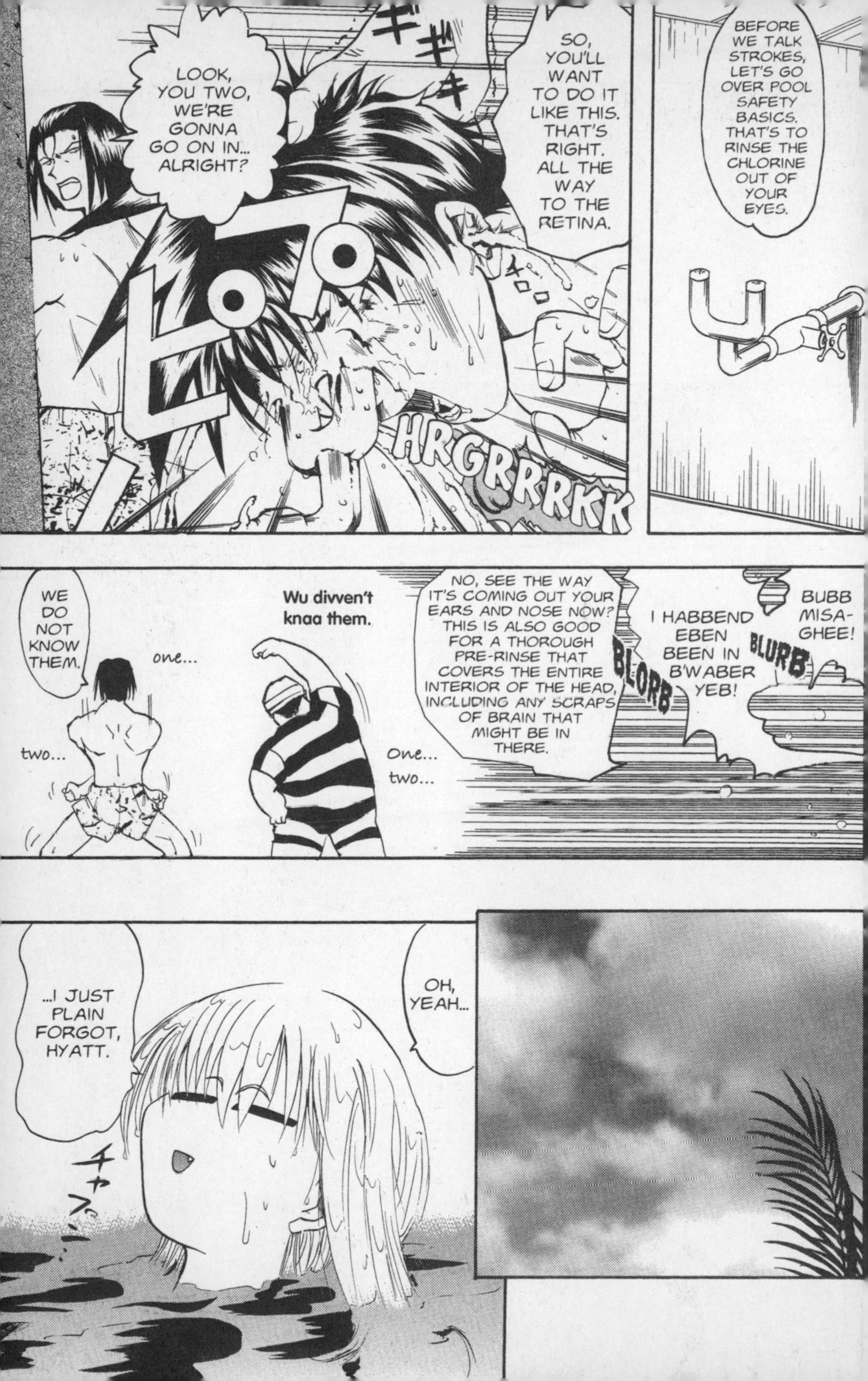
BEFORE WE TALK STROKES, LET'S GO OVER POOL SAFETY BASICS. THAT'S TO RINSE THE CHLORINE OUT OF YOUR EYES.
SO, YOU'LL WANT TO DO IT LIKE THIS. THAT'S RIGHT. ALL THE WAY TO THE RETINA.
LOOK, YOU TWO, WE'RE GONNA GO ON IN... ALRIGHT?
HRGRRRRKK
BUBB MISA-GHEE!
BLURB
I HABBEND EBEN BEEN IN B'WABER YEB!
BLORB
NO, SEE THE WAY IT'S COMING OUT YOUR EARS AND NOSE NOW? THIS IS ALSO GOOD FOR A THOROUGH PRE-RINSE THAT COVERS THE ENTIRE INTERIOR OF THE HEAD, INCLUDING ANY SCRAPS OF BRAIN THAT MIGHT BE IN THERE.
Wu divven't knaa them.
One... two...
WE DO NOT KNOW THEM.
one...
two...
OH, YEAH...
...I JUST PLAIN FORGOT, HYATT.

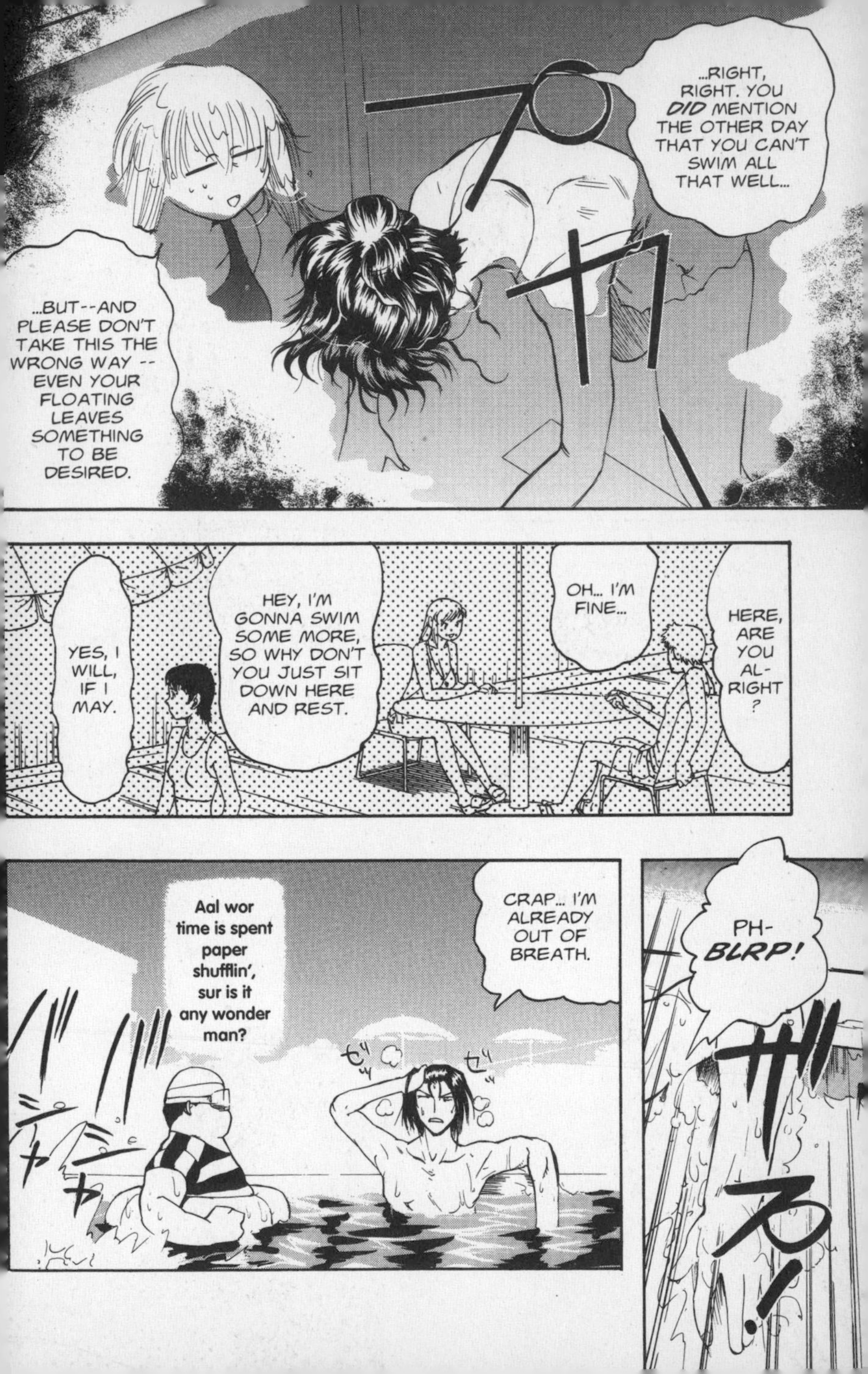
...RIGHT, RIGHT. YOU *DID* MENTION THE OTHER DAY THAT YOU CAN'T SWIM ALL THAT WELL...
...BUT--AND PLEASE DON'T TAKE THIS THE WRONG WAY -- EVEN YOUR FLOATING LEAVES SOMETHING TO BE DESIRED.
HERE, ARE YOU AL-RIGHT?
OH... I'M FINE...
HEY, I'M GONNA SWIM SOME MORE, SO WHY DON'T YOU JUST SIT DOWN HERE AND REST.
YES, I WILL, IF I MAY.
PH-*BLRP!*
CRAP... I'M ALREADY OUT OF BREATH.
Aal wor time is spent paper shufflin', sur is it any wonder man?

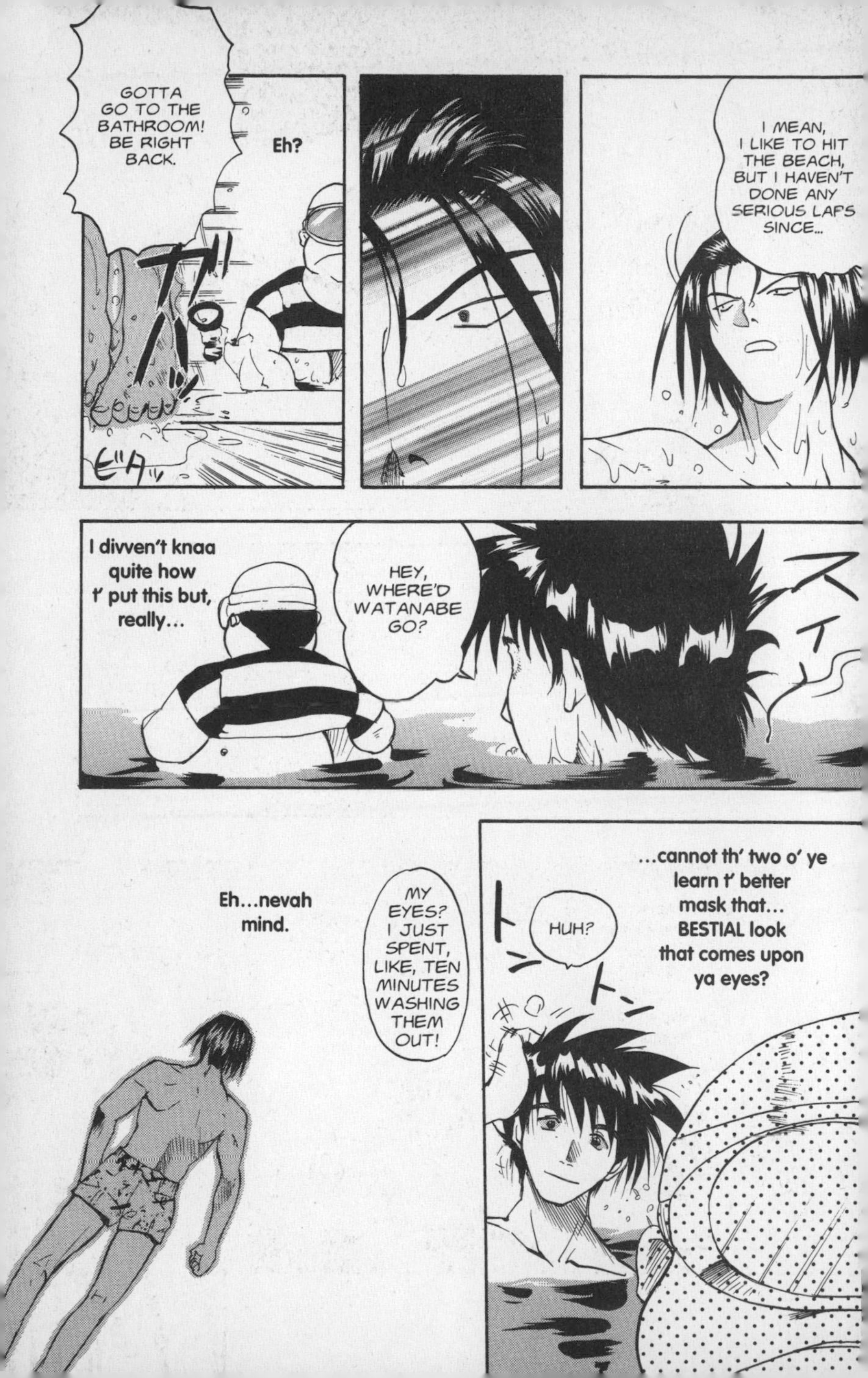
I MEAN, I LIKE TO HIT THE BEACH, BUT I HAVEN'T DONE ANY SERIOUS LAPS SINCE...
Eh?
GOTTA GO TO THE BATHROOM! BE RIGHT BACK.
HEY, WHERE'D WATANABE GO?
I divven't knaa quite how t' put this but, really…
…cannot th' two o' ye learn t' better mask that… BESTIAL look that comes upon ya eyes?
HUH?
MY EYES? I JUST SPENT, LIKE, TEN MINUTES WASHING THEM OUT!
Eh…nevah mind.

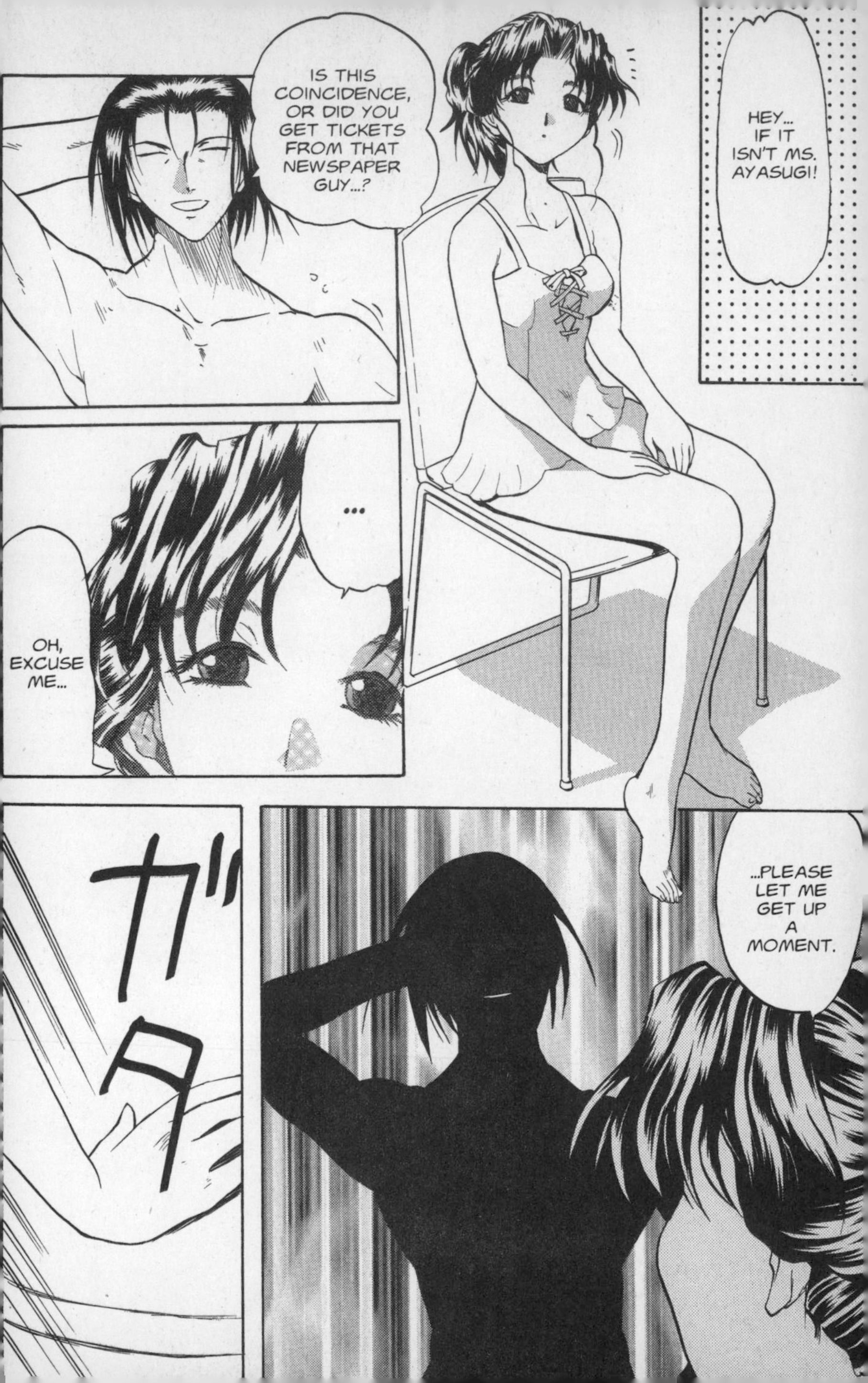
HEY... IF IT ISN'T MS. AYASUGI!
IS THIS COINCIDENCE, OR DID YOU GET TICKETS FROM THAT NEWSPAPER GUY...?
...
OH, EXCUSE ME...
...PLEASE LET ME GET UP A MOMENT.
ガタ

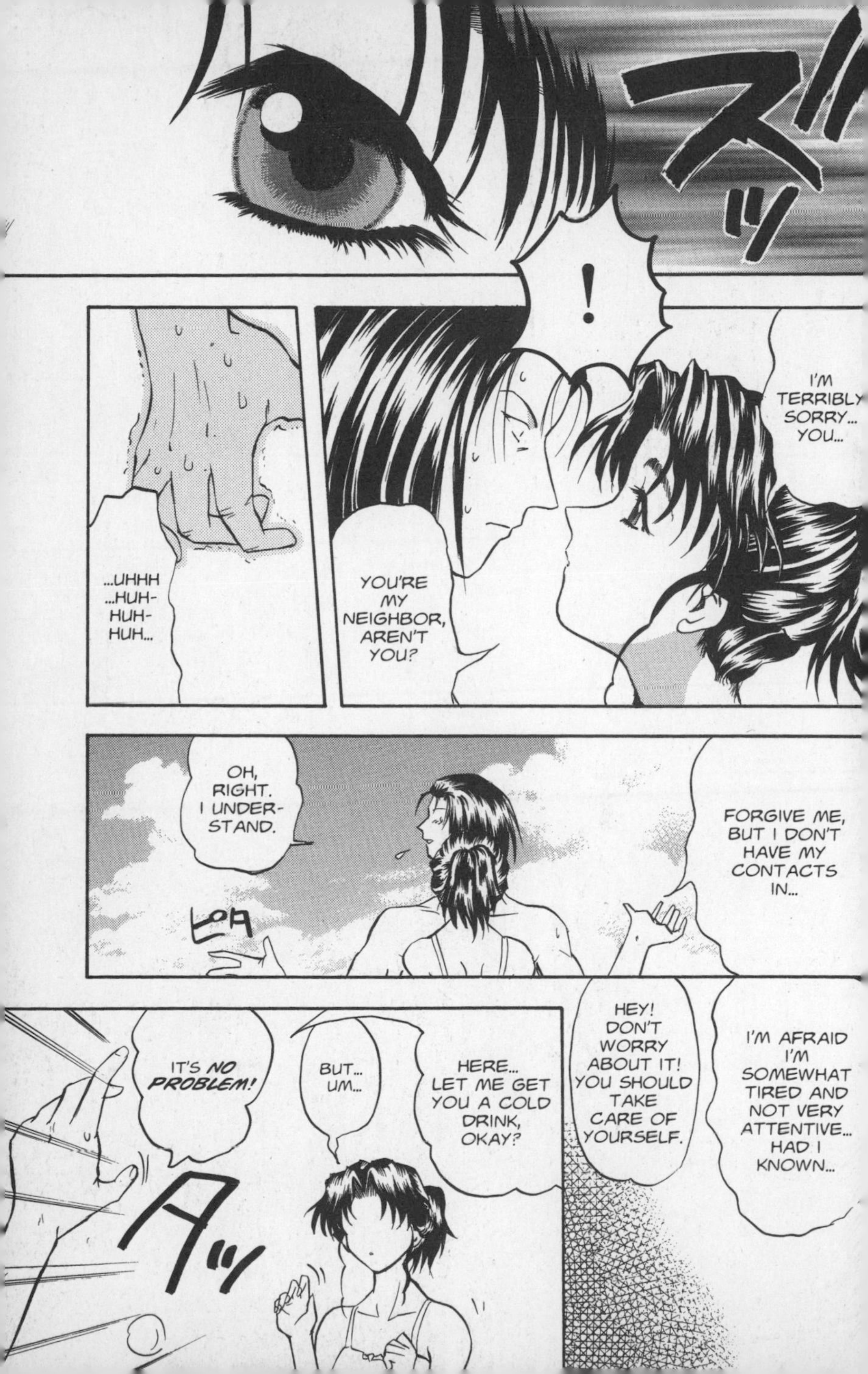
ズッ
!
I'M TERRIBLY SORRY... YOU...
YOU'RE MY NEIGHBOR, AREN'T YOU?
...UHHH ...HUH-HUH-HUH...
FORGIVE ME, BUT I DON'T HAVE MY CONTACTS IN...
OH, RIGHT. I UNDER-STAND.
I'M AFRAID I'M SOMEWHAT TIRED AND NOT VERY ATTENTIVE... HAD I KNOWN...
HEY! DON'T WORRY ABOUT IT! YOU SHOULD TAKE CARE OF YOURSELF.
HERE... LET ME GET YOU A COLD DRINK, OKAY?
BUT... UM...
IT'S *NO PROBLEM!*
ダッ

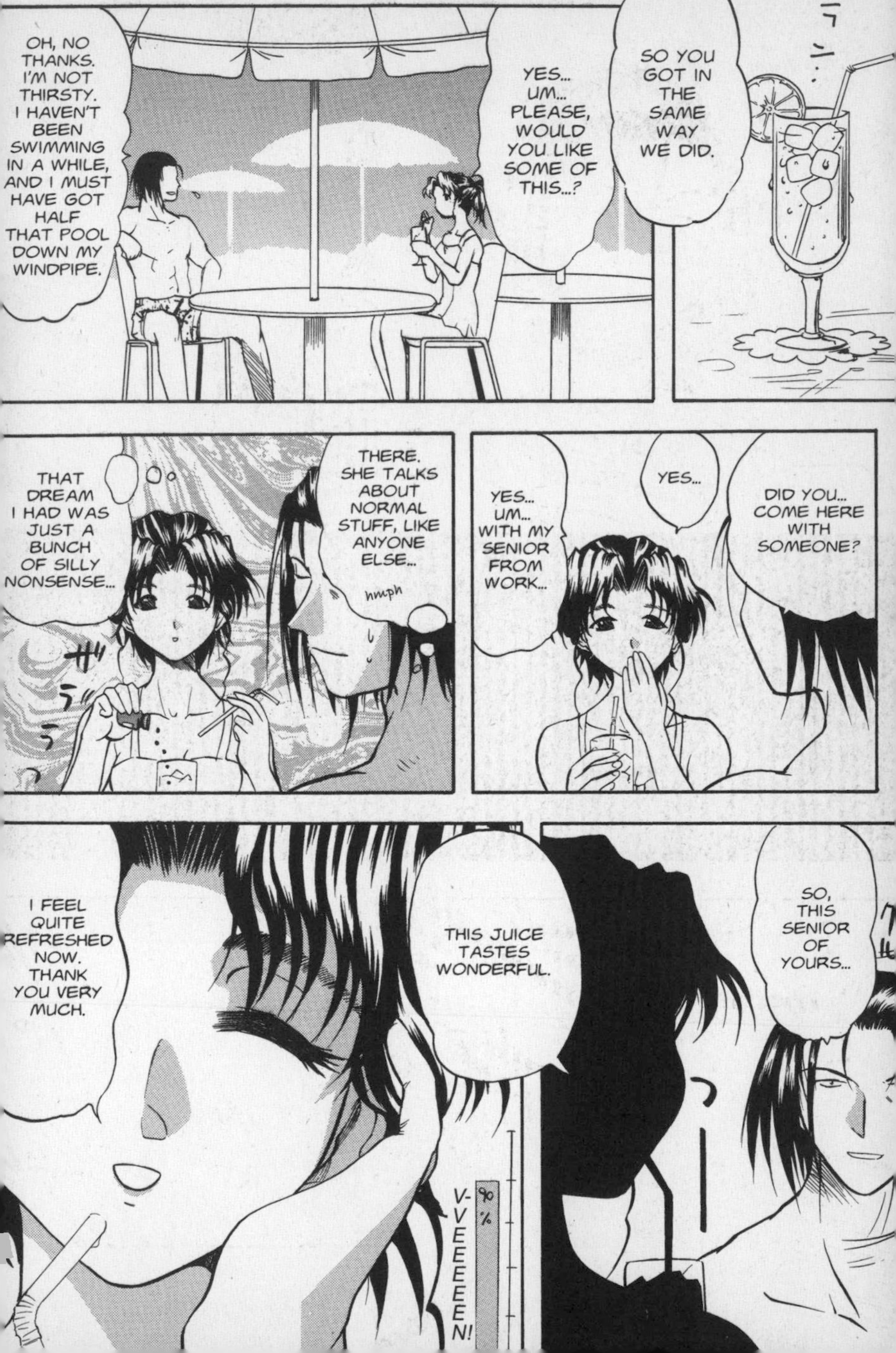
SO YOU GOT IN THE SAME WAY WE DID.
YES... UM... PLEASE, WOULD YOU LIKE SOME OF THIS...?
OH, NO THANKS. I'M NOT THIRSTY. I HAVEN'T BEEN SWIMMING IN A WHILE, AND I MUST HAVE GOT HALF THAT POOL DOWN MY WINDPIPE.
DID YOU... COME HERE WITH SOMEONE?
YES...
YES... UM... WITH MY SENIOR FROM WORK...
THERE. SHE TALKS ABOUT NORMAL STUFF, LIKE ANYONE ELSE...
hmph
THAT DREAM I HAD WAS JUST A BUNCH OF SILLY NONSENSE...
SO, THIS SENIOR OF YOURS...
THIS JUICE TASTES WONDERFUL.
V-VEEEEEEN!
90%
I FEEL QUITE REFRESHED NOW. THANK YOU VERY MUCH.

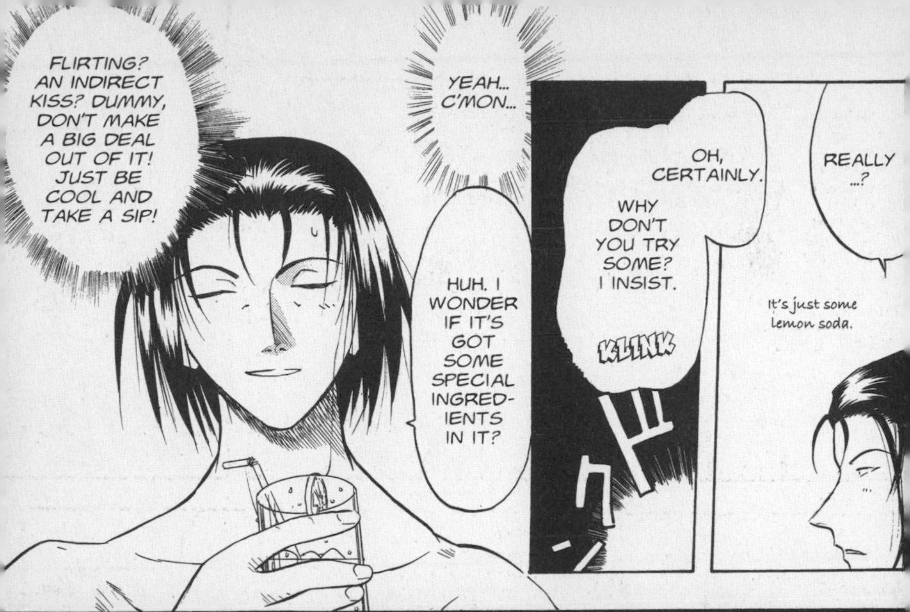
REALLY ...?
It's just some lemon soda.
OH, CERTAINLY.
WHY DON'T YOU TRY SOME? I INSIST.
KLINK
YEAH... C'MON...
HUH. I WONDER IF IT'S GOT SOME SPECIAL INGREDIENTS IN IT?
FLIRTING? AN INDIRECT KISS? DUMMY, DON'T MAKE A BIG DEAL OUT OF IT! JUST BE COOL AND TAKE A SIP!

[redacted]

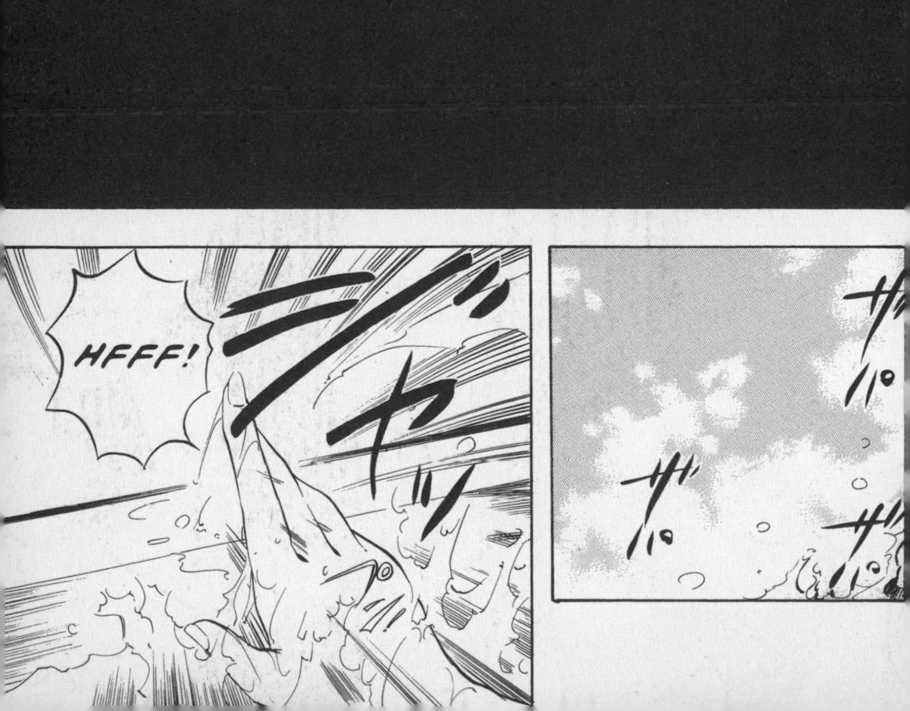
HFFF!

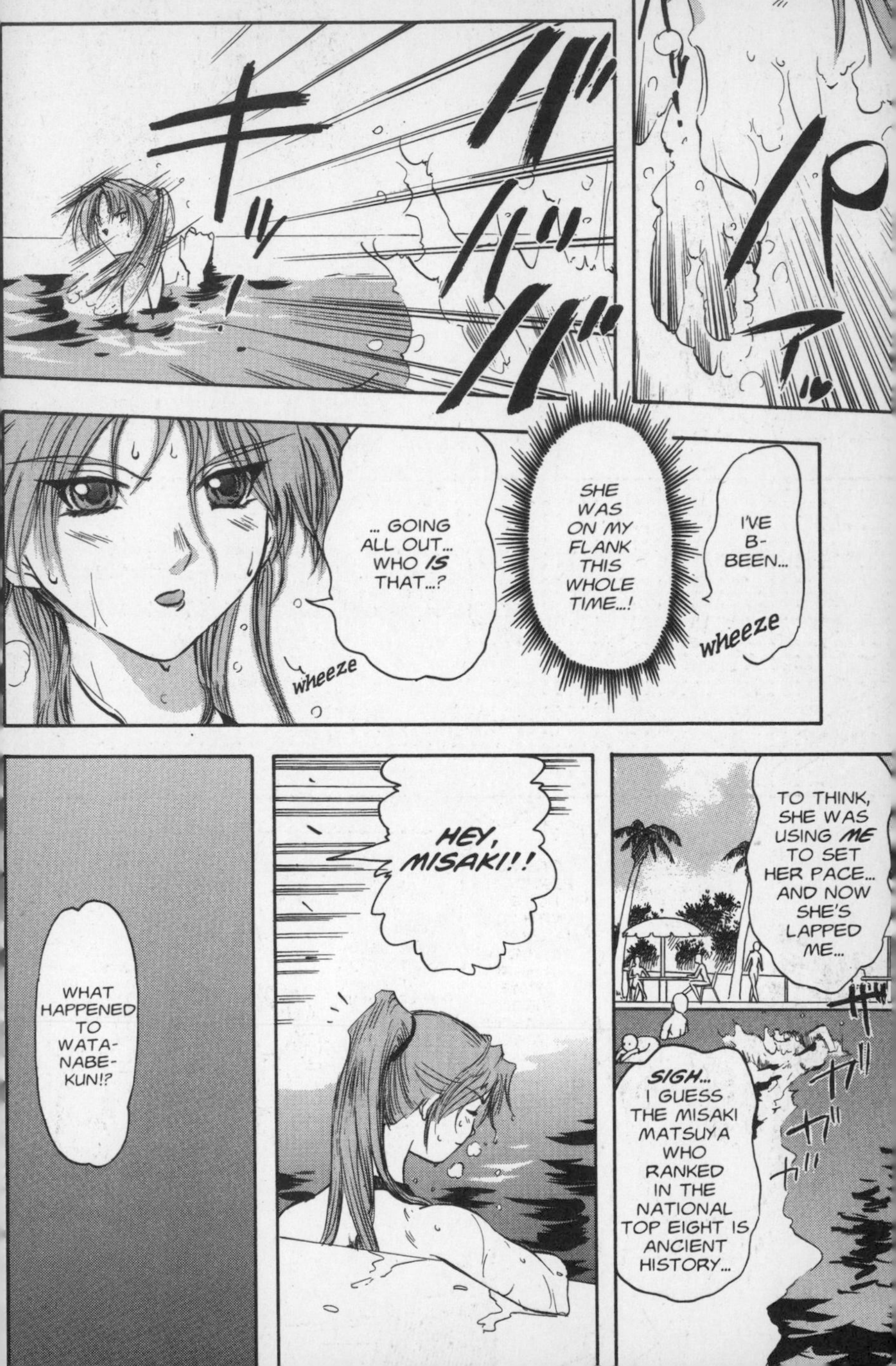
I'VE B-BEEN...
wheeze
SHE WAS ON MY FLANK THIS WHOLE TIME...!
... GOING ALL OUT... WHO IS THAT...?
wheeze
TO THINK, SHE WAS USING ME TO SET HER PACE... AND NOW SHE'S LAPPED ME...
SIGH... I GUESS THE MISAKI MATSUYA WHO RANKED IN THE NATIONAL TOP EIGHT IS ANCIENT HISTORY...
HEY, MISAKI!!
WHAT HAPPENED TO WATA-NABE-KUN!?

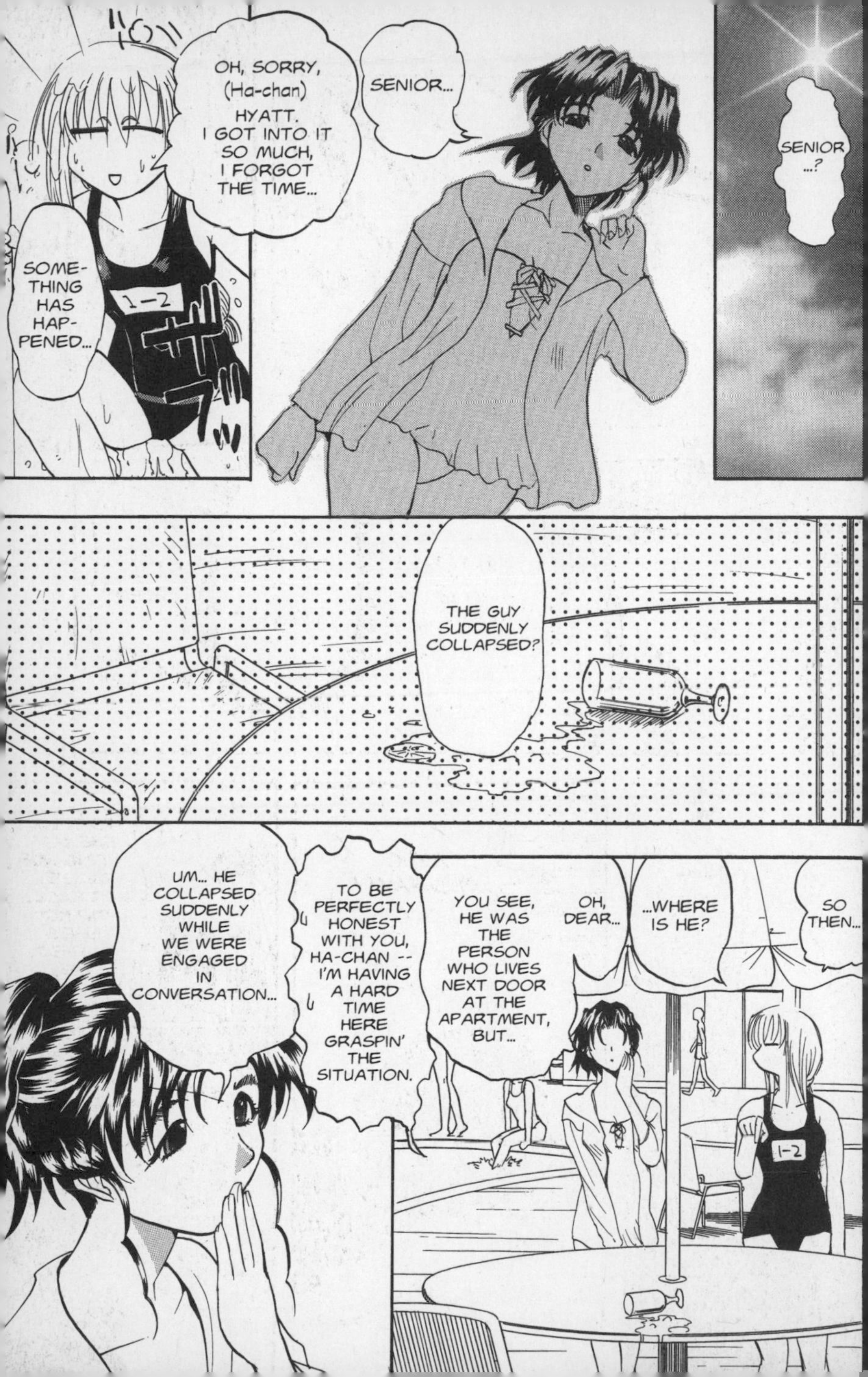
SENIOR ...?
SENIOR...
OH, SORRY, (Ha-chan) HYATT. I GOT INTO IT SO MUCH, I FORGOT THE TIME...
SOME-THING HAS HAP-PENED...
THE GUY SUDDENLY COLLAPSED?
SO THEN...
...WHERE IS HE?
OH, DEAR...
YOU SEE, HE WAS THE PERSON WHO LIVES NEXT DOOR AT THE APARTMENT, BUT...
TO BE PERFECTLY HONEST WITH YOU, HA-CHAN -- I'M HAVING A HARD TIME HERE GRASPIN' THE SITUATION.
UM... HE COLLAPSED SUDDENLY WHILE WE WERE ENGAGED IN CONVERSATION...

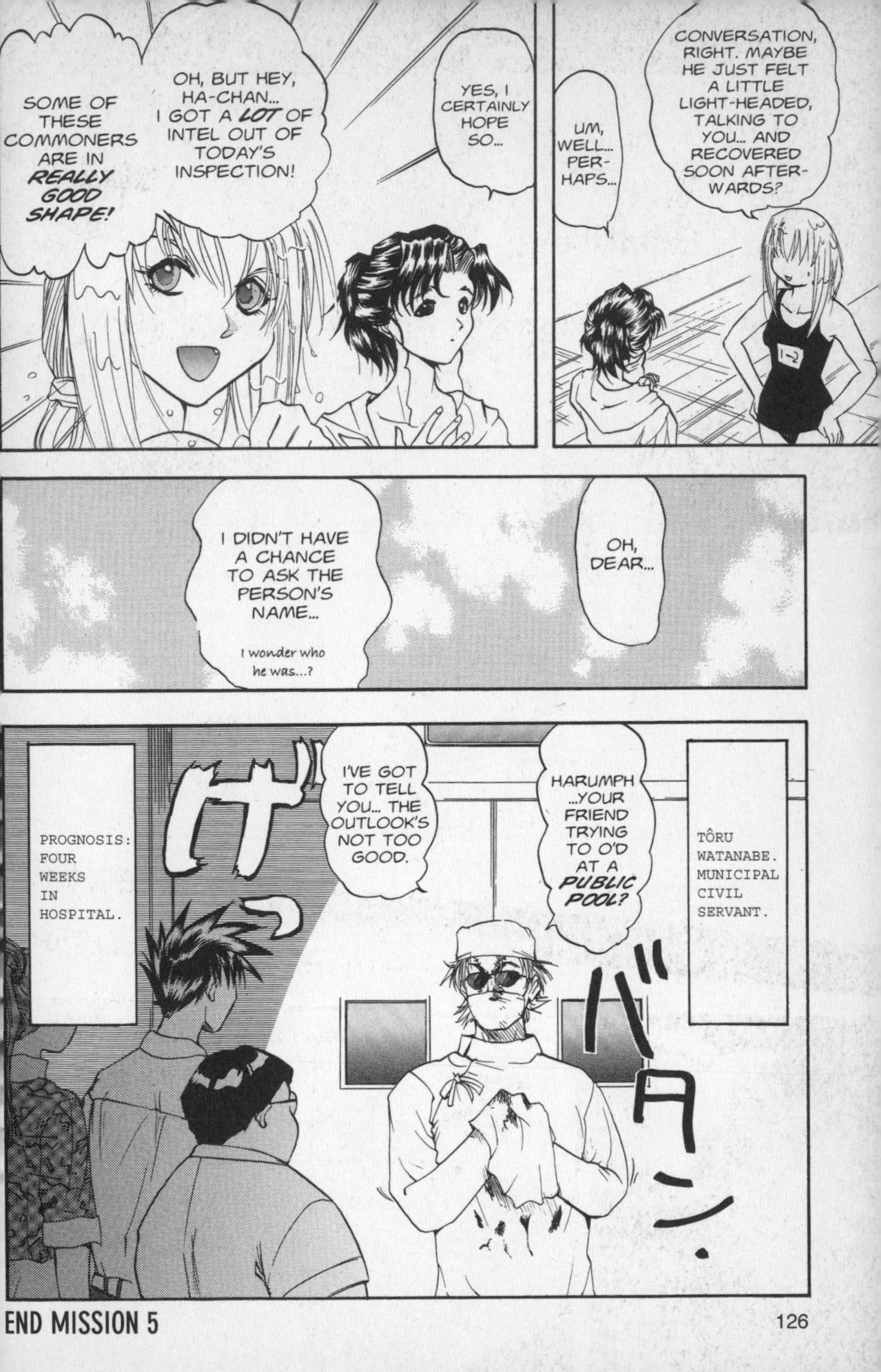
CONVERSATION, RIGHT. MAYBE HE JUST FELT A LITTLE LIGHT-HEADED, TALKING TO YOU... AND RECOVERED SOON AFTER-WARDS?
UM, WELL... PER-HAPS...
YES, I CERTAINLY HOPE SO...
OH, BUT HEY, HA-CHAN... I GOT A LOT OF INTEL OUT OF TODAY'S INSPECTION!
SOME OF THESE COMMONERS ARE IN REALLY GOOD SHAPE!
1-2
OH, DEAR...
I DIDN'T HAVE A CHANCE TO ASK THE PERSON'S NAME...
I wonder who he was...?
TÔRU WATANABE. MUNICIPAL CIVIL SERVANT.
バタン
HARUMPH ...YOUR FRIEND TRYING TO O'D AT A PUBLIC POOL?
I'VE GOT TO TELL YOU... THE OUTLOOK'S NOT TOO GOOD.
PROGNOSIS: FOUR WEEKS IN HOSPITAL.

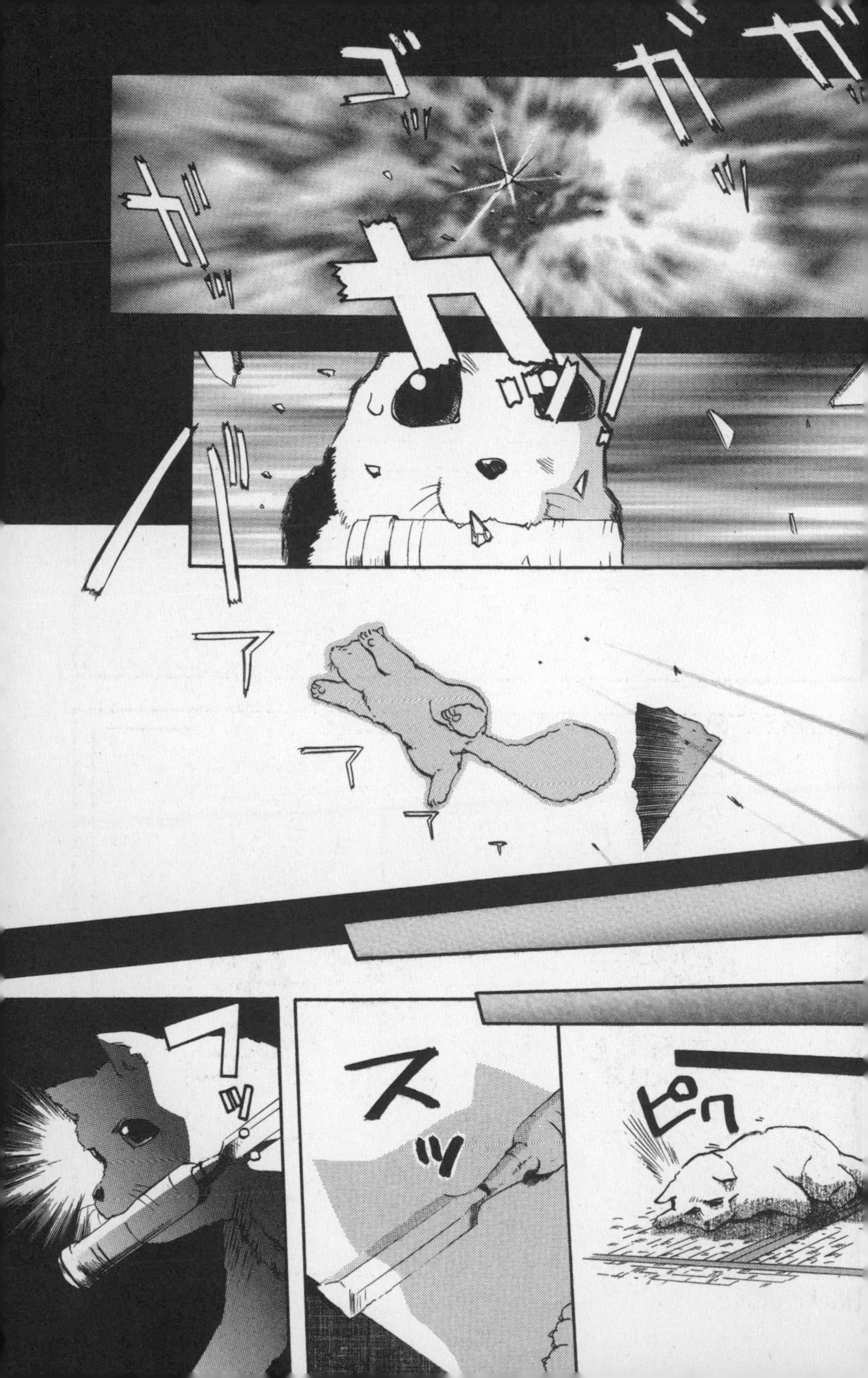
ガガッ
ゴッ
ガッ
カッ
アアアァ
ピク
スッ
フッ

MISSION 6
INTO THE LABYRINTH

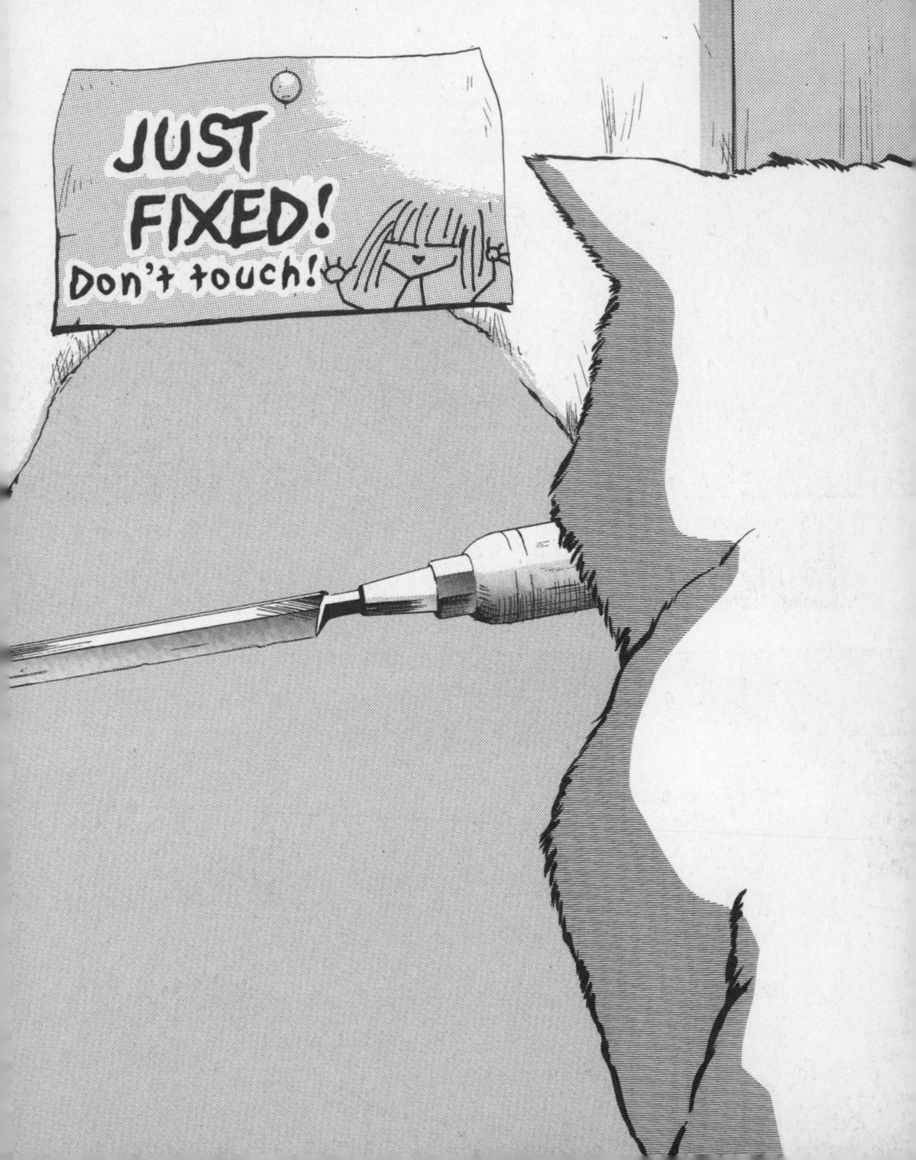
JUST FIXED!
Don't touch!

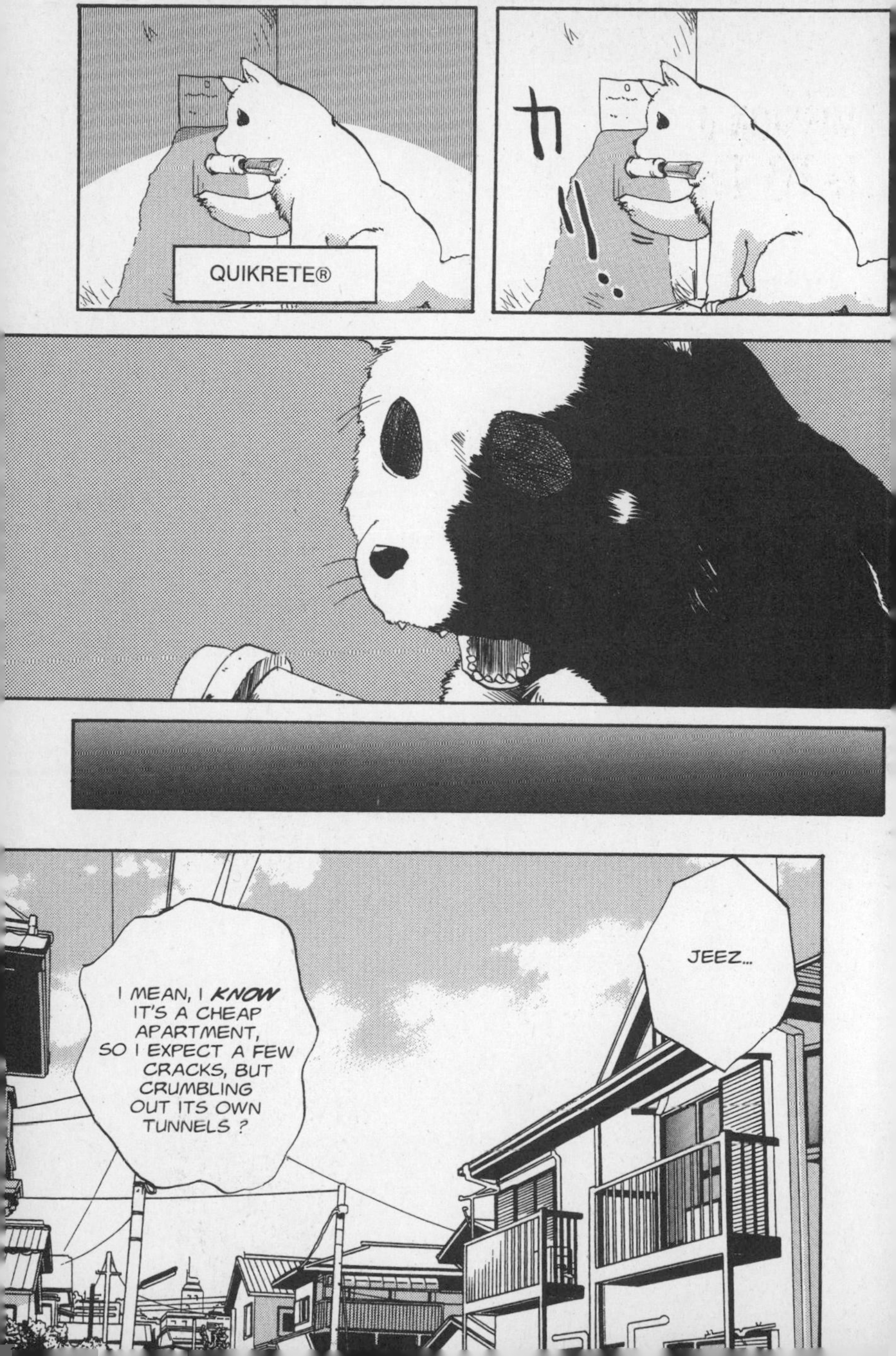
カリ
QUIKRETE®
JEEZ...
I MEAN, I *KNOW* IT'S A CHEAP APARTMENT, SO I EXPECT A FEW CRACKS, BUT CRUMBLING OUT ITS OWN TUNNELS ?

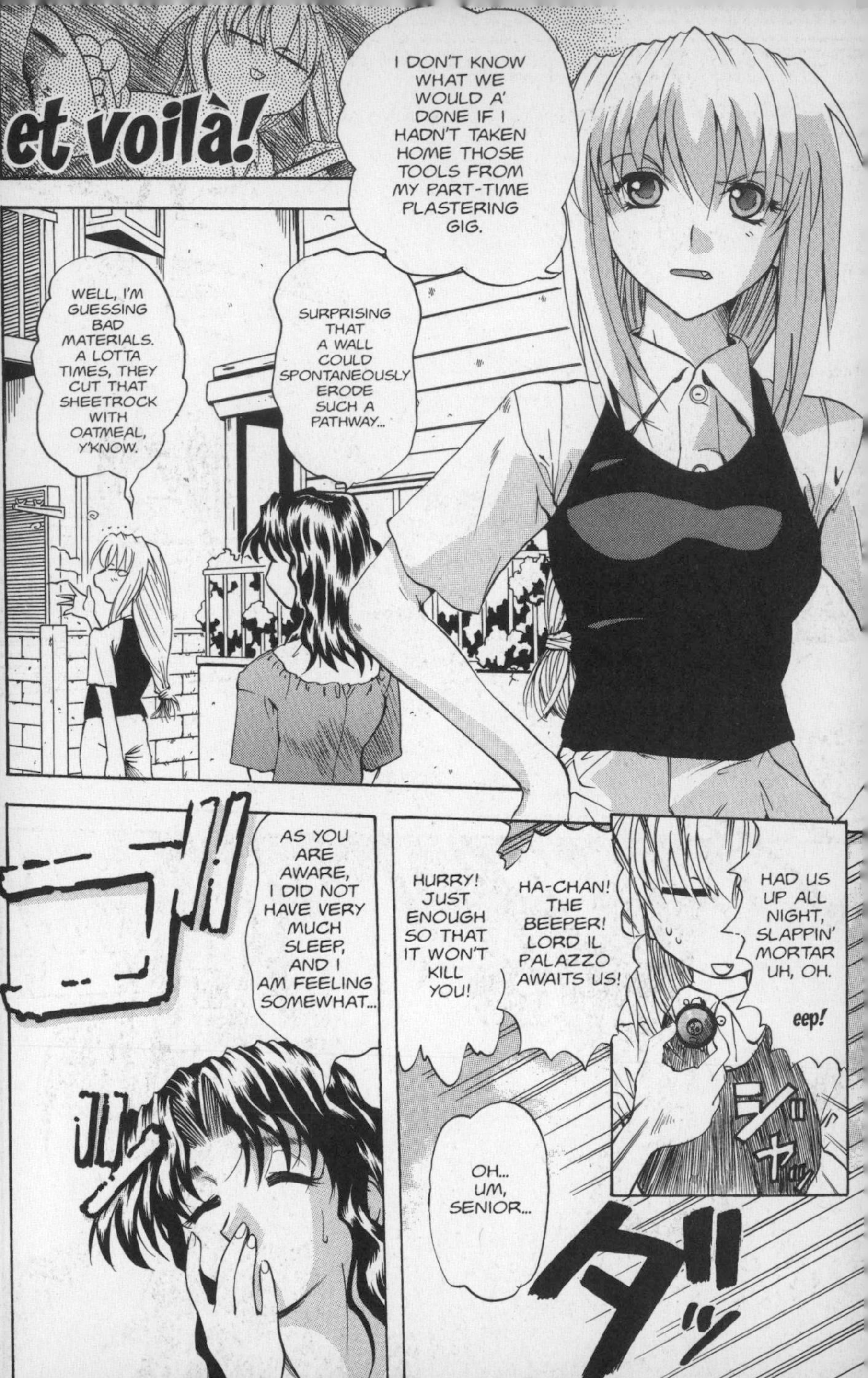
et voilà!
I DON'T KNOW WHAT WE WOULD A' DONE IF I HADN'T TAKEN HOME THOSE TOOLS FROM MY PART-TIME PLASTERING GIG.
SURPRISING THAT A WALL COULD SPONTANEOUSLY ERODE SUCH A PATHWAY...
WELL, I'M GUESSING BAD MATERIALS. A LOTTA TIMES, THEY CUT THAT SHEETROCK WITH OATMEAL, Y'KNOW.
HAD US UP ALL NIGHT, SLAPPIN' MORTAR UH, OH.
eep!
HA-CHAN! THE BEEPER! LORD IL PALAZZO AWAITS US!
HURRY! JUST ENOUGH SO THAT IT WON'T KILL YOU!
OH... UM, SENIOR...
AS YOU ARE AWARE, I DID NOT HAVE VERY MUCH SLEEP, AND I AM FEELING SOMEWHAT...

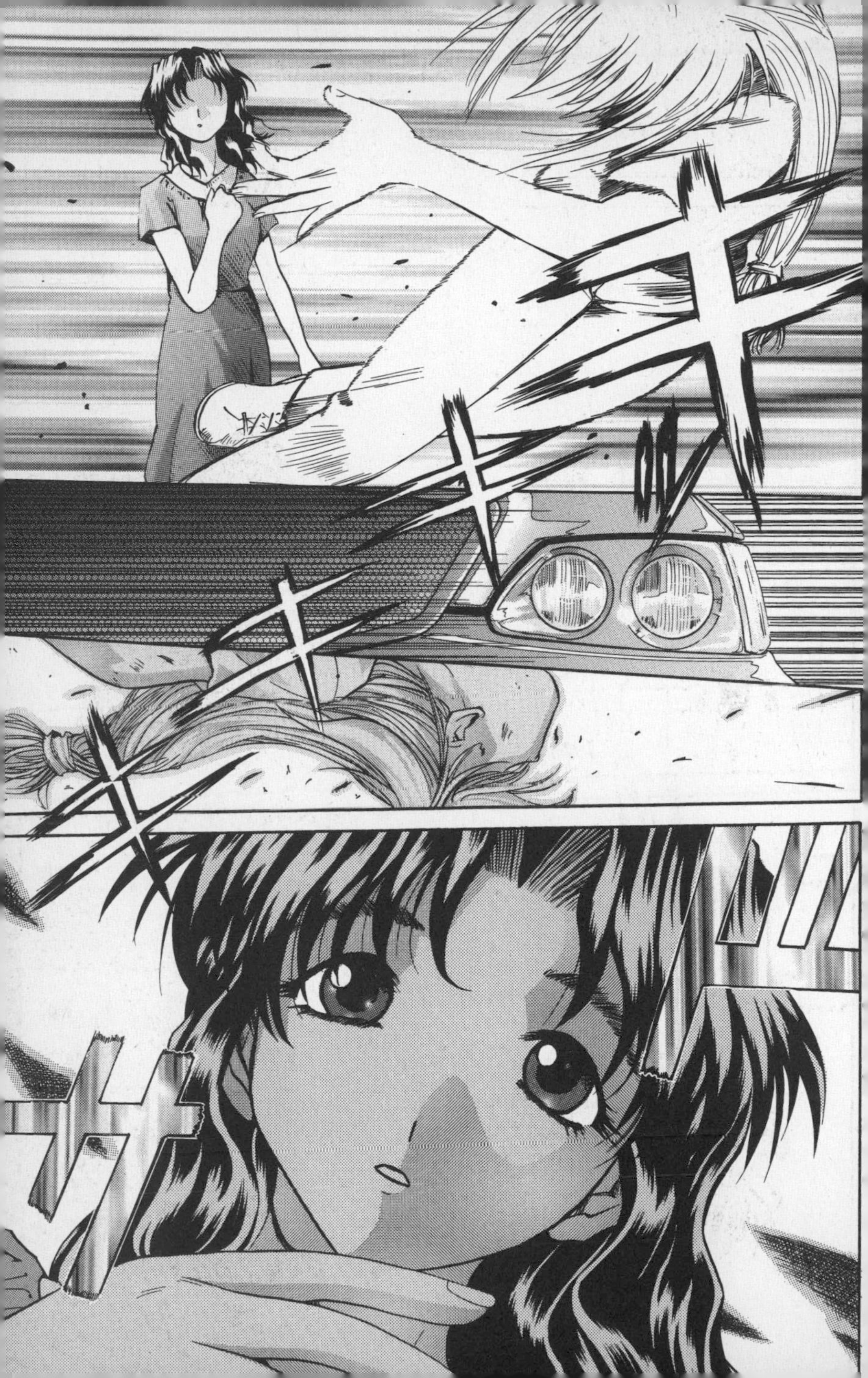

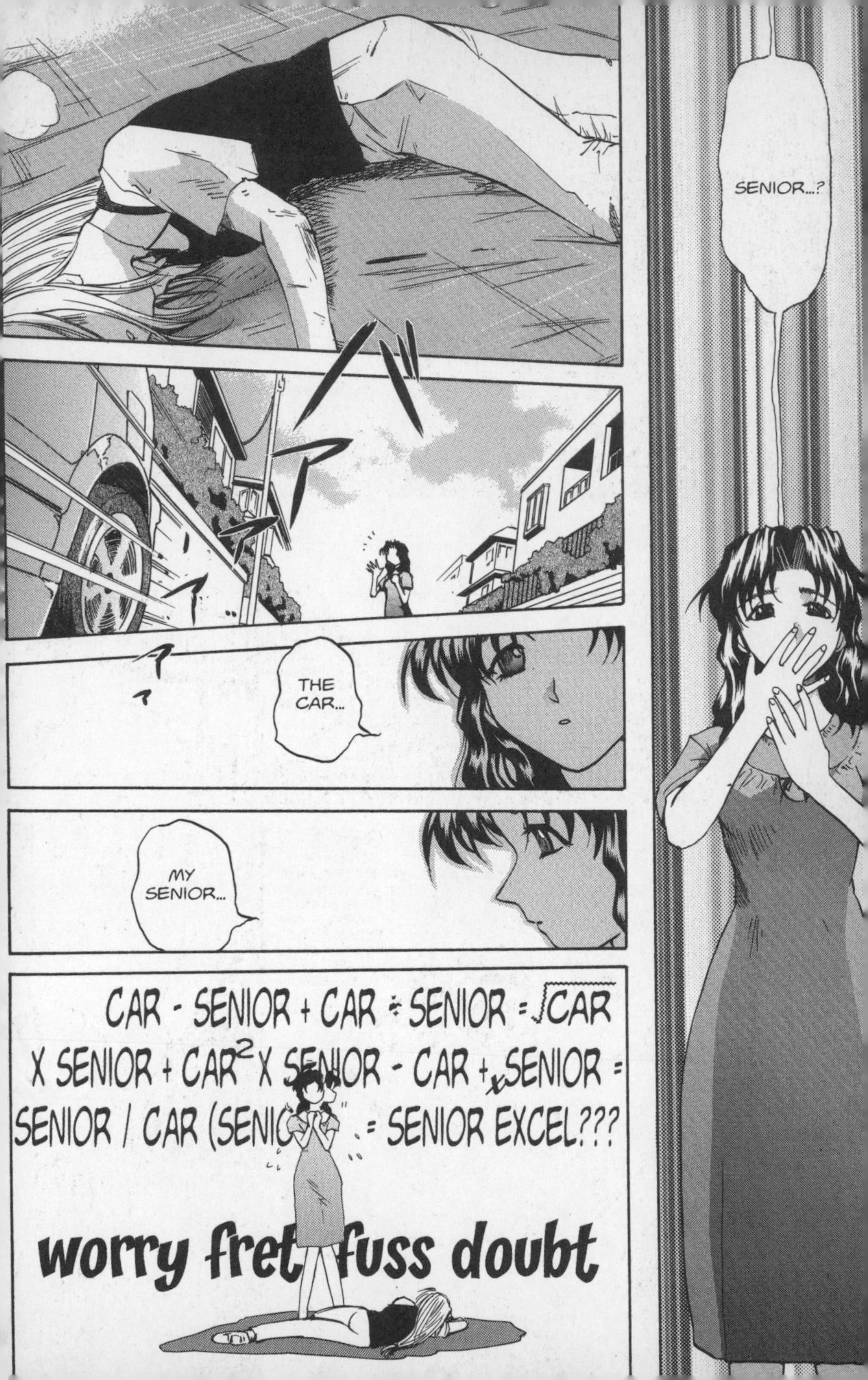
SENIOR...?
THE CAR...
MY SENIOR...
CAR - SENIOR + CAR ÷ SENIOR = √CAR
X SENIOR + CAR^{2} X SENIOR - CAR + SENIOR =
= SENIOR EXCEL???
worry fret fuss doubt

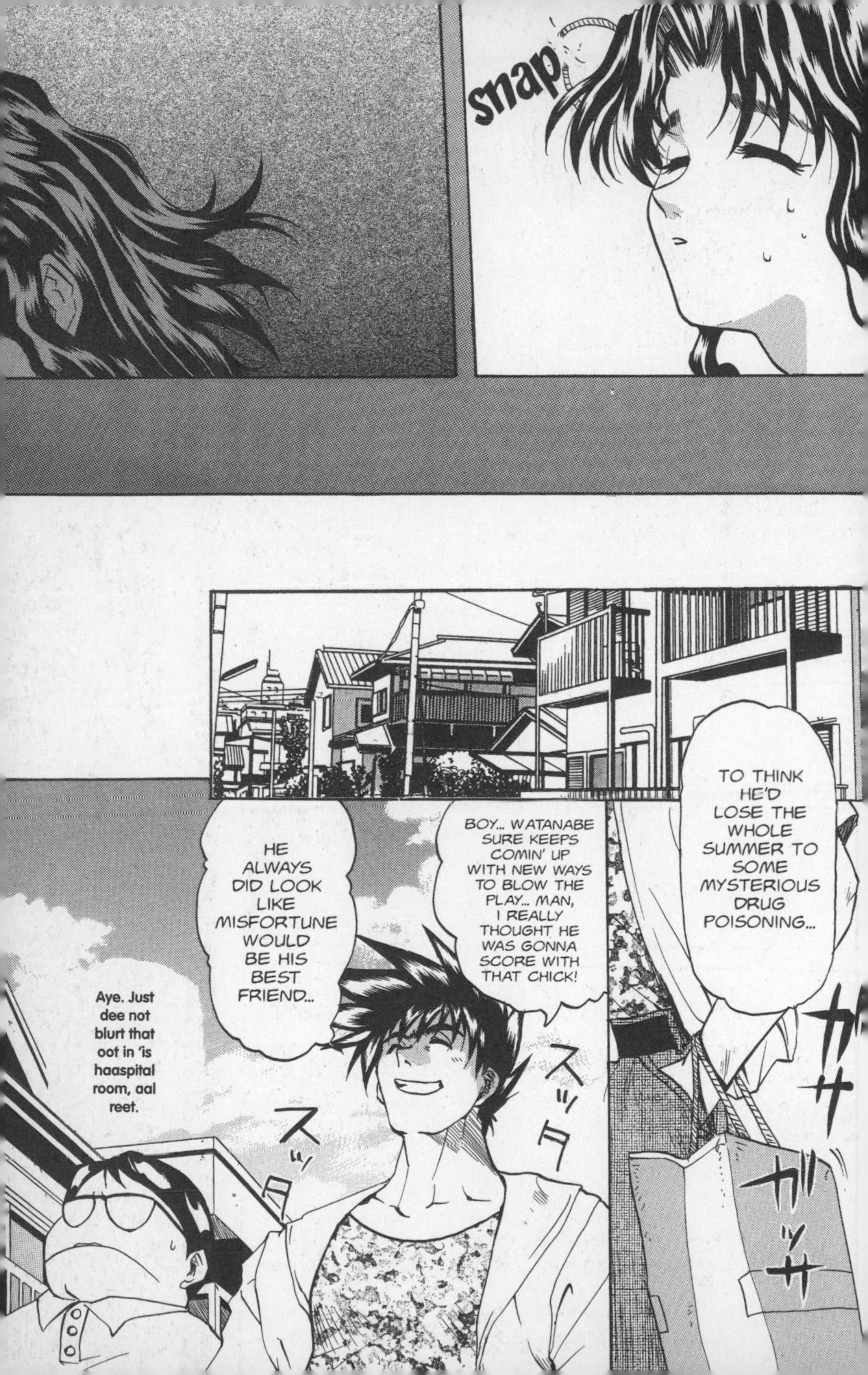
snap
TO THINK HE'D LOSE THE WHOLE SUMMER TO SOME MYSTERIOUS DRUG POISONING...
ガサ
ガッサ
BOY... WATANABE SURE KEEPS COMIN' UP WITH NEW WAYS TO BLOW THE PLAY... MAN, I REALLY THOUGHT HE WAS GONNA SCORE WITH THAT CHICK!
スッタ
HE ALWAYS DID LOOK LIKE MISFORTUNE WOULD BE HIS BEST FRIEND...
スッタ
Aye. Just dee not blurt that oot in 'is haaspital room, aal reet.

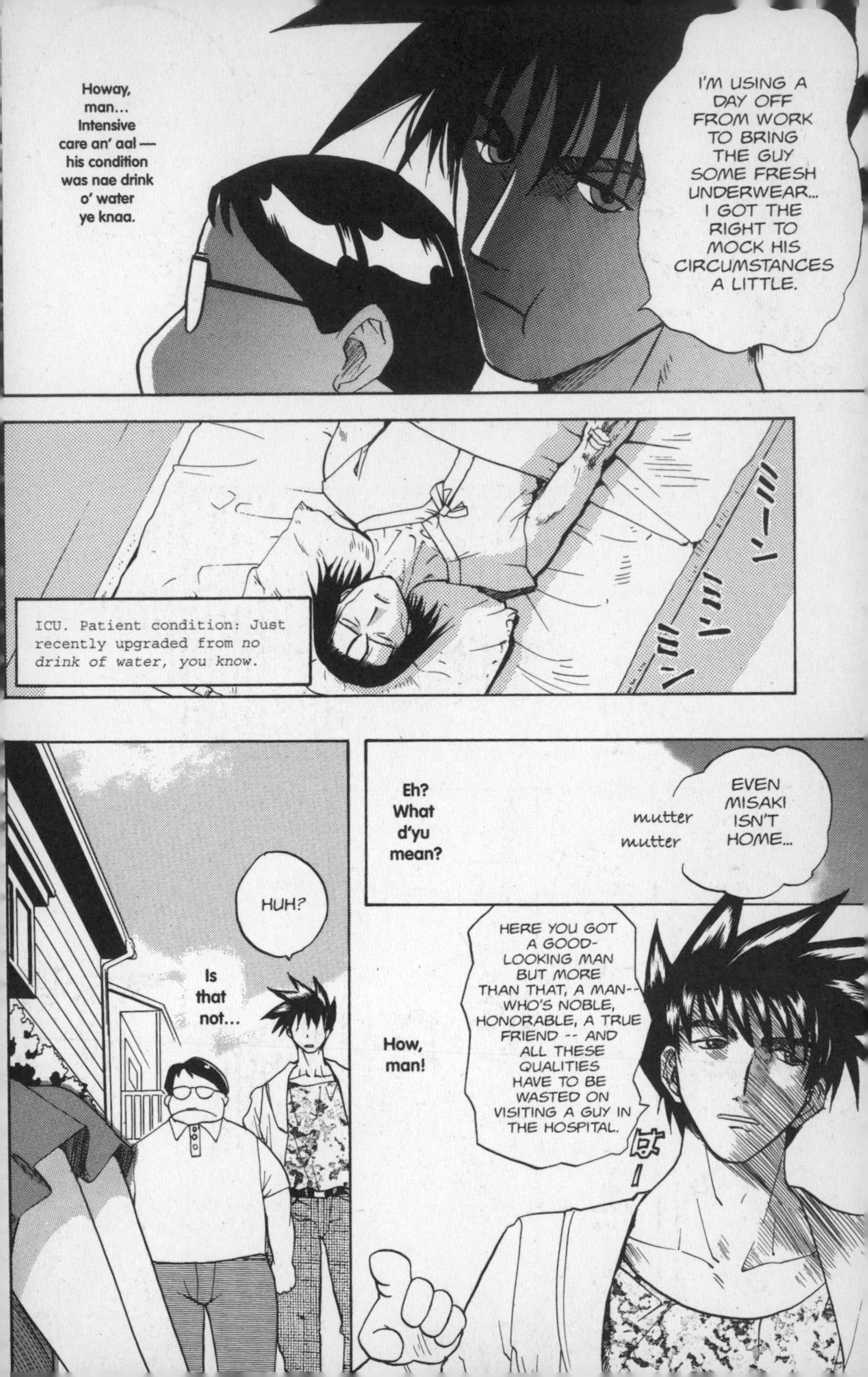

I'M USING A DAY OFF FROM WORK TO BRING THE GUY SOME FRESH UNDERWEAR... I GOT THE RIGHT TO MOCK HIS CIRCUMSTANCES A LITTLE.
Howay, man... Intensive care an' aal — his condition was nae drink o' water ye knaa.
ICU. Patient condition: Just recently upgraded from *no drink of water, you know.*
EVEN MISAKI ISN'T HOME...
mutter mutter
Eh? What d'yu mean?
HERE YOU GOT A GOOD-LOOKING MAN BUT MORE THAN THAT, A MAN-- WHO'S NOBLE, HONORABLE, A TRUE FRIEND -- AND ALL THESE QUALITIES HAVE TO BE WASTED ON VISITING A GUY IN THE HOSPITAL.
How, man!
HUH?
Is that not...

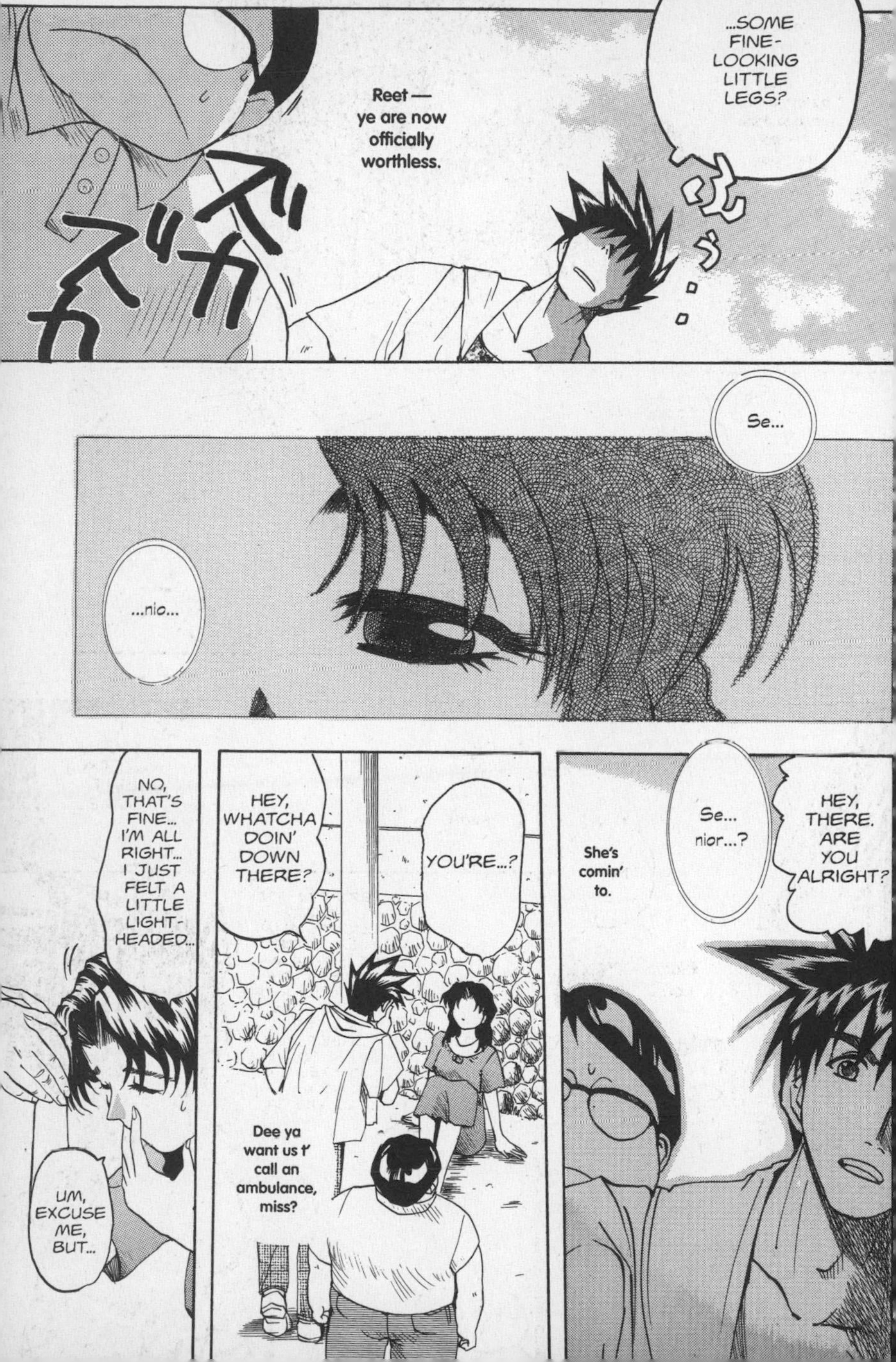
...SOME FINE-LOOKING LITTLE LEGS?
Reet — ye are now officially worthless.
Se...
...nio...
HEY, THERE. ARE YOU ALRIGHT?
Se... nior...?
She's comin' to.
YOU'RE...?
HEY, WHATCHA DOIN' DOWN THERE?
Dee ya want us t' call an ambulance, miss?
NO, THAT'S FINE... I'M ALL RIGHT... I JUST FELT A LITTLE LIGHT-HEADED...
UM, EXCUSE ME, BUT...

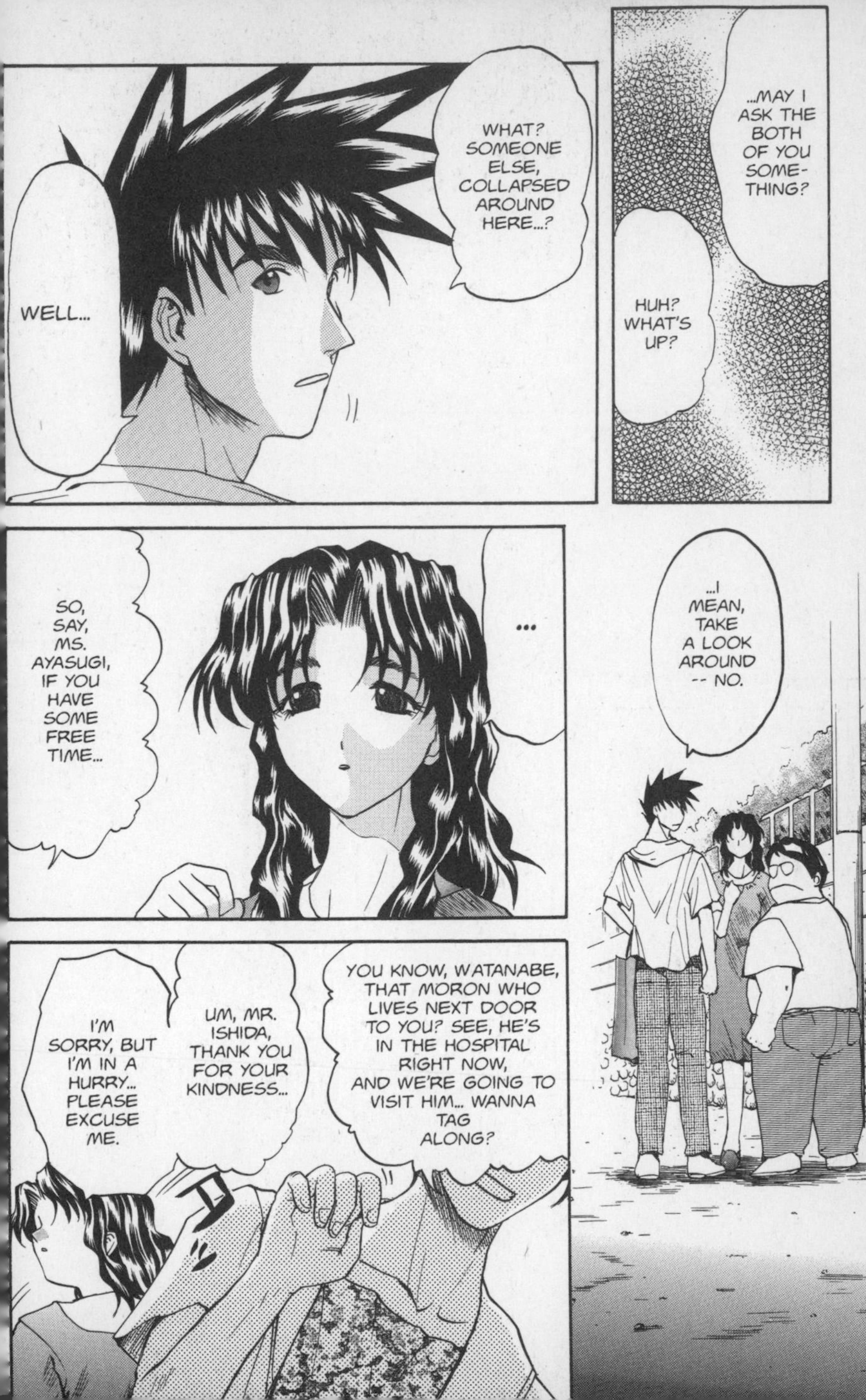
...MAY I ASK THE BOTH OF YOU SOME-THING?
HUH? WHAT'S UP?
WHAT? SOMEONE ELSE, COLLAPSED AROUND HERE...?
WELL...
...I MEAN, TAKE A LOOK AROUND -- NO.
...
SO, SAY, MS. AYASUGI, IF YOU HAVE SOME FREE TIME...
YOU KNOW, WATANABE, THAT MORON WHO LIVES NEXT DOOR TO YOU? SEE, HE'S IN THE HOSPITAL RIGHT NOW, AND WE'RE GOING TO VISIT HIM... WANNA TAG ALONG?
UM, MR. ISHIDA, THANK YOU FOR YOUR KINDNESS...
I'M SORRY, BUT I'M IN A HURRY... PLEASE EXCUSE ME.

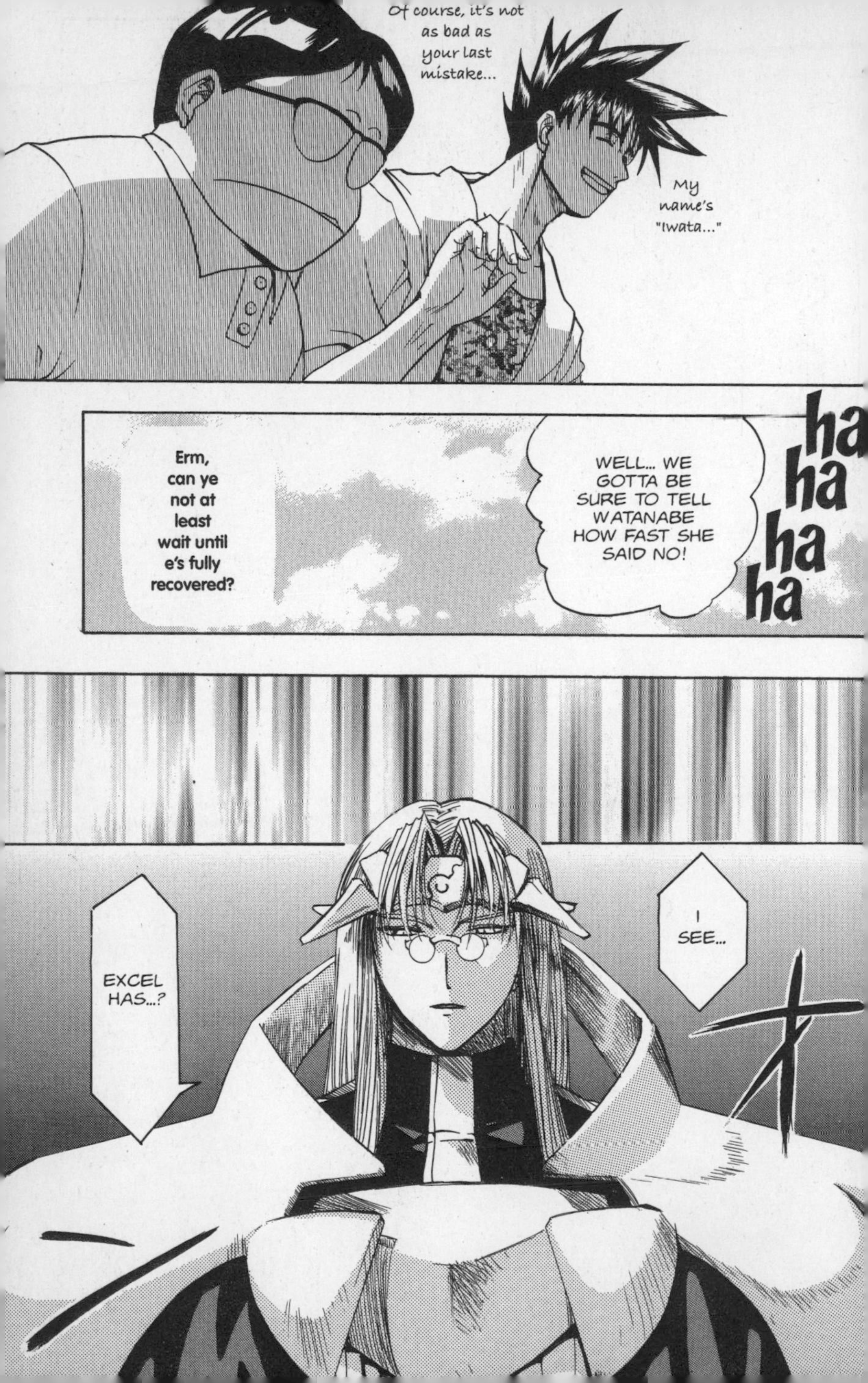
My name's "Iwata..."
Of course, it's not as bad as your last mistake...
hahahaha
WELL... WE GOTTA BE SURE TO TELL WATANABE HOW FAST SHE SAID NO!
Erm, can ye not at least wait until e's fully recovered?
I SEE...
EXCEL HAS...?

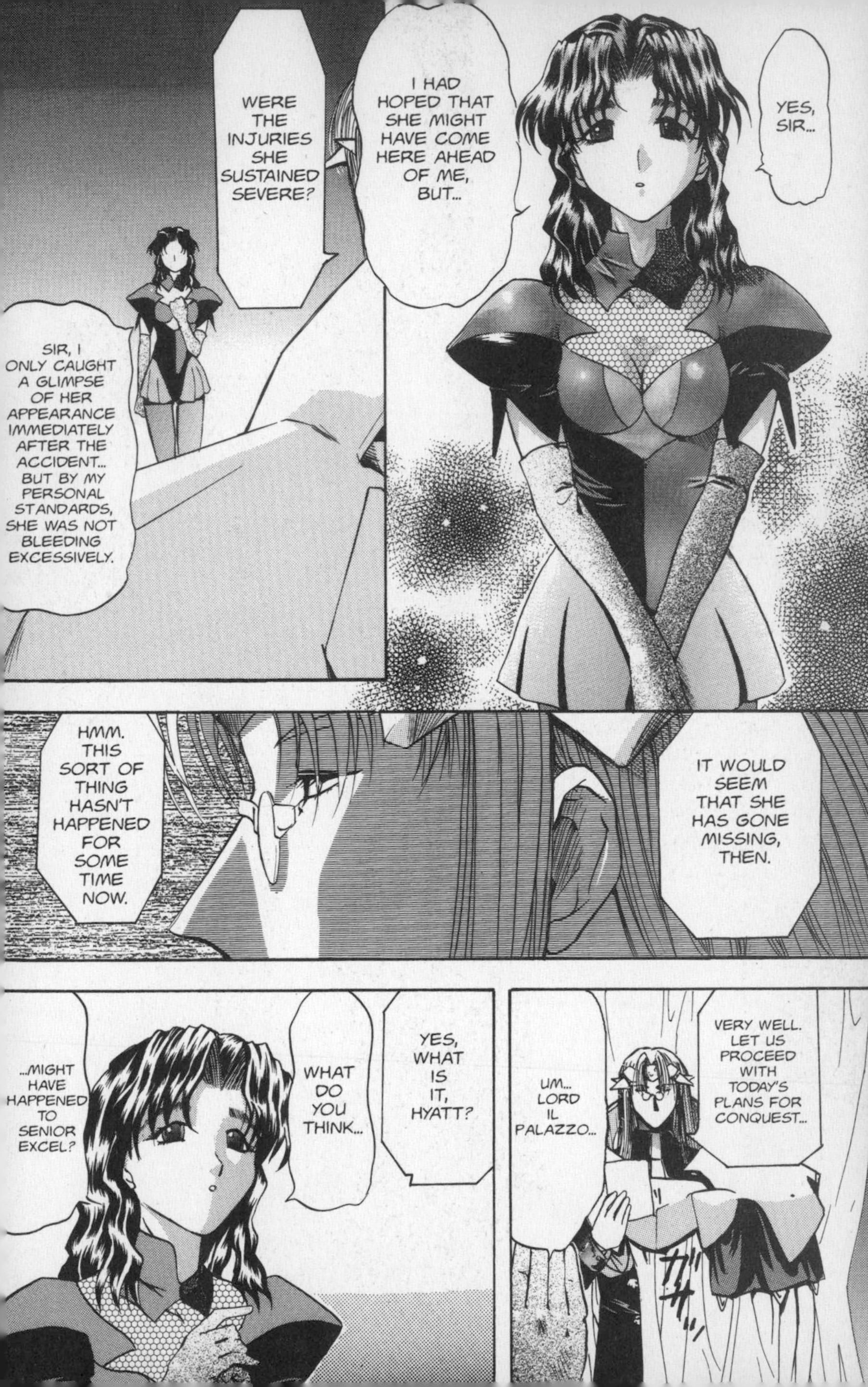
I HAD HOPED THAT SHE MIGHT HAVE COME HERE AHEAD OF ME, BUT...
YES, SIR...
WERE THE INJURIES SHE SUSTAINED SEVERE?
SIR, I ONLY CAUGHT A GLIMPSE OF HER APPEARANCE IMMEDIATELY AFTER THE ACCIDENT... BUT BY MY PERSONAL STANDARDS, SHE WAS NOT BLEEDING EXCESSIVELY.
IT WOULD SEEM THAT SHE HAS GONE MISSING, THEN.
HMM. THIS SORT OF THING HASN'T HAPPENED FOR SOME TIME NOW.
VERY WELL. LET US PROCEED WITH TODAY'S PLANS FOR CONQUEST...
UM... LORD IL PALAZZO...
YES, WHAT IS IT, HYATT?
WHAT DO YOU THINK...
...MIGHT HAVE HAPPENED TO SENIOR EXCEL?

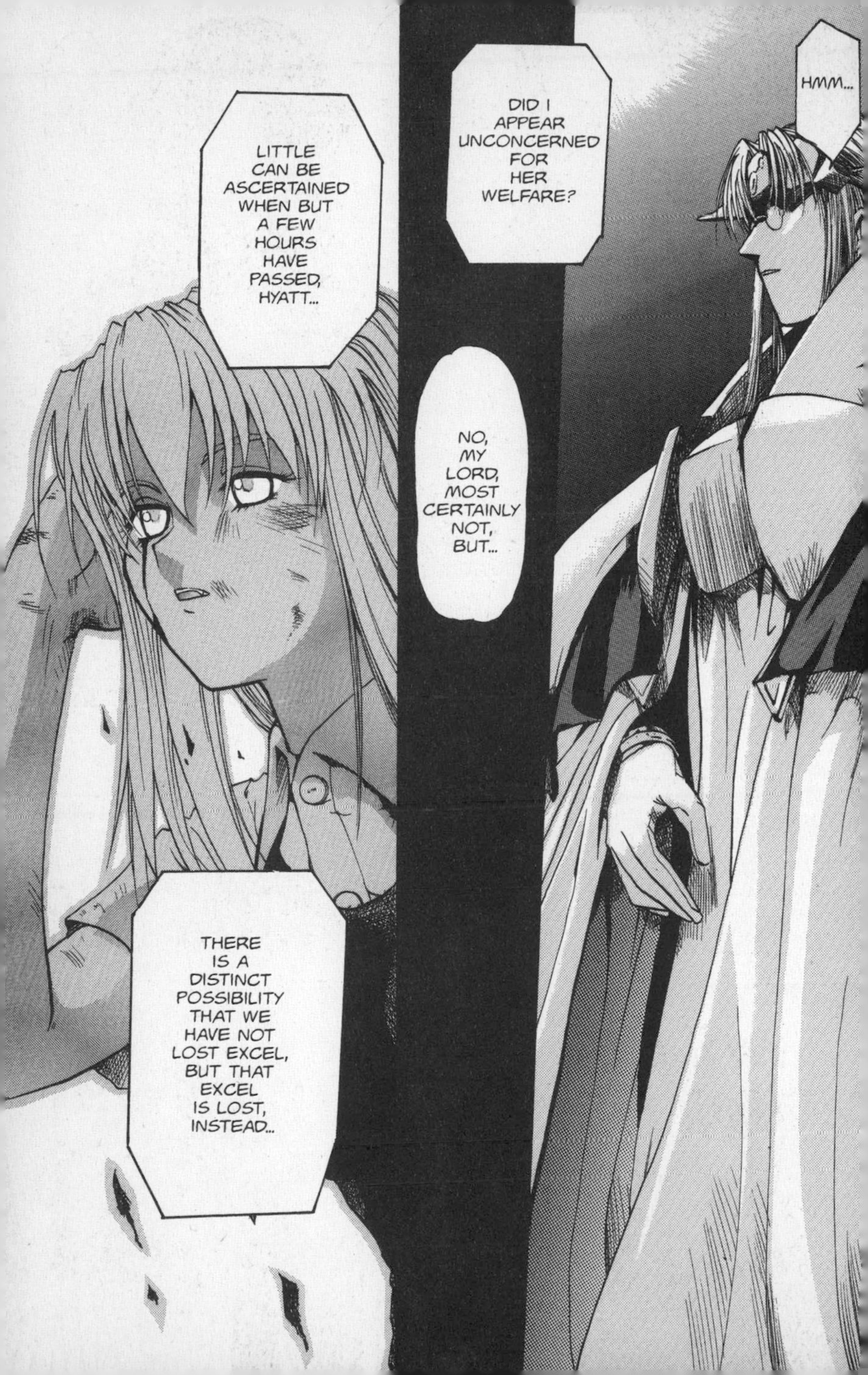
HMM...
DID I APPEAR UNCONCERNED FOR HER WELFARE?
NO, MY LORD, MOST CERTAINLY NOT, BUT...
LITTLE CAN BE ASCERTAINED WHEN BUT A FEW HOURS HAVE PASSED, HYATT...
THERE IS A DISTINCT POSSIBILITY THAT WE HAVE NOT LOST EXCEL, BUT THAT EXCEL IS LOST, INSTEAD...

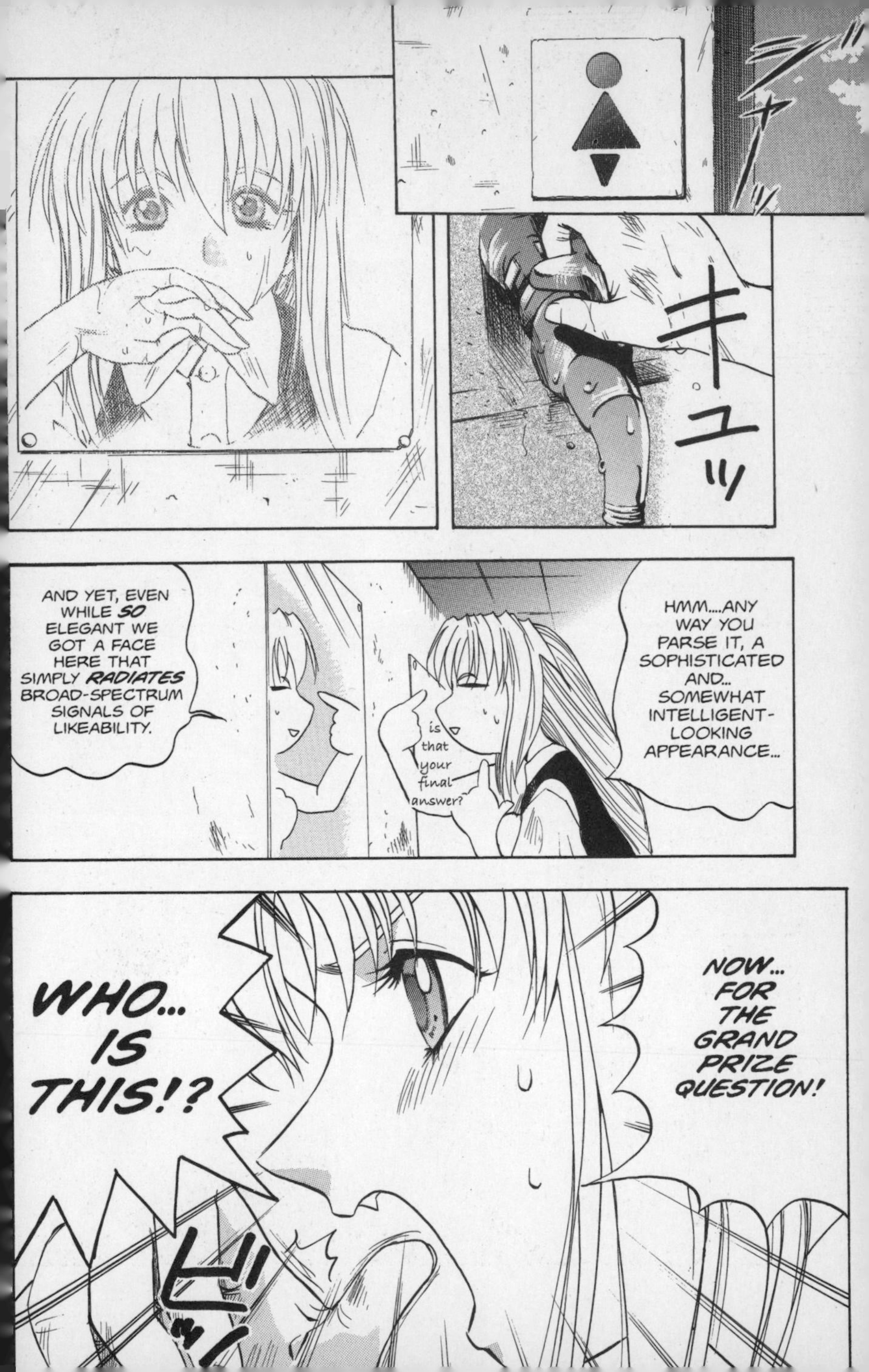
キュッ
HMM....ANY WAY YOU PARSE IT, A SOPHISTICATED AND... SOMEWHAT INTELLIGENT-LOOKING APPEARANCE...
is that your final answer?
AND YET, EVEN WHILE SO ELEGANT WE GOT A FACE HERE THAT SIMPLY RADIATES BROAD-SPECTRUM SIGNALS OF LIKEABILITY.
NOW... FOR THE GRAND PRIZE QUESTION!
WHO... IS THIS!?

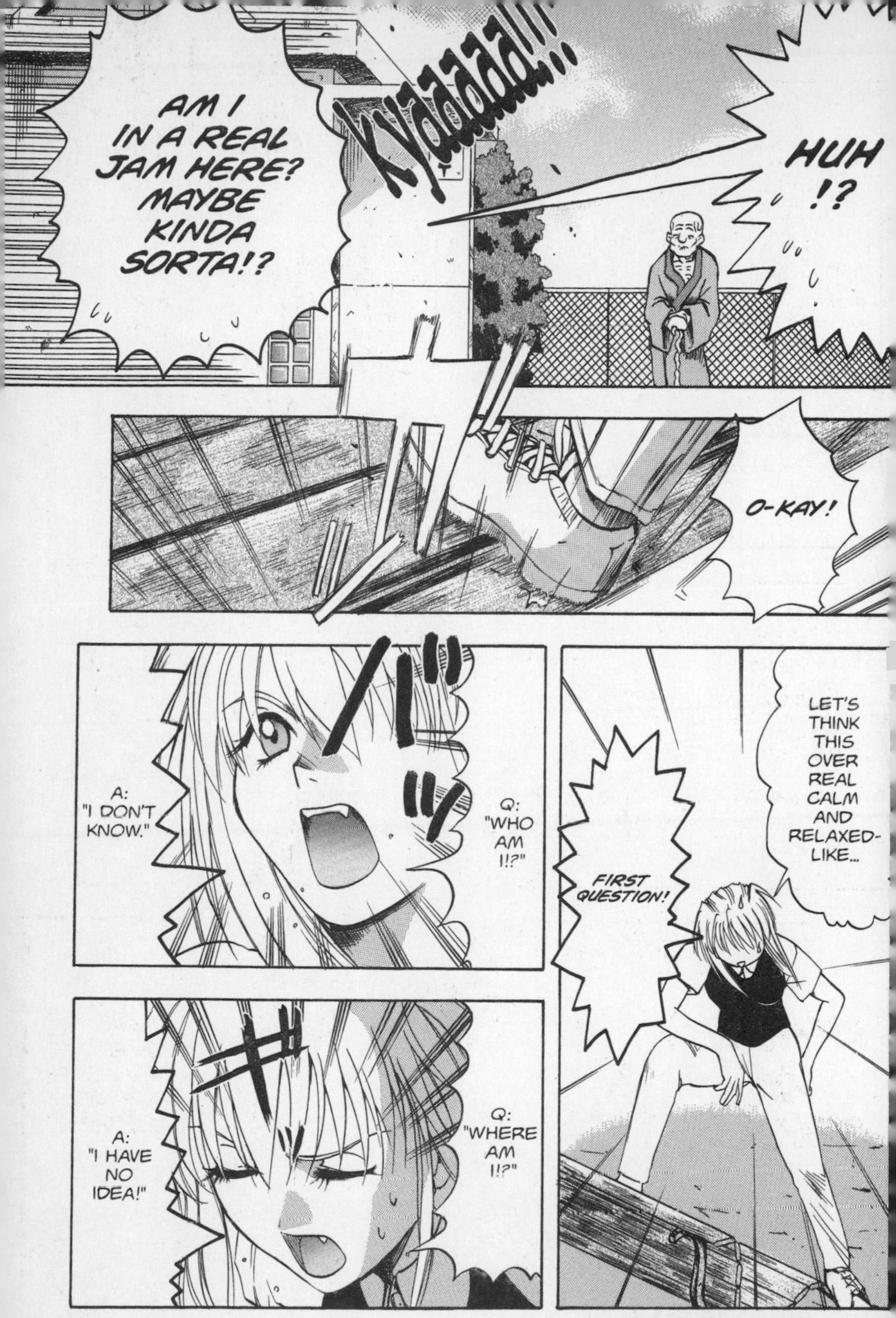
KYAAAAA!!!
HUH !?
AM I IN A REAL JAM HERE? MAYBE KINDA SORTA!?
O-KAY!
LET'S THINK THIS OVER REAL CALM AND RELAXED-LIKE...
FIRST QUESTION!
Q: "WHO AM I!?"
A: "I DON'T KNOW."
Q: "WHERE AM I!?"
A: "I HAVE NO IDEA!"

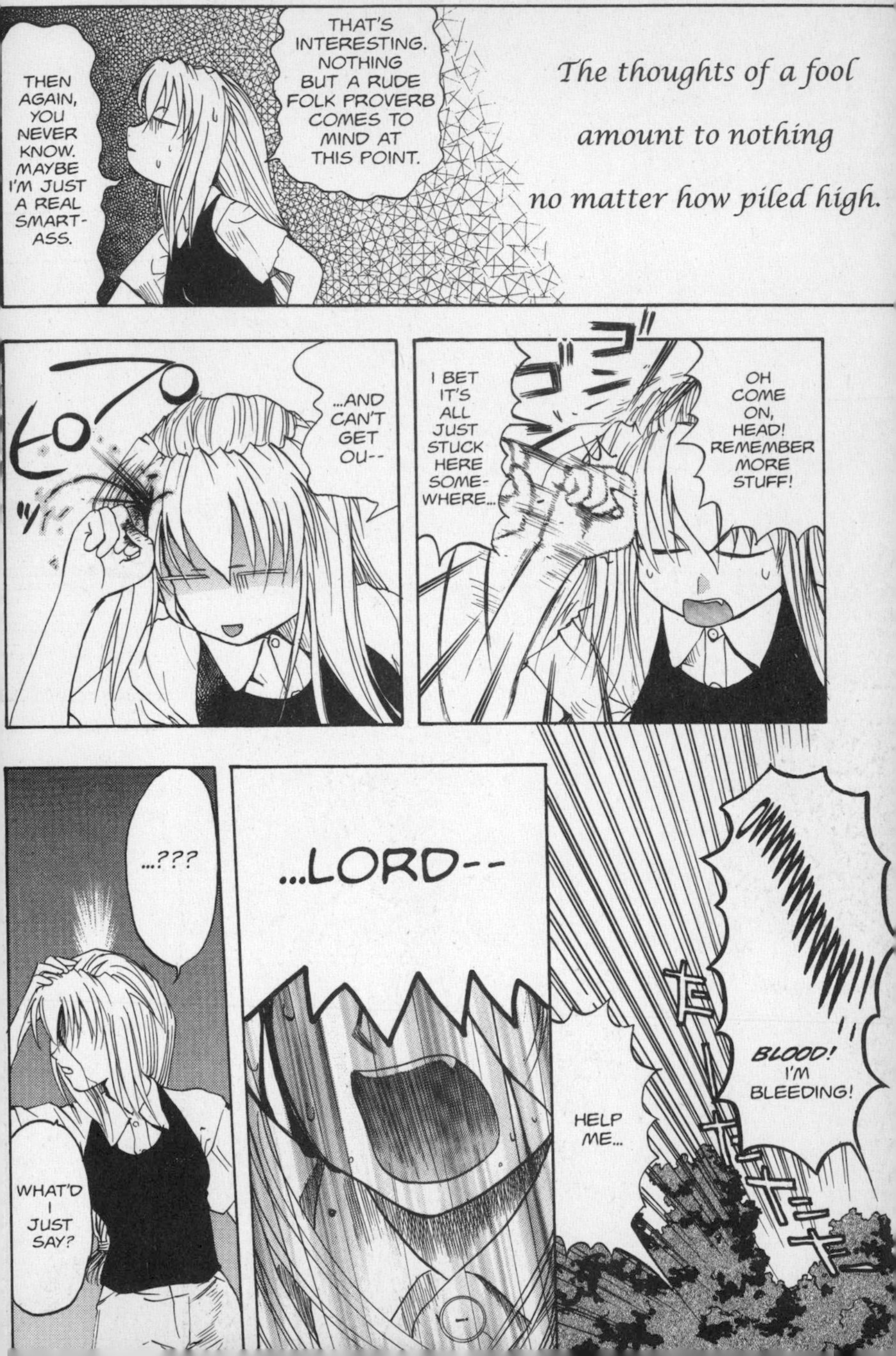
The thoughts of a fool amount to nothing no matter how piled high.
THAT'S INTERESTING. NOTHING BUT A RUDE FOLK PROVERB COMES TO MIND AT THIS POINT.
THEN AGAIN, YOU NEVER KNOW. MAYBE I'M JUST A REAL SMART-ASS.
OH COME ON, HEAD! REMEMBER MORE STUFF!
I BET IT'S ALL JUST STUCK HERE SOMEWHERE...
...AND CAN'T GET OU--
BLOOD! I'M BLEEDING!
HELP ME...
...LORD--
...???
WHAT'D I JUST SAY?

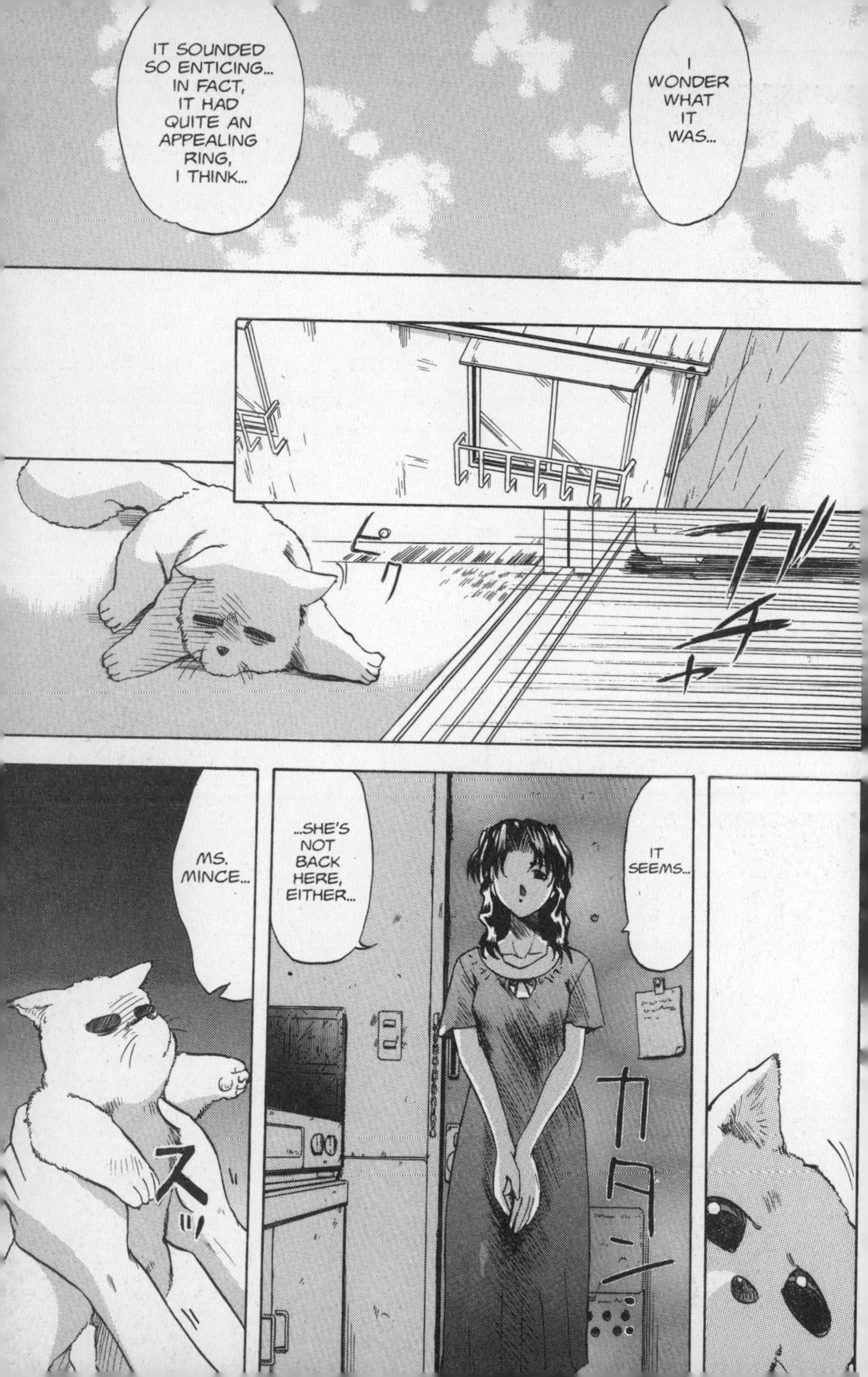
I WONDER WHAT IT WAS...
IT SOUNDED SO ENTICING... IN FACT, IT HAD QUITE AN APPEALING RING, I THINK...
ガチャ
ピク
カタン
IT SEEMS...
...SHE'S NOT BACK HERE, EITHER...
MS. MINCE...
スッ

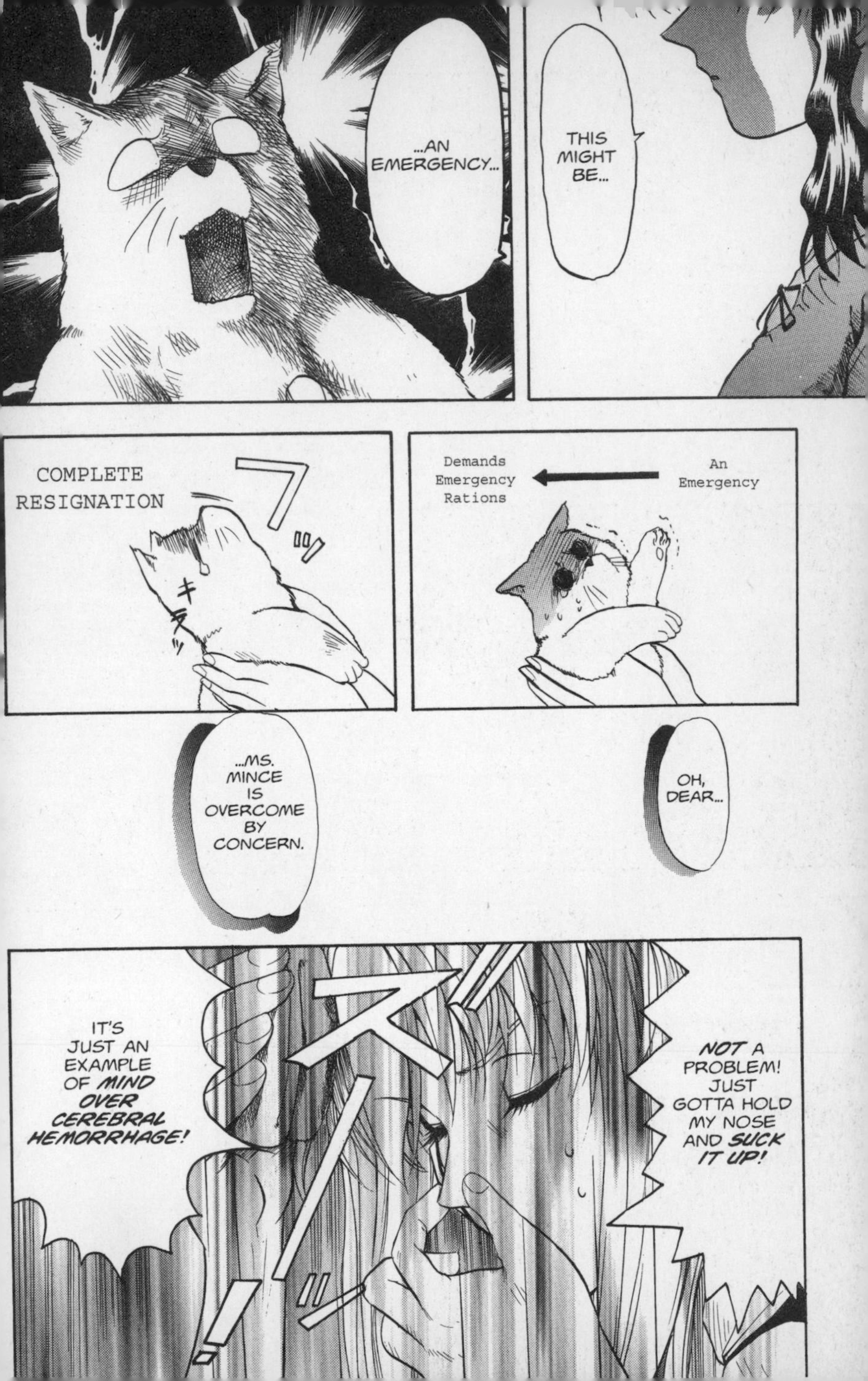

THIS MIGHT BE...
...AN EMERGENCY...
An Emergency
Demands Emergency Rations
COMPLETE RESIGNATION
OH, DEAR...
...MS. MINCE IS OVERCOME BY CONCERN.
NOT A PROBLEM! JUST GOTTA HOLD MY NOSE AND *SUCK IT UP!*
IT'S JUST AN EXAMPLE OF *MIND OVER CEREBRAL HEMORRHAGE!*

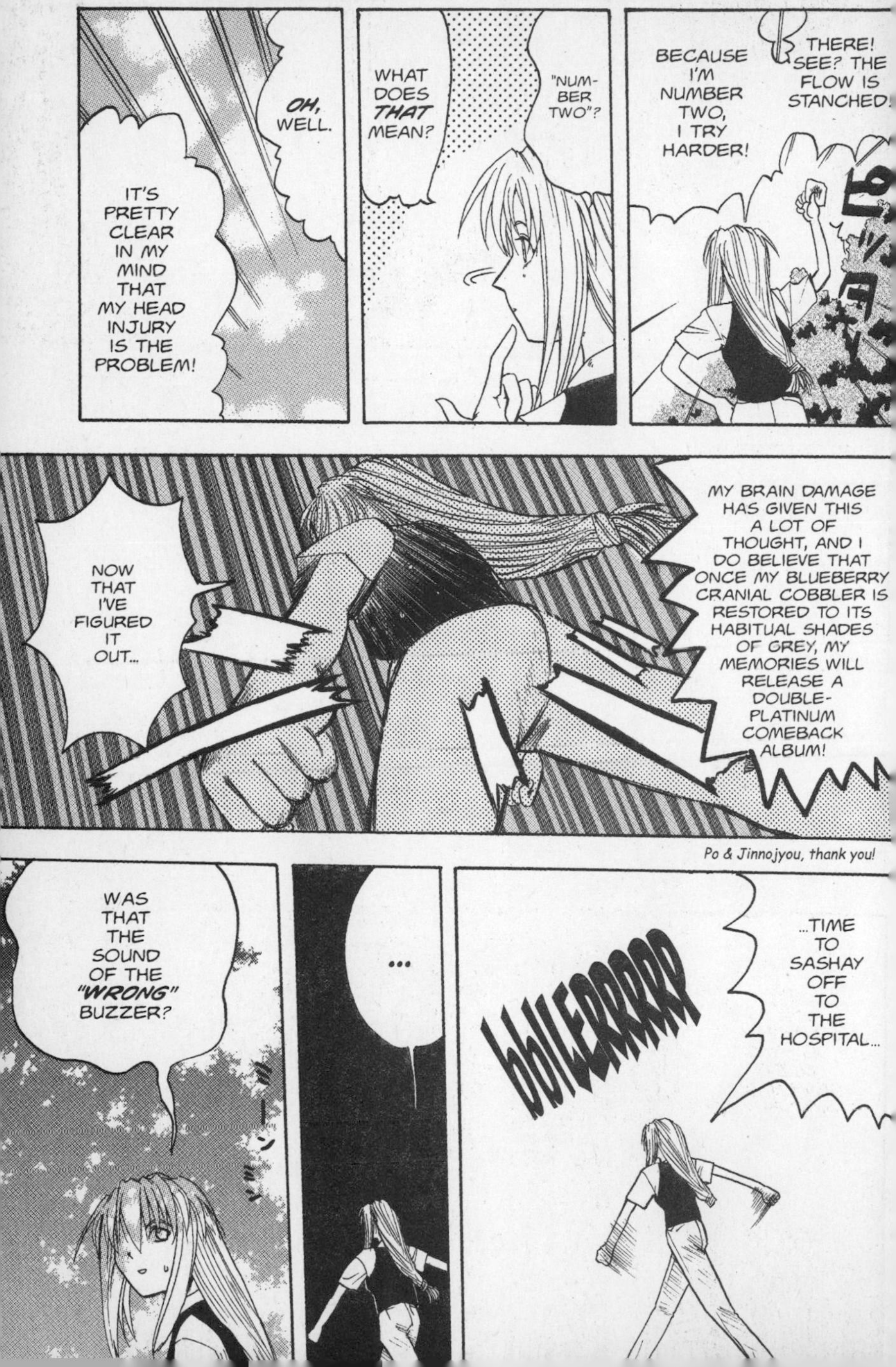
THERE! SEE? THE FLOW IS STANCHED!
BECAUSE I'M NUMBER TWO, I TRY HARDER!
"NUMBER TWO"?
WHAT DOES THAT MEAN?
OH, WELL.
IT'S PRETTY CLEAR IN MY MIND THAT MY HEAD INJURY IS THE PROBLEM!
MY BRAIN DAMAGE HAS GIVEN THIS A LOT OF THOUGHT, AND I DO BELIEVE THAT ONCE MY BLUEBERRY CRANIAL COBBLER IS RESTORED TO ITS HABITUAL SHADES OF GREY, MY MEMORIES WILL RELEASE A DOUBLE-PLATINUM COMEBACK ALBUM!
NOW THAT I'VE FIGURED IT OUT...
...TIME TO SASHAY OFF TO THE HOSPITAL...
bbLERRRRP
...
WAS THAT THE SOUND OF THE "WRONG" BUZZER?

Po & Jinnojyou, thank you!

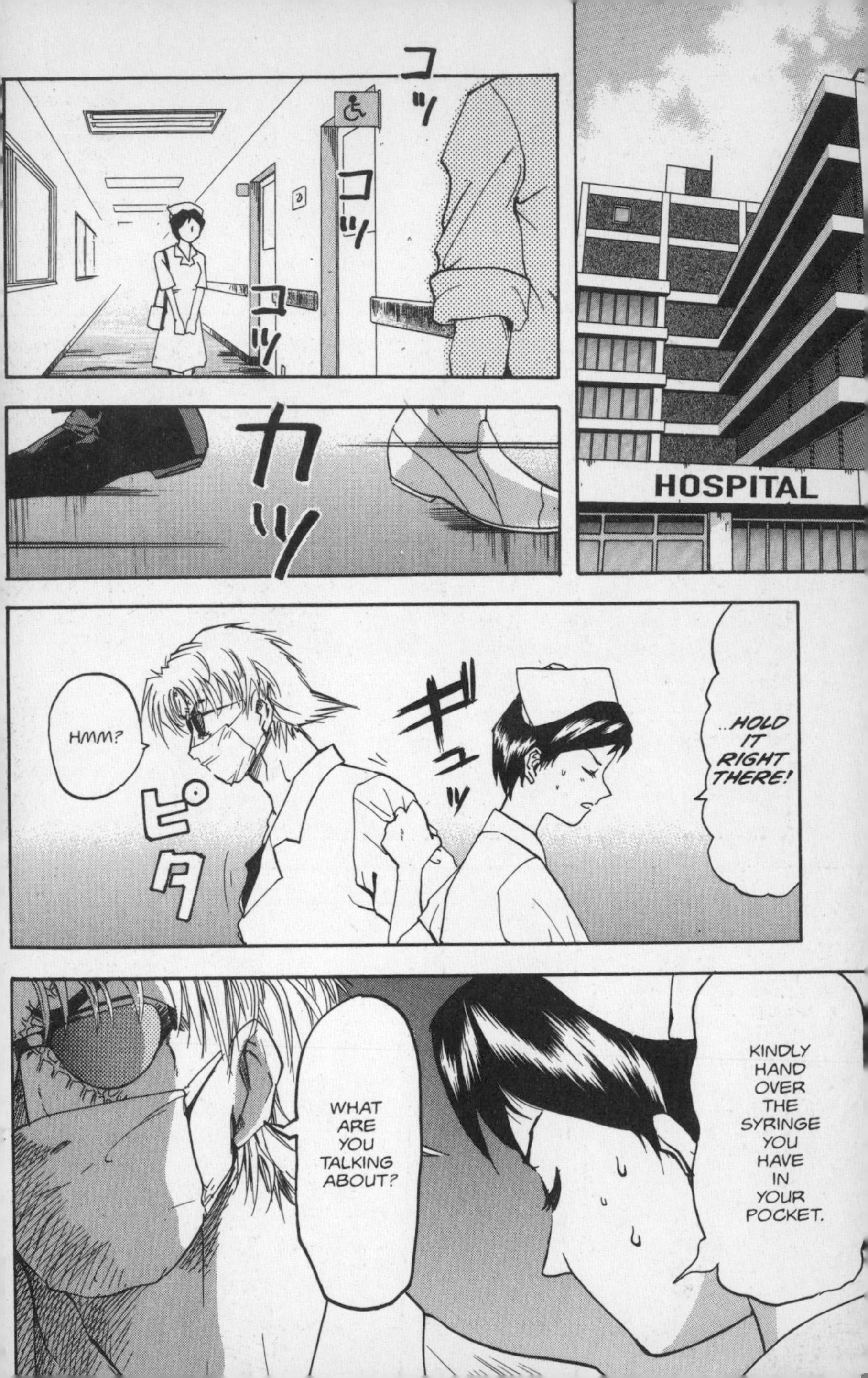
HOSPITAL
コッ
コッ
コッ
カッ
...HOLD IT RIGHT THERE!
ギュッ
HMM?
ピタ
KINDLY HAND OVER THE SYRINGE YOU HAVE IN YOUR POCKET.
WHAT ARE YOU TALKING ABOUT?

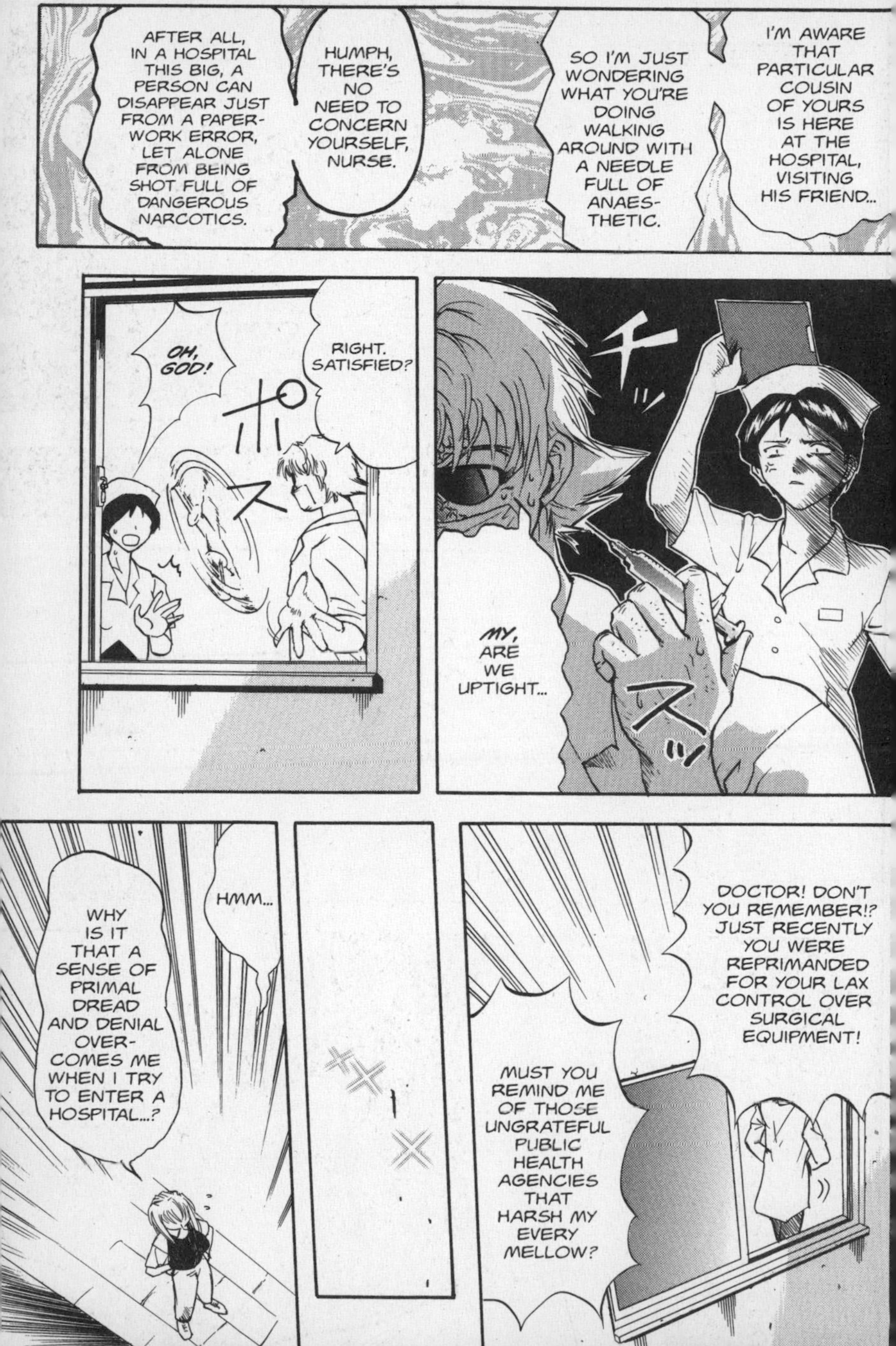
I'M AWARE THAT PARTICULAR COUSIN OF YOURS IS HERE AT THE HOSPITAL, VISITING HIS FRIEND...
SO I'M JUST WONDERING WHAT YOU'RE DOING WALKING AROUND WITH A NEEDLE FULL OF ANAES-THETIC.
HUMPH, THERE'S NO NEED TO CONCERN YOURSELF, NURSE.
AFTER ALL, IN A HOSPITAL THIS BIG, A PERSON CAN DISAPPEAR JUST FROM A PAPER-WORK ERROR, LET ALONE FROM BEING SHOT FULL OF DANGEROUS NARCOTICS.
MY, ARE WE UPTIGHT...
RIGHT. SATISFIED?
OH, GOD!
DOCTOR! DON'T YOU REMEMBER!? JUST RECENTLY YOU WERE REPRIMANDED FOR YOUR LAX CONTROL OVER SURGICAL EQUIPMENT!
MUST YOU REMIND ME OF THOSE UNGRATEFUL PUBLIC HEALTH AGENCIES THAT HARSH MY EVERY MELLOW?
HMM...
WHY IS IT THAT A SENSE OF PRIMAL DREAD AND DENIAL OVER-COMES ME WHEN I TRY TO ENTER A HOSPITAL...?

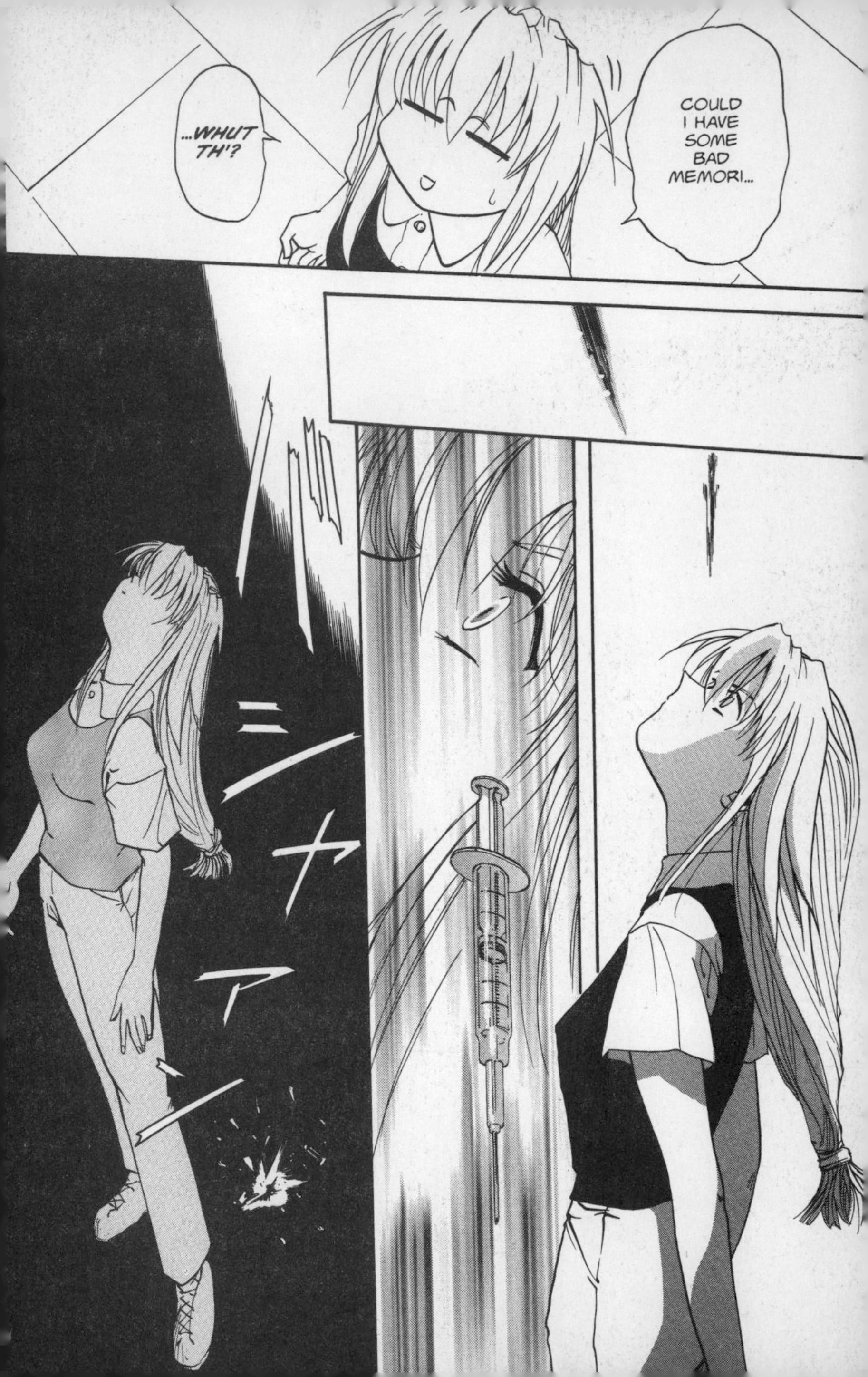
COULD I HAVE SOME BAD MEMORI...
...WHUT TH'?

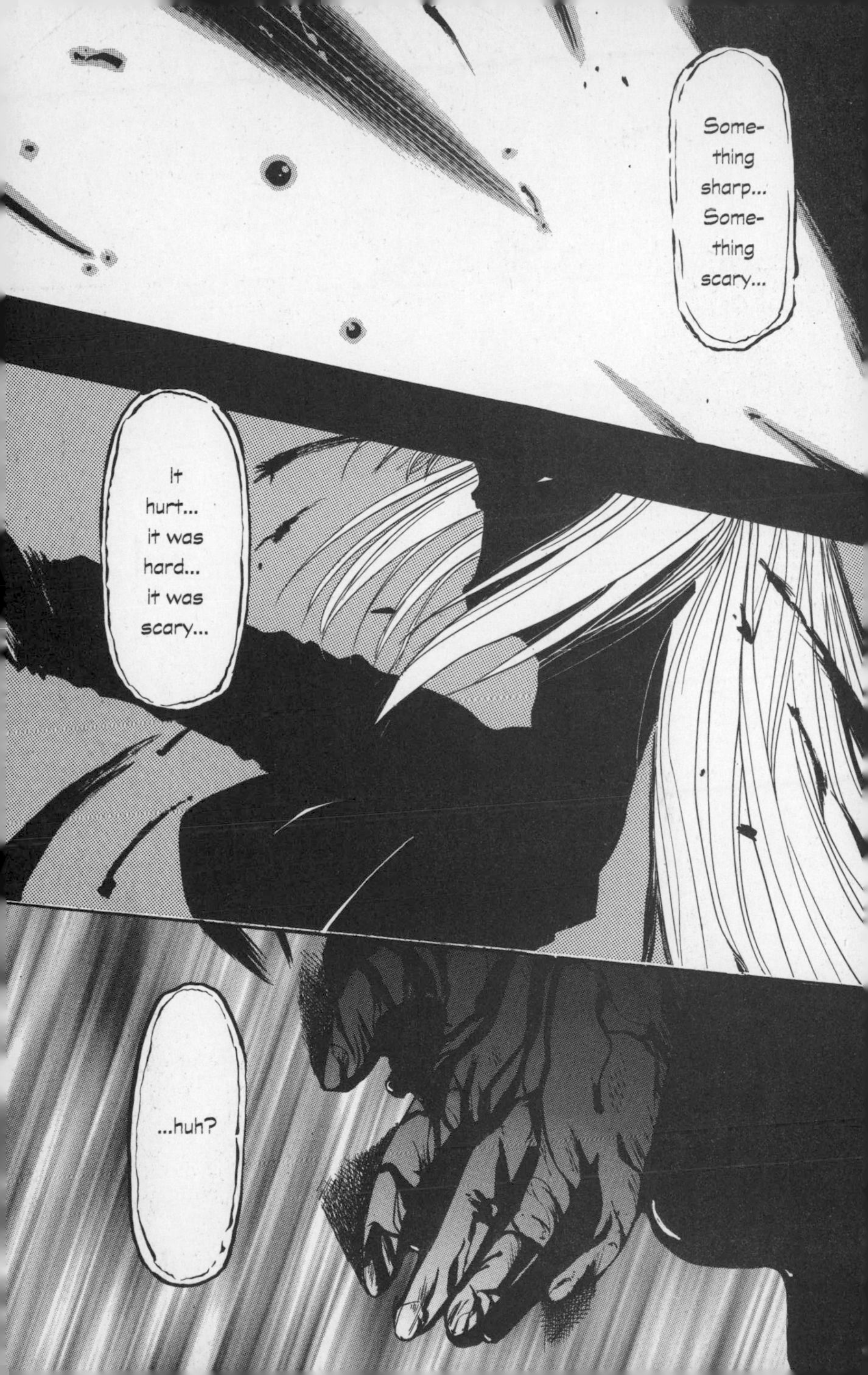
Some-thing sharp... Some-thing scary...
It hurt... it was hard... it was scary...
...huh?

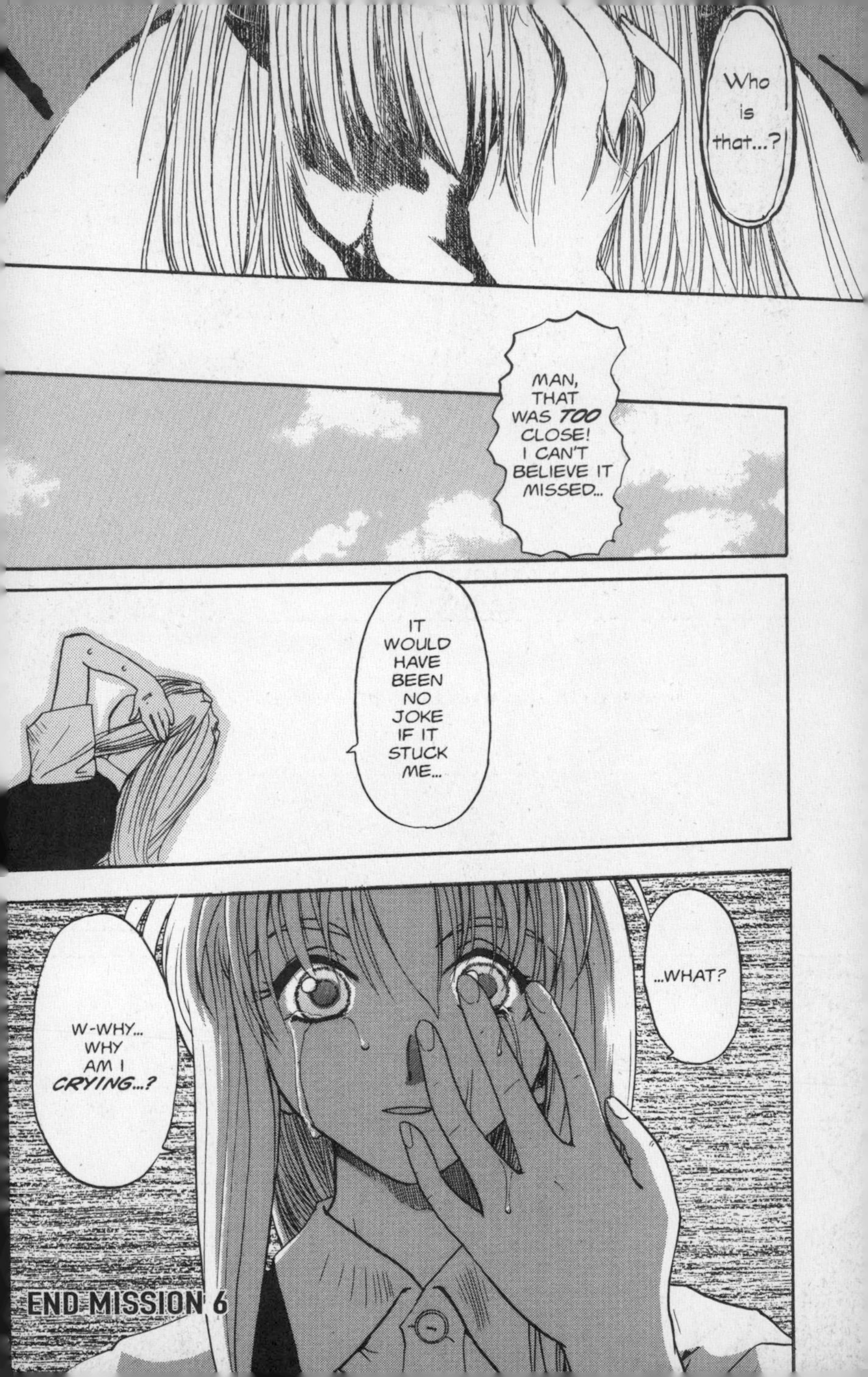
Who is that...?
MAN, THAT WAS *TOO* CLOSE! I CAN'T BELIEVE IT MISSED...
IT WOULD HAVE BEEN NO JOKE IF IT STUCK ME...
...WHAT?
W-WHY... WHY AM I *CRYING*...?
END MISSION 6

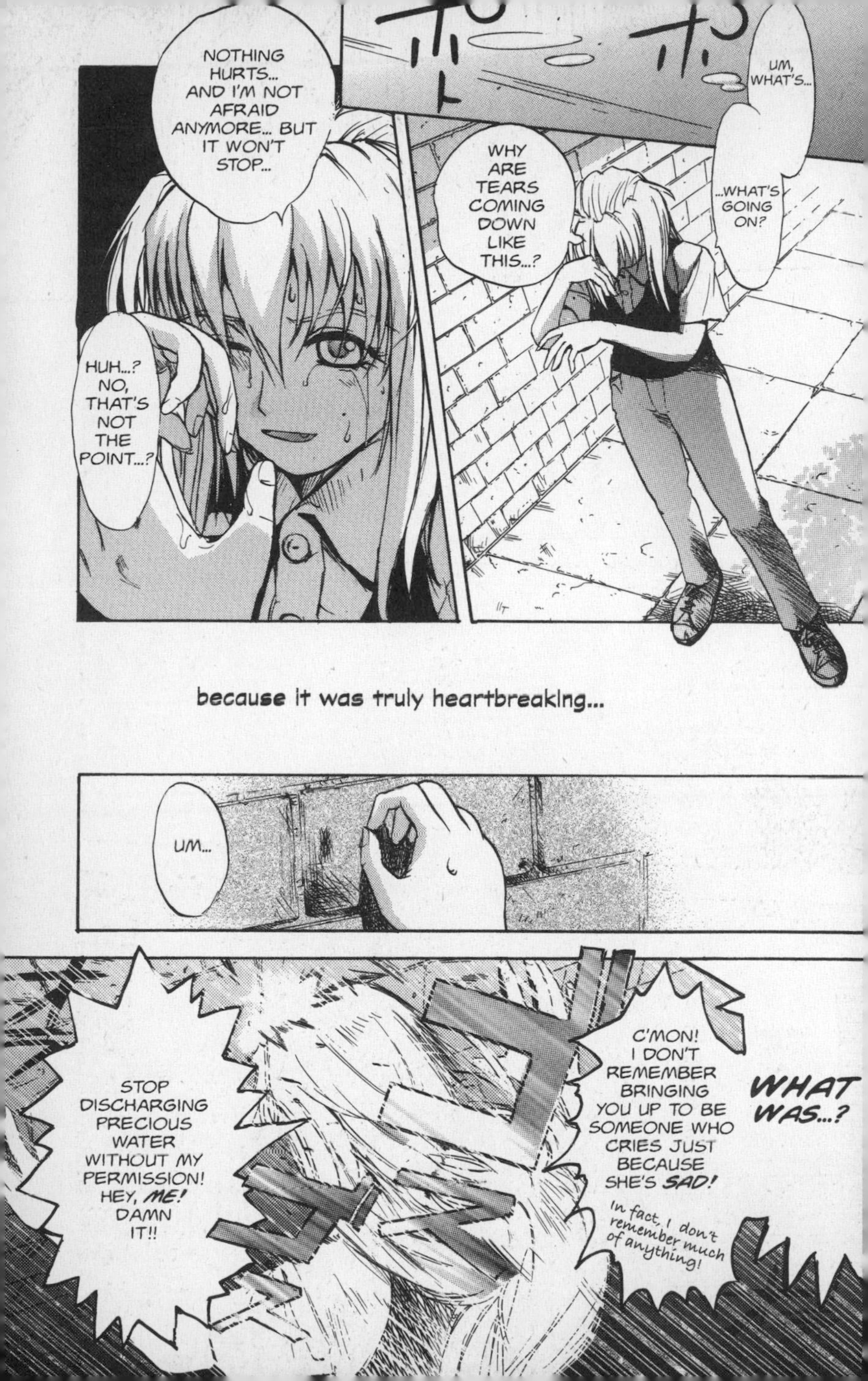
UM, WHAT'S...
...WHAT'S GOING ON?
WHY ARE TEARS COMING DOWN LIKE THIS...?
NOTHING HURTS... AND I'M NOT AFRAID ANYMORE... BUT IT WON'T STOP...
HUH...? NO, THAT'S NOT THE POINT...?
because it was truly heartbreaking...
UM...
WHAT WAS...?
C'MON! I DON'T REMEMBER BRINGING YOU UP TO BE SOMEONE WHO CRIES JUST BECAUSE SHE'S *SAD!*
In fact, I don't remember much of anything!
STOP DISCHARGING PRECIOUS WATER WITHOUT MY PERMISSION! HEY, *ME!* DAMN IT!!

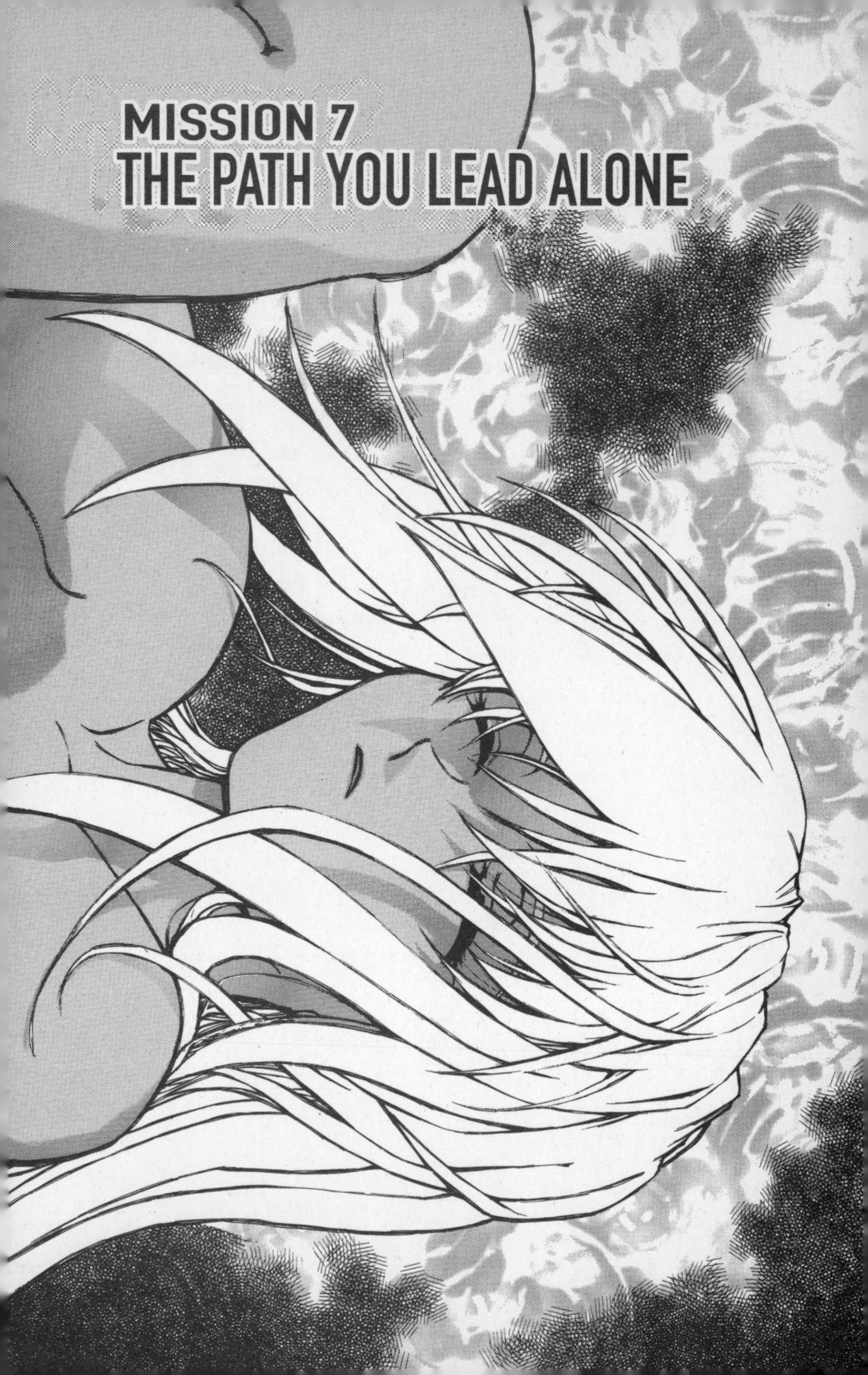
MISSION 7
THE PATH YOU LEAD ALONE

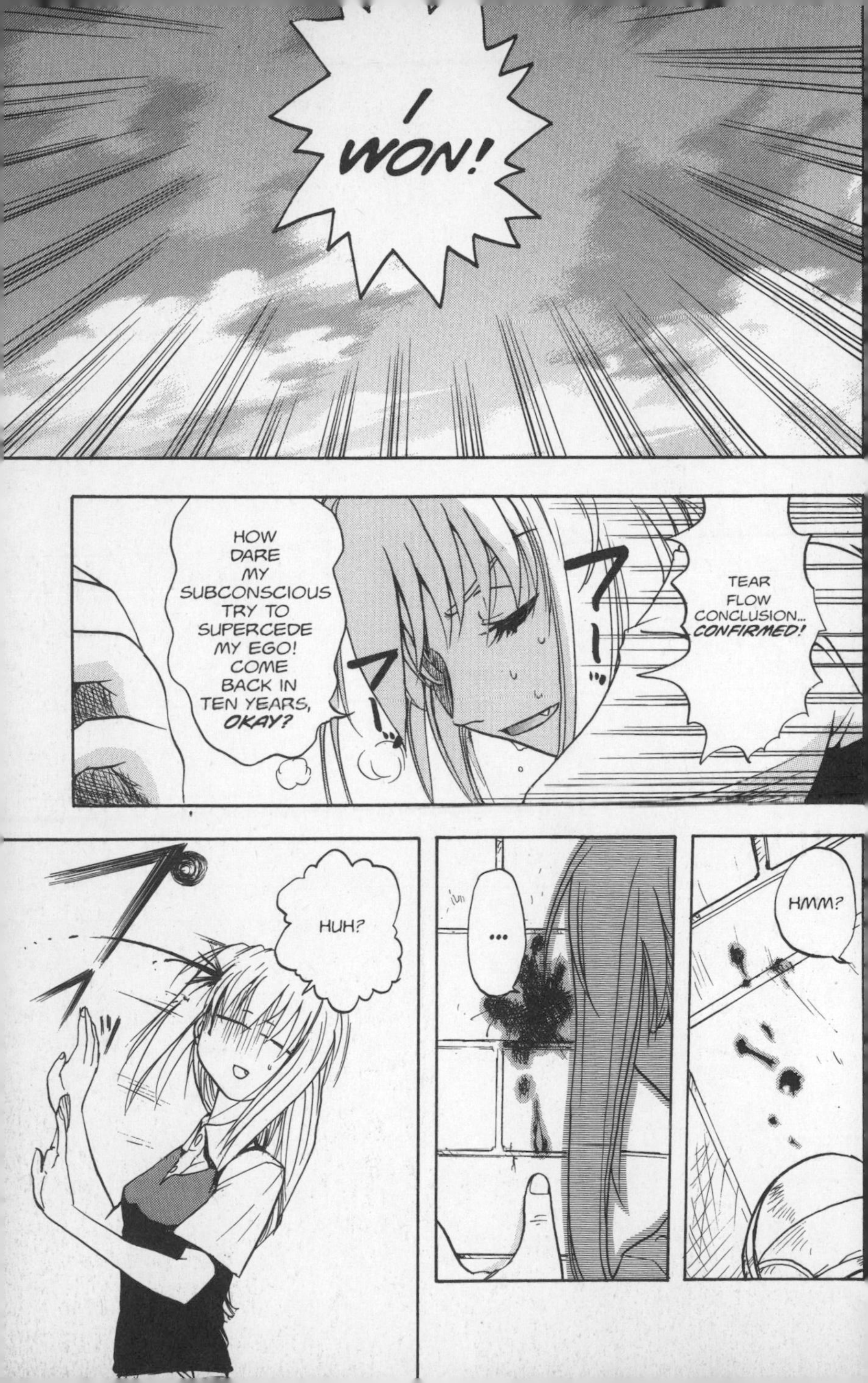
I WON!
TEAR FLOW CONCLUSION... CONFIRMED!
HOW DARE MY SUBCONSCIOUS TRY TO SUPERCEDE MY EGO! COME BACK IN TEN YEARS, OKAY?
HMM?
...
HUH?

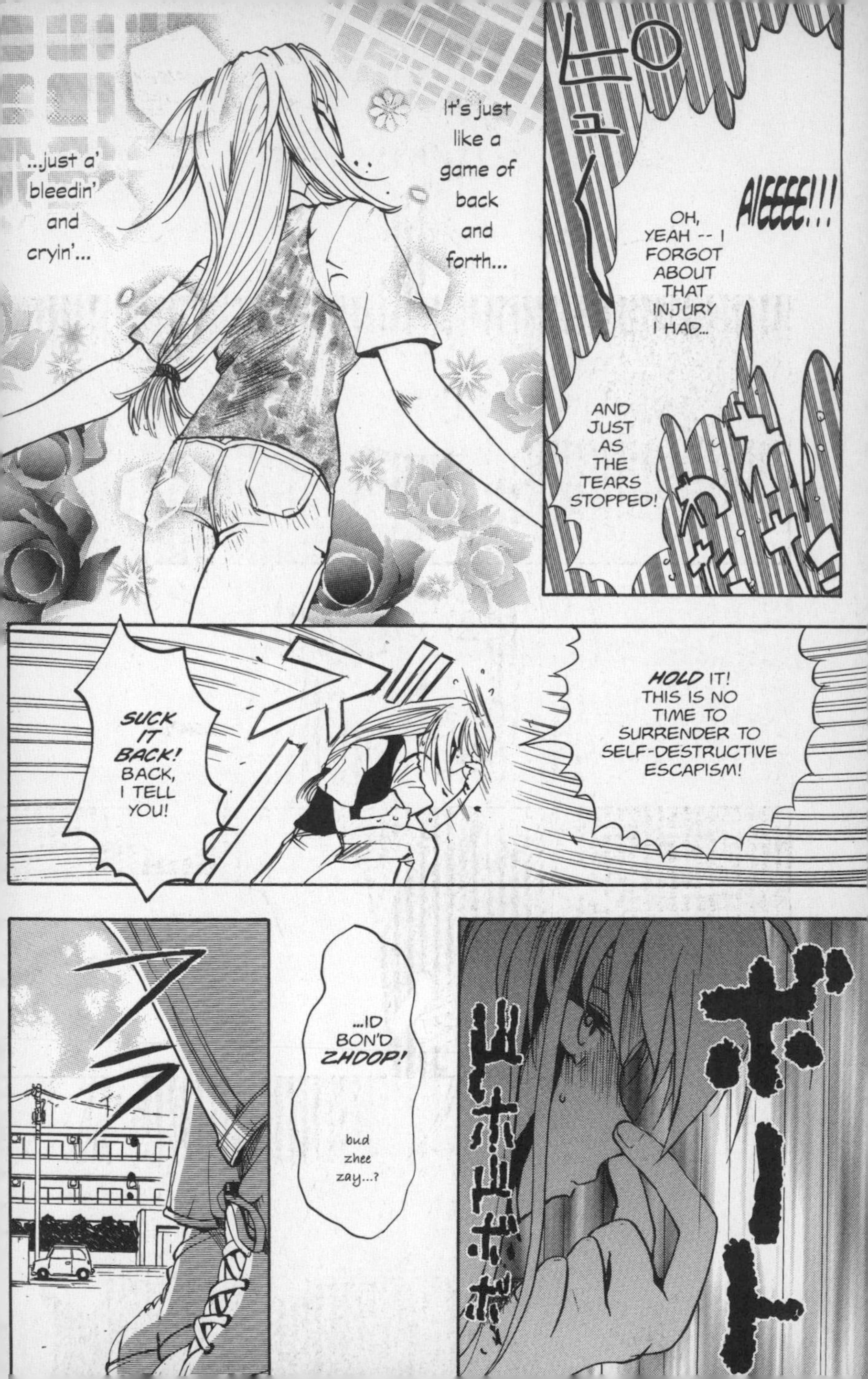
AIEEEE!!!
OH, YEAH -- I FORGOT ABOUT THAT INJURY I HAD...
AND JUST AS THE TEARS STOPPED!
It's just like a game of back and forth...
...just a' bleedin' and cryin'...
HOLD IT! THIS IS NO TIME TO SURRENDER TO SELF-DESTRUCTIVE ESCAPISM!
SUCK IT BACK! BACK, I TELL YOU!
...ID BON'D ZHDOP!
bud zhee zay...?

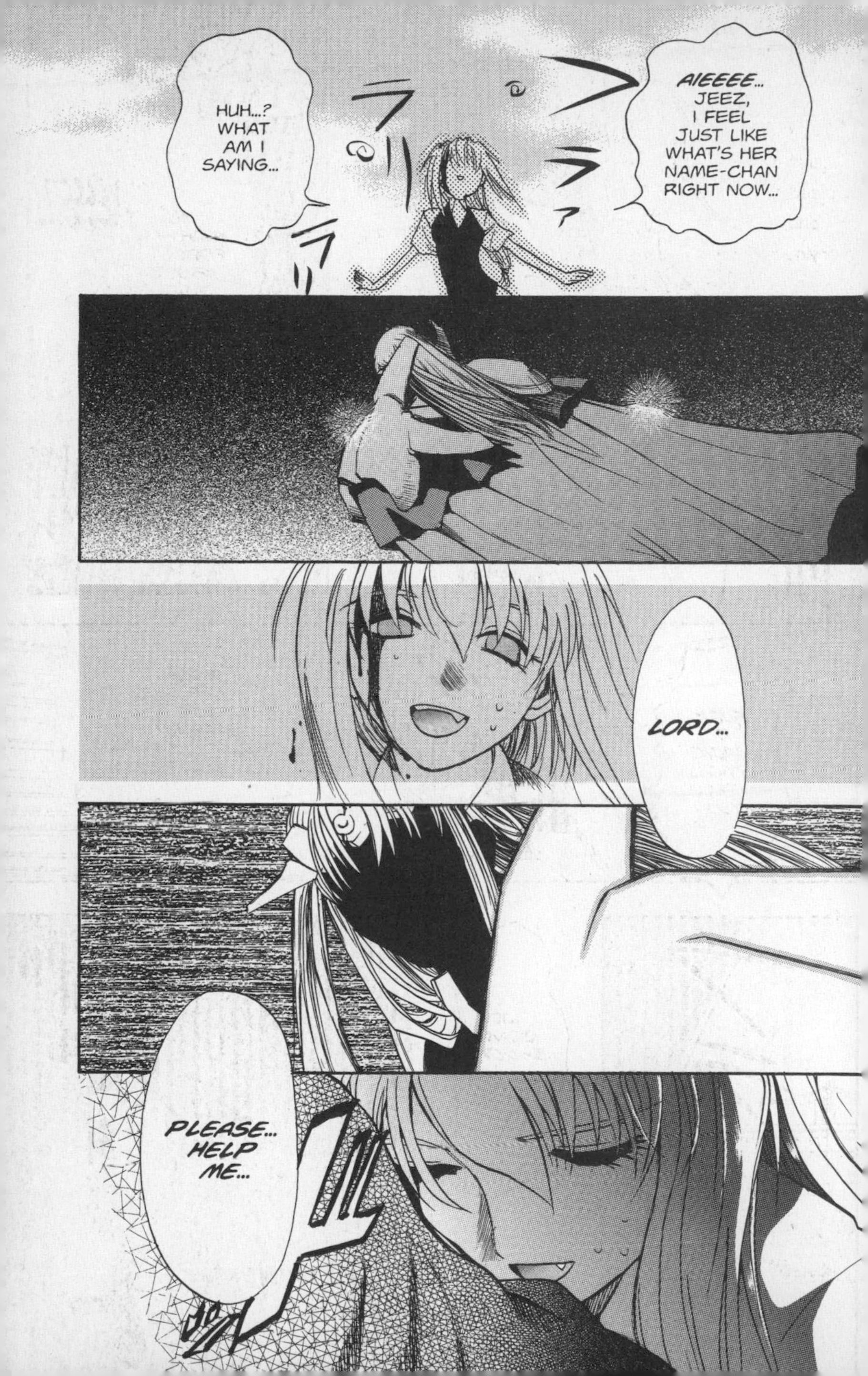
AIEEEE... JEEZ, I FEEL JUST LIKE WHAT'S HER NAME-CHAN RIGHT NOW...
HUH...? WHAT AM I SAYING...
LORD...
PLEASE... HELP ME...

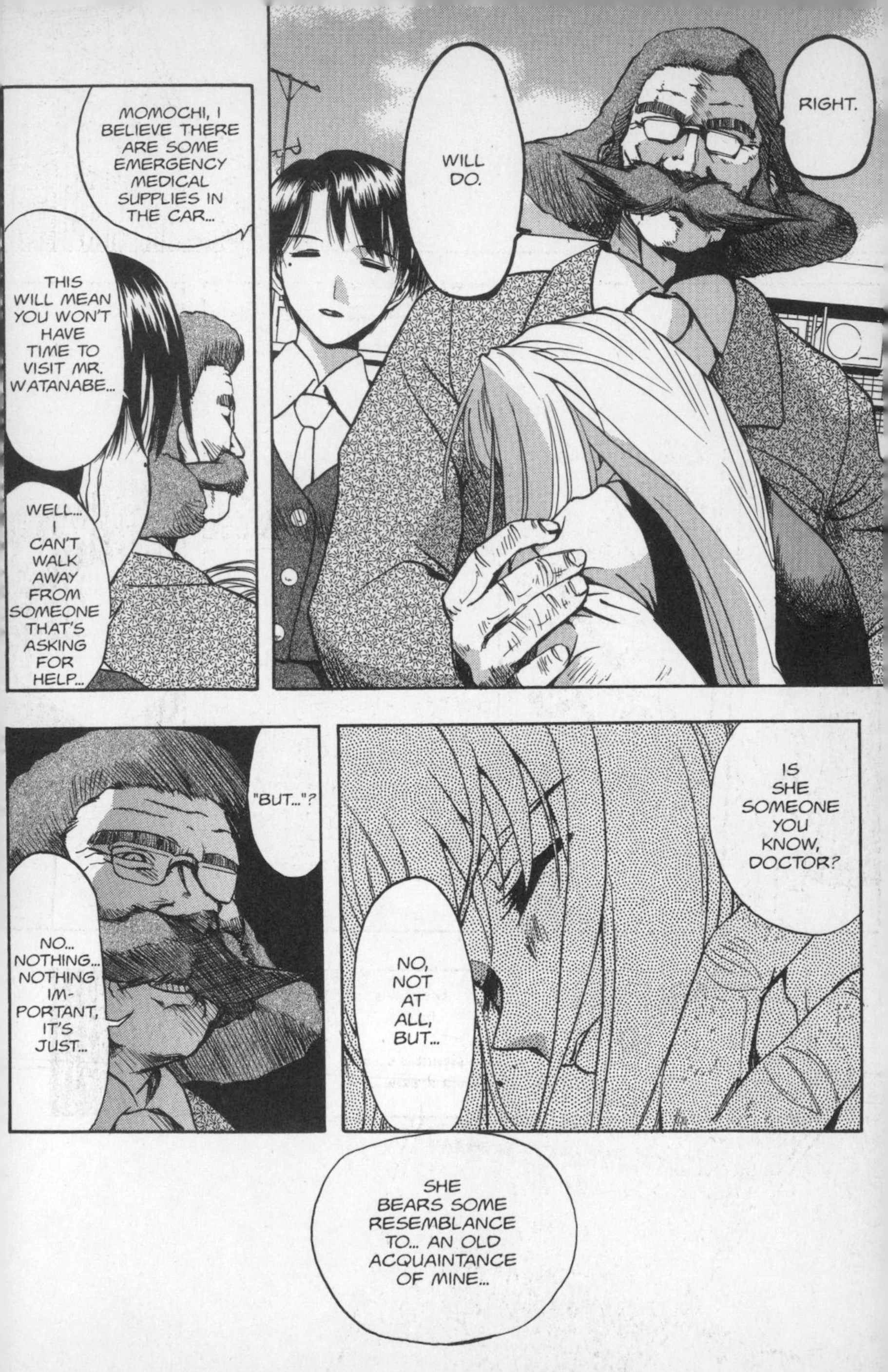
RIGHT.
WILL DO.
MOMOCHI, I BELIEVE THERE ARE SOME EMERGENCY MEDICAL SUPPLIES IN THE CAR...
THIS WILL MEAN YOU WON'T HAVE TIME TO VISIT MR. WATANABE...
WELL... I CAN'T WALK AWAY FROM SOMEONE THAT'S ASKING FOR HELP...
IS SHE SOMEONE YOU KNOW, DOCTOR?
NO, NOT AT ALL, BUT...
"BUT..."?
NO... NOTHING... NOTHING IM-PORTANT, IT'S JUST...
SHE BEARS SOME RESEMBLANCE TO... AN OLD ACQUAINTANCE OF MINE...

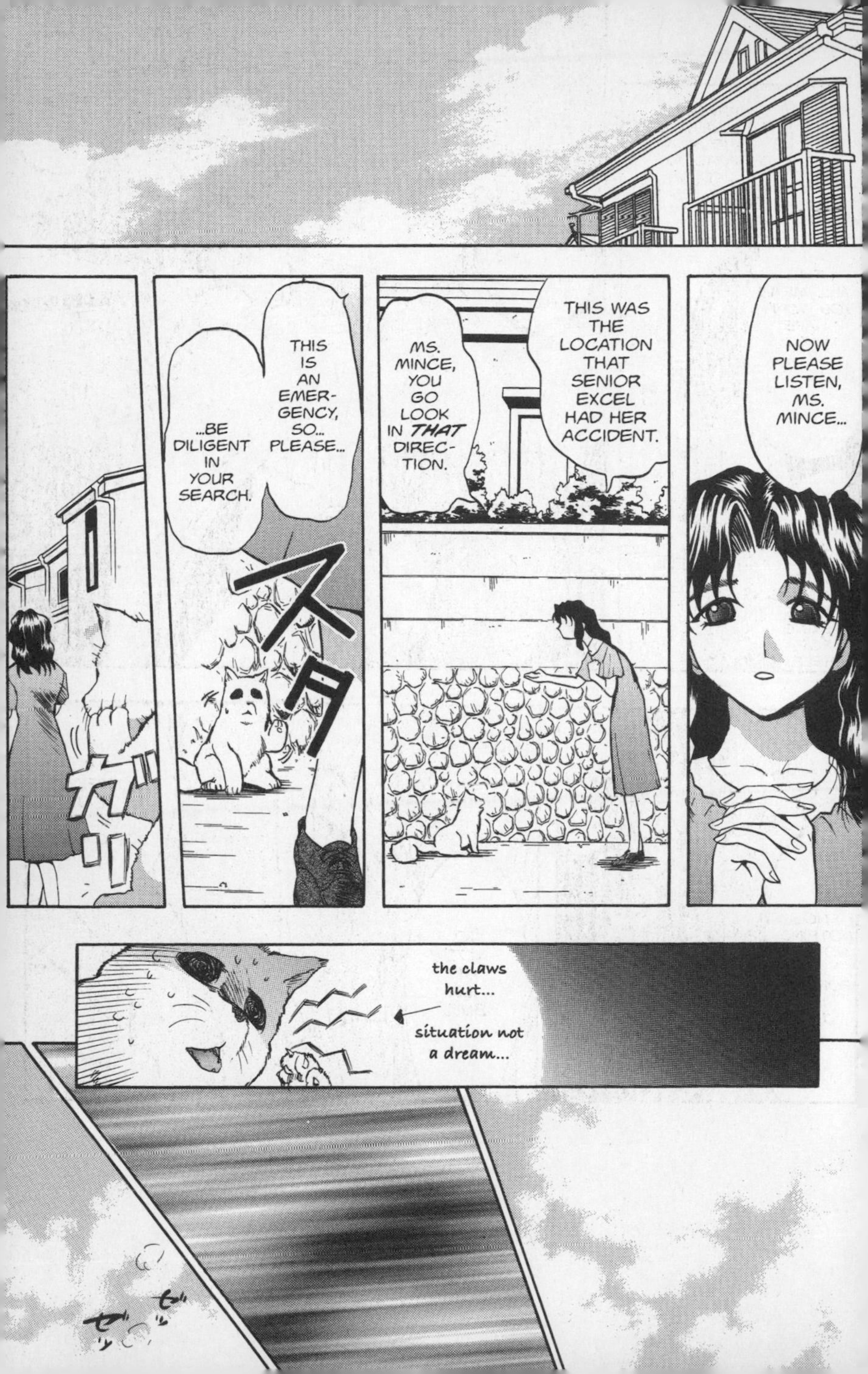
NOW PLEASE LISTEN, MS. MINCE...
THIS WAS THE LOCATION THAT SENIOR EXCEL HAD HER ACCIDENT.
MS. MINCE, YOU GO LOOK IN *THAT* DIRECTION.
THIS IS AN EMERGENCY, SO... PLEASE...
...BE DILIGENT IN YOUR SEARCH.
スタ
the claws hurt...
situation not a dream...

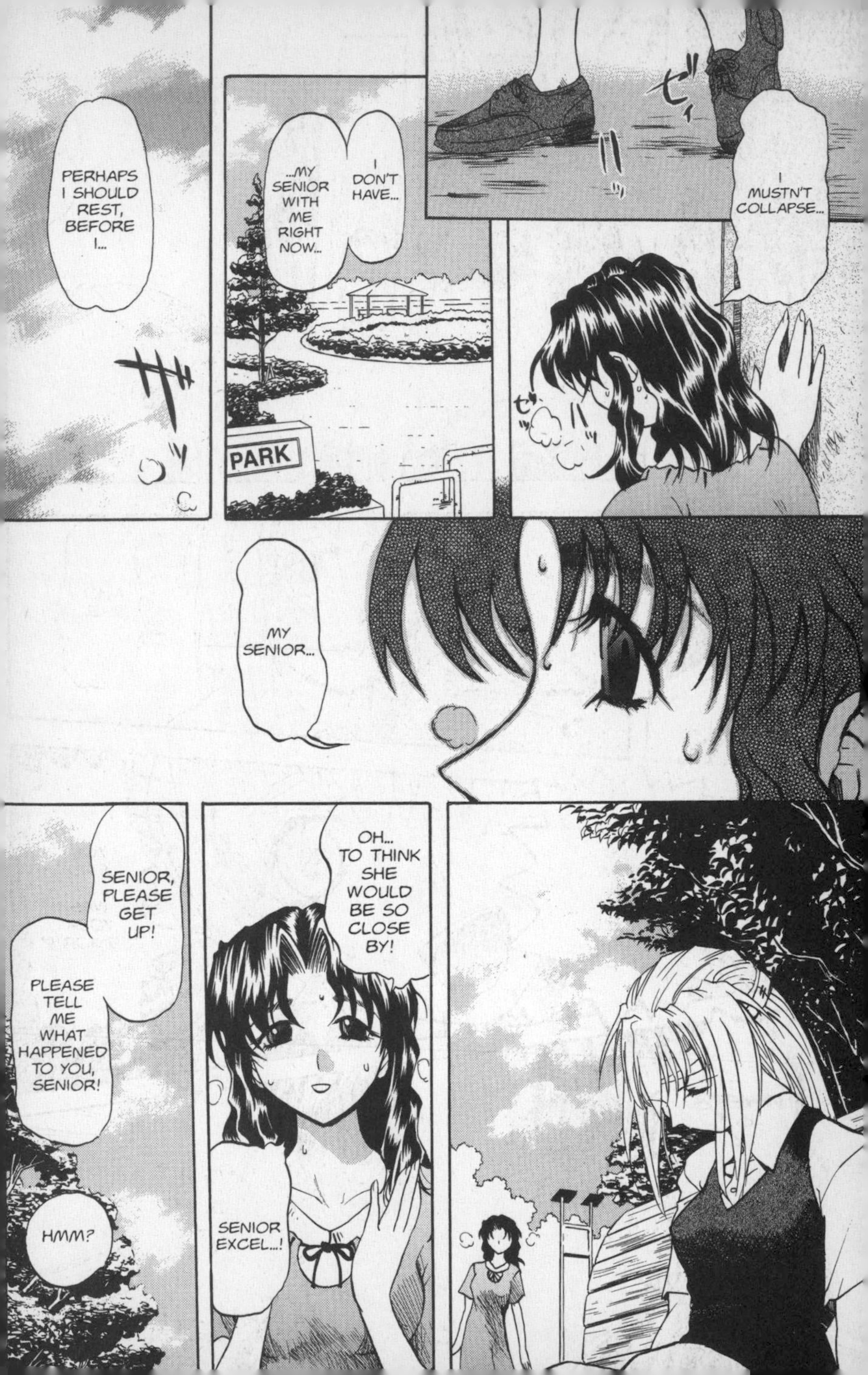
I MUSTN'T COLLAPSE...
I DON'T HAVE...
...MY SENIOR WITH ME RIGHT NOW...
PARK
PERHAPS I SHOULD REST, BEFORE I...
MY SENIOR...
OH... TO THINK SHE WOULD BE SO CLOSE BY!
SENIOR EXCEL...!
SENIOR, PLEASE GET UP!
PLEASE TELL ME WHAT HAPPENED TO YOU, SENIOR!
HMM?

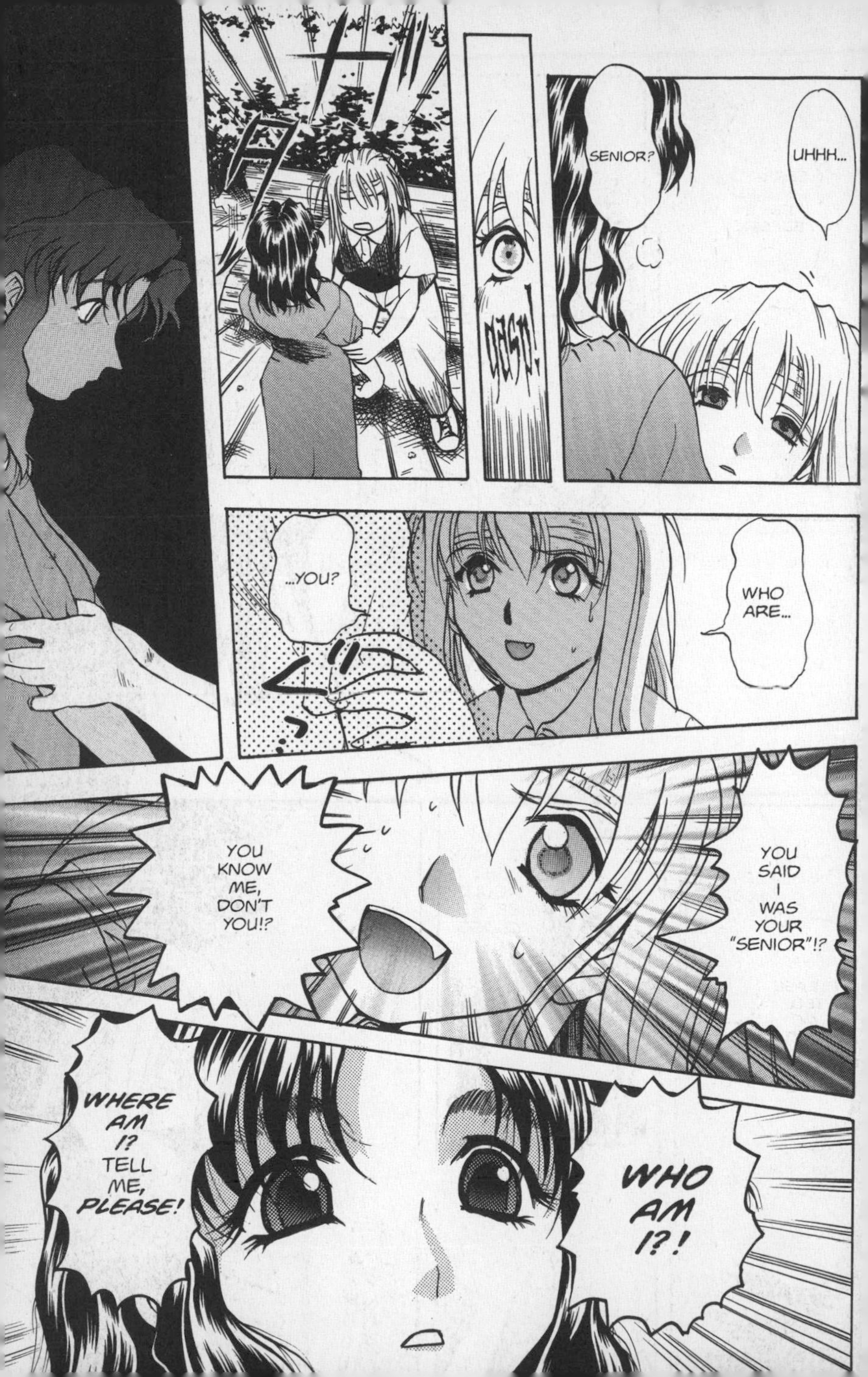
UHHH...
SENIOR?
gasp!
WHO ARE...
...YOU?
YOU SAID I WAS YOUR "SENIOR"!?
YOU KNOW ME, DON'T YOU!?
WHO AM I?!
WHERE AM I? TELL ME, PLEASE!

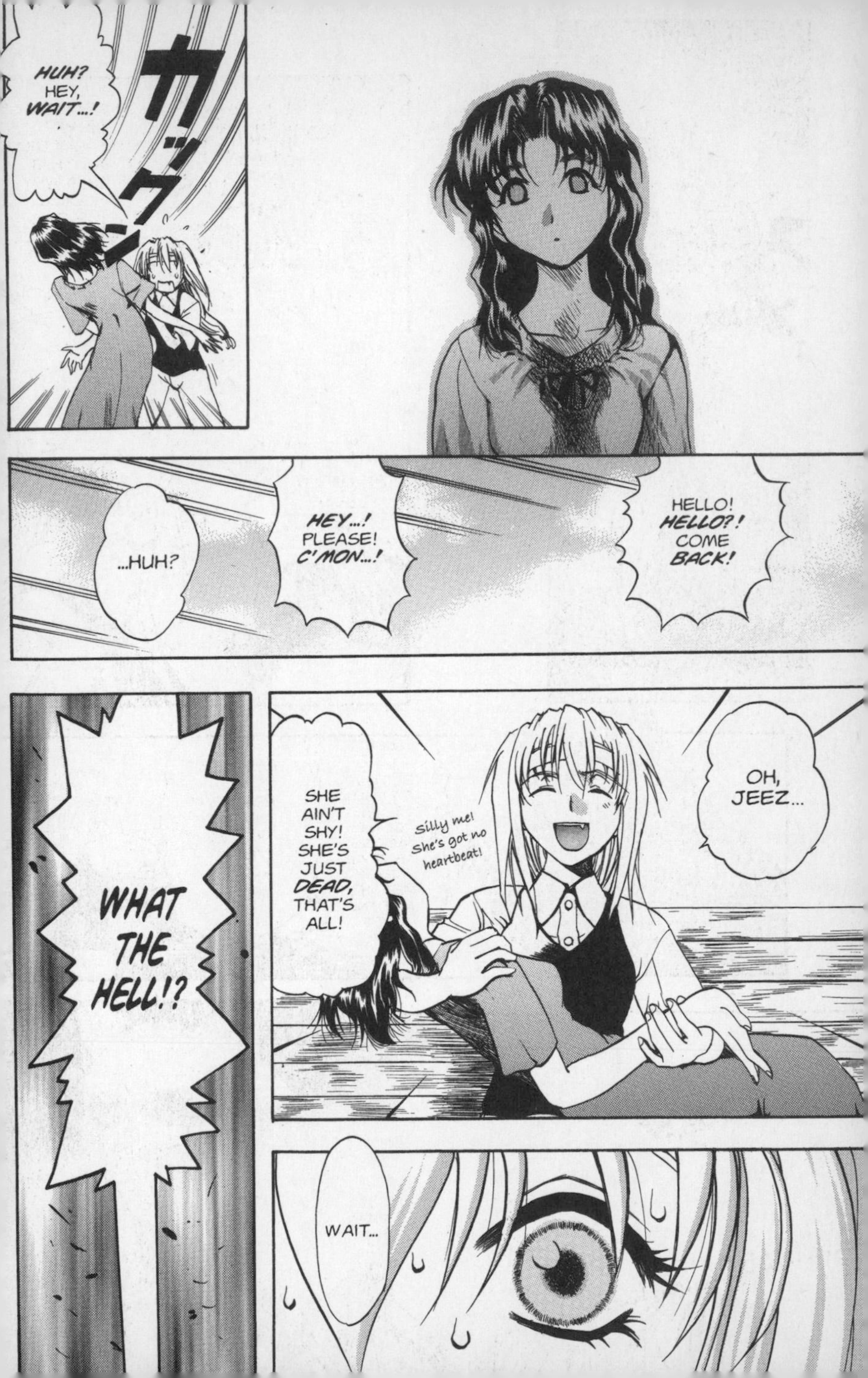
HUH? HEY, WAIT...!
カックン
HELLO! HELLO?! COME BACK!
HEY...! PLEASE! C'MON...!
...HUH?
OH, JEEZ...
Silly me! She's got no heartbeat!
SHE AIN'T SHY! SHE'S JUST DEAD, THAT'S ALL!
WAIT...
WHAT THE HELL!?

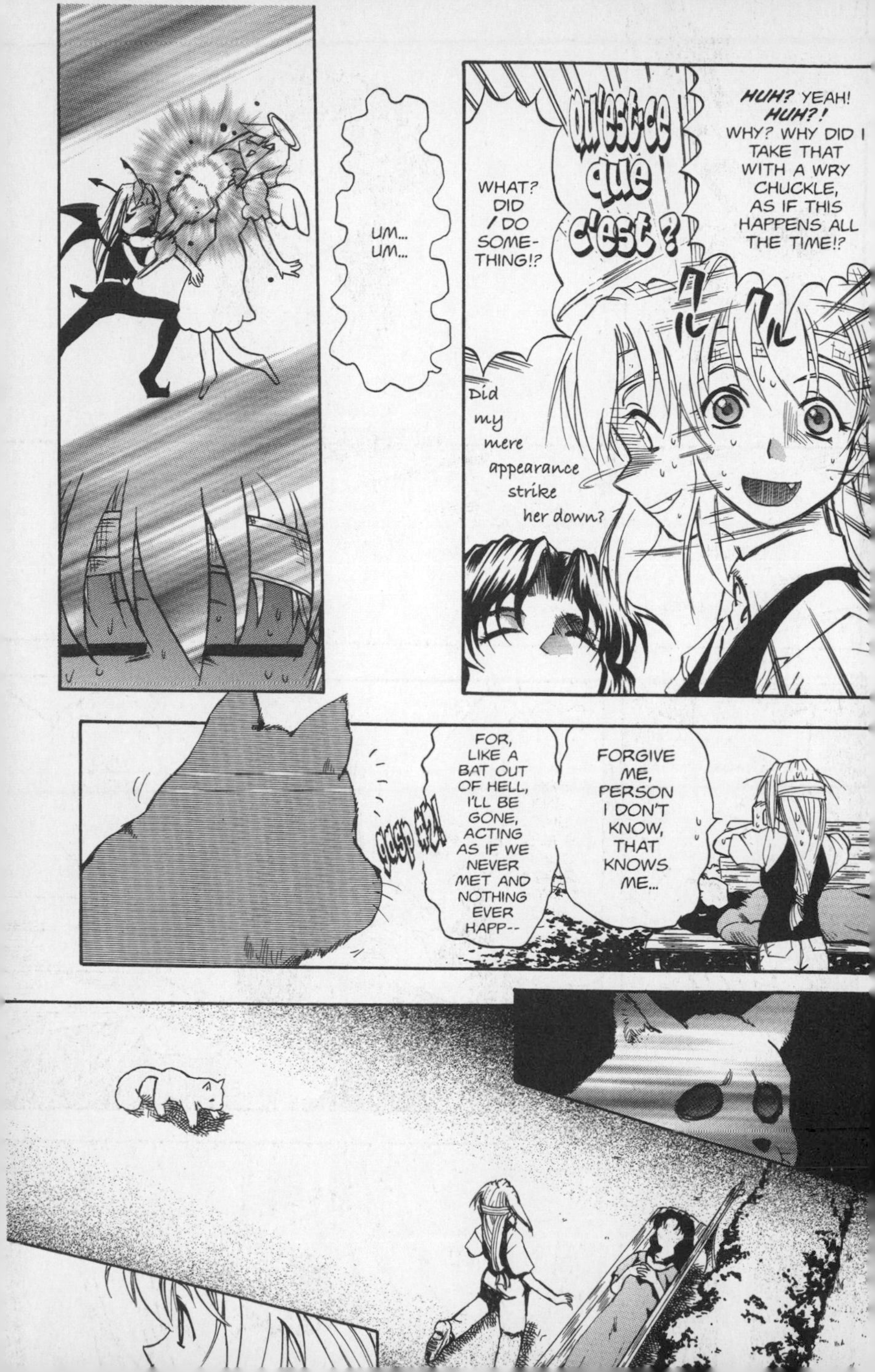
HUH? YEAH! HUH?! WHY? WHY DID I TAKE THAT WITH A WRY CHUCKLE, AS IF THIS HAPPENS ALL THE TIME!?
Qu'est-ce que c'est ?
WHAT? DID I DO SOMETHING!?
Did my mere appearance strike her down?
UM... UM...
FORGIVE ME, PERSON I DON'T KNOW, THAT KNOWS ME...
FOR, LIKE A BAT OUT OF HELL, I'LL BE GONE, ACTING AS IF WE NEVER MET AND NOTHING EVER HAPP--
gasp #2!

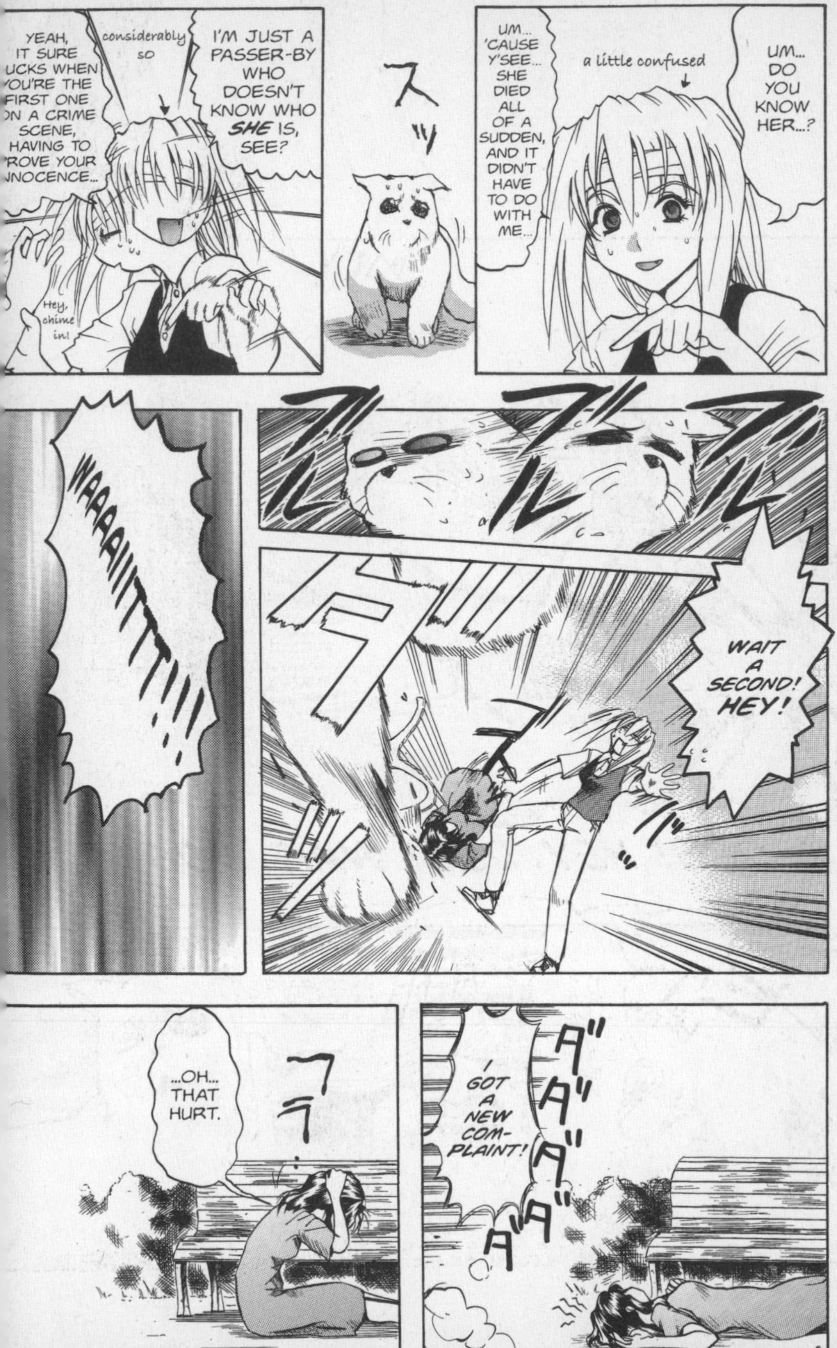
UM... DO YOU KNOW HER...?
a little confused
UM... 'CAUSE Y'SEE... SHE DIED ALL OF A SUDDEN, AND IT DIDN'T HAVE TO DO WITH ME...
スッ
I'M JUST A PASSER-BY WHO DOESN'T KNOW WHO SHE IS, SEE?
considerably so
YEAH, IT SURE UCKS WHEN OU'RE THE FIRST ONE N A CRIME SCENE, HAVING TO ROVE YOUR NNOCENCE...
Hey, chime in!
ブルブル
WAIT A SECOND! HEY!
WAAAAIIITTT!!!
I GOT A NEW COM-PLAINT!
...OH... THAT HURT.

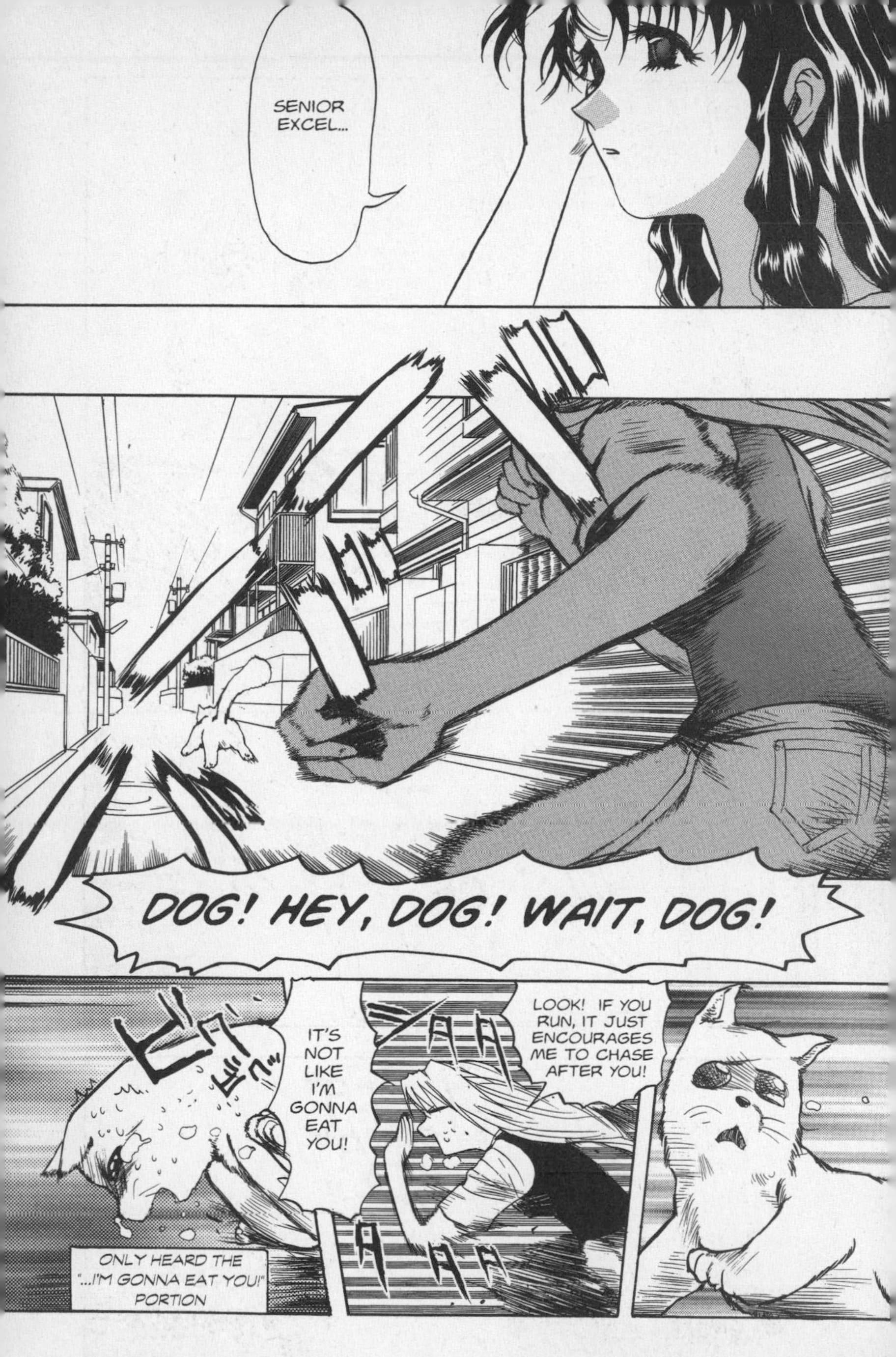
SENIOR EXCEL...
DOG! HEY, DOG! WAIT, DOG!
LOOK! IF YOU RUN, IT JUST ENCOURAGES ME TO CHASE AFTER YOU!
IT'S NOT LIKE I'M GONNA EAT YOU!
ONLY HEARD THE "...I'M GONNA EAT YOU!" PORTION

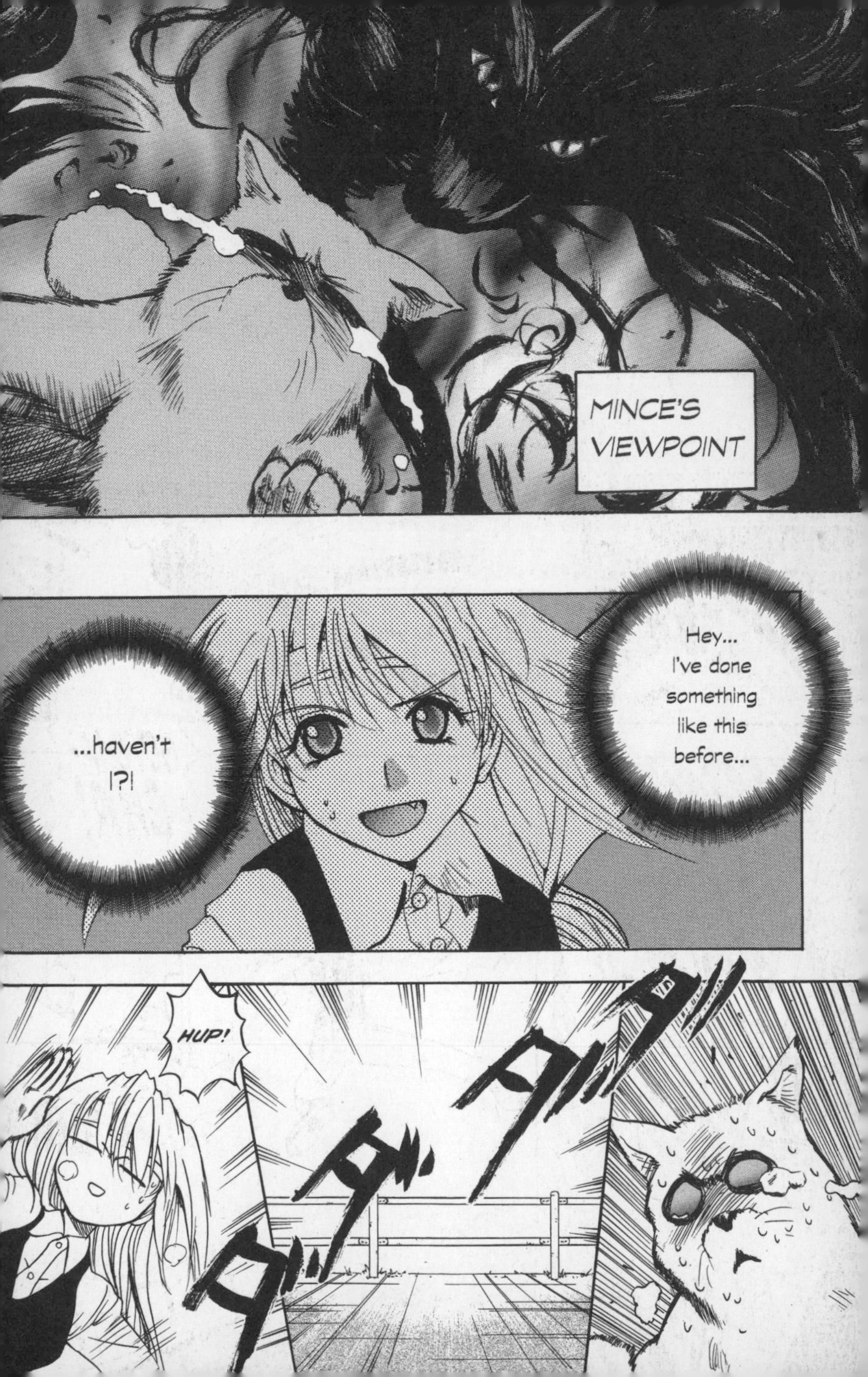
MINCE'S VIEWPOINT
Hey... I've done something like this before...
...haven't I?!
HUP!

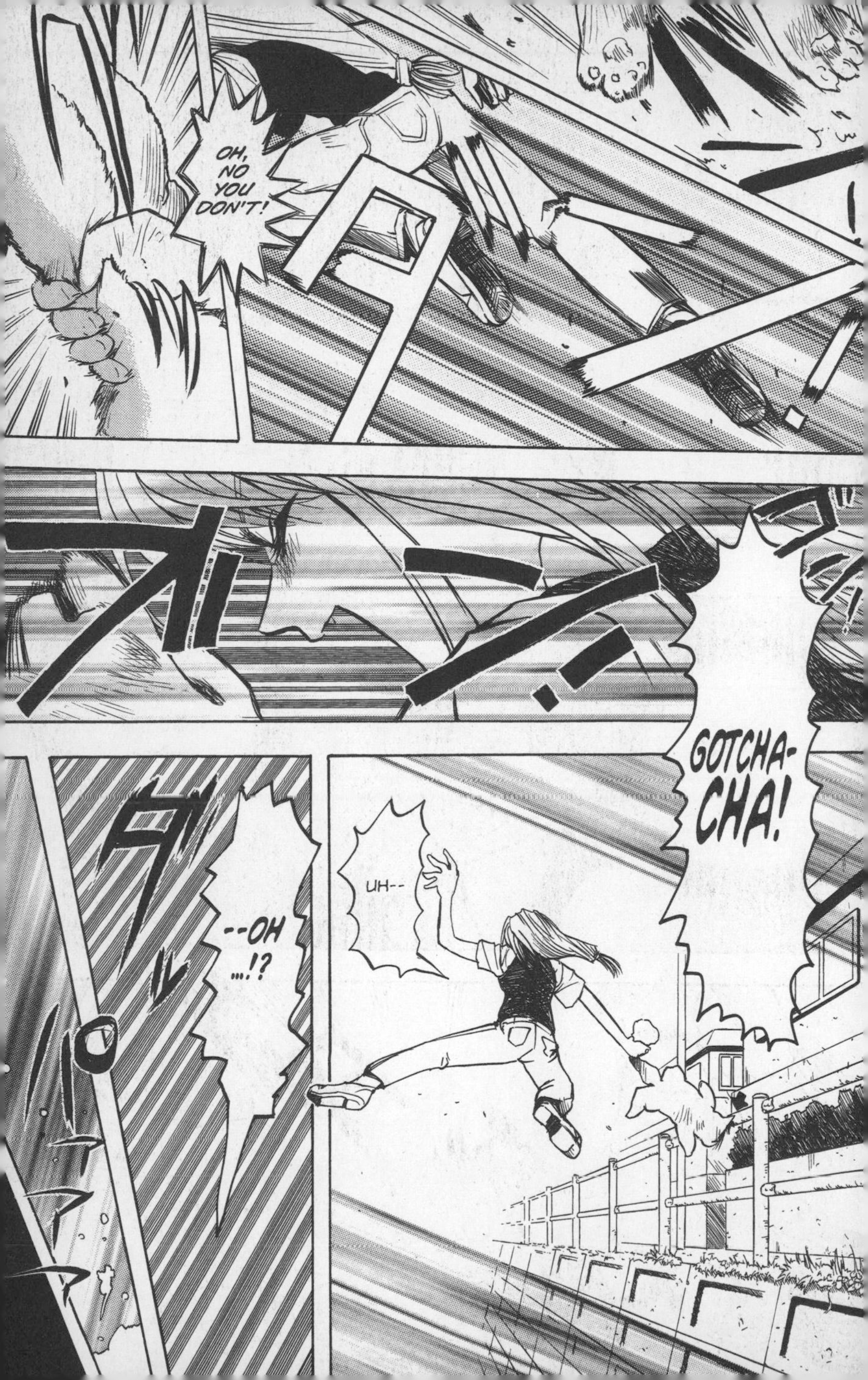
OH, NO YOU DON'T!
GOTCHA-CHA!
UH--
--OH ...!?

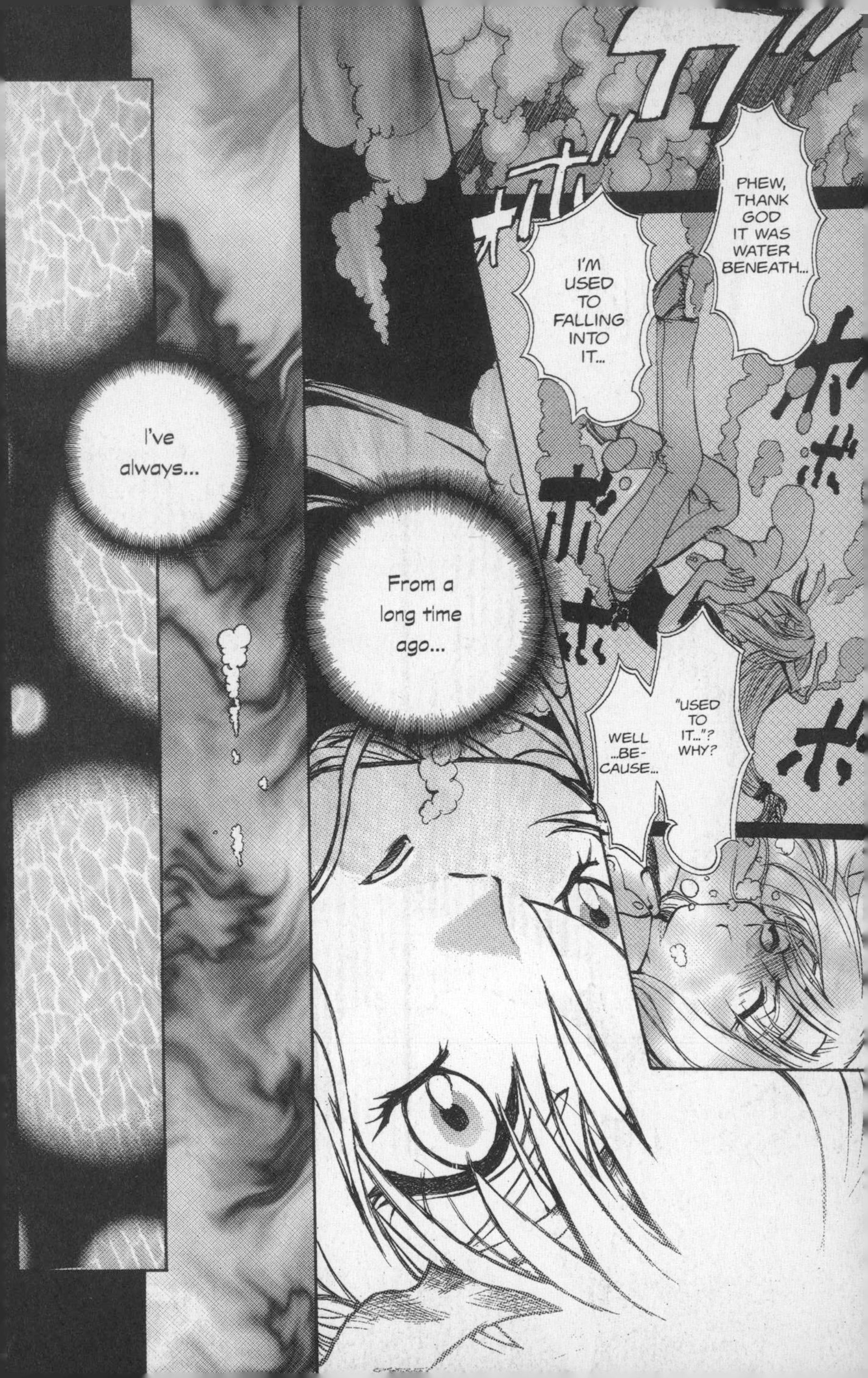
PHEW, THANK GOD IT WAS WATER BENEATH...
I'M USED TO FALLING INTO IT...
"USED TO IT..."? WHY?
WELL ...BE-CAUSE...
From a long time ago...
I've always...

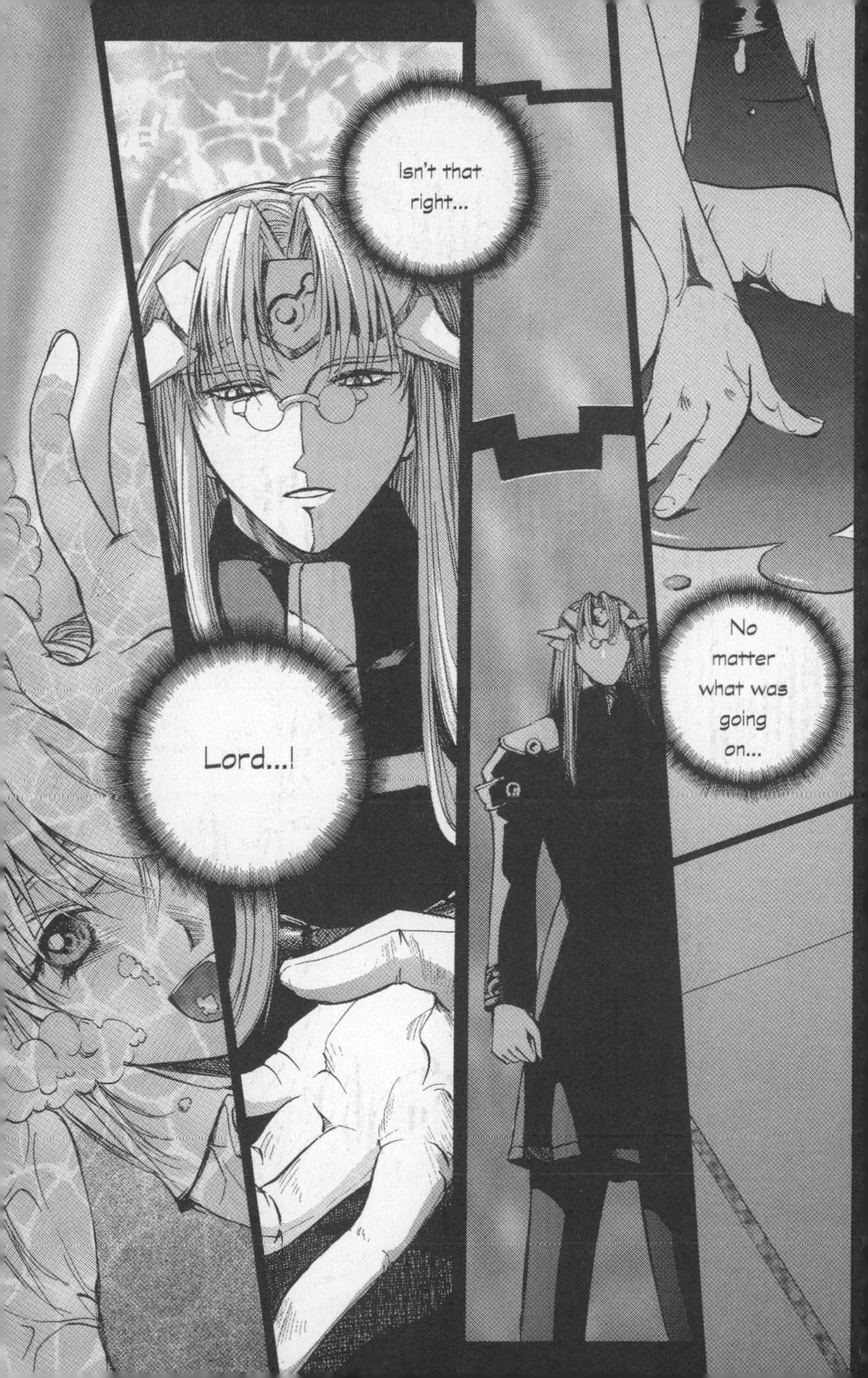
No matter what was going on...
Isn't that right...
Lord...!

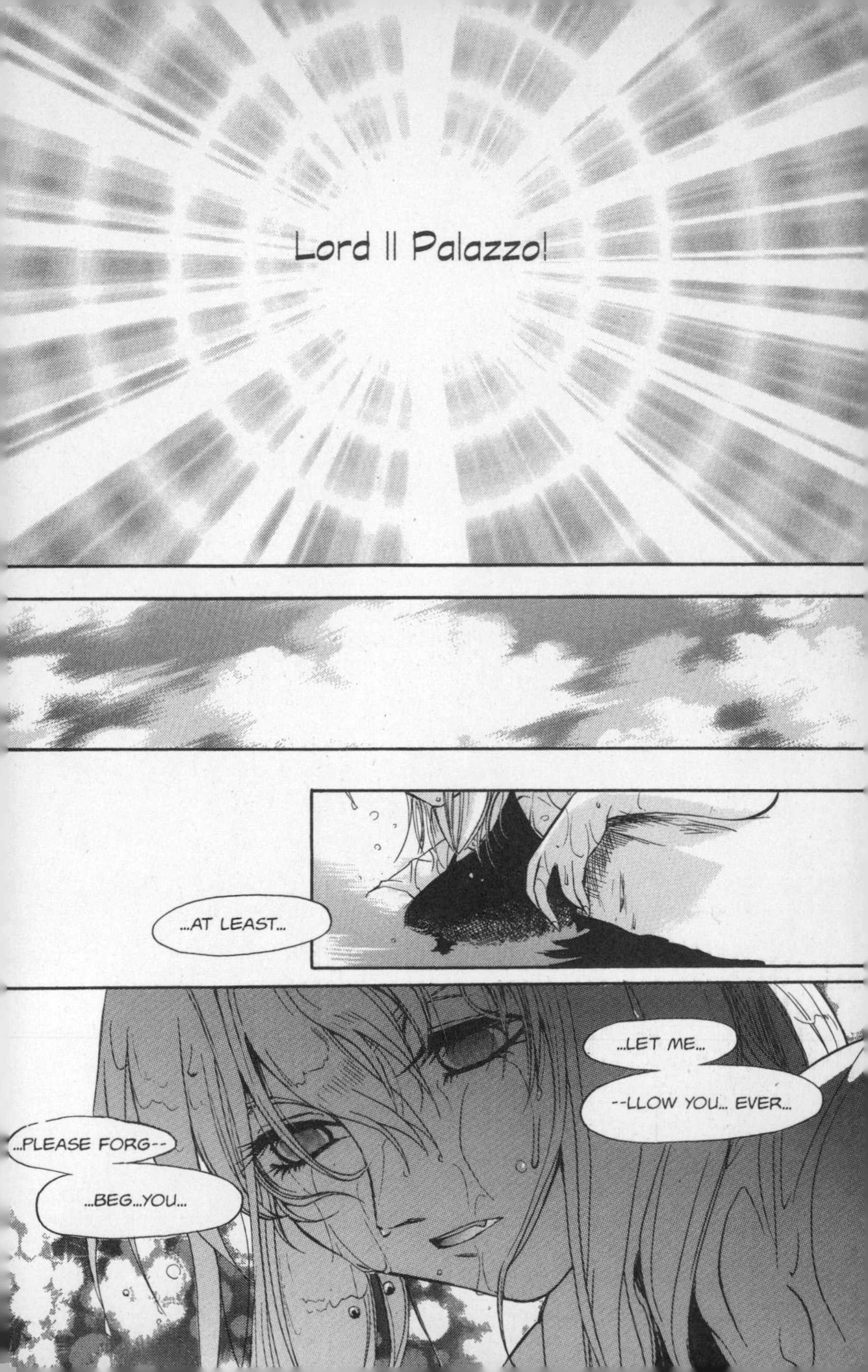
Lord Il Palazzo!
...AT LEAST...
...LET ME...
--LLOW YOU... EVER...
...PLEASE FORG--
...BEG...YOU...

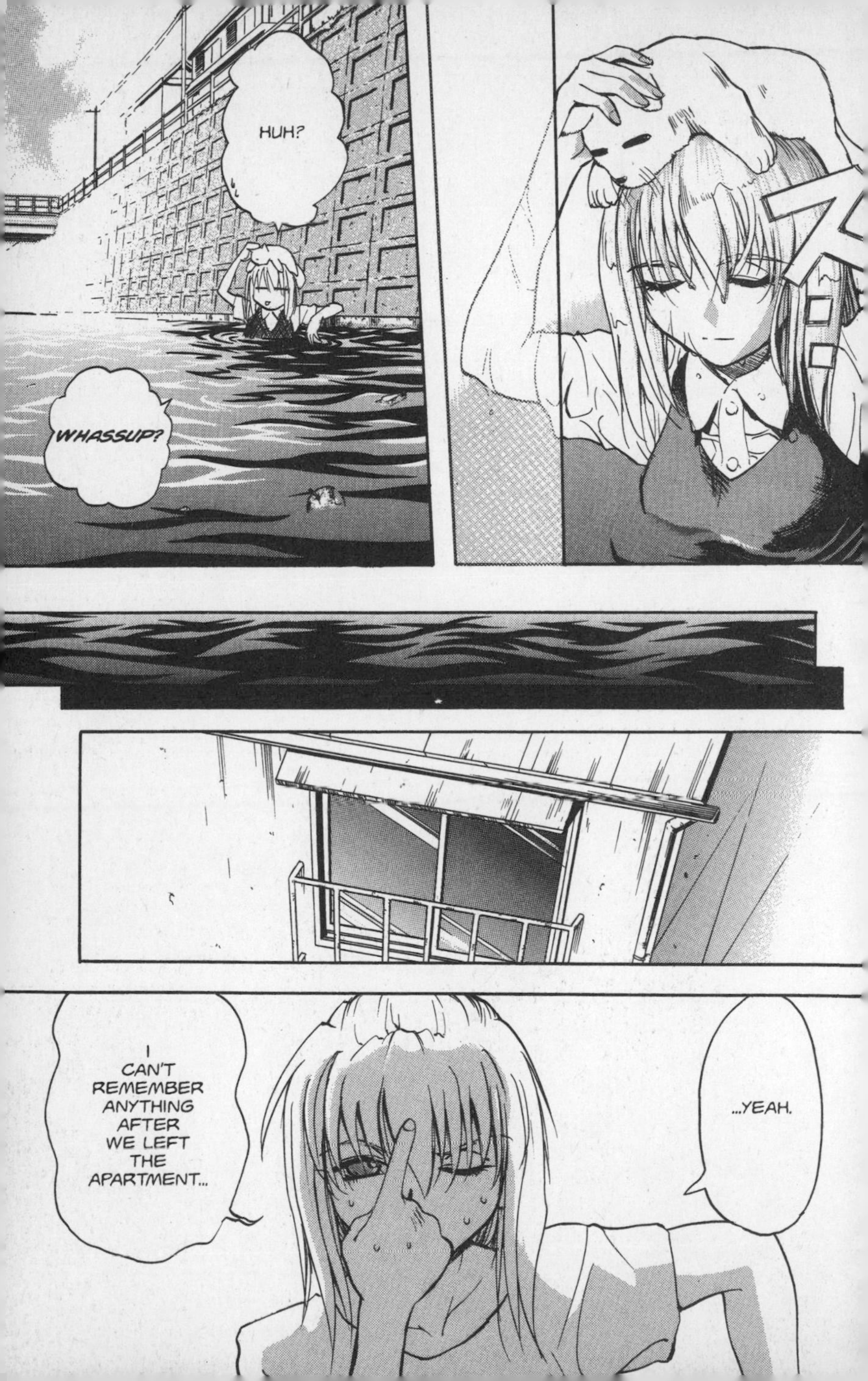
HUH?
WHASSUP?
I CAN'T REMEMBER ANYTHING AFTER WE LEFT THE APARTMENT...
...YEAH.

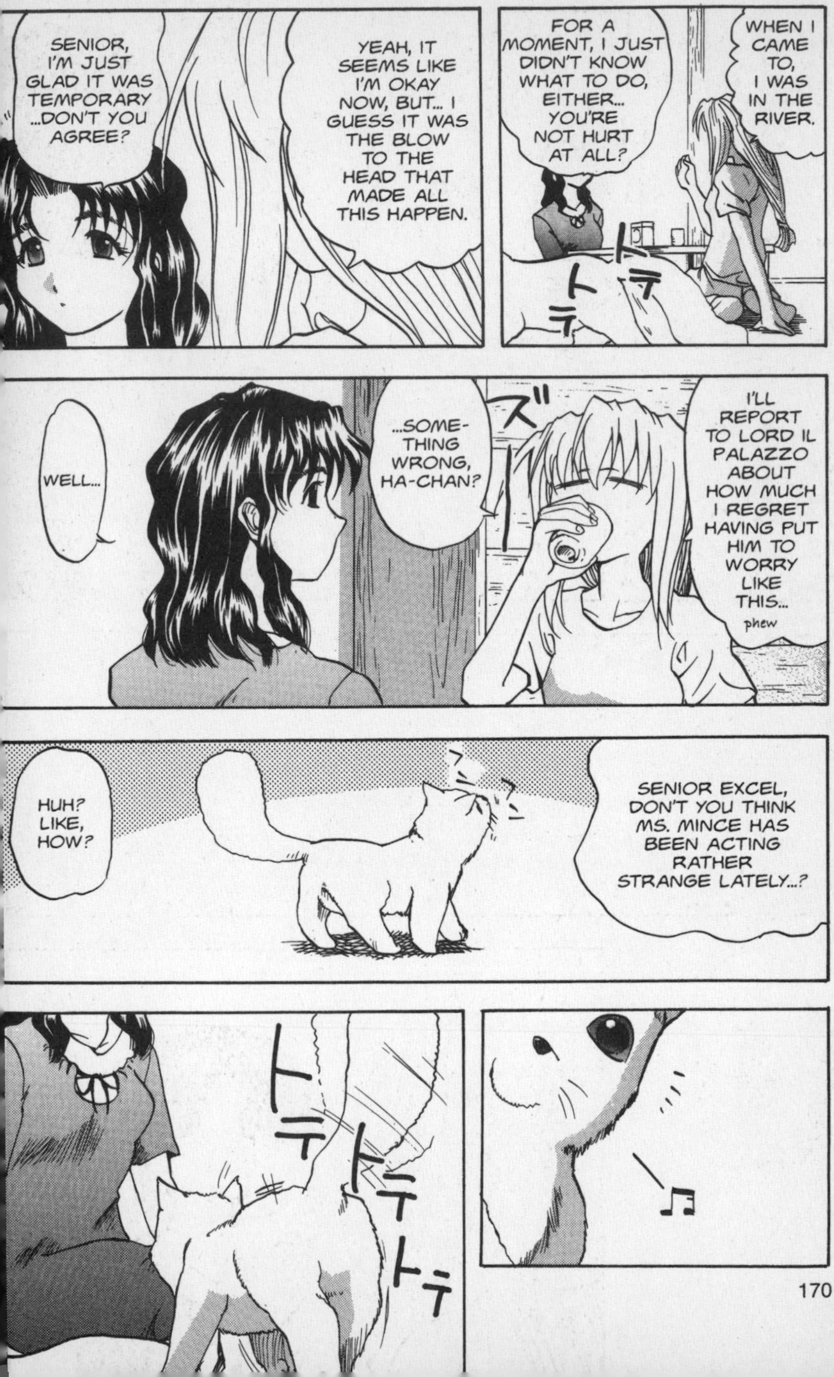
WHEN I CAME TO, I WAS IN THE RIVER.
FOR A MOMENT, I JUST DIDN'T KNOW WHAT TO DO, EITHER... YOU'RE NOT HURT AT ALL?
トテ トテ
YEAH, IT SEEMS LIKE I'M OKAY NOW, BUT... I GUESS IT WAS THE BLOW TO THE HEAD THAT MADE ALL THIS HAPPEN.
SENIOR, I'M JUST GLAD IT WAS TEMPORARY ...DON'T YOU AGREE?
I'LL REPORT TO LORD IL PALAZZO ABOUT HOW MUCH I REGRET HAVING PUT HIM TO WORRY LIKE THIS...
phew
ズー
...SOME-THING WRONG, HA-CHAN?
WELL...
SENIOR EXCEL, DON'T YOU THINK MS. MINCE HAS BEEN ACTING RATHER STRANGE LATELY...?
HUH? LIKE, HOW?
♫
トテトテ トテトテ

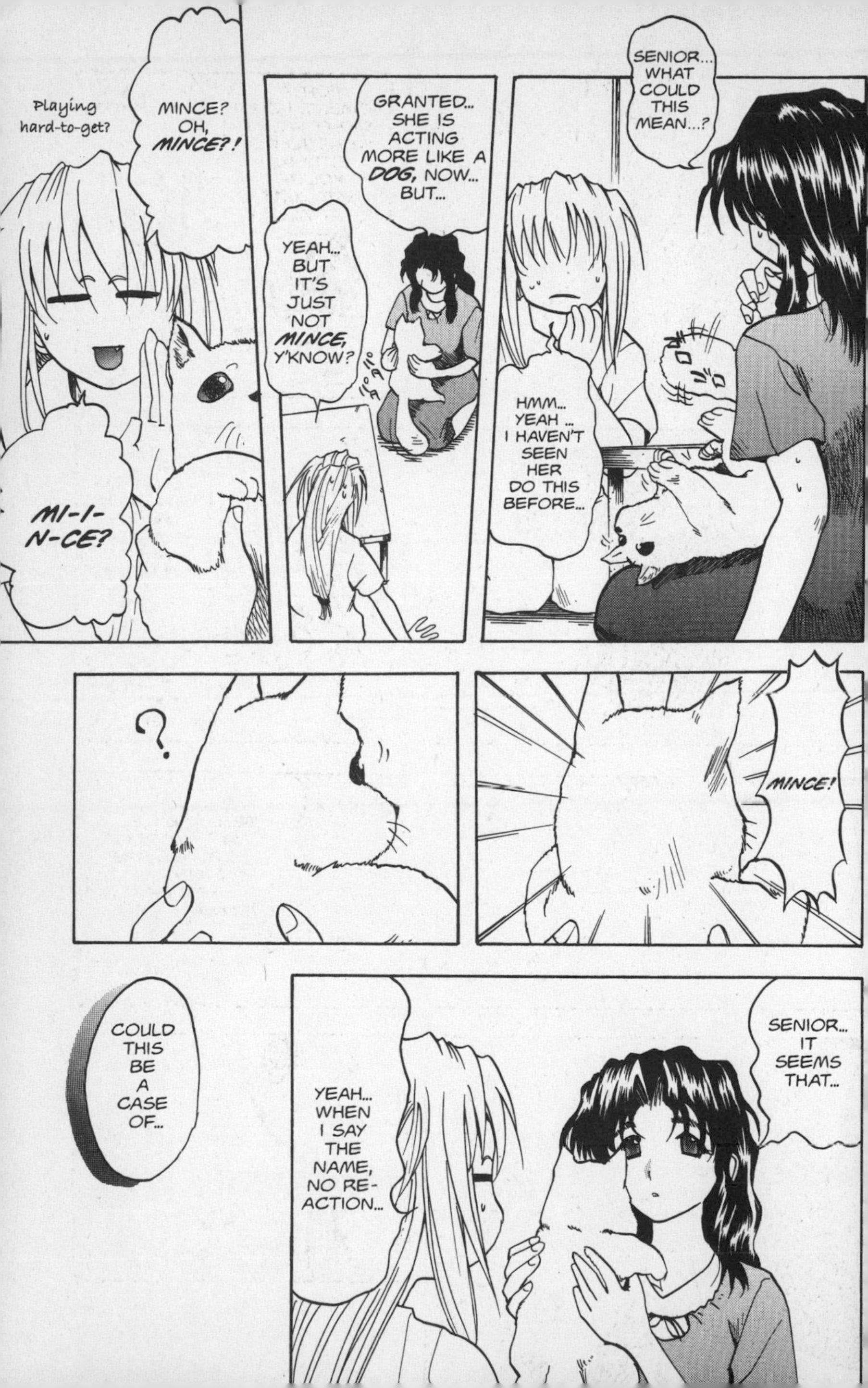
SENIOR... WHAT COULD THIS MEAN...?
HMM... YEAH ... I HAVEN'T SEEN HER DO THIS BEFORE...
GRANTED... SHE IS ACTING MORE LIKE A DOG, NOW... BUT...
YEAH... BUT IT'S JUST NOT MINCE, Y'KNOW?
MINCE? OH, MINCE?!
Playing hard-to-get?
MI-I-N-CE?
MINCE!
?
SENIOR... IT SEEMS THAT...
YEAH... WHEN I SAY THE NAME, NO RE-ACTION...
COULD THIS BE A CASE OF...

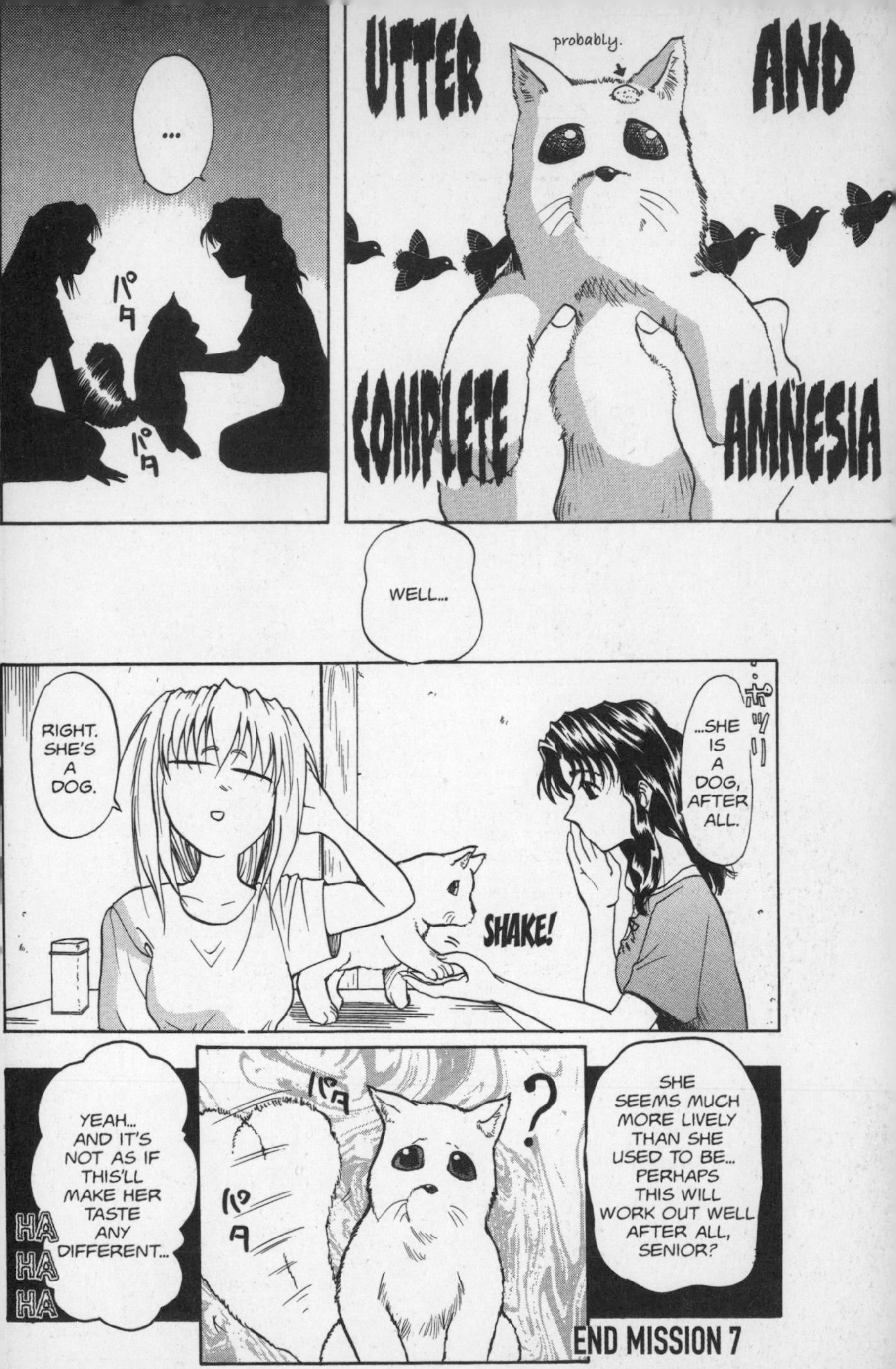
probably.
UTTER AND COMPLETE AMNESIA
...
パタ
パタ
WELL...
ポツリ
...SHE IS A DOG, AFTER ALL.
SHAKE!
RIGHT. SHE'S A DOG.
SHE SEEMS MUCH MORE LIVELY THAN SHE USED TO BE... PERHAPS THIS WILL WORK OUT WELL AFTER ALL, SENIOR?
?
パタ
パタ
YEAH... AND IT'S NOT AS IF THIS'LL MAKE HER TASTE ANY DIFFERENT...
HA HA HA
END MISSION 7

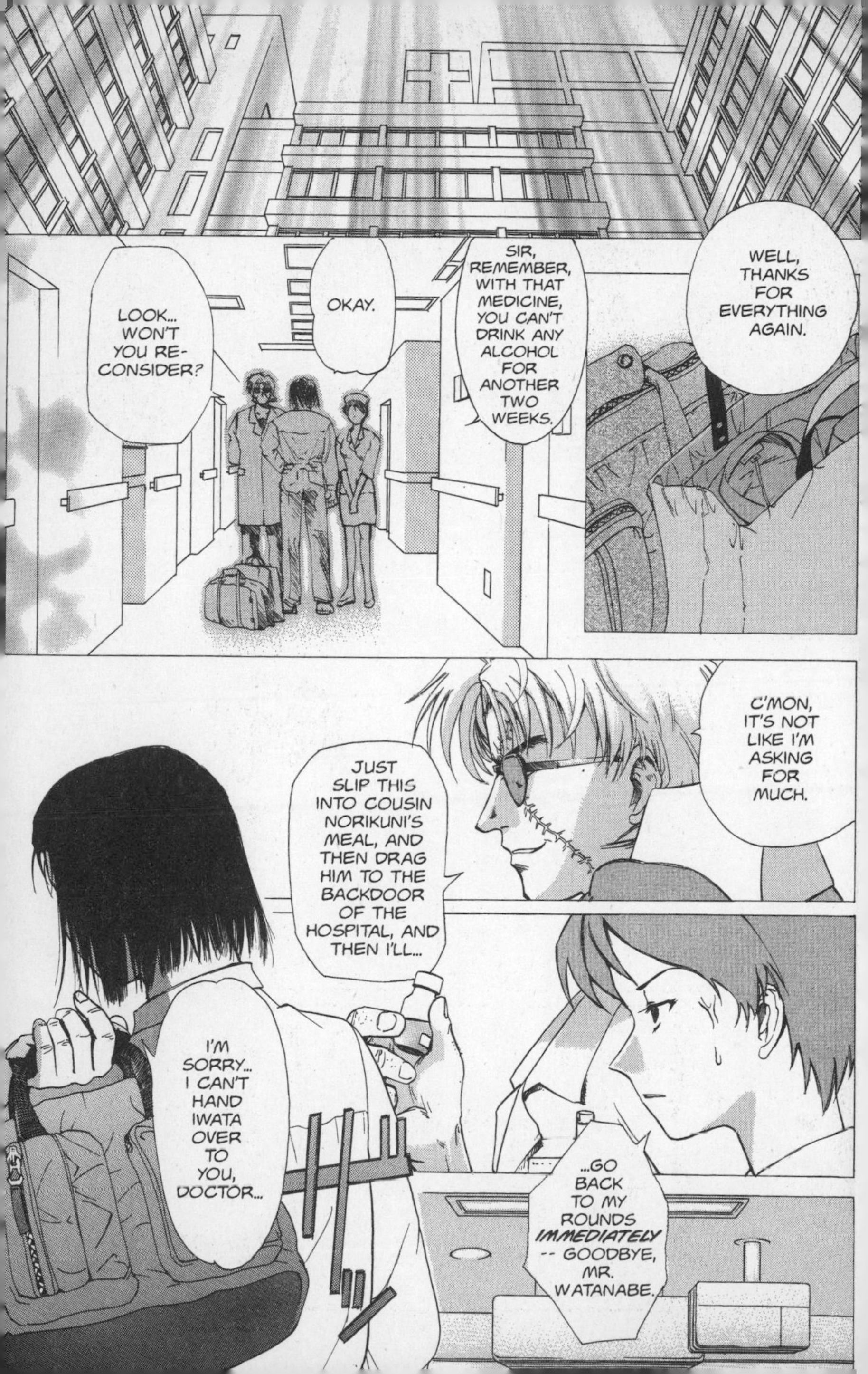
WELL, THANKS FOR EVERYTHING AGAIN.
SIR, REMEMBER, WITH THAT MEDICINE, YOU CAN'T DRINK ANY ALCOHOL FOR ANOTHER TWO WEEKS.
OKAY.
LOOK... WON'T YOU RE-CONSIDER?
C'MON, IT'S NOT LIKE I'M ASKING FOR MUCH.
JUST SLIP THIS INTO COUSIN NORIKUNI'S MEAL, AND THEN DRAG HIM TO THE BACKDOOR OF THE HOSPITAL, AND THEN I'LL...
I'M SORRY... I CAN'T HAND IWATA OVER TO YOU, DOCTOR...
...GO BACK TO MY ROUNDS *IMMEDIATELY* -- GOODBYE, MR. WATANABE.

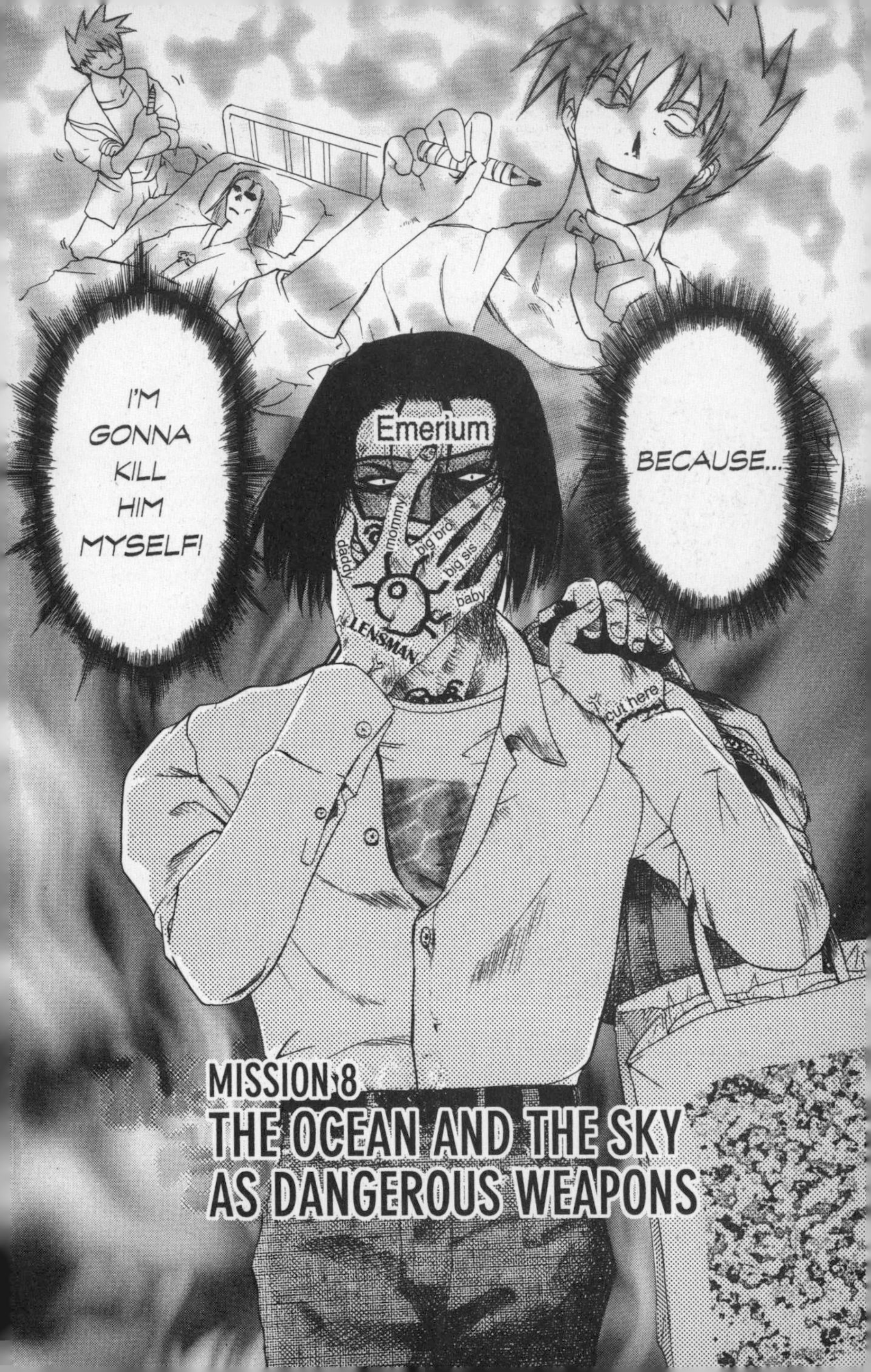
BECAUSE...
I'M GONNA KILL HIM MYSELF!
Emerium
mommy
daddy
big bro
big sis
baby
LENSMAN
cut here
MISSION 8
THE OCEAN AND THE SKY AS DANGEROUS WEAPONS

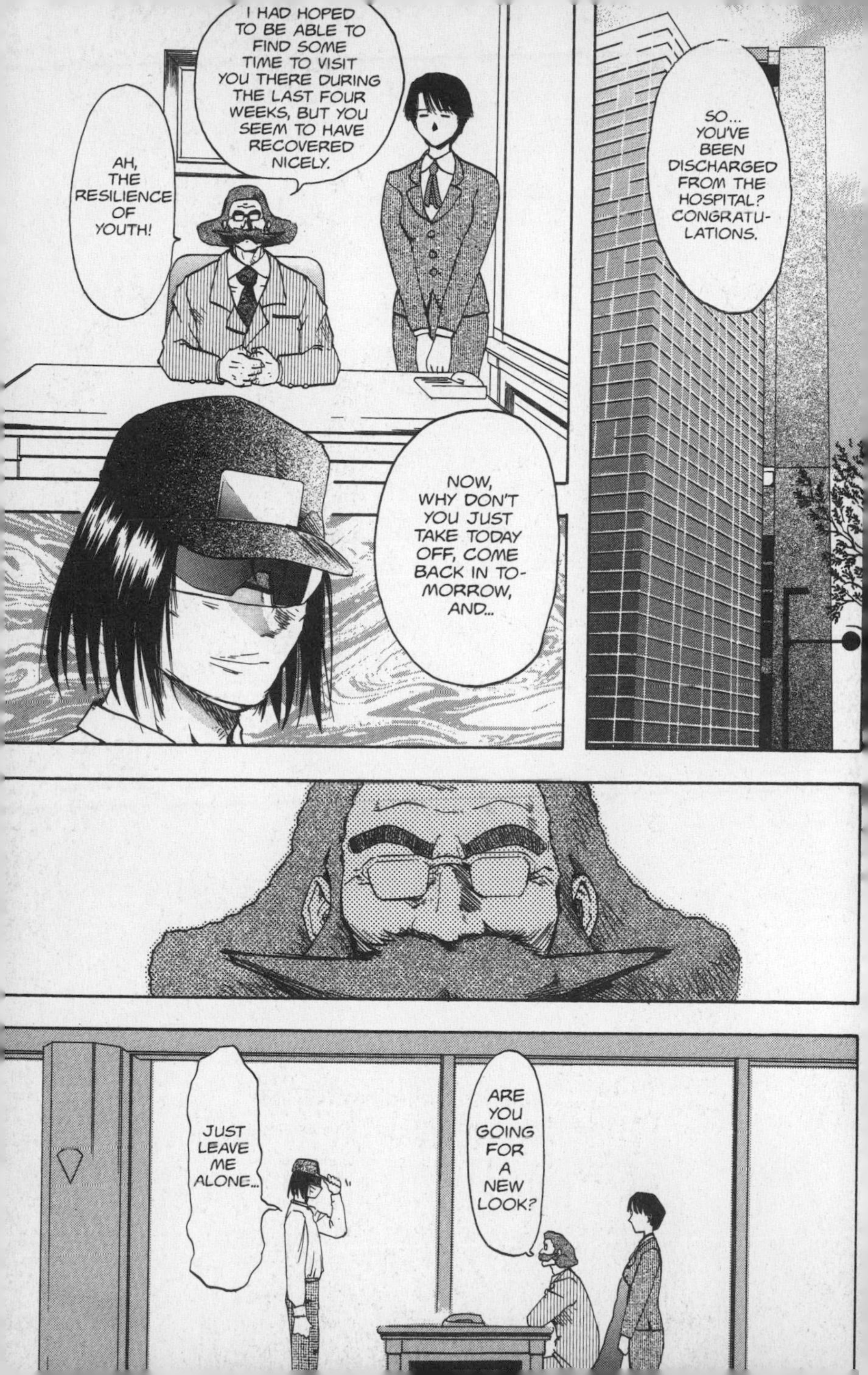
SO... YOU'VE BEEN DISCHARGED FROM THE HOSPITAL? CONGRATULATIONS.
I HAD HOPED TO BE ABLE TO FIND SOME TIME TO VISIT YOU THERE DURING THE LAST FOUR WEEKS, BUT YOU SEEM TO HAVE RECOVERED NICELY.
AH, THE RESILIENCE OF YOUTH!
NOW, WHY DON'T YOU JUST TAKE TODAY OFF, COME BACK IN TOMORROW, AND...
ARE YOU GOING FOR A NEW LOOK?
JUST LEAVE ME ALONE...

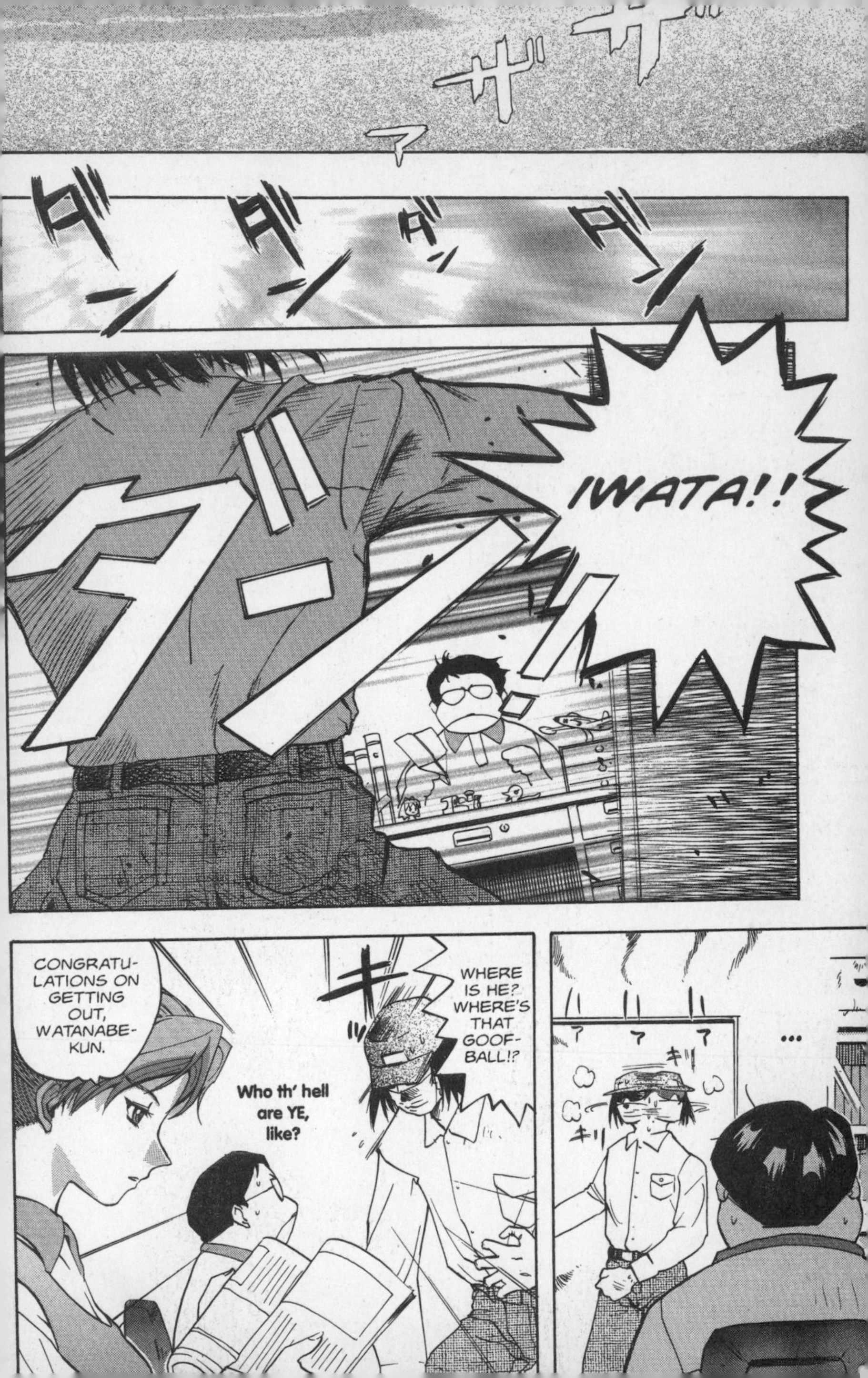
IWATA!!
...
WHERE IS HE? WHERE'S THAT GOOF-BALL!?
CONGRATU-LATIONS ON GETTING OUT, WATANABE-KUN.
Who th' hell are YE, like?

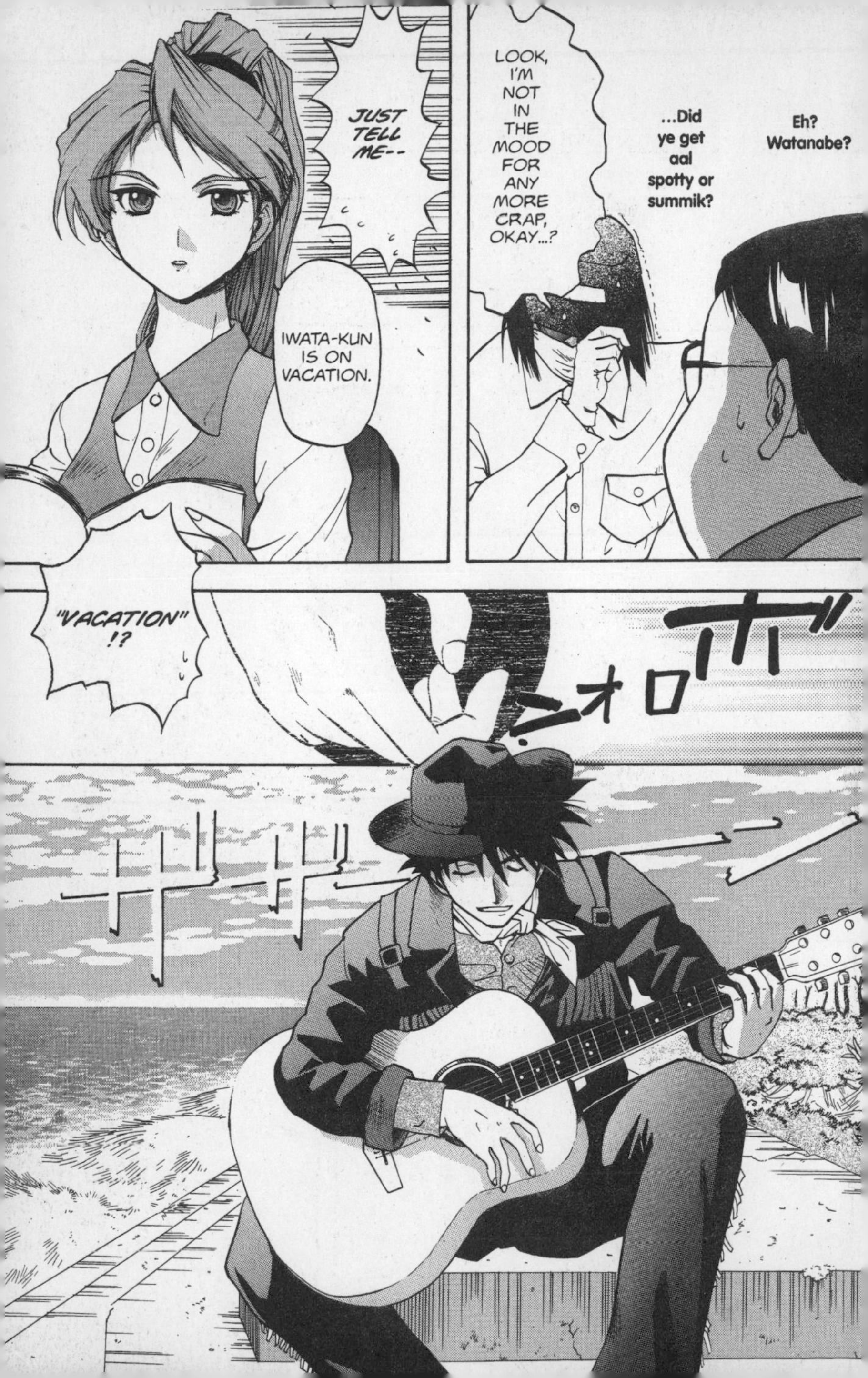
Eh? Watanabe?
...Did ye get aal spotty or summik?
LOOK, I'M NOT IN THE MOOD FOR ANY MORE CRAP, OKAY...?
JUST TELL ME--
IWATA-KUN IS ON VACATION.
"VACATION" !?

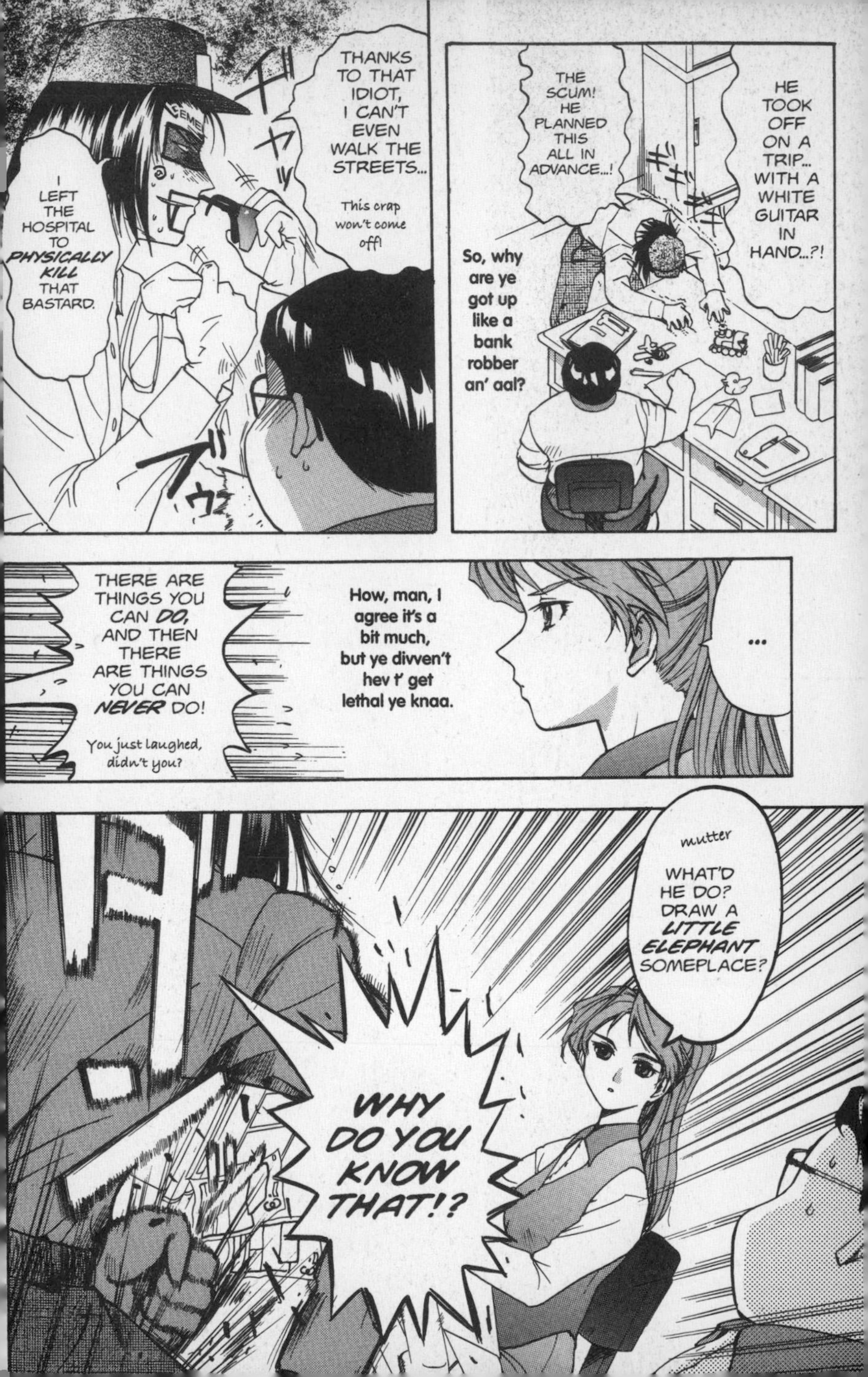
HE TOOK OFF ON A TRIP... WITH A WHITE GUITAR IN HAND...?!
THE SCUM! HE PLANNED THIS ALL IN ADVANCE...!
So, why are ye got up like a bank robber an' aal?
THANKS TO THAT IDIOT, I CAN'T EVEN WALK THE STREETS...
This crap won't come off!
I LEFT THE HOSPITAL TO PHYSICALLY KILL THAT BASTARD.
...
How, man, I agree it's a bit much, but ye divven't hev t' get lethal ye knaa.
THERE ARE THINGS YOU CAN DO, AND THEN THERE ARE THINGS YOU CAN NEVER DO!
You just laughed, didn't you?
mutter
WHAT'D HE DO? DRAW A LITTLE ELEPHANT SOMEPLACE?
WHY DO YOU KNOW THAT!?

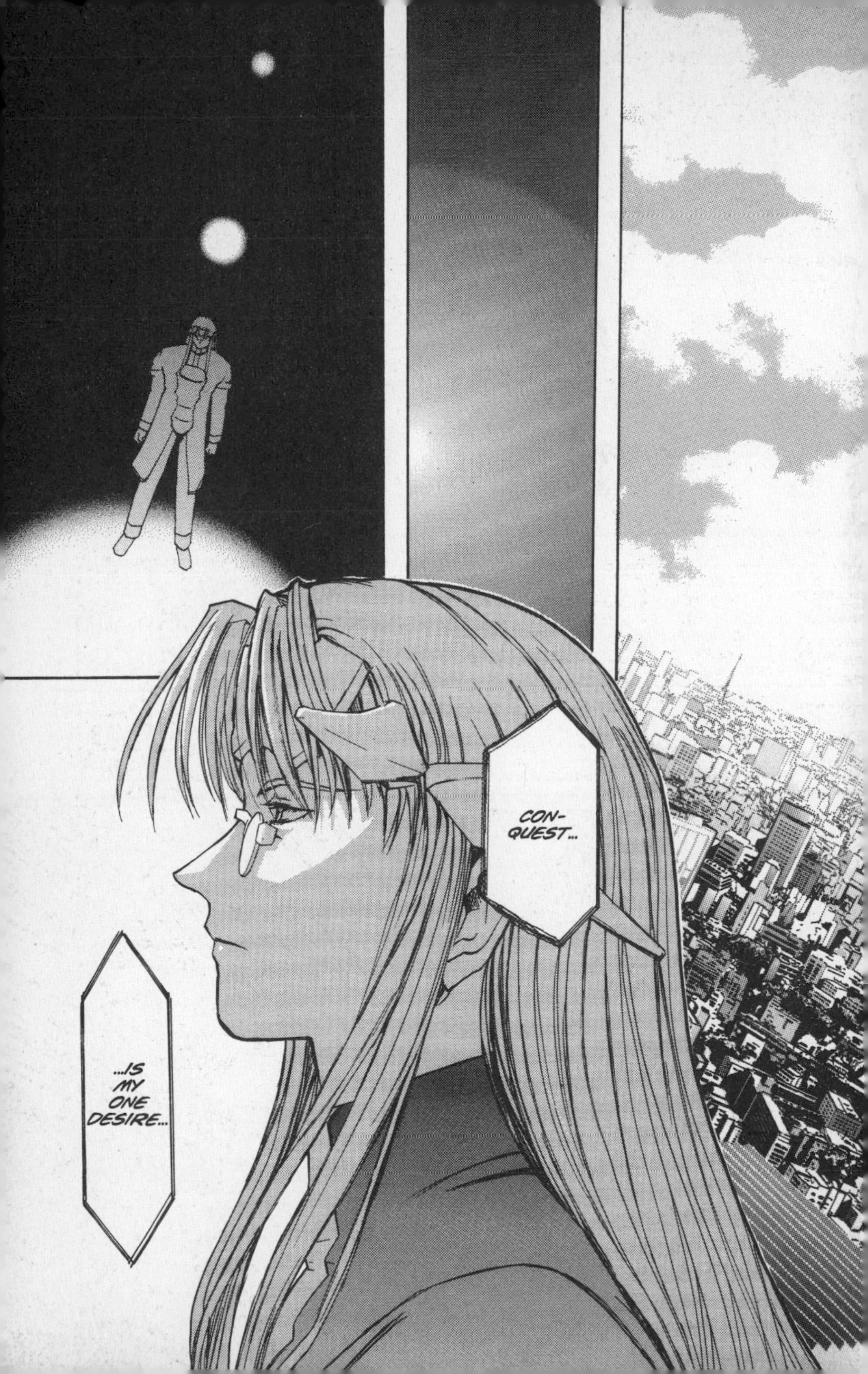
CON-QUEST...
...IS MY ONE DESIRE...

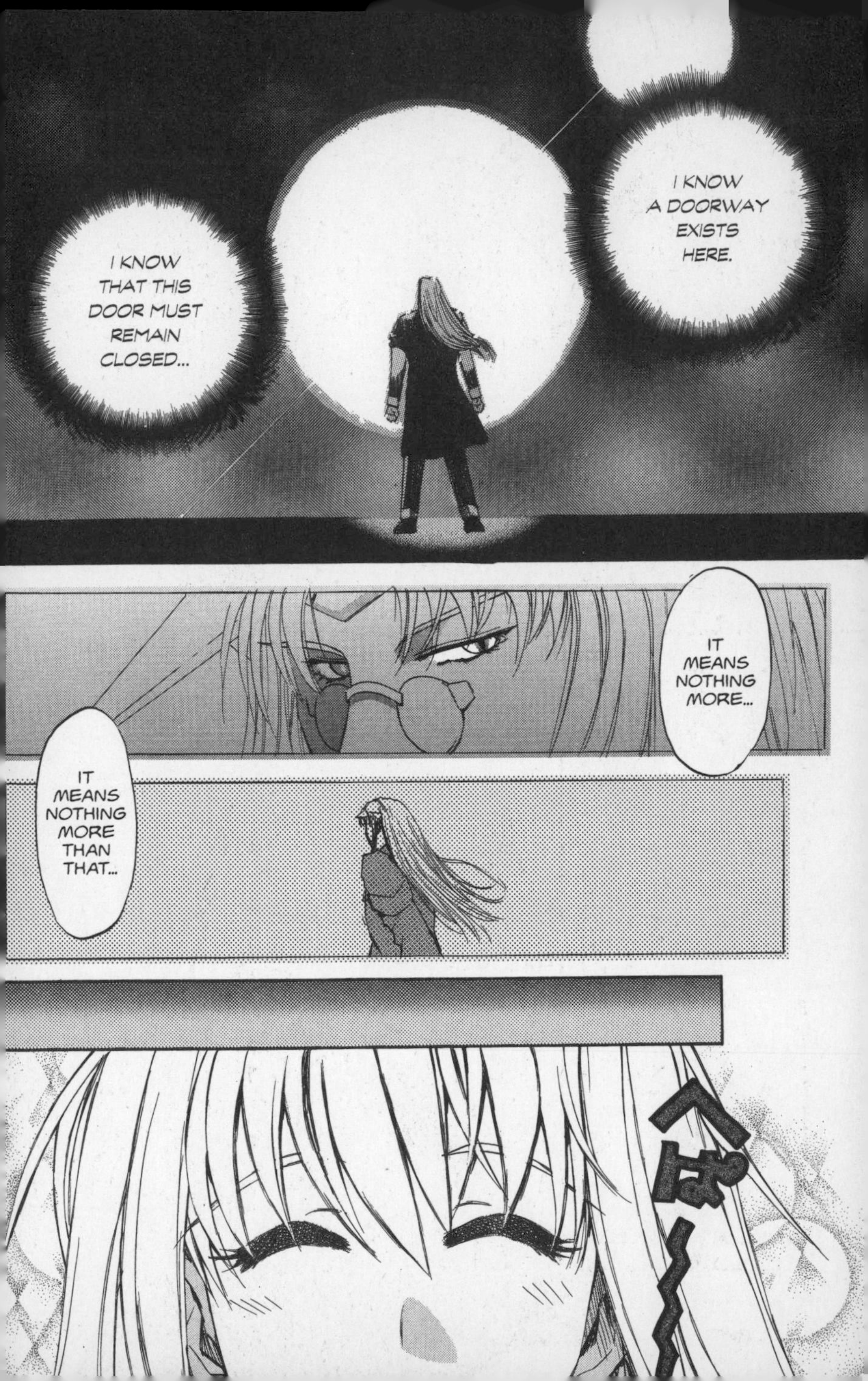
I KNOW A DOORWAY EXISTS HERE.
I KNOW THAT THIS DOOR MUST REMAIN CLOSED...
IT MEANS NOTHING MORE...
IT MEANS NOTHING MORE THAN THAT...
へぱ～～

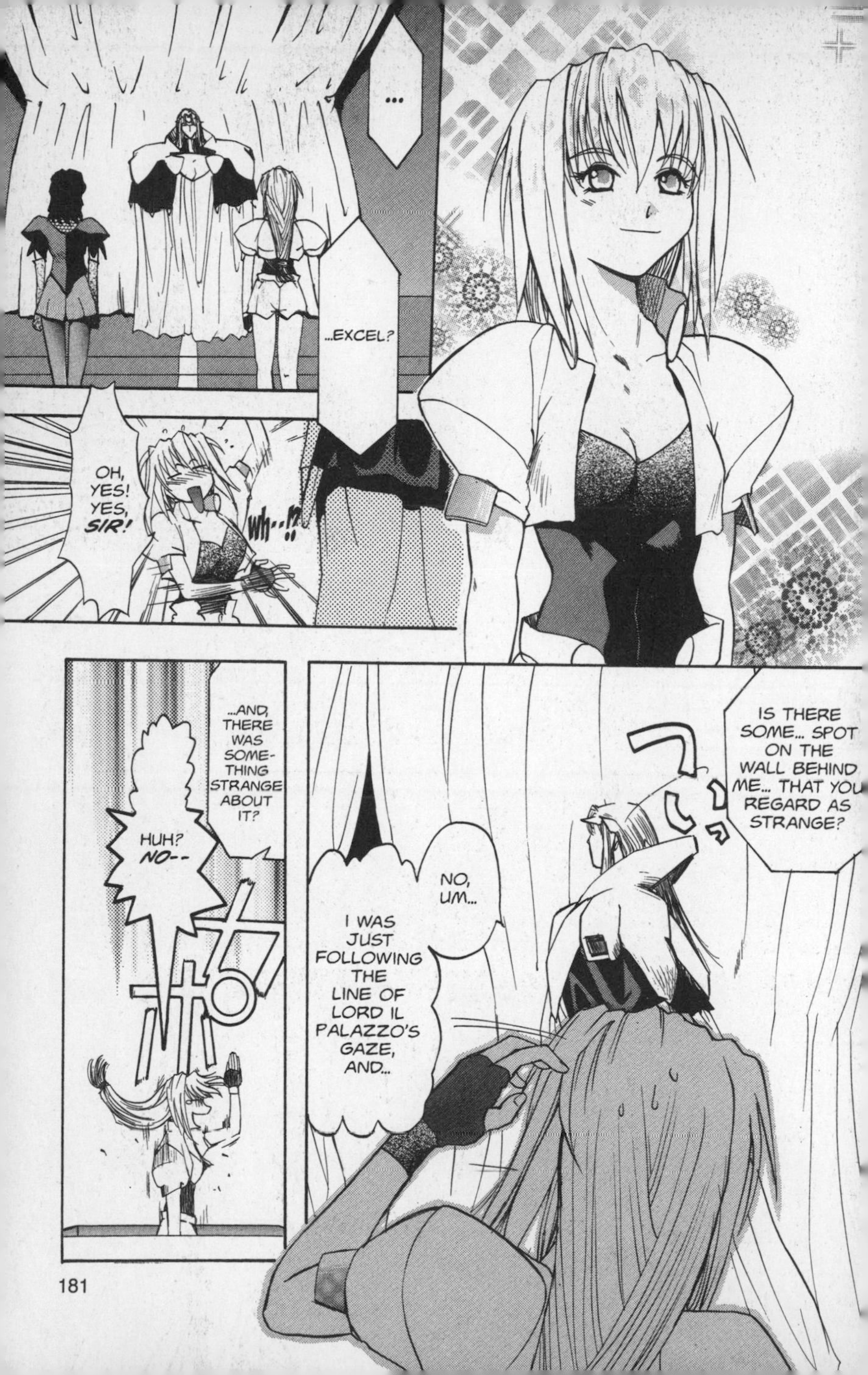
...
...EXCEL?
OH, YES! YES, *SIR!*
Wh--!?
IS THERE SOME... SPOT ON THE WALL BEHIND ME... THAT YOU REGARD AS STRANGE?
NO, UM...
I WAS JUST FOLLOWING THE LINE OF LORD IL PALAZZO'S GAZE, AND...
...AND, THERE WAS SOME-THING STRANGE ABOUT IT?
HUH? *NO--*

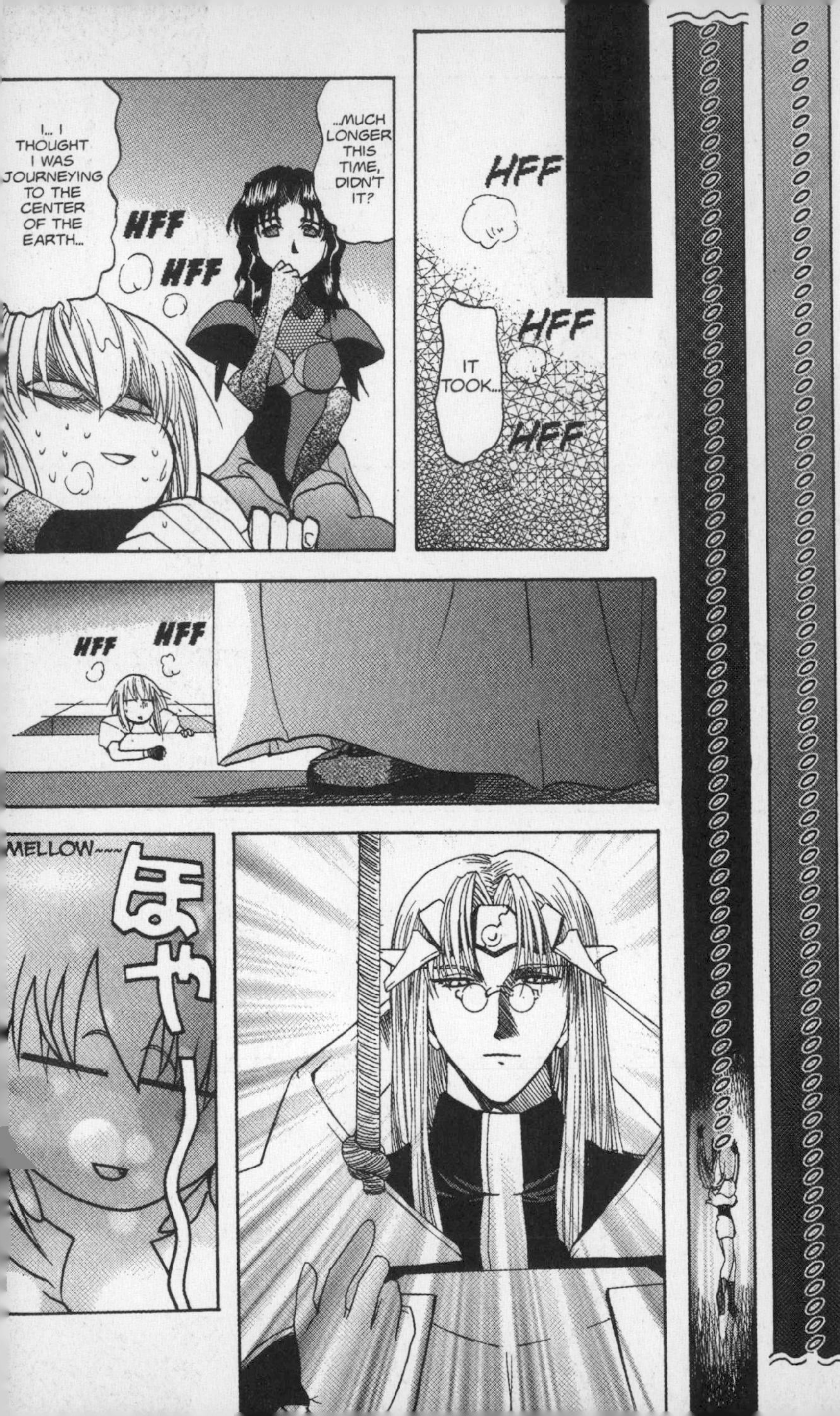
HFF
IT TOOK...
HFF
HFF
...MUCH LONGER THIS TIME, DIDN'T IT?
I... I THOUGHT I WAS JOURNEYING TO THE CENTER OF THE EARTH...
HFF
HFF
HFF
HFF
MELLOW~~~
ほや

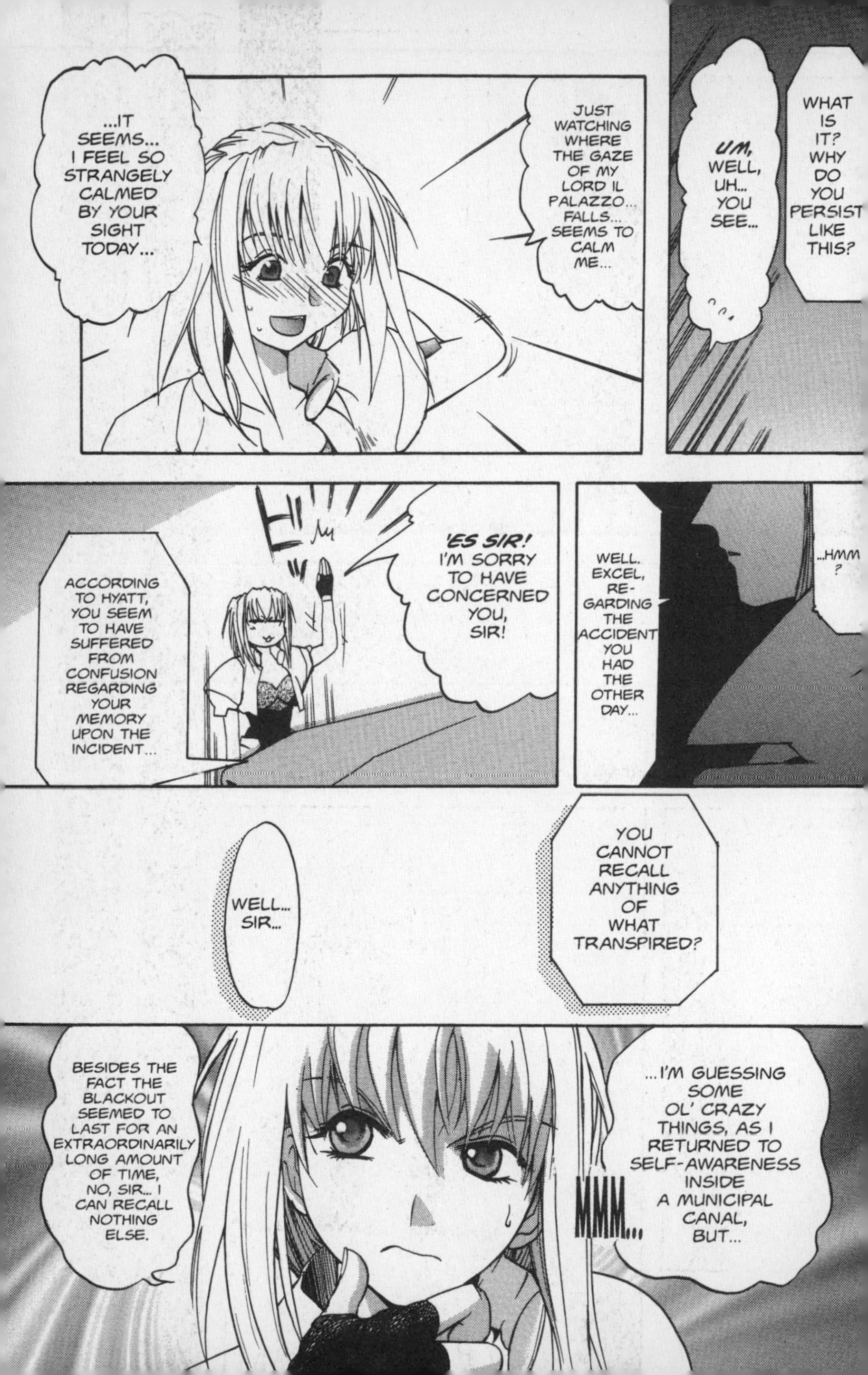
WHAT IS IT? WHY DO YOU PERSIST LIKE THIS?
UM, WELL, UH... YOU SEE...
JUST WATCHING WHERE THE GAZE OF MY LORD IL PALAZZO... FALLS... SEEMS TO CALM ME...
...IT SEEMS... I FEEL SO STRANGELY CALMED BY YOUR SIGHT TODAY...
...HMM ?
WELL. EXCEL, RE-GARDING THE ACCIDENT YOU HAD THE OTHER DAY...
'ES SIR! I'M SORRY TO HAVE CONCERNED YOU, SIR!
ACCORDING TO HYATT, YOU SEEM TO HAVE SUFFERED FROM CONFUSION REGARDING YOUR MEMORY UPON THE INCIDENT...
YOU CANNOT RECALL ANYTHING OF WHAT TRANSPIRED?
WELL... SIR...
...I'M GUESSING SOME OL' CRAZY THINGS, AS I RETURNED TO SELF-AWARENESS INSIDE A MUNICIPAL CANAL, BUT...
MMM...
BESIDES THE FACT THE BLACKOUT SEEMED TO LAST FOR AN EXTRAORDINARILY LONG AMOUNT OF TIME, NO, SIR... I CAN RECALL NOTHING ELSE.

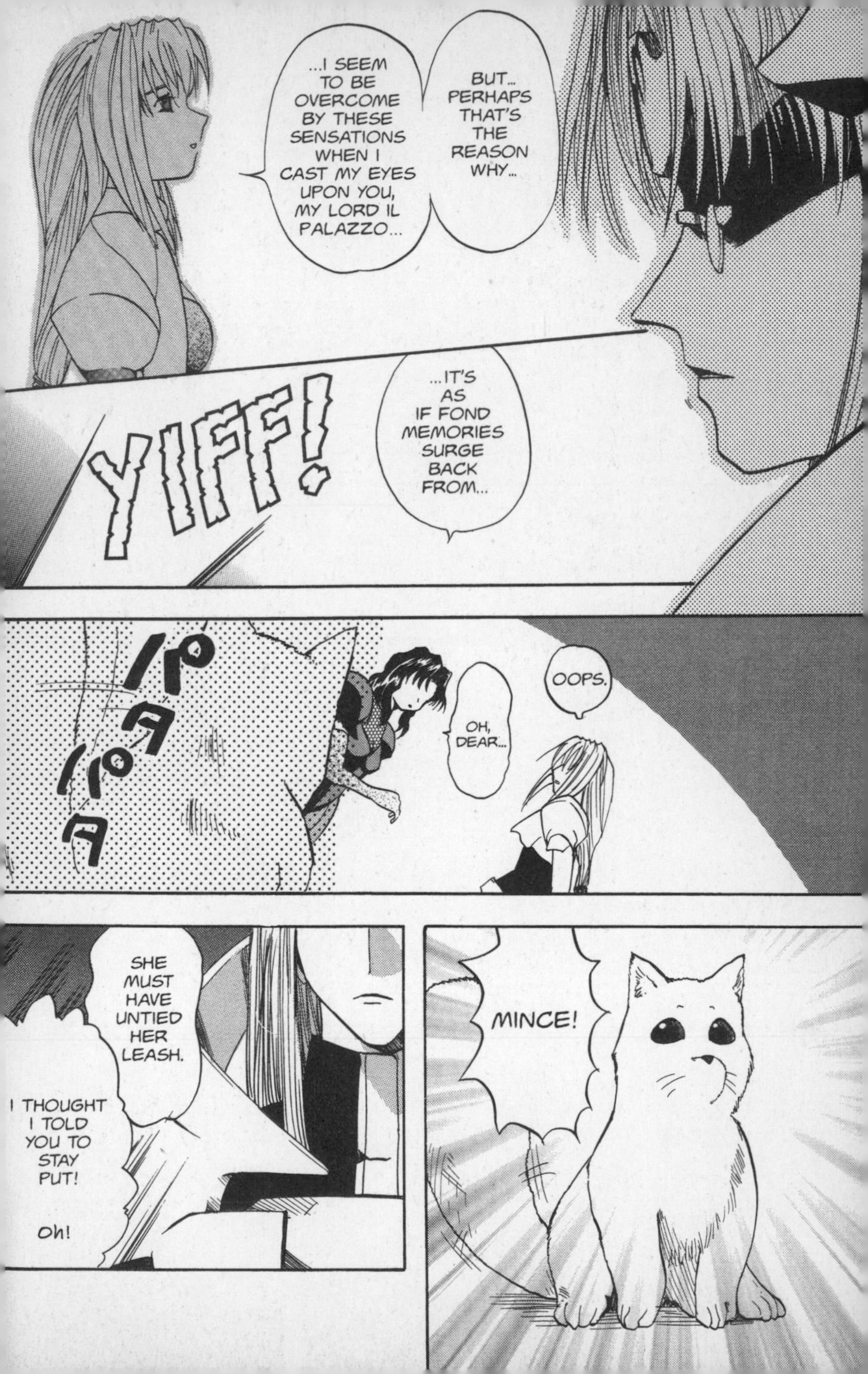
BUT... PERHAPS THAT'S THE REASON WHY...
...I SEEM TO BE OVERCOME BY THESE SENSATIONS WHEN I CAST MY EYES UPON YOU, MY LORD IL PALAZZO...
...IT'S AS IF FOND MEMORIES SURGE BACK FROM...
YIFF!
OOPS.
OH, DEAR...
パタパタ
MINCE!
SHE MUST HAVE UNTIED HER LEASH.
I THOUGHT I TOLD YOU TO STAY PUT!
Oh!

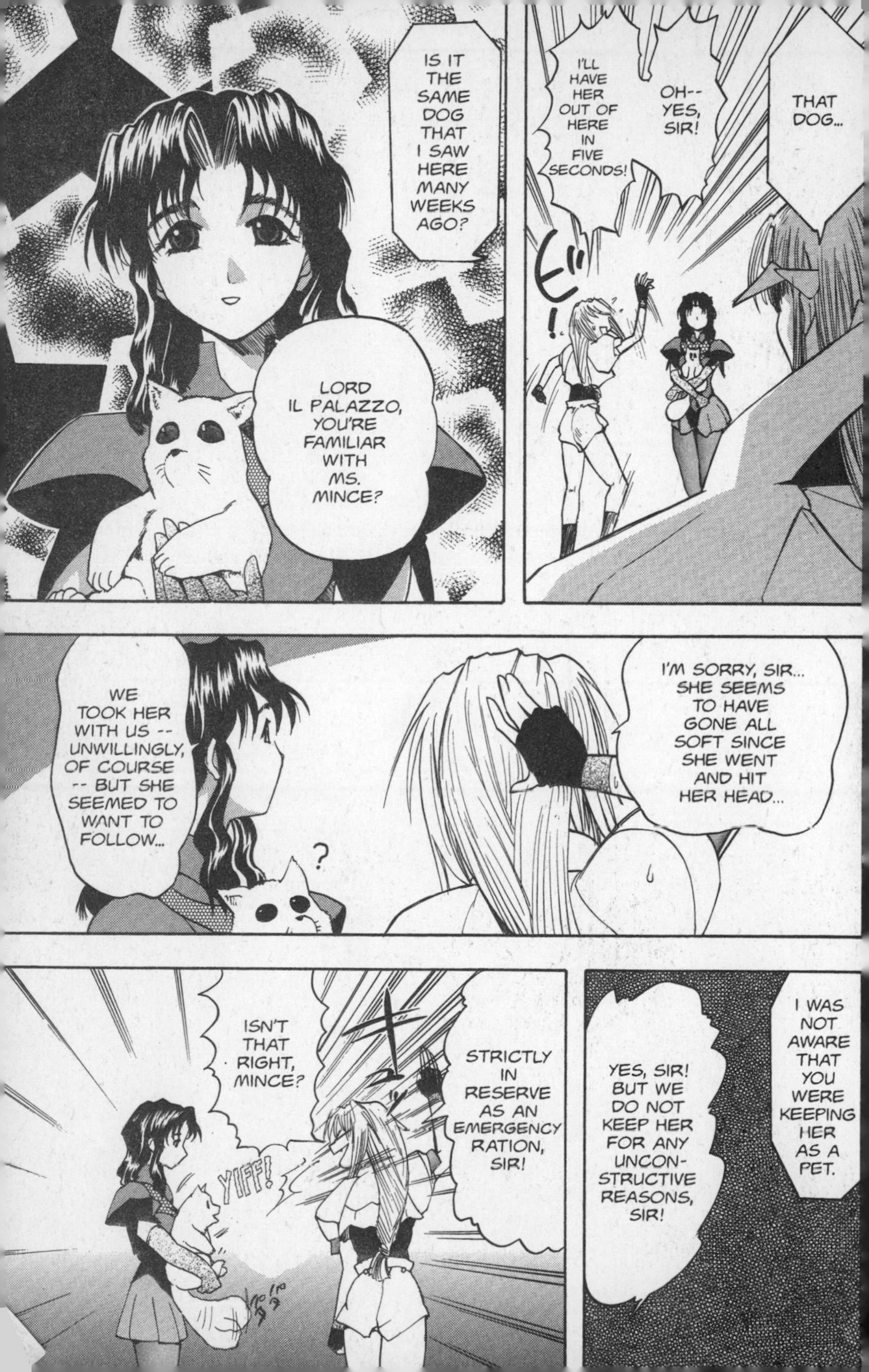
THAT DOG...
OH-- YES, SIR!
I'LL HAVE HER OUT OF HERE IN FIVE SECONDS!
IS IT THE SAME DOG THAT I SAW HERE MANY WEEKS AGO?
LORD IL PALAZZO, YOU'RE FAMILIAR WITH MS. MINCE?
I'M SORRY, SIR... SHE SEEMS TO HAVE GONE ALL SOFT SINCE SHE WENT AND HIT HER HEAD...
?
WE TOOK HER WITH US -- UNWILLINGLY, OF COURSE -- BUT SHE SEEMED TO WANT TO FOLLOW...
I WAS NOT AWARE THAT YOU WERE KEEPING HER AS A PET.
YES, SIR! BUT WE DO NOT KEEP HER FOR ANY UNCON-STRUCTIVE REASONS, SIR!
STRICTLY IN RESERVE AS AN EMERGENCY RATION, SIR!
ISN'T THAT RIGHT, MINCE?
YIFF!

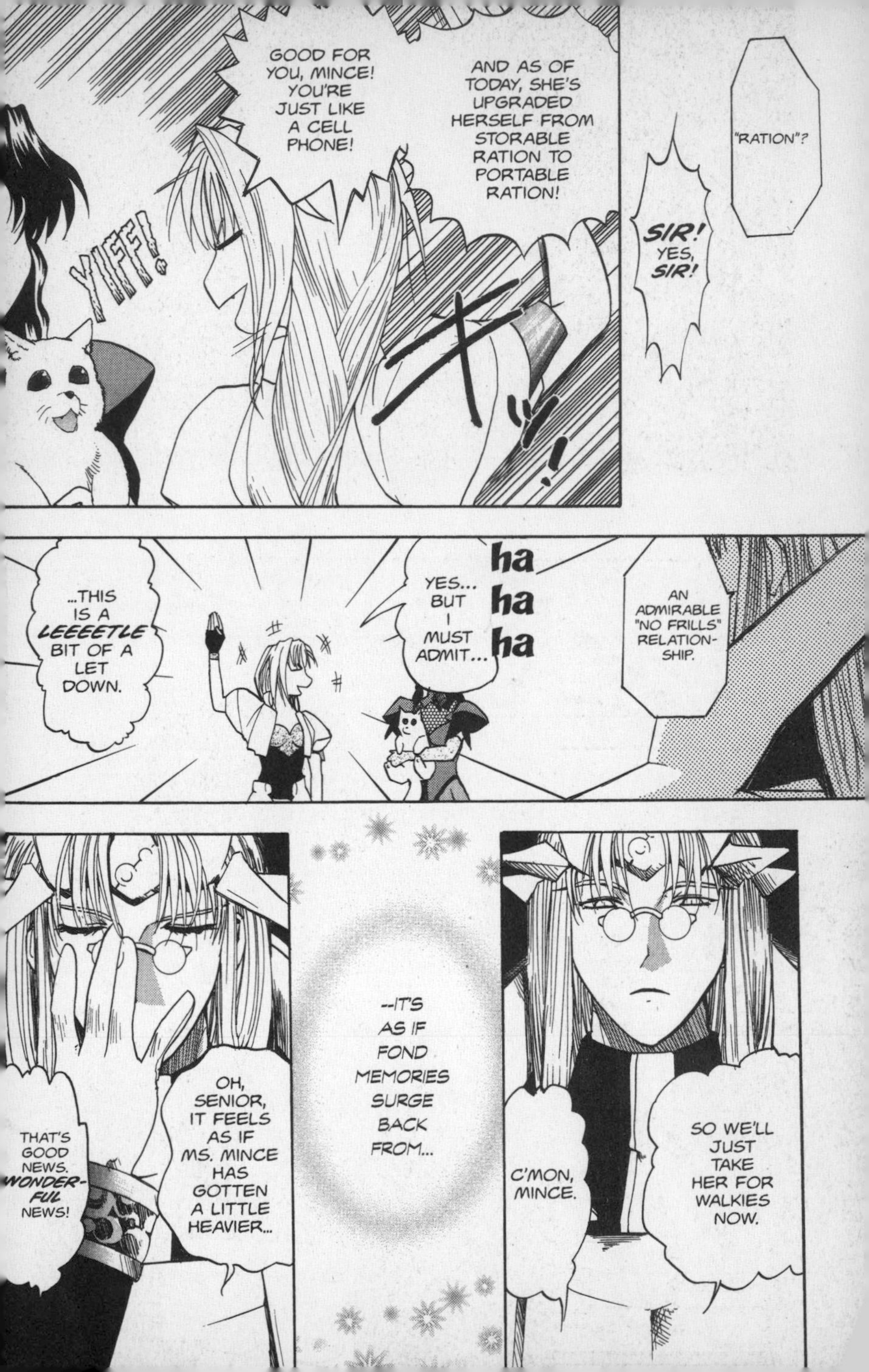
"RATION"?
SIR! YES, SIR!
AND AS OF TODAY, SHE'S UPGRADED HERSELF FROM STORABLE RATION TO PORTABLE RATION!
GOOD FOR YOU, MINCE! YOU'RE JUST LIKE A CELL PHONE!
YIFF!
AN ADMIRABLE "NO FRILLS" RELATIONSHIP.
ha ha ha
YES... BUT I MUST ADMIT...
...THIS IS A LEEEETLE BIT OF A LET DOWN.
SO WE'LL JUST TAKE HER FOR WALKIES NOW.
C'MON, MINCE.
--IT'S AS IF FOND MEMORIES SURGE BACK FROM...
OH, SENIOR, IT FEELS AS IF MS. MINCE HAS GOTTEN A LITTLE HEAVIER...
THAT'S GOOD NEWS. WONDERFUL NEWS!

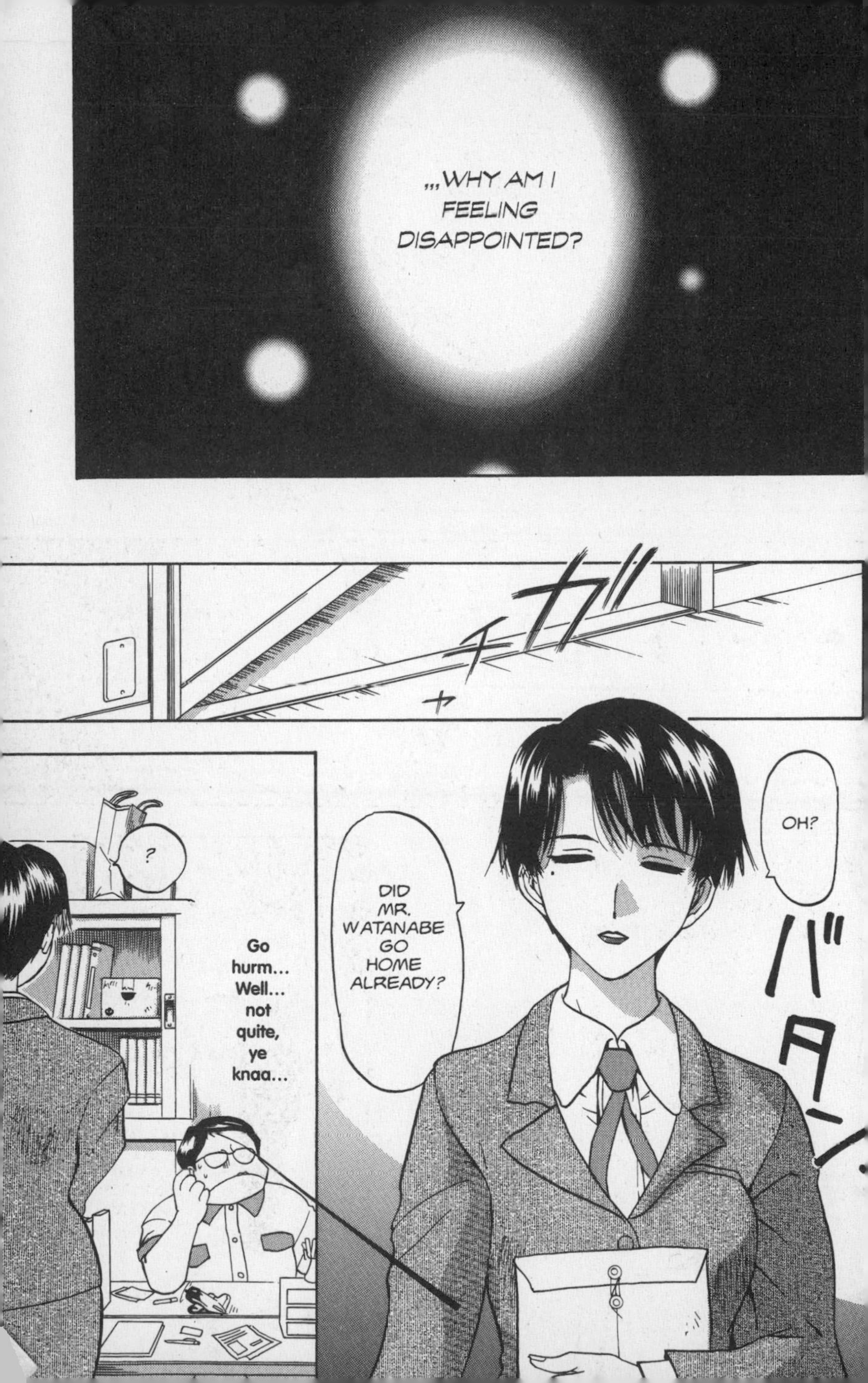
...WHY AM I FEELING DISAPPOINTED?
ガチャ
OH?
DID MR. WATANABE GO HOME ALREADY?
バター!
?
Go hurm... Well... not quite, ye knaa...

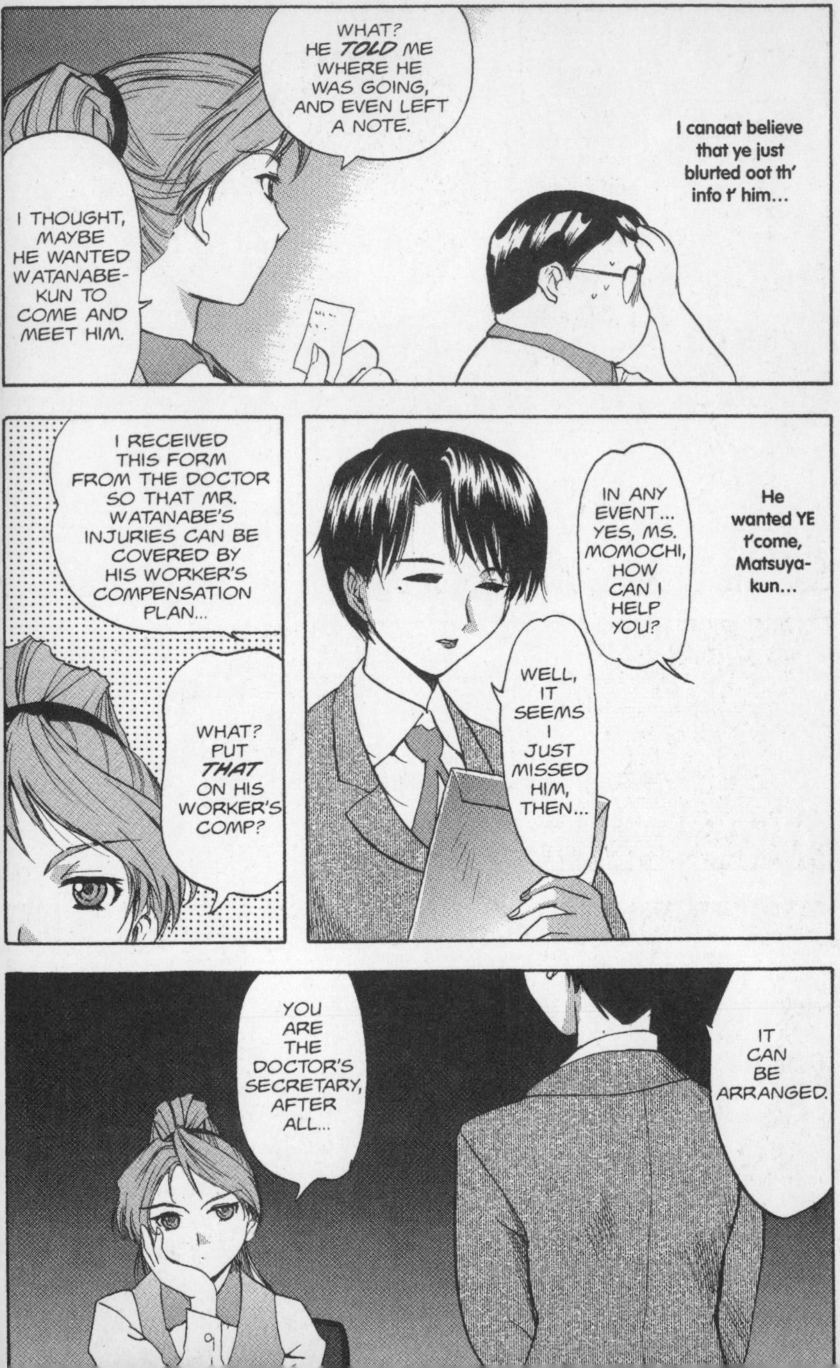
WHAT? HE *TOLD* ME WHERE HE WAS GOING, AND EVEN LEFT A NOTE.
I canaat believe that ye just blurted oot th' info t' him...
I THOUGHT, MAYBE HE WANTED WATANABE-KUN TO COME AND MEET HIM.
He wanted YE t'come, Matsuya-kun...
IN ANY EVENT... YES, MS. MOMOCHI, HOW CAN I HELP YOU?
WELL, IT SEEMS I JUST MISSED HIM, THEN...
I RECEIVED THIS FORM FROM THE DOCTOR SO THAT MR. WATANABE'S INJURIES CAN BE COVERED BY HIS WORKER'S COMPENSATION PLAN...
WHAT? PUT *THAT* ON HIS WORKER'S COMP?
YOU ARE THE DOCTOR'S SECRETARY, AFTER ALL...
IT CAN BE ARRANGED.

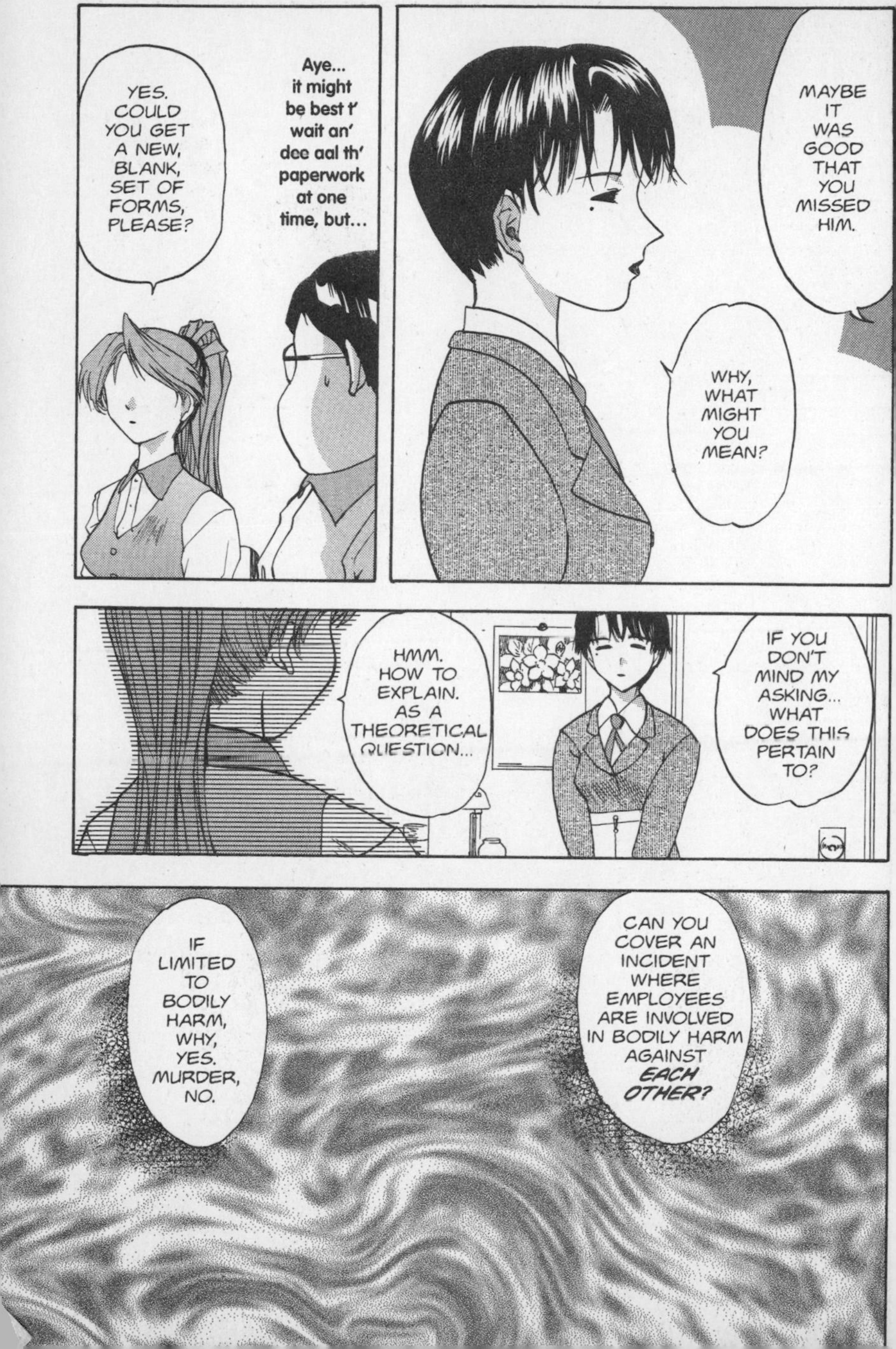
MAYBE IT WAS GOOD THAT YOU MISSED HIM.
WHY, WHAT MIGHT YOU MEAN?
Aye... it might be best t' wait an' dee aal th' paperwork at one time, but...
YES. COULD YOU GET A NEW, BLANK, SET OF FORMS, PLEASE?
IF YOU DON'T MIND MY ASKING... WHAT DOES THIS PERTAIN TO?
HMM. HOW TO EXPLAIN. AS A THEORETICAL QUESTION...
CAN YOU COVER AN INCIDENT WHERE EMPLOYEES ARE INVOLVED IN BODILY HARM AGAINST *EACH OTHER?*
IF LIMITED TO BODILY HARM, WHY, YES. MURDER, NO.

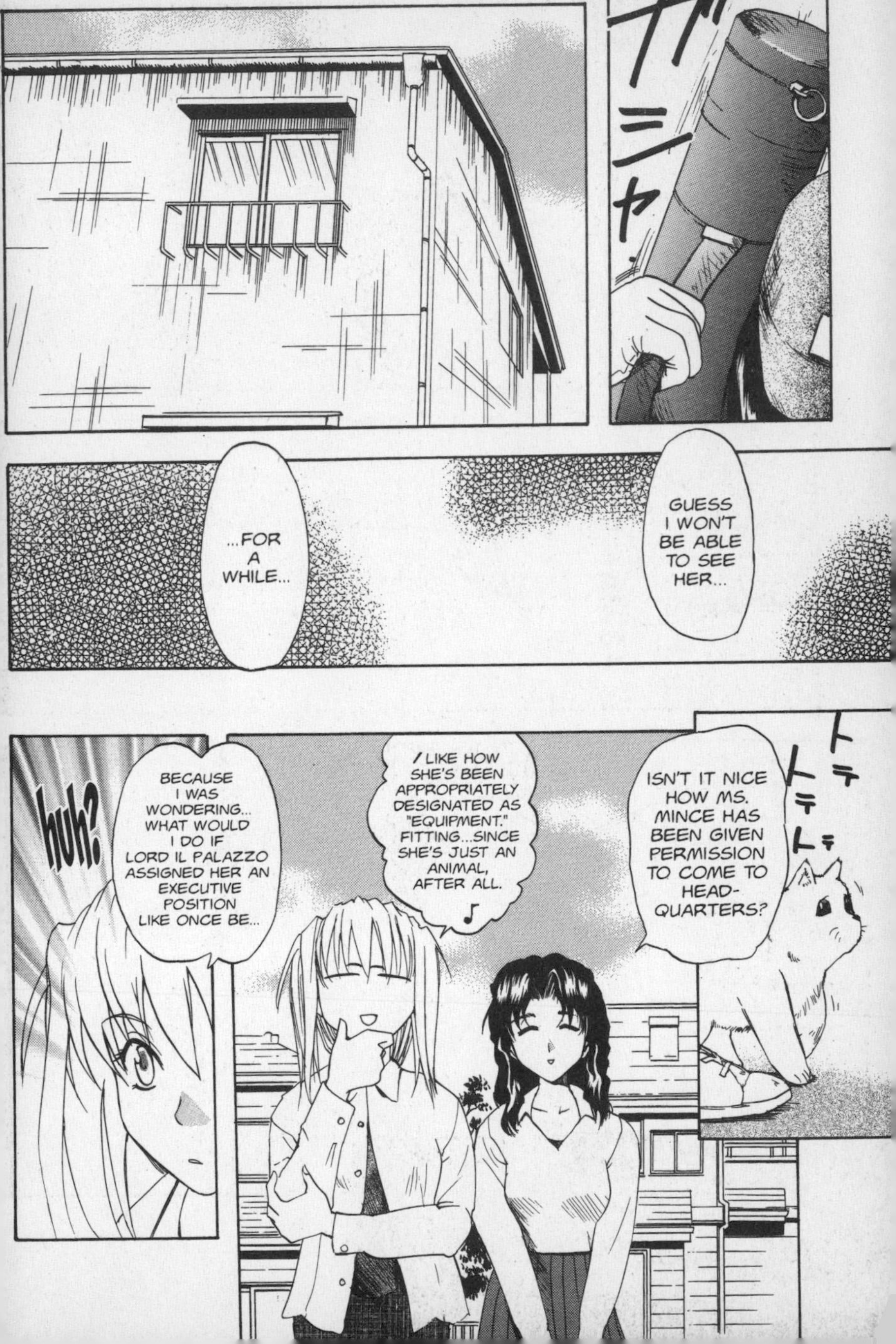
ガシャ
GUESS I WON'T BE ABLE TO SEE HER...
...FOR A WHILE...
トテトテト
ISN'T IT NICE HOW MS. MINCE HAS BEEN GIVEN PERMISSION TO COME TO HEAD-QUARTERS?
I LIKE HOW SHE'S BEEN APPROPRIATELY DESIGNATED AS "EQUIPMENT." FITTING...SINCE SHE'S JUST AN ANIMAL, AFTER ALL. ♪
huh?
BECAUSE I WAS WONDERING... WHAT WOULD I DO IF LORD IL PALAZZO ASSIGNED HER AN EXECUTIVE POSITION LIKE ONCE BE...

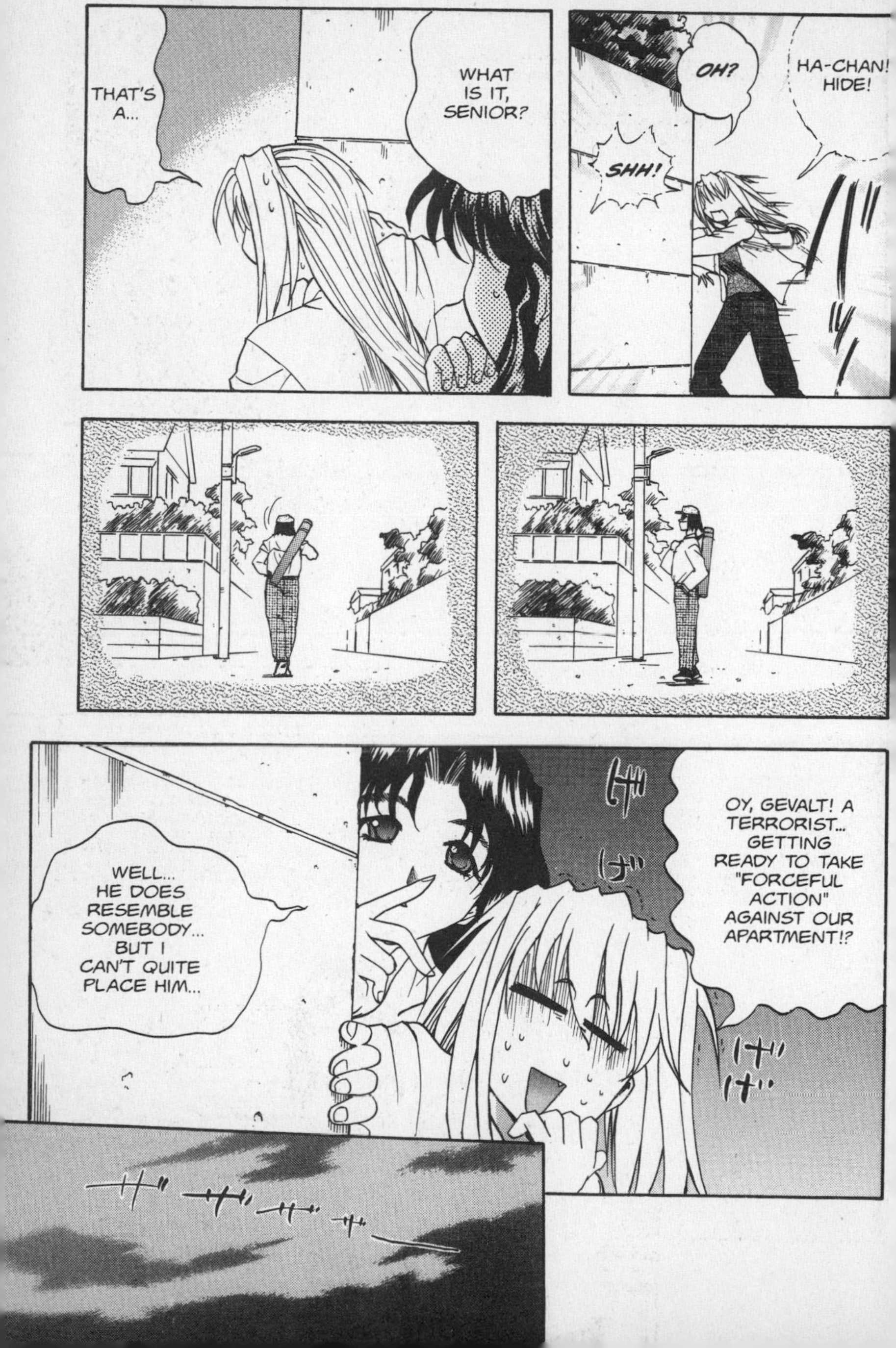
HA-CHAN! HIDE!
OH?
SHH!
WHAT IS IT, SENIOR?
THAT'S A...
OY, GEVALT! A TERRORIST... GETTING READY TO TAKE "FORCEFUL ACTION" AGAINST OUR APARTMENT!?
WELL... HE DOES RESEMBLE SOMEBODY... BUT I CAN'T QUITE PLACE HIM...

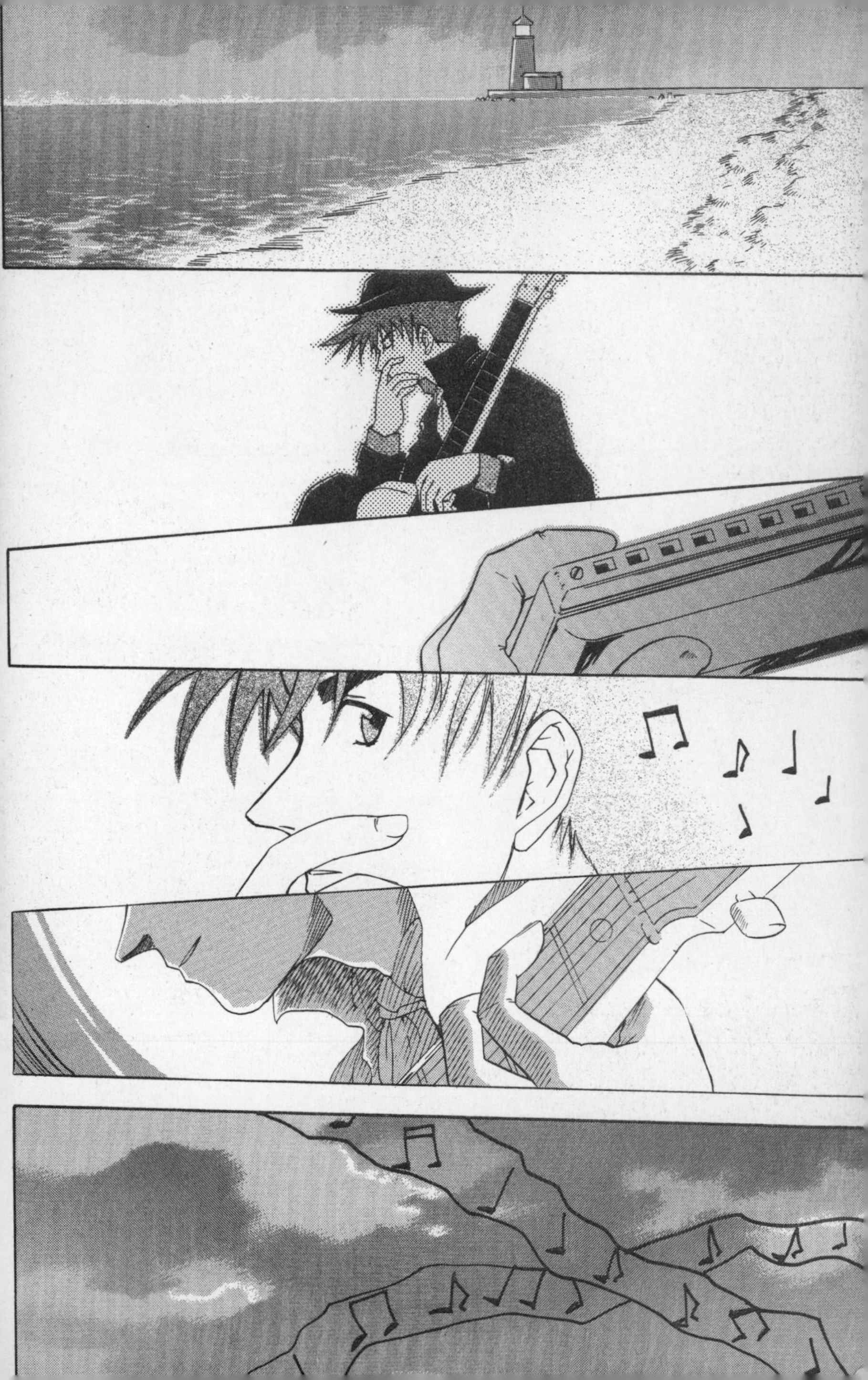

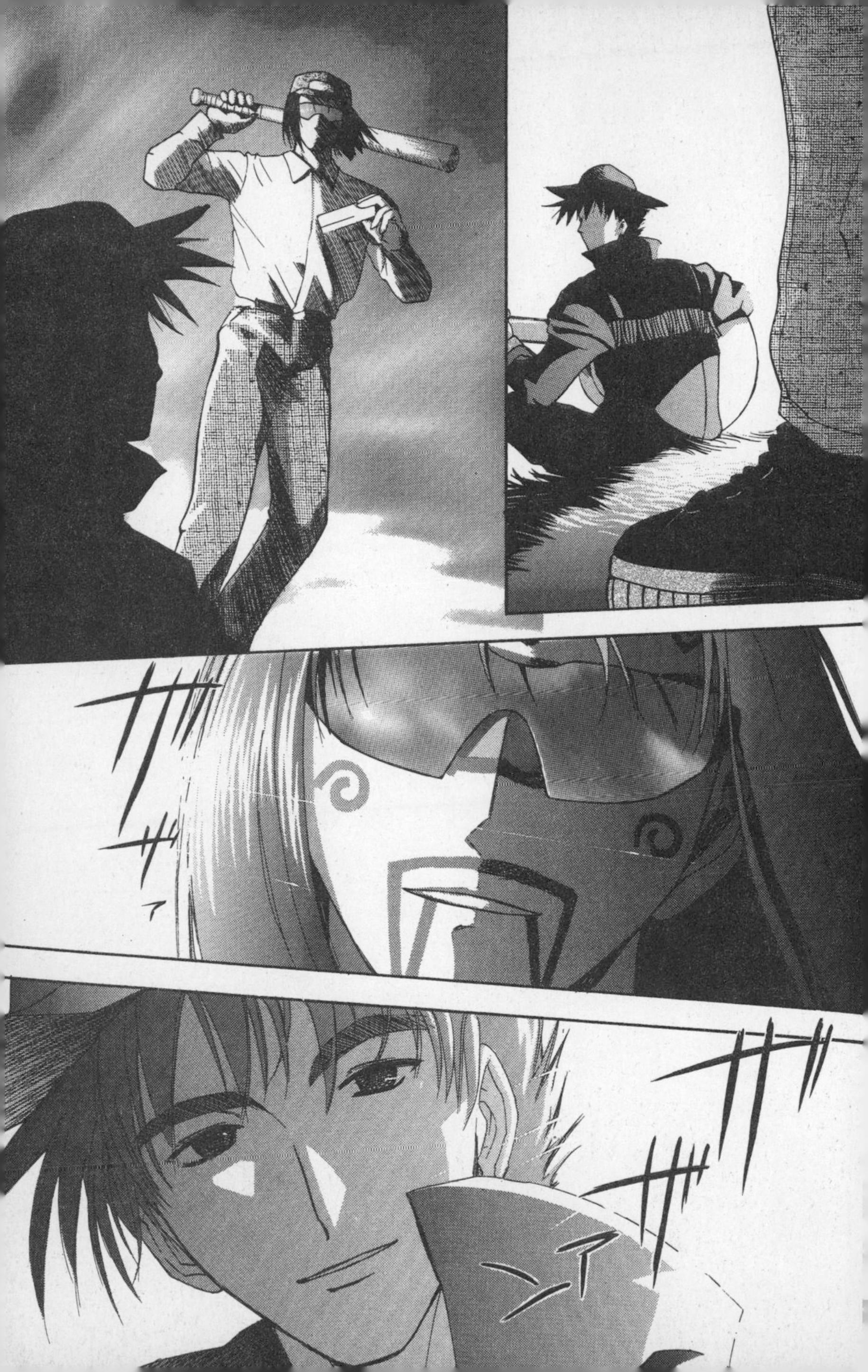

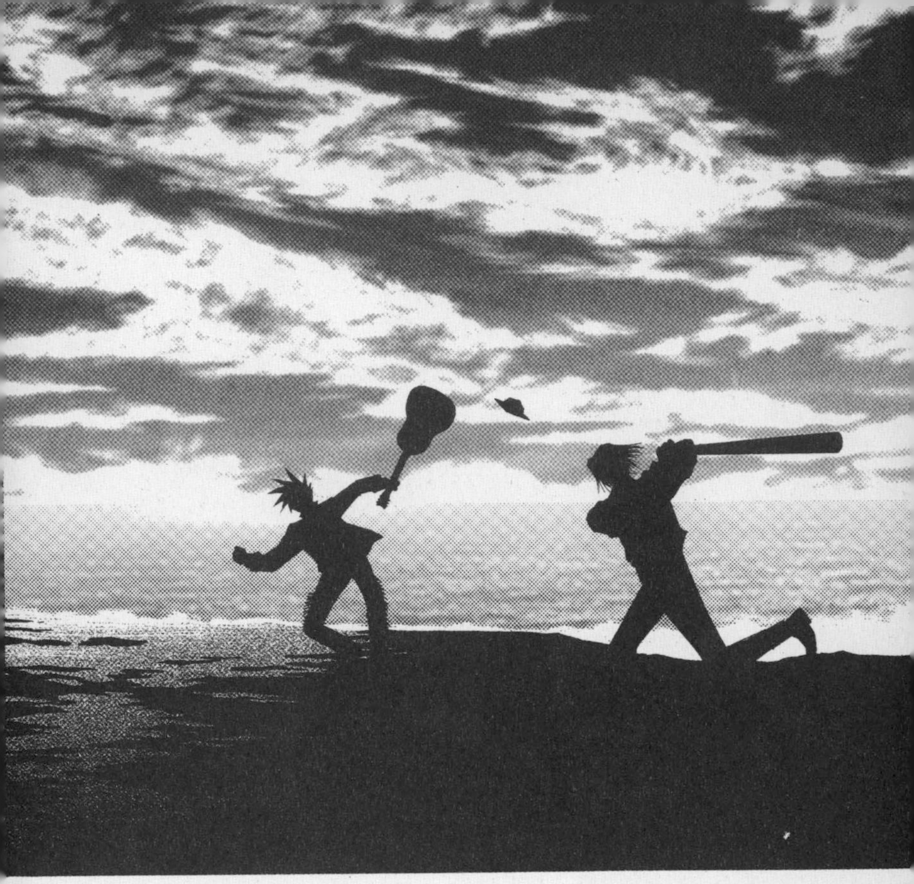

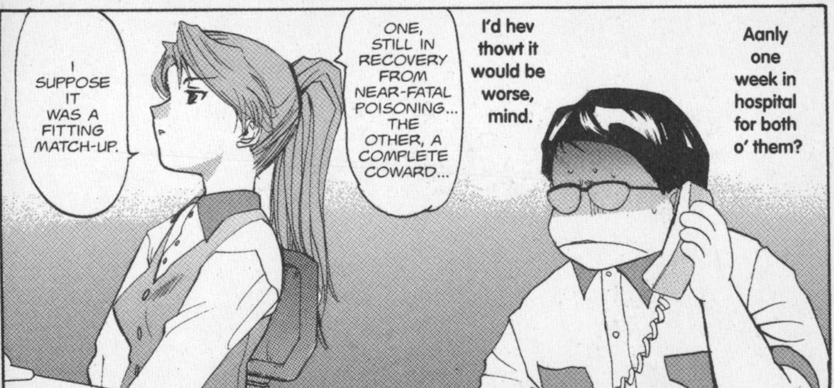
Aanly one week in hospital for both o' them?
I'd hev thowt it would be worse, mind.
ONE, STILL IN RECOVERY FROM NEAR-FATAL POISONING... THE OTHER, A COMPLETE COWARD...
I SUPPOSE IT WAS A FITTING MATCH-UP.

END MISSION 8

EXCEL SAGA

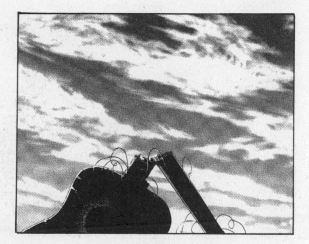

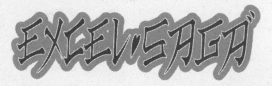

Scenes from the Personal Life of Rikdo Koshi Vol.⑤

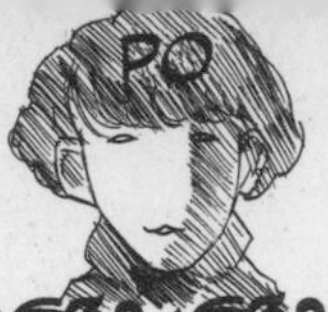
PO

We Who Push the Envelope

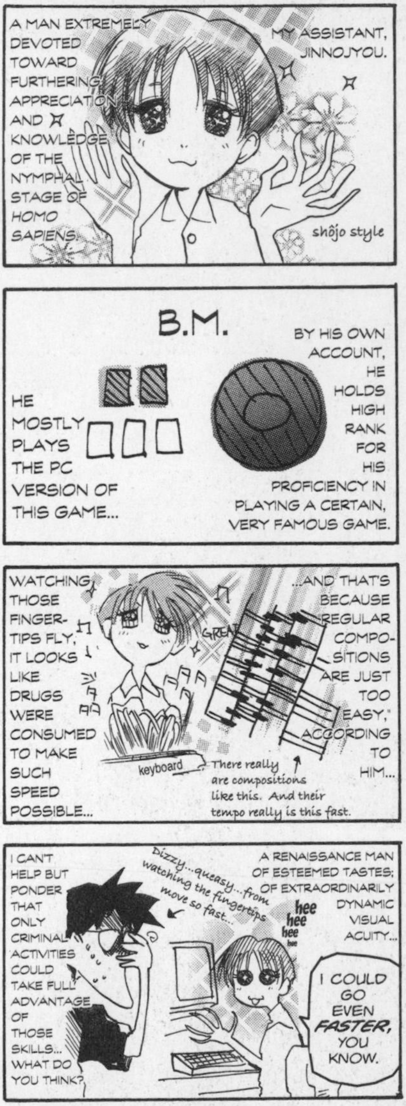
MY ASSISTANT, JINNOJYOU.
A MAN EXTREMELY DEVOTED TOWARD FURTHERING APPRECIATION AND KNOWLEDGE OF THE NYMPHAL STAGE OF *HOMO SAPIENS*.
shôjo style
BY HIS OWN ACCOUNT, HE HOLDS HIGH RANK FOR HIS PROFICIENCY IN PLAYING A CERTAIN, VERY FAMOUS GAME.
B.M.
HE MOSTLY PLAYS THE PC VERSION OF THIS GAME...
...AND THAT'S BECAUSE "REGULAR COMPOSITIONS ARE JUST TOO EASY," ACCORDING TO HIM...
WATCHING THOSE FINGERTIPS FLY, IT LOOKS LIKE DRUGS WERE CONSUMED TO MAKE SUCH SPEED POSSIBLE...
keyboard
There really are compositions like this. And their tempo really is this fast.
A RENAISSANCE MAN OF ESTEEMED TASTES; OF EXTRAORDINARILY DYNAMIC VISUAL ACUITY...
hee hee hee hee
I COULD GO EVEN *FASTER,* YOU KNOW.
Dizzy...queasy...from watching the fingertips move so fast...
I CAN'T HELP BUT PONDER THAT ONLY CRIMINAL ACTIVITIES COULD TAKE FULL ADVANTAGE OF THOSE SKILLS... WHAT DO YOU THINK?

We Who Can Fly

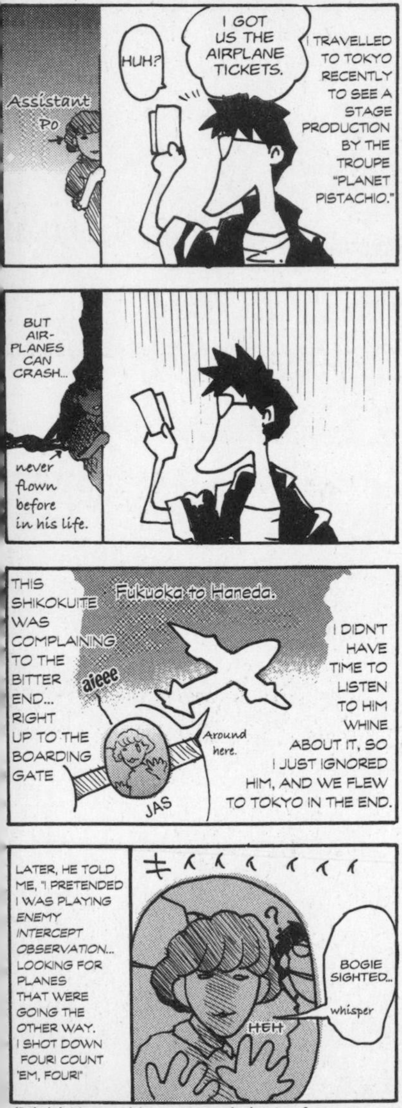
I TRAVELLED TO TOKYO RECENTLY TO SEE A STAGE PRODUCTION BY THE TROUPE "PLANET PISTACHIO."
I GOT US THE AIRPLANE TICKETS.
HUH?
Assistant Po
BUT AIRPLANES CAN CRASH...
never flown before in his life.
I DIDN'T HAVE TIME TO LISTEN TO HIM WHINE ABOUT IT, SO I JUST IGNORED HIM, AND WE FLEW TO TOKYO IN THE END.
Fukuoka to Haneda.
THIS SHIKOKUITE WAS COMPLAINING TO THE BITTER END... RIGHT UP TO THE BOARDING GATE
aieee
Around here.
JAS
キィィィィィィ
BOGIE SIGHTED...
whisper
HEH
LATER, HE TOLD ME, "I PRETENDED I WAS PLAYING *ENEMY INTERCEPT OBSERVATION*... LOOKING FOR PLANES THAT WERE GOING THE OTHER WAY. I SHOT DOWN FOUR! COUNT 'EM, FOUR!"

(Rikdo) Hey, at least ***someone's*** *having fun...*

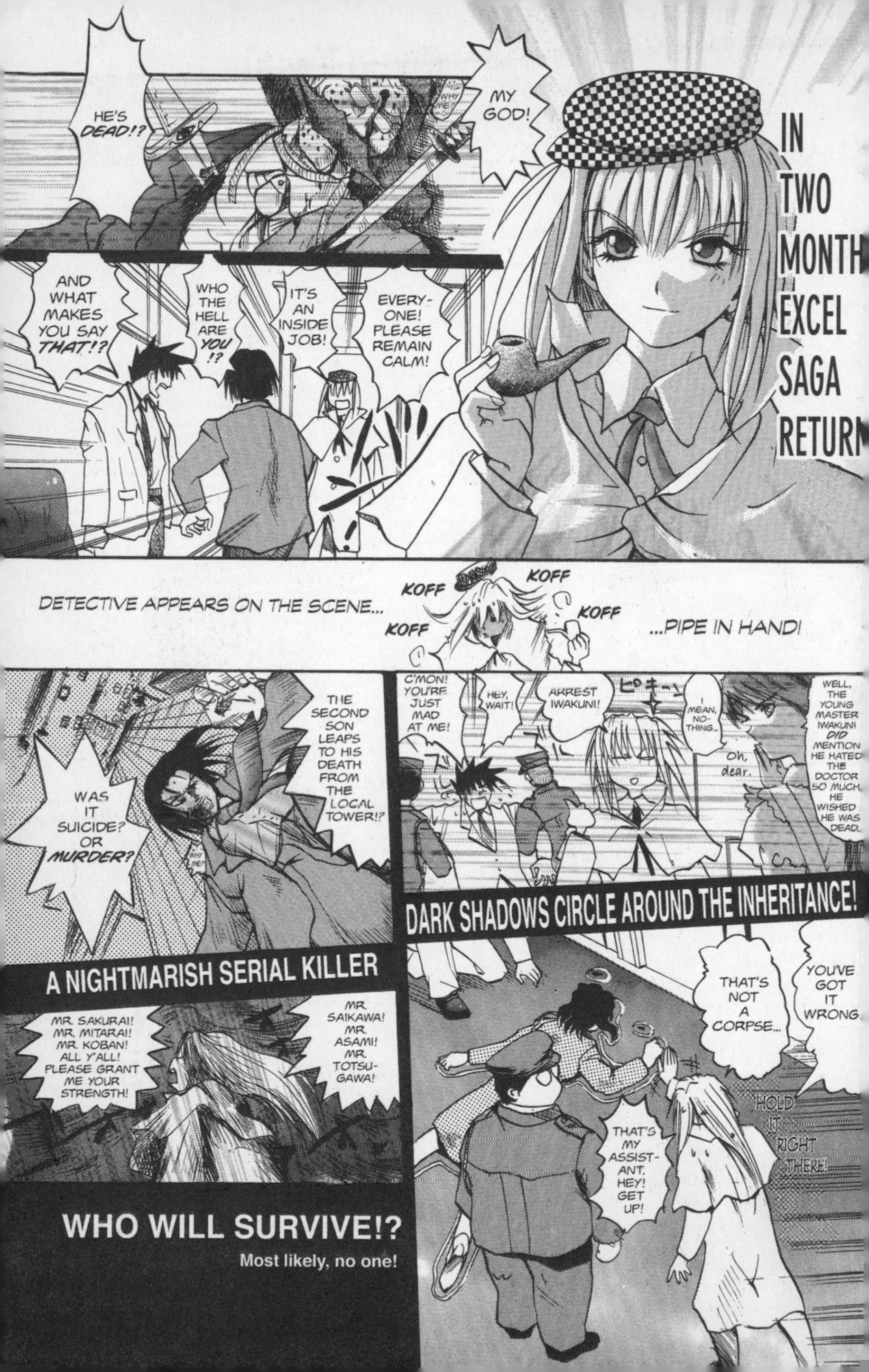
IN TWO MONTH EXCEL SAGA RETURN
MY GOD!
WHY ME?
HE'S DEAD!?
EVERY-ONE! PLEASE REMAIN CALM!
IT'S AN INSIDE JOB!
WHO THE HELL ARE YOU!?
AND WHAT MAKES YOU SAY THAT!?
DETECTIVE APPEARS ON THE SCENE...
KOFF
KOFF
KOFF
KOFF
...PIPE IN HAND!
WELL, THE YOUNG MASTER IWAKUNI DID MENTION HE HATED THE DOCTOR SO MUCH, HE WISHED HE WAS DEAD...
Oh, dear.
I MEAN, NO-THING...
ARREST IWAKUNI!
HEY, WAIT!
C'MON! YOU'RE JUST MAD AT ME!
DARK SHADOWS CIRCLE AROUND THE INHERITANCE!
THE SECOND SON LEAPS TO HIS DEATH FROM THE LOCAL TOWER!?
WAS IT SUICIDE? OR MURDER?
WHY ME?
A NIGHTMARISH SERIAL KILLER
YOU'VE GOT IT WRONG.
THAT'S NOT A CORPSE...
HOLD IT RIGHT THERE!
THAT'S MY ASSIST-ANT. HEY! GET UP!
MR. SAIKAWA! MR. ASAMI! MR. TOTSU-GAWA!
MR. SAKURAI! MR. MITARAI! MR. KOBAN! ALL Y'ALL! PLEASE GRANT ME YOUR STRENGTH!
WHO WILL SURVIVE!?
Most likely, no one!

Guide to *Excel Saga* 04's Sound Effects!

8-2-1 ——FX ph´WooWoosh

8-2-2 ——FX wup´LASHsh!

8-3-1 ——FX th´RAAAAASHshshsh (zararara, sound)

8-3-2 ——FX k´chak k´chak k´chak (gacha cha, sound, something opening and closing)

8-4-1 ——FX th´raash (gasha, sound)

8-4-2 ——FX zz´rak zz´rak (zyari zyari, sound, loose stones like)

8-5-1 ——FX k´chak (ga´cha, sound, clasping sound)

8-5-2 ——FX zz´rak (zyari, sound, loose stones like)

9-1-1 ——FX zZINGg´ (zya´, depiction and movement, fast movement followed by sudden stop)

9-1-2 ——FX (ou!, dialog, mixture of the expletive for exertion (ou) and the Chinese character for responding)

9-2 ——FX pSSH´t pSSH´t pSSH´t (hi´, sound, plosive release sound)

9-3 ——FX hup! (dialog)

10-4 ——FX zsh´SHINGg! (babi´, depiction)

10-5-1—FX ´es, Sir...! (dialog)

10-5-2—FX bow (heko, movement)

12-3-1—FX Hmmph (dialog)

12-3-2—FX k´cha´t (cha´, sound, mechanical)

12-4-1—FX ggg (gu´, squeeze)

12-4-2—FX klik (kacha, trigger pull)

12-5 ——FX ph´AAAp´! (baa´, depiction, burst of energy)

13-3 ——FX bustle bustle (doya, sound and depiction, noises particular to a lively group of people)

13-4 ——FX tok tok! (kon, sound)

Most of Rikdo Koshi's original sound FX are left in their original Japanese in the Viz edition of Excel Saga; exceptions being handwritten dialogue and "drawn" notes that have the character of captions. Although these sounds are all listed as "FX," they are of two types: onomatopoeia (in Japanese, *giseigo*) where the writing is used in an attempt to imitate the actual sound of something happening, and mimesis (in Japanese, *gitaigo*) where the writing is used to attempt to convey rhetorically a state, mood, or condition.

Whereas the first type of FX will invariably be portrayed with kana, the second may use kana and/or kanji. One should note that there is often overlap between these two types. Onomatopoeia notes: Sound refers to audible sounds being generated somehow. Movement refers to the physical movement, or lack of movement, of something; not audible or mostly not audible. Depiction refers to the psychological state of something or someone. In the unlikely event the matter slipped your mind during the two-month gap between vol. 03 and 04, all numbers are given in the original Japanese reading order: right-to-left.

Thanks to Matt Greenfield, Monica Rial, Brett Weaver, and all y'all other speakers and attendees (my memory is a trifle unclear) at the Excel Saga panel for Anime Weekend Atlanta this last September! If you have any ol' crazy things to relate, please write *Oubliette* c/o Excel Saga, VIZ, LLC, P.O. Box 77064, San Francisco, CA, 94107.

23-1-2 –FX wheeze whezz wheeze (ze~, sound)

23-2 —FX huff huff (ha, sound)

24-2 —FX b'thump! (batan, sound)

24-3-1 –FX kla'chak! (gacha', sound)

24-3-2 –FX klang klang klang (kan, sound)

24-4 —FX shake shake shake (buru, movement, violent shaking)

24-5 —FX zz'rk zzraak (zu' zuu', sound, dragging something)

24-6 —FX A'RRTH! (basa', sound and depiction, clothing or cloths being moved about)

25-1 —Mince (out of wb) Phew...

25-2 —FX cha'Ching! (zya', depiction, brandishing something)

25-3 —FX k'thak (ka', sound, digging)

25-4 —FX wh'thak! (ga', sound, digging, reinforced)

25-5 —FX k'thak! k'thak! k'thak! (ka', sound, digging)

26-5 —FX GASP (ha', depiction)

30-4 —FX klak klak klak (kotsu, sound)

31-3 —FX v'Vwhooshwoosh... (ooo, sound and depiction, sense of elation and unearthly presence)

31-4-1 –FX th'CRAK! (bishi!, sound)

31-4-2 –FX t'thatatatatatat (da'ta~, depiction and movement, running continuously)

34-3 —FX flap flap (pata pata, movement)

34-5 —FX (lower left) k'thok (koto, sound)

35-1 —FX SCREECH (kikiki~, sound)

35-2 —FX SKRE'SKRE'SKREEECH (gyagyagya!, sound, squealing tires)

35-3 —FX vV'RRRRROM (baoooo, sound)

36-1-1 –FX vrrrmmm (barooo, sound, Doppler Effect-lower pitch)

13-5 —FX kla'chak! (gacha!, sound)

14-2 —FX fidget fidget (sowa, depiction and movement)

15-5 —FX zsh'SHINGg! (babi', depiction)

18-1 —FX ph'ump (bo', depiction, lighting something)

18-2-1 –FX kla'chak (gacha, sound)

18-2-2 –FX ph'ffft (pu~, depiction, smoke)

18-4-1 –FX zz'rak! (za', sound)

18-4-2 –FX w'THUDD (gomu', sound, dull)

19-1 —FX zz't (zi', sound, hissing from charring)

19-3-1 –FX b'thump (batan, sound)

19-3-2 –FX klak klak (katsu, sound)

19-4-1 –FX klak klak klak (katsu, sound)

19-4-2 –FX fssk fssk fssk (suta, depiction, rapid walking -> movement)

21-1-1 –FX klak klak (katsu, sound)

21-1-2 –FX klak (katsu, sound)

21-1-3 –FX k'lak k'lak (kotsu, sound, lighter)

21-5 —FX th'chakk cha'chakk th'chakk (gasa goso gasa..., sound and depiction, moving things about)

22-1-1 –FX k'thak k'thak k'thak (ka', sound, digging)

22-1-2 –FX sk'RApe sk'RApe (gari ga, sound digging)

22-2-1 –FX klang klang klang (kan, sound)

22-2-2 –FX kla'chak kla'chak (gacha, sound)

22-2-3 –FX th-THUMp (biku', depiction)

22-3 —FX rustle bustle (bata bata bata, depiction)

22-4 —FX klatch (gacha', loud door opening)

23-1-1 –FX pSSH't (bi', sound, plosive release sound)

44-1——FX b'BrAK! (ga!, sound, hitting something)

44-3——FX k'THAK'thunk (dogakan, sound, crashing about)

44-4-1–FX wh'THUD (doka, sound)

44-4-2–FX k'Kthak'lunk (garan, sound, crashing and rolling about)

44-6——FX th-THUMp (biku', depiction)

45-1——FX klakklakklak (katatata, depiction and movement, shivering)

45-2-1–FX vV'Wooorommm˜ (gooo, sound)

45-2-2–FX kreek kreek (kiko, sound)

45-3——FX fade… (suu, depiction, something fading away)

45-4——FX zl'Shak (zyara, sound, loose items)

45-5——FX 'rrMmmm (ooonn, sound, residual)

46-2/3–FX klk klk klk klk (chikikikiki…, sound, wheel rotating)

47-1——FX aA'RaTH! (gaba!, depiction)

47-2——FX ggrip (gu', depiction)

49-1——FX aA'RuTH aA'RuTH (basa, sound, flapping of bird's wings)

49-2-1–FX aA'RuTH aA'RuTH (basa, sound, flapping of bird's wings)

49-2-2–FX aA'RuTH aA'RuTH aA'RuTH (basa, sound, flapping of bird's wings)

49-3——FX hgn'k (gokuri, depiction, swallowing)

49-4——FX k'thonk (koto, depiction, falling like flies)

49-6——FX t'thut t'thut (ta', depiction and sound, brisk running)

49-7——FX t'thut (as above)

52-4——FX g'ThuDd wh'ThuDd! (gatan, sound)

36-1-2–FX kR'clacla… (kara…, sound, opening sliding door resting on bearings)

36-2——FX bustle bustle (bata bata, depiction, moving about)

36-3——FX kla'crashsh (kashaaan, sound, brittle breaking sound-glass)

37-4——FX v'rmmm… (ooo, sound, residual)

38-2——FX TA-DAMM!! (don!, depiction, strong reinforcement)

38-3-1–FX zZINGg' (za', depiction and movement, pulling something out)

38-3-2–FX ph'FFFFFFT (hyu˜, sound, air movement)

38-4/6–FX ph'vWooW000˜˜

39-1——FX GASP (ha', depiction)

39-2——FX wobble (yoro, depiction and movement)

39-4——FX k'thak… k'thak… (katsu˜, sound, chipping away at hard surface)

39-5——FX sh'ZINGg' (bishi, depiction and movement, fast movement followed by sudden stop)

39-6——FX z'CHAk! (za', depiction, readying something)

40-1——FX ph'rOrOrOrO˜˜˜˜ (hirororo, sound)

41-3——FX sSK'REECH! (gya!, sound)

41-4——FX zya'krrkrrkrrk ('zyaaa, sound, smooth bicycle gear sounds)

42-2——FX g'GVRoommm (girororo, sound, strange caustic sound of car engine)

42-3——FX 'Rmmm (ooo, sound, residual)

42-4——FX zz'RTH (zu', sound and depiction, movement of clothing)

42-5——FX GLARE (ki', depiction)

43-1——FX 'Rmmm (ooo, sound, residual)

43-5——FX ggrip (ga', depiction)

53-1—FX quiver quiver (kako kako, depiction)

53-3—FX snap (pori, sound and depiction)

53-5-1–FX k'thud (gata', sound)

53-5-2–FX zz'rak (zu', sound and movement, abrasive)

54-1—FX wh'THUD (gatan, sound)

54-3—FX umph... (kata, sound, moving about -> expletive describing exertion)

54-4—FX fssk fssk fssk (ka', movement, sudden)

55-4—FX ph'TiNG! (biku', depiction, alarm)

56-1—FX t'thut t'thut (da', sound, brisk running)

56-2—FX t'thut t'thut (da', sound, brisk running)

56-4—FX vGRGGGROARRR (gooooo, sound, fire)

57-4-1–FX k'KRASH (gasha, sound)

57-4-2–FX vGROARRR (goo, sound, fire)

57-4-3–FX fret fret (hara hara, depiction)

57-4-4–FX k'THUD (dokan, sound)

57-4-5–FX fret (hara, depiction)

57-4-6–FX rROARRRrr (booo, sound, fire, residual)

58-2—FX ROOOAARRR (guoooo, sound, fire)

59-3—FX rroarrrr (ooo, sound, residual)

63-5-1–FX huff (dialog)

63-5-2–FX bustle bustle panic panic (ata futa ata futa, depiction and movement)

64-1—FX fret fret fret (oro oro, depiction)

64-2—FX t'tht t'tht t'tht (tototo, depiction and movement, quick walk)

64-3—FX t'tht t'tht t'tht (tototo, depiction and movement, quick walk)

64-4—FX Here, ma'am! (dialog)

66-1—FX hg'gnk (gokuri, sound, swallowing)

66-2—FX ta-dum! (depiction)

66-3—FX du-DUMMn (don, depiction, dramatic reinforcement)

67-1—FX k'thak (koton, sound, putting something down–i.e., a pen)

67-3—FX kla'chak (gacha, sound)

67-6—FX GASP (ha', depiction)

67-7—FX b'thump (batan! sound)

68-2-1–FX bon (depiction)

68-2-2–FX whisper whisper whisper (boso boso, depiction)

68-4—FX Oh boy [or Dear God] (dialog)

69-3—FX b'thump (batan, sound)

69-5-1–FX whRRRRR (uiiin, sound, mechanical)

69-5-2–FX kla'chak zz'chak (gasha, sound, moving things about)

70-1-1–FX thBPLth (bu', sound, plosive bilabial)

70-1-2–FX kla'CHAKk! (zyaki!, sound)

70-1-3–FX fph'WAP! (paan!, sound)

70-5—FX k'thok k'thok (kon, sound, knocking)

71-3—FX kl'chak cha'chak (kaki, sound, mechanical, fitting something)

71-5-1—FX cla'CHAK (zui', movement and depiction, getting close -> sound)

71-5-2—FX wRRRR! (chui', sound)

71-6-1—FX kK'thud' (gata', sound)

71-6-2—FX wh'THUDd (gataan, sound)

72-1—FX tt'ZuTHh (da', movement, dashing movement)

79-6-2 —FX wWHACK (bakan, sound)

79-6-3 —FX sp'LRSHsh (boshu, sound, something spilling out)

80-3 ——FX sscrsh sscrsh (shaka, sound, scrubbing something)

84-3 ——FX t'tht t'tht t'tht (ta', sound, running)

84-4 ——FX t'tht t'tht (ta', sound, running)

85-3 ——FX SMILE (nika, depiction)

86-3 ——FX ch'THnK! (puchin!, sound)

86-4 ——FX kr'THnK k'THnK (putsun patsun, sound)

87-2-1 —FX vV'CHANKk! (dobutsun!, sound and depiction)

87-2-2 —FX th'thup thup thup' (boto to to', depiction, liquid spilling, small amount)

87-3-1 —FX k'THrKsh (gasha, sound)

87-3-2 —FX struggle struggle (zita bata, depiction)

88-2 ——FX k'REEk (gishi, sound)

88-5-1 —FX klak… (kotsu, sound)

88-5-2 —FX a-hahaha (dialog)

89-3 ——FX glare (ki', depiction)

90-2-1 —FX (black, lower left) K'AUFF CAUFF (geho, sound, coughing)

90-2-2 —FX (black, upper left) t'thut t'thut t'thut (suta, movement, quick)

90-3 ——FX klak (kotsu, sound)

90-4 ——FX fssk (su', movement)

91-2 ——FX klak klak klak (katsu, sound)

91-5-1 —FX kreek kreek kreek (kori, sound and depiction, moving about)

91-5-2 —FX kK'Grk! (gori', sound and depiction, shoving something in)

72-4 ——FX ggrip! (gashi', depiction)

72-5 ——FX aA'RuTHh (gaba, movement)

73-2 ——FX Phew… (ho, sound and depiction)

73-4 ——FX v'WHRRR (chyuun, sound)

74-2 ——FX fssk (su, movement)

74-3 ——FX sh'sloch sh'sloch (guzyu, sound and depiction)

74-5 ——FX ggrip'chak (guri', movement)

74-6-1 —FX vV'WHrREEE (gyun!, sound)

74-6-2 —FX vVRRRM' RM' RM' (gyrururu, sound)

74-6-3 —FX zZ'RAAAK (zugogo, sound)

74-6-4 —FX zDRlLz zDRILLz (gori gori, depiction and sound)

74-6-5 —FX vW'Hreee … (ziiii, sound)

75-1-1 —FX …Whrrr… (ii, sound, residual)

75-1-2 —FX fssk (su, movement)

75-2-1 —FX k'thok (kako, sound, knocking)

75-2-2 —FX wWhEEEZz wWhEEEZz (dialog)

76-1-1 —FX vz~~~~ (zi~, sound mechanical)

76-1-2 —FX k'clk (kakon, sound, mechanical)

76-3 ——FX gDRILLg gDRILLg (geri, depiction, comic, drilling about)

77-3 ——FX glare (gya', depiction)

77-4 ——FX kla'chak'SHING (shaki~n, depiction)

77-5 ——FX k'thud k'thud (gata, sound)

78-2 ——FX slip (zuru, depiction)

78-3-1 —FX wh'THUDD! (dogaga', sound)

78-3-2 —FX k'KRNCH (bori, depiction)

79-1 ——FX aA'RuTH (gaba, movement)

79-6-1 —FX wh'THUMPTt! (dobomu, sound)

102-1-2-FX   p'fap (patan, sound and depiction, closing something)

102-2—FX   k'thud (gata, sound)

102-4—FX   fssk (su', depiction)

103-2—FX   ho~nk (paan, sound)

103-3-1-FX   h'honk (bupu~, sound)

103-3-2-FX   v'vRrmm (buroro, sound)

104-5—FX   k'THUD! (dan!, sound)

106-3—FX   z'SHING! (zuwa', movement)

107-1—FX   z'SHING!! (za!, movement)

108-2—FX   GASP! (depiction)

110-1-1-FX   (black) ph'unk! (pun', depiction, sudden movement)

110-1-2-FX   (toned) thr'PLASH! (dopaa!, sound, splashing sound)

110-1-3-FX   (second left) shlshlshlshlshl (zozozozo, depiction, the tentacales reaching over)

110-2-1-FX   k'rnch k'rnch (meri meri, depiction, something squeezing and putting pressure on something)

110-2-2-FX   sup'LASH! (basha', sound)

111-3-1-FX   bustle bustle (doya doya, depiction)

111-3-2-FX   bustle (doya, depiction)

111-4—FX   ph'thap! (peshi!, sound)

112-2—FX   Urgrgrg!! (aaaaa', dialog)

112-3—FX   SHINE (kan, depiction, bright sun)

113-1—FX   ph'thapt (peta, sound, wet)

114-1—FX   fssk! (ki', movement)

114-3—FX   t'that (ta', sound)

114-4—FX   SUR'PLASH (za'pu-n, sound)

115-1—FX   rustle rustle (zawa, depiction)

92-2—FX   kla'chak (gacha, sound)

92-3-1—FX   kreek (gishi', sound)

92-3-2-FX   b'thump (batan, sound)

92-4—FX   pip pip (pi', sound, electronic)

92-5—FX   kla'chak (gacha, sound)

94-2—FX   pip (pi', sound)

95-2—FX   trickle trickle (zoro, movement and depiction)

96-2—FX   zz'LURp (zu', sound)

96-4—FX   bustle bustle (zawa, depiction)

96-5—FX   k'snap (pakin, sound)

97-1-1—FX   k'klaaaak (kako~n, sound, slow running)

97-1-2—FX   k'klaaaak (kako~n, sound, slow running)

97-2—FX   k'thud (gata', sound)

97-4—FX   munch munch (mori, depiction, eating a lot)

97-5—FX   kk'lank (karan, sound)

98-3—FX   ggrip (gu', depiction)

98-4—FX   ppop (poko, sound)

99-3-1—FX   pB'Llerrrt (buryuu, snd and dpct)

99-3-2—FX   ooze (murkiriri, dpct)

99-4—FX   k'thunk (katan, sound)

99-5—FX   kla'chakk (kacha, sound)

99-6—FX   mmunch (mofu, depiction)

101-1/2FX   kla'chak (gacha, sound)

101-6—FX   flap (bara, depiction)

101-7—FX   thh'thaff (kasa…, depiction, moving something light but rigid)

102-1-1-FX   kla'chak (gacha', sound)

122-5-1-FX   turn (kuru, movement)

122-5-2-FX   thththth'lurp (tsu~, sound, sucking)

123-2—FX   th-thump (dokun, depiction)

123-5—FX   thr'splash thr'splash thr'splash (zapa, sound)

123-6-1-FX   zz'PLASH (zya', sound and depiction)

123-6-2-FX   (white) t'thutt (pun!, sound)

124-1-1-FX   phBLrp! (pa', sound, plosive bilabial)

124-1-2-FX   huff! (ha'!, dialog)

124-2-1-FX   th'plashplashplash (bababa, sound)

124-2-2-FX   glare (ki', depiction)

124-4—FX   th'plashplashplash (zagagaga, sound)

125-2-1-FX   huff huff (ha~, sound)

125-2-2-FX   p'plashss (zabu', sound, getting out of body of water)

126-4-1-FX   b'thump (batan, sound)

126-4-2-FX   GAK (dialog)

127-1-1-FX   k'thak (ka', sound, digging)

127-1-2-FX   k'thak (ka', sound, digging)

127-1-3-FX   g'thak (ga', sound, digging)

127-1-4-FX   k'thak (ka', sound, digging)

127-2—FX   k'thakk!! (ka'!, sound, digging)

127-3—FX   v'WHOOSH… (baa~, movement)

127-6—FX   ph'ting! (piku, depiction)

127-7—FX   fssk (su, motion)

127-8—FX   humph… (dialog)

129-1—FX   sc'rthk… (kari, sound, abrasive)

115-2—FX   zz'sSHING (zan!, depiction, posing)

115-5—FX   sh'ZINGg' (bi', depiction and movement, fast movement followed by sudden stop)

116-2—FX   ph'ting! (piki, depiction)

116-5—FX   ph'fft (pon, depiction)

117-2-1-FX   (black) ggri~~p (gigigi, depiction)

117-2-2-FX   (black, next to ear) dribble dribble (chiroro, depiction)

117-2-3-FX   (white) p'SHSHSH~~~ (pupi~, depiction, gushing water, comic)

117-5—FX   sp'lsh… (chapun, sound)

118-1—FX   blblmp (puka~, depiction, floating, dead in the water)

118-3—FX   th'PLASH! (zapu!, sound)

118-4-1-FX   wheez wheez (ze', sound)

118-4-2-FX   thrplash thrplash (basha basha, sound)

119-3-1-FX   p'plashss (gapa, sound, getting out of body of water)

119-3-2-FX   ph'thap (bita', sound)

119-4—FX   fssk (sui', movement)

119-5—FX   thok thok (ton, sound)

120-6—FX   k'thud (gata, sound)

121-1—FX   zz'rak (zu', sound and movement, abrasive)

121-4—FX   p'ting (pita, depiction, sudden freeze)

121-6—FX   t'thut (ta, movement)

122-1—FX   k'lankk… (karan, sound, ice turning)

122-4—FX: zth'chakchak (zara', sound and depiction, moving things about)

130-4—FX zZINGg' (zya', depiction and movement, fast movement followed by sudden stop)

130-5—FX t'thut!! (da!!, sound, running start)

130-6—FX WH'UD (go', sound)

131-1/4FX sKK'REEECH (ki'kikiki, sound)

131-4—FX wh'THUD (dosa, sound)

132-2/4 FX v'VROOMmm (baa, sound)

133-5—FX th'chakk th'chakk (gasa, sound)

133-6—FX t'thutt t'thutt (su'ta, sound, walking, somewhat comic)

134-2—FX mM'EEEM mM'IM mM'IM (sound, Japanese cicada)

134-4—FX hm~~~fff (ha~, sound, sigh)

135-1-1-FX hmfff (fuu, sound, sigh)

135-1-2-FX zz'thut zz'thut (zuka, sound, reinforced walking)

136-5—FX t'thut (ta', sound)

137-4—FX v'VRm! (nn', depiction, dramatic appearance)

138-4—FX thh'chakk (gasa, sound and depiction, moving things about)

140-1—FX th'plasssh' (zya~, sound, running water)

140-2—FX kreekk (kyu', sound, tightening something)

140-5—FX zZINGg' (bi', depiction and movement, fast movement followed by sudden stop)

141-2—FX K'THAKK (ga', sound)

141-4—FX a'RhuTH' (ba', sound and depiction, dramatic movement)

141-5—FX zz'SHING' (gi', depiction and motion, another pose)

142-2—FX g'thog g'thog (gon, sound)

142-3—FX p'SHSHT (pupi', depiction, gushing water, comic)

142-4—FX t'thththut (ta~tatata, sound, running)

143-3-1-FX kla'chak (gacha', sound)

143-3-2-FX ph'ting (piku, depiction, reaction)

143-5—FX k'thunkk (katan, sound, door closing)

143-6—FX fssk (su, motion)

144-4-1-FX humph (dialog)

144-4-2-FX sparkle (kira, depiction, light reflecting off of tears)

144-6—FX zzz'zrk (zu~~~'!, sound, sucking noise)

145-1—FX ph'tink!! (pi'ta', depiction, complete stoppage)

145-4—FX rth'SHING (nba, depiction, dramatic standing

145-7FX mM'EEEM mM'IM (sound, Japanese cicada)

146-2—FX klak klak klak (ko', sound)

146-3—FX klakk (katsu, sound)

146-4-1-FX ggrip (gyu, depiction)

146-4-2-FX p'ting (pita, depiction, sudden freeze)

147-2-1-FX tsk (dialog)

147-2-2-FX fssk (su', motion)

147-3—FX toss (posu, motion, comic)

148-5—FX Kla'SMASHKk (bashaan, sound)

151-1—FX poink ppoink (po poto, sound)

151-6-1-FX g'THUD g'THUD (gosu, sound)

151-6-2-FX c'mon!! (dialog)

153-2—FX huff fuff (dialog)

162-5-1-FX   A'RATH (ba', motion)

162-5-2-FX   g'THUD (goto, sound)

162-5-3-FX   th'THUT (da', motion)

162-7—FX   t'thuthuthuthut (dadada, sound, running)

162-8—FX   wobble (fura, sound)

163-2—FX   v'thudthudthud (babababa, sound, running)

163-4-1-FX   ph'thuthuthut (shutata, sound, fast running)

163-4-2-FX   thuthuthut… (tatata, sound)

163-5—FX   th'thumpthump (bikubiku, depiction, changed perspective)

164-4/5   FX v'thudthudthud (dadada, sound, running)

165-1—FX   v'WHOOSH (ba', motion)

165-2—FX   vV'WHOOSHt (dan, motion)

165-3—FX   ggrip (gu', depiction)

165-4-1-FX   k'thud! (gon!, sound)

165-4-2-FX   v'SWING (bun!, motion)

165-6—FX   TH'… (da', sound)

165-7/8   FX …PLASH! (paan, sound)

166-1/2   FX blub glub vlub (gaboo, sound)

166-2—FX   blub blub blub (bobobo, sound)

169-1—FX   fssk (depiction)

170-1—FX   t'thut t'thut (tote tote, motion, walking, comic)

170-3—FX   z'lurrrrp (zu ~, sound)

170-4—FX   sniff sniff (funn funn, sound)

170-6—FX   t'thut t'thut t'thut (tote tote, motion, walking, comic)

153-5—FX   p'SHT' (pufu', depiction, gushing water, starting, comic)

154-1-1-FX   (upper left) p'SHSHSH~~~ (pyu~, depiction, gushing water, comic)

154-1-2-FX   (lower right) panic panic (wata, depiction)

154-4—FX   zzz'zrk (zu~~~'!, sound, sucking noise)

154-5-1-FX   bla'blpt (boto, depiction, blood flow)

154-5-2-FX   th'blpblpblpblp (dobobob, depiction, massive blood flow)

154-7—FX   wobble (fura, motion and depiction)

155-1-1-FX   whobble (fura, depiction and movement)

155-1-2   FX dizzy (rari, depiction, brain chemical imbalance induced stupor)

155-5—FX   t'thud (do', sound)

157-4—FX   t'thut (suta, sound)

157-5—FX   zsc'rthk… (kari, sound, abrasive)

157-9—FX   wheez wheez (dialog)

158-1—FX   wheez wheez (dialog)

158-2—FX   wheez wheez (dialog)

158-4—FX   zz'rak (za', sound)

159-3—FX   k'thud (gata', sound)

159-4—FX   ggrip (gu', depiction)

160-2—FX   k'thunk (kakkun, motion, collapsing)

161-2—FX   turn turn (kuru, motion)

162-2—FX   fssk (su', depiction)

162-4—FX   shake shake shake (buru, motion)

171-1—FX snuggle snuggle (goro goro, depiction)

171-2—FX flap flap (pata, movement)

172-2—FX flap flap (pata pata, motion)

172-4—FX murmur (potsuri, depiction)

172-5—FX flap flap (as 172-2)

173-6—FX zz'chak (za', sound)

176-1—FX zz'plashzz zz'plashzz (zaza, sound)

176-2—FX g'thud g'thud g'thud g'thud (dan, sound)

176-3—FX vV'UMP!! (dan!, sound, opening door, reinforced)

176-4-1-FX huff huff huff (dialog)

176-4-2-FX k'reek k'reek (kiri, motion, fast mechanical type turning of head)

176-5—FX glare (ki', depiction)

177-3—FX ta'thmbthmbmmmn (boroon, sound, guitar)

177-4—FX zz'plash~~~ (zaza~n, sound)

178-1—FX GrGrGrGr (gigig, depiction and sound, building anger as well as scraping the table top)

178-2-1-FX ch'lak (zya', sound and depiction, removing)

178-2-2-FX thBPLth (dialog, plosive bilabial)

178-4—FX WH'THUDD! (dan', sound)

180-5—FX beam ~~~ (hepa~, depiction, smiling, comic)

181-4—FX fssk (tsui', motion)

181-5—FX kla'chunk (kapo, depiction, something opening, comic)

183-4—FX zz'shing (bi', depiction, going into pose)

184-3—FX flap flap (pata pata, motion)

185-1—FX zsh'SHINGg! (babi', depiction)

185-5-1-FX fssk (kyu', motion)

185-5-2-FX flap flap (pata, motion)

186-1—FX fssk! (ki', depiction, glare -> changed to movement)

187-2—FX kla'chak (gacha', sound)

187-3—FX b'thump (batan, sound)

190-1—FX cha'chak (gasha, sound)

190-4—FX t'thut t'thut t'thut (tote tote, motion, walking, comic)

191-1—FX A'RATH! (ba'!, motion)

191-5—FX gak gak gak agak (dialog)

191-6—FX zz'plashzz'plashzz (zazazaza, sound)

193-3—FX zz'plashzz (zaza, sound)

193-4—FX zz'plashzz'plashzz (zazann, sound)

196-3-1-FX th'att th'att th'att th'att (tatatata, sound)

196-3-2-FX k'att th'att th'att th'att th'att (jitatatata, sound)

196-7—FX v'REEE (mi~~~ (nasal), sound, comic engine sound)

196-8—FX (on top) phK'IIIII (kiiii, sound, high pitch flying sound)

197-3—FX b'thump! (ban!, sound)

197-5-1-FX sh'SHING! (piki~n, depiction, shining eyes -> fast pose)

197-5-2-FX zz'drag (zuru, depiction, being dragged away)

197-5-3-FX zz'drag (zuru, depiction, being dragged away)

197-10-FX ph'VROooARRRoaR (goooo, sound, strong powerful storm winds)

World War they were very much known infor-
mally as the "Thought Police," arresting, jailing,
torturing, and if deemed necessary, murdering
those Japanese among the tens of thousands of
whom spoke out (or even gave the appearance
of speaking out) against the policies of their
own government. The scarred man shadowing
Chiyoko in Satoshi Kon's wonderful recent
anime film Millennium Actress (now available in
the U.S. on DVD from DreamWorks!) is, in his
20th century "incarnation," a Tokkô agent.

Japan At War: An Oral History by Haruko Taya
Cook & Theodore F. Cook, includes first-hand
accounts of Tokkô repression; but *Japan At War*
is recommended beyond this, as a very acces-
sible and balanced way to find out what the
Second World War was like through the memories of the Japanese people who actually lived
it. The Cooks talked to dozens of people representing all sectors of Japanese civilian and
military life in the 1930s and 40s—from ordinary students and soldiers, to manga artists,
diplomats, would-be kamikaze pilots, the real
officers in charge of "The Bridge on the River
Kwai"—even a man who served in the infa-
mous Unit 731 that tested horrific biological
weapons on thousands of living Chinese,
Russian, Korean, and—yes— American sub-
jects.

31-4 Original reference speaks not of a "runner's high," but the considerably more tran-
scendent-sounding Japanese equivalent, the
"Realm of the Divinity."

34-1 Wire transfer is the most common method
by which people pay utility and other common
monthly bills in Japan. Checks are employed in
Japan mostly for interbusiness transactions,
and are rarely used by everyday consumers.
You need not have a bank account to do a wire
transfer in Japan; you simply go to a financial

5-5: Of what, we can't say here.

12-1: Year of the current Emperor, Akihito,
whose reign was inaugurated with the name
Heisei ("Achieved Peace"). Year 9 is 1997 (see
Excel Saga Vol. 03, note for page 18-2).
Although this type of usage may sound a bit
archaic to American ears ("Between the years
when the oceans drank Atlantis and the rise of
the sons of Aryas...") it is in fact quite common in Japan. Sometimes it is used in con-
junction with the Western equivalent, and
sometimes alone; for example, the original
Japanese edition of Excel Saga Vol. 04 bears
only the print date of "Heisei Year 11," not
1999.

16-7-2: The Japanese economy has been suf-
fering from a prolonged recession, and one
crucial reason for this has to do with all the—
to use the industry's delicate phrase—"non-
performing" loans that the banks are saddled
with. Robert Whiting, in *Tokyo Underworld* (see
Excel Saga Vol. 03, note for page 24-3-3)
maintains that many such loans represent
money lent to yakuza-owned concerns; which
in turn suggests the manga *Sanctuary*'s idea of
reform among Japanese gangsters as a necessary precondition to reform Japan is no less
true for it being absurd. There has been and
continues to be a lot of debate over how to
overhaul the Japanese banking system, and
injection of public funds into it has been a
source of endless controversy.

29-6 The Tokkô, short for Tokubetsu Koto
Keisatsu; also translated as the Special Secret
Service Police; whatever you called them, they
were, in the words of translator Dan
Kanemitsu, "a very scary group of people."
Founded in 1901, the Tokkô was the civilian
counterpart to Japanese military intelligence
(the Kempeitai), and by the time of the Second

chance that the Japanese postal service in the near future will look nothing like it is today.

40-1 As Excel explained it to Mince on page 77 of Excel Saga Vol. 1, a shinme is a horse that the gods ride about on. The Go in Goshime is a prefix that reinforces the notion of something as being sacred or special or superior.

42-4 Members of a traditional Japanese organized crime gang (the yakuza) often address each other figuratively as older or younger brother, depending on their seniority in the organization. However, these two actually are brothers.

52-4-1: The original phrase was kono amaa zettai. Ama (here stretched out a little in the gangsta gangsta's angry diction) by itself might be no worse than "slut," but combined with kono (here having the meaning of "You…!") and zettai ("total and complete"), you really have to bring out the big battalions. I might note that ama also means "nun" in Japanese, a fact that no doubt leads to all kinds of wacky ruler-slappings among those in Japanese Catholic schools. This kind of language might seem a little out of place in Excel Saga, what with its lighthearted attitude towards subversion and conquest. And so it is; but this exception helps to prove the general rule that there isn't much serious swearing in this particular manga. Personally, I think big brother was trying to drop some Al Pacino lines from *Scarface*, but messed up and did *Glengarry Glen Ross* instead. If you would like to learn more bad words, I highly recommend *Banana Fish* by Akimi Yoshida, also available from Viz.

52-4-2: This is supposed to not make sense. The proper syntax of this statement should have been: "I'll stick my hand into your mouth through your ear and make your teeth rattle!" This is a strong threatening statement that's often used by gangsters, and gangster wannabes.

institution, the local post office, or even a convenience store, and you can do it right there with cash (you pay them cash and they will wire the money for a minimum fee.) See 36-4 below regarding the relationship between the Post Office and financial institutions in Japan.

34-6 Perhaps you think this is merely another bit of absurdité to underscore the dubious material circumstances of our dear Excel. Let it be known that a good percentage of the sandwiches sold in Japan are with the crust cut away: cheap bags of such orphan crust are in fact therefore available in many stores.

36-4 Japan Post—the Japanese post office system—offers a wide variety of services that their American counterparts do not, most particularly financial services—savings accounts, loans, CDs. As mentioned above, one can also make utility payments at the post office: in effect, they function as miniature municipal services outlets. These aspects of Japan Post arose as part of the particular circumstances of economic development in during the reign of the Emperor Meiji (1867-1912), Japan's great period of post-feudal modernization. The idea of having people bank at their local post office came about at the beginning of the 20th century, as a way for the Japanese government to acquire urgently needed new investment capital. For many years, the postal service was an important factor in meeting financial development needs, most particularly for rural Japan; but today, a century later, Japan Post (which offers almost negligible interest on accounts) faces competition from a large and fully developed private banking and investment sector, not to mention the many money-management services available through the convenience stores and Internet. Japan Post is currently in the midst of restructuring and reorganization, and there is a good knew rose above the horizon, and then the next evening you watched for the same star to rise, you would find (if you had timed it) that it took not 24 hours, but 23 hours, 56 minutes, and 4 seconds. Trust Dr. Kabapu not to have an ordinary day like the rest of us.

92-3-1 Some readers familiar with the original version of the manga may wonder why when Kabapu adds the suffix "-kun" in the Japanese Excel Saga, it is dropped from the English version, whereas when Misaki uses it, it is included. The translator notes the reason lies in a wish to communicate the relative nature of interpersonal relationships within the quite vertical hierarchy that is Japanese society. When Kabapu adds the suffix "-kun" against someone lower than him (i.e. his workers, or someone younger than him) it designates his view of their inferior position. But when Misaki uses it towards Watanabe and Sumiyoshi, it simply designates a proper politeness, rather than talking down to someone. If Kabapu were to be addressing the Mayor as, say, "my dear Rikdo-kun," it would be left as is, but if Misaki were to say, for instance, "-kun" against her younger brother, it would be dropped in English.

Mr. Kanemitsu wishes to underscore that while Japanese name suffixes such as kun do certainly have some meaning in of themselves (and he included a translation table in Excel Saga Vol. 2, note for page 115-1-3), they do not exist in a vacuum; indeed, the default assumptions of inequality built into much of Japanese speech requires that the "proper meaning," and hence the desirable translation, of such terms, can only be known when we also know exactly who is talking to whom. Kanemitsu notes, "I'm not trying to reproduce every word that was spoken in the Japanese version into English, but rather, I am trying to recreate and preserve the relative social relationships in English; and to do that, it

54-2: This statement has no real meaning beyond giving context to the situation. According to the translator's sources, Noma is a part of Fukuoka that's removed from the city somewhat. Mr. Kanemitsu suggests, "In the context of San Francisco, it would be like saying: "My aunt in Walnut Creek wore the worst makeup at Thanksgiving last year." Ahem.

59-6-1: Original expression was "bodily injury resulting in death."

66-2: Remember, Japan has a national health insurance program as, does, come to think of it, almost every other advanced nation on Earth…

75-4: In Japanese, X-ray machines are known as Rentogens, a name derived from its inventor, the German scientist Wilhelm Konrad Roentgen. Dr. Iwata makes another reference about Roentgen later, so this has to be here, or the following reference won't make sense.

81-5: They're watching the movie version of the cop show *Odoru Sousamou* ("The Dancing Dragnet"). The line about "Cases happen at the scene of the crime…" is a catchphrase of Aoshima-kun, the junior detective in the show. Aestheticism.com notes, "The series has been a source of much yaoi fodder to Japanese and foreign viewers alike, including the *Kizuna* artist, Kodaka Kazuma." That is to say, it's inspired a lot of gay fan-fiction; gay here also having the meaning of homosexual.

83: 23 hours, 56 minutes, and 4 seconds is—as Animerica Extra and (astronomy student)'s William Flanagan could tell you—the length of a sidereal day. The 24-hour day is of course the time it takes the Earth to turn around once with respect to the sun. But the sidereal day is the time it takes with respect to the stars in the sky. Speaking roughly, if in the evening, you waited to see at exactly what time a particular star you

106-1-1 Since, of course, the intrusion was actually from the "upper world," this inversion is a deliberate one on Il Palazzo's part; he is using "lower" in a philosophical sense, as ACROSS represents a "higher conception" for the ordering of society.

113-4-2 Excel's swimwear looks suspiciously like the standard issue for PE swimming classes in Japanese grades 7-12. The "1-2" would designate that Excel is in the first grade (of either junior high school or high school), and in home room class #2.

174-1 "Emerium," as everyone knows, is the name of the ray that Ultra Seven shoots.

191-5-1 Japanese student radicals of the late 1960s and early 70s did in fact use the German loan-word *Gewalt*, or *gevalt*, meaning "force," when they talked about taking action. The original 1971-72 *Lupin III* TV series (not the second one, the one airing on Adult Swim of late, which despite its dub, is from 1977-80—can you imagine any classic American TV show of the 1970s having its re-runs dubbed over with contemporary references in an attempt to make people think it's a recent show?), whose first half was a big influence on *Cowboy Bebop*, has been described as having its era's "cool gevalt" ("radical chic," if you like) style.

196-7-1 Haneda is Tokyo's other major airport; much closer to downtown than Narita, it is used almost exclusively for domestic traffic.

196-7-2 Shikokuite, a person from Shikoku (the term has just been made up by the translator). See note in Excel Saga Vol. 2 for page 35-5-2.

requires that sometimes the '-kun' is dropped. Why? Because referring to someone without '-kun' sounds more rude than when it's there."

96-1 The sign says *kaiten zushi*. Japanese people usually pronounce sushi *zushi*—the nonvocal "s" becoming the vocal "z"—in such cases when another word (here called a conditioner) is added at the top to form a distinct meaning. A kaiten zushi restaurant of course is a conveyor-belt sushi establishment; a plain old ordinary sushi restaurant would just be pronounced "sushi."

102-5-1 There are two types of taxis available in Japan; the standard variety comparable to the ordinary American cruising or radio-dispatched cab, and an upscale version referred to in Japan as haiya, or "hired cars." They are quite high-end in their luxury, so it was thought a limo service would better convey the notion in U.S. terms.

105 "The Season Faraway From The Sun" is probably a reference to *The Season of the Sun*, a 1955 novel by Shintaro Ishihara. Written when he was 23 (and supposedly, in three days), *Season of the Sun* was seen as representing a Japanese equivalent to other contemporaneous post-war youth rebellion artistic scenes, such as the Beats in the United States or the "Angry Young Men" of Britain. Today Ishihara, as governor of Tokyo, is the most controversial political figure in Japan—accused of being a neo-nationalist and racist, but also admired among many in the electorate for shaking up politics as usual. He is also the chairman of the "Tokyo International Anime Fair," an annual film festival held at Tokyo Big Sight, the same venue as the famous twice-yearly doujinshi meet Comic Market. Ishihara's welcome message to attendees is "We firmly believe that you too will be able to fully experience the power of Anime from Tokyo that keeps on inspiring limitless dreams and possibilities in the new millennium."

If you enjoy EXCEL SAGA, the editor recommends, also from VIZ:

SANCTUARY

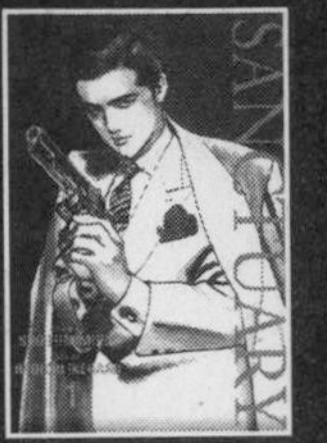
SANCTUARY

© 1990 Sho Fumimura/ Ryoichi Ikegami/ Shogakukan, Inc.

"You can't be a politician if you're embarrassed to show your ass...a politician has no need for common sense." And I *quote* from the first of nine volumes of *Sanctuary*, which illustrates (art by Ryoichi Ikegami) and describes (story by Sho Fumimura) that *Excel Saga*'s portrayal of corruption and absurdity in Japanese politics is more realistic than cynical. And unlike Excel's relatively nonviolent ways (no doubt from being unable to afford even Wal-Mart prices on ammunition), in *Sanctuary*'s world all your problems are solved with a pop pop, another politician drop, and you feel relief like plop, plop, fizz.

BLACK JACK

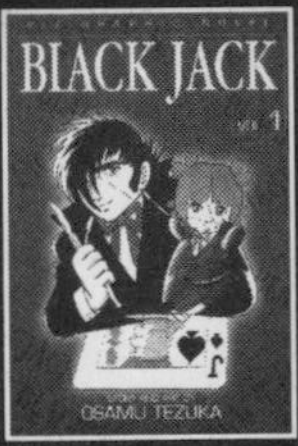
BLACK JACK
OSAMU TEZUKA

© 2003 Tezuka Productions

You're old enough, and it's time you knew who Dr. Iwata is in fact based on: Black Jack, the medical mercenary created by Osamu Tezuka (*Phoenix*) in his manga of the same name. Tezuka—in his spare time from being the modern manga industry's greatest pioneer—earned a medical degree, and in *Black Jack* created the story of a mysterious, scarred drifter/surgeon rejected by the health-care establishment, yet able to work miracles on baffling wounds and conditions when all hope is lost. Really sort of the complete opposite of Dr. Iwata; now that I think about it, I guess Rikdo-san was right.

FLOWERS AND BEES

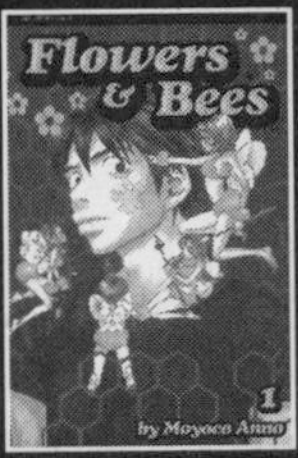
Flowers & Bees
1
by Moyoco Anno

© 2000 Moyoco Anno/Kodansha Ltd.

Unlike *Sanctuary* or *Black Jack*, this manga is brand new—so it *must* be good! You may have noticed that in *Excel Saga* there's no time for love, Dr. Jones. But just for the sake of variety I kind of admire Excel and Hyatt's more spiritual infatuation with Il Palazzo; you don't see them having a high-school crush over him (although that happens in *Excel Saga* Vol. 10) or cooking and cleaning for him like a punk (although that happens in *No Need For Tenchi!*). Every once in a while, though, you want to read a manga about teenage affairs of the heart and other, more "M"-rated organs. You'll find it in *Flowers and Bees* Vol. 1, out just now—maybe even on the same collapsible cardboard rack where you found this very book! It may even be shrink-wrapped, which makes it all the more enticing, doesn't it?

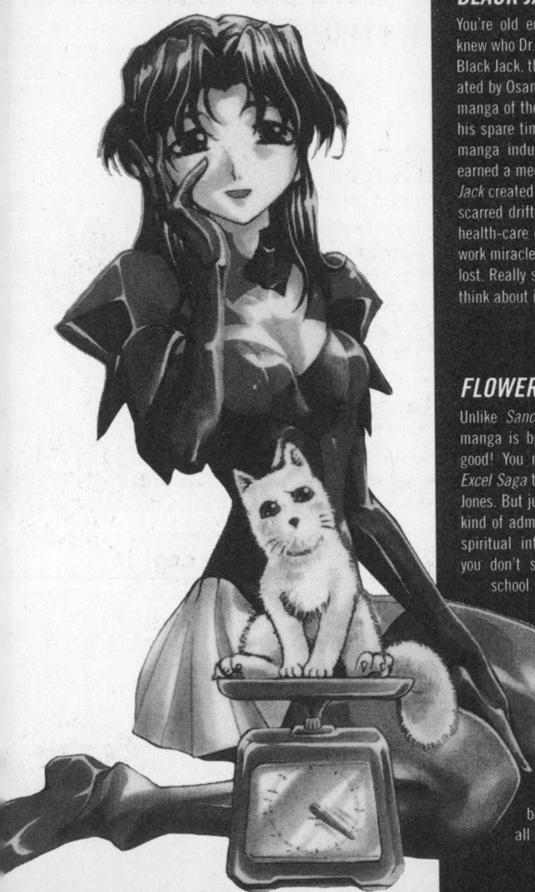

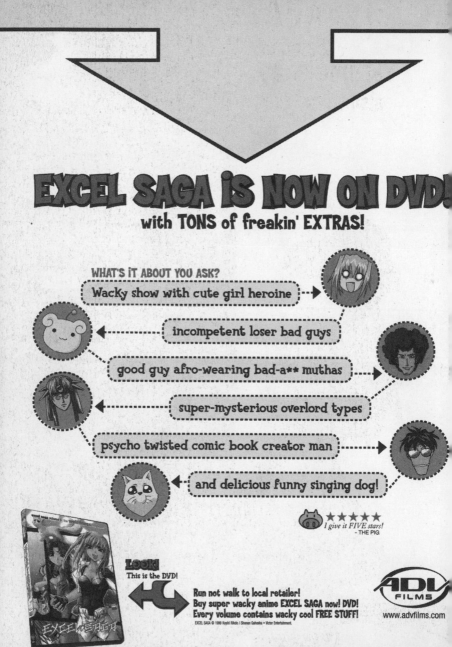

COMPLETE OUR SURVEY AND LET
US KNOW WHAT YOU THINK!

☐ Please check here if you DO NOT wish to receive information or future offers from VIZ

Name: _____

Address: _____

City: _____ State: _____ Zip: _____

E-mail: _____

☐ Male ☐ Female   Date of Birth (mm/dd/yyyy): ___ / ___ / ___   (Under 13? Parental consent required)

What race/ethnicity do you consider yourself? (please check one)

☐ Asian/Pacific Islander   ☐ Black/African American   ☐ Hispanic/Latino

☐ Native American/Alaskan Native ☐ White/Caucasian   ☐ Other: _____

What VIZ product did you purchase? (check all that apply and indicate title purchased)

☐ DVD/VHS _____

☐ Graphic Novel _____

☐ Magazines _____

☐ Merchandise _____

Reason for purchase: (check all that apply)

☐ Special offer   ☐ Favorite title   ☐ Gift

☐ Recommendation   ☐ Other _____

Where did you make your purchase? (please check one)

☐ Comic store   ☐ Bookstore   ☐ Mass/Grocery Store

☐ Newsstand   ☐ Video/Video Game Store ☐ Other: _____

☐ Online (site: _____)

What other VIZ properties have you purchased/own? _____

_____

How many anime and/or manga titles have you purchased in the last year? How many were VIZ titles? (please check one from each column)

ANIME	MANGA	VIZ
☐ None	☐ None	☐ None
☐ 1-4	☐ 1-4	☐ 1-4
☐ 5-10	☐ 5-10	☐ 5-10
☐ 11+	☐ 11+	☐ 11+

I find the pricing of VIZ products to be: (please check one)

☐ Cheap ☐ Reasonable ☐ Expensive

What genre of manga and anime would you like to see from VIZ? (please check two)

☐ Adventure ☐ Comic Strip ☐ Science Fiction ☐ Fighting

☐ Horror ☐ Romance ☐ Fantasy ☐ Sports

What do you think of VIZ's new look?

☐ Love It ☐ It's OK ☐ Hate It ☐ Didn't Notice ☐ No Opinion

Which do you prefer? (please check one)

☐ Reading right-to-left

☐ Reading left-to-right

Which do you prefer? (please check one)

☐ Sound effects in English

☐ Sound effects in Japanese with English captions

☐ Sound effects in Japanese only with a glossary at the back

THANK YOU! Please send the completed form to:

NJW Research
42 Catharine St.
Poughkeepsie, NY 12601

All information provided will be used for internal purposes only. We promise not to sell or otherwise divulge your information.